Mind's Eye

DALLAS MUSEUM OF ART • DISTRIBUTED BY YALE UNIVERSITY PRESS, NEW HAVEN AND LONDON

Mind's Eye

Masterworks on Paper
from David to Cézanne

Edited by *Olivier Meslay* and *William B. Jordan*

WITH CONTRIBUTIONS BY

Esther Bell
Richard R. Brettell
Alessandra Comini
Dakin Hart
William B. Jordan
Felix Krämer
Laurence Lhinares
Heather MacDonald
Olivier Meslay
Jed Morse
Steven Nash
Sylvie Patry
Louis-Antoine Prat
Richard Rand
George T. M. Shackelford
Richard Shiff
Kevin W. Tucker
Charles Wylie

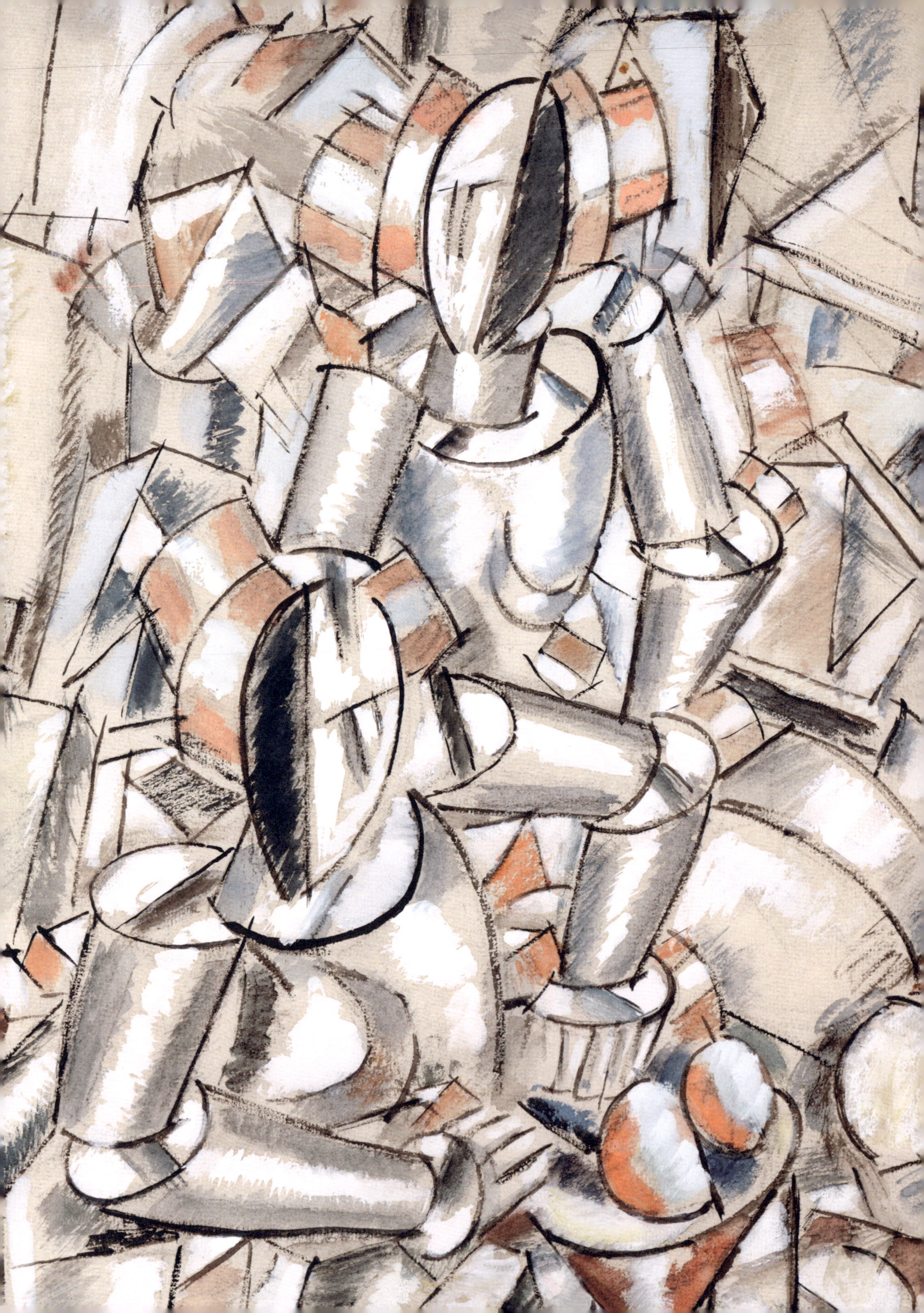

Contents

Lenders to the Exhibition

Nona and Richard Barrett Collection
Richard R. Brettell
Mr. and Mrs. Thomas C. Campbell
Dowell Family Collection
William B. Jordan and Robert Dean Brownlee
Mr. and Mrs. Barron U. Kidd
Lon Elliott Leva
Mary Ralph Lowe
Charlene and Tom Marsh
George T. M. Shackelford
Jeremy and Wendy Strick
And several generous lenders who wish to remain anonymous

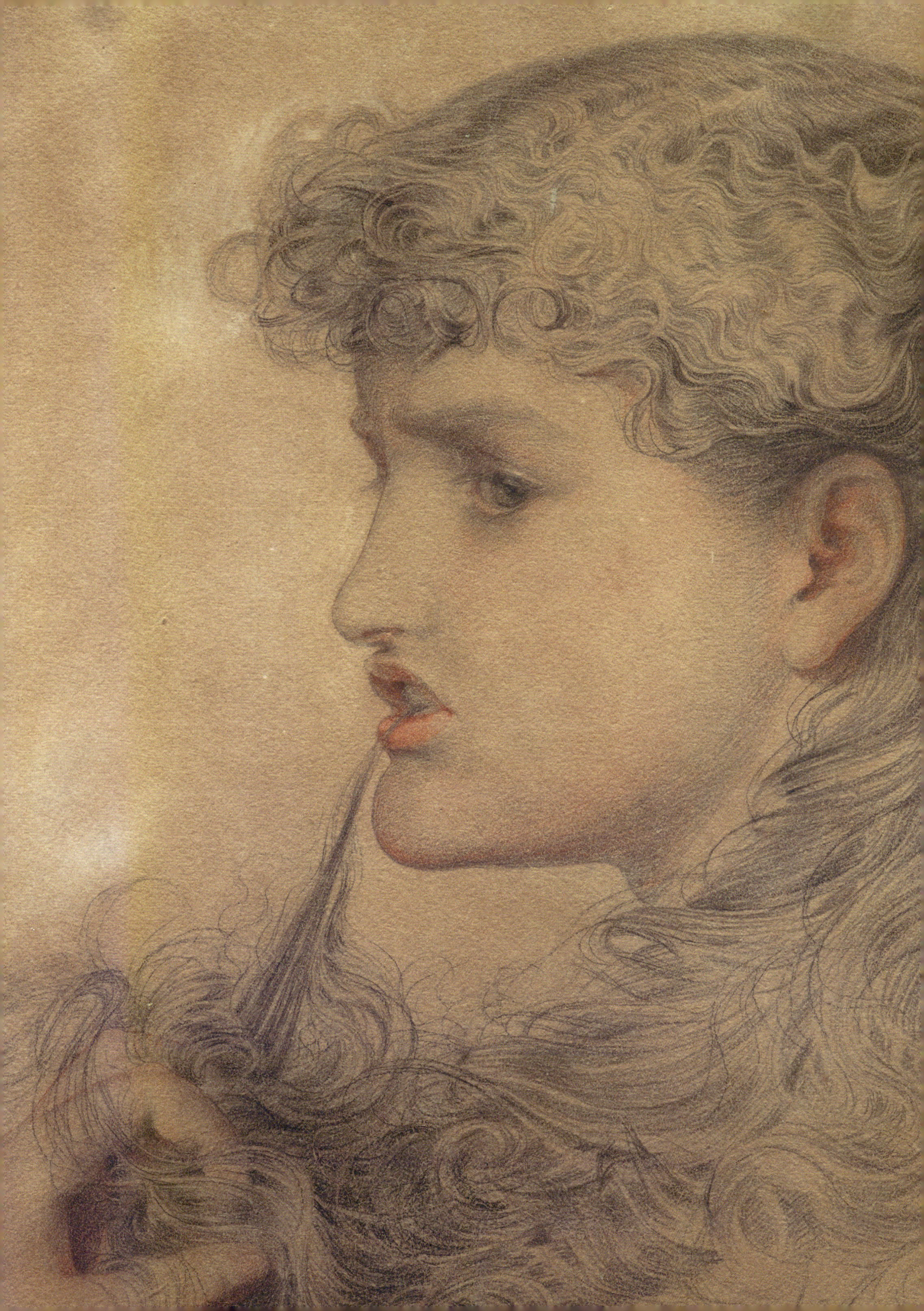

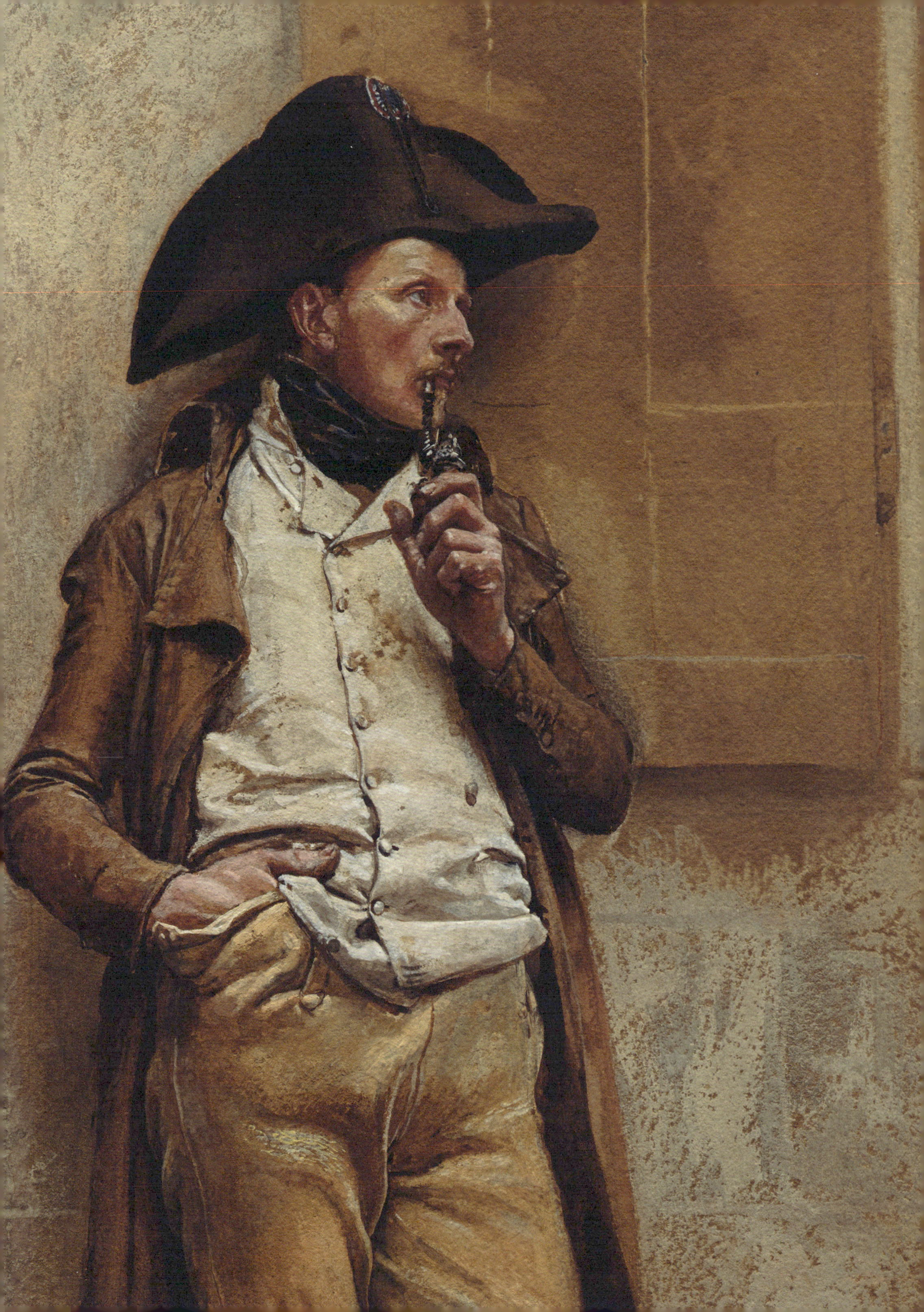

Director's Foreword

The collecting and connoisseurship of drawings were for centuries pleasures associated with the privileged, the educated, or artists themselves, and the skills derived from these activities eventually formed the basis of modern art history. For this reason, drawings usually have been an integral part of the curatorial alignment of most great art museums. Through museums, a larger public has come to enjoy and value these most intimate of artists' expressions.

The Dallas Museum of Art has never had a curator focused solely on works on paper. Yet collecting in this area has gone on throughout the DMA's 111-year history, mostly by collectors who have gravitated around it. Some have given or bequeathed their drawings; others have continued to collect despite the absence of organized encouragement on the Museum's part. *Mind's Eye: Masterworks on Paper from David to Cézanne* is the first exhibition to take stock of what has been achieved by this largely random process, and it is meant as a tribute to the generations of collectors who have brought these drawings to North Texas—the last place in the world most of their creators would ever have imagined they would wind up. The show and its catalogue are also intended as a sign of the Board of Trustees' commitment, expressed in the Museum's 2013 Strategic Plan, to incorporate the field of works on paper more fully into its collecting and exhibition strategy. As we look to the future, we hope to proceed with a well-rounded and historically based program that honors and builds upon our legacy.

We are fortunate to have as the co-curators of *Mind's Eye* Olivier Meslay, the DMA's Associate Director of Curatorial Affairs, Senior Curator of European and American Art, and The Barbara Thomas Lemmon Curator of European Art, and William B. Jordan, former Director of the Meadows Museum and Deputy Director of the Kimbell Art Museum, as well as a current trustee of both the DMA and the Foundation for the Arts. Both of these seasoned professionals are lifelong drawing connoisseurs with ties to the other drawing specialists throughout the world, many of whom they called upon for assistance with this scholarly catalogue.

One of the core missions of the Museum is to encourage collecting within the community. I can think of no better example of how to do this than to highlight the DMA's graphic holdings together with those that have been assembled in private homes throughout our area. *Mind's Eye* presents a rich and fascinating array of works in various media by artists from the Austro-Hungarian, Belgian, British, Dutch, French, German, Spanish, and Swiss schools, spanning nearly 150 years—from the French Revolution to the dawn of modernism. Its scholarly yet highly readable catalogue springs from a lively dialogue among scholars and curators and an active partnership between its organizer, the Dallas Museum of Art, and collectors in North Texas, most of them living in Dallas or Fort Worth. We wish to express our deepest gratitude to the numerous lenders who were willing to relinquish these magnificent works for the exhibition. It is our hope that among the public discovering these normally inaccessible treasures will be some new collectors inspired to join the ranks of those who have enriched their own lives in this way.

An impressive team of international scholars have contributed substantive object entries to the catalogue: Esther Bell, Curator of European Paintings, Drawings, and Sculpture, Cincinnati Art Museum; Richard R. Brettell, The Margaret McDermott Distinguished Chair, School of Arts and Humanities, University of Texas at Dallas; Alessandra Comini, Distinguished Professor of Art History Emerita at Southern Methodist University in Dallas; Dakin Hart, Senior Curator, the Noguchi Museum, New York; William B. Jordan; Felix Krämer, Head of Modern Art at the Städel Museum, Frankfurt; Laurence Lhinares, Research Fellow at the Département des Arts graphiques, Musée du Louvre, Paris; Heather MacDonald, The Lillian and James H. Clark Associate Curator of European Art at the DMA; Olivier Meslay; Jed Morse, Chief Curator at the Nasher Sculpture Center in Dallas; Steven Nash, Director of the Palm Springs Art Museum; Sylvie Patry, Curator of Paintings, Musée d'Orsay, Paris; Louis-Antoine Prat, Curatorial Advisor at the Département des Arts graphiques, Musée du Louvre, Professor at the École du Louvre, and Vice President of Les Amis du Louvre, Paris; Richard Rand, Senior Curator and Curator of Paintings and Sculpture, Sterling and Francine Clark Art Institute, Williamstown, Massachusetts; George T.M. Shackelford, Deputy Director and Chief Curator, Kimbell Art Museum, Fort Worth; Richard Shiff, The Effie Marie Cain Regents Chair in Art and Director, Center for the Study of Modernism, University of Texas at Austin; Kevin W. Tucker, The Margot B. Perot Senior Curator of Decorative Arts and Design at the DMA; and Charles Wylie, formerly The Lupe Murchison Curator of Contemporary Art at the DMA and currently an independent scholar and art historian in Dallas. We thank them for their incisive texts, filled with fresh research, new attributions, and sage reflections, all of which have greatly enhanced this publication.

Within the DMA, recognition and thanks must go to all those whose hard work and skills contributed to the success of the exhibition and its accompanying publication: Anne Bergeron, Associate Director of External Affairs; Jill Bernstein, Director of Public Relations; Giselle Castro-Brightenburg, Imaging Manager; Mandy Engleman, Director of Creative Services; Brad Flowers, Head Photographer; Jessica Harden, Director of Exhibition Design; Michael Hartman, McDermott Curatorial Intern for European Art; Sara Hignite, Associate Registrar, Exhibitions; John Lendvay, Head Preparator; Mary Leonard, Librarian; Andrea Lesovsky, Exhibitions Assistant; Stacey Lizotte, Head of Adult Programs and Multimedia Services; Martha MacLeod, Curatorial Administrative Assistant, European and American Art; Liz Menz, Manager of Adult Programming; Brooke Molinaroli, Director of Marketing; Kevin Parmer, Associate Exhibitions Graphic Designer; Chad Redmon, Assistant Photographer; Chip Sims, Head Carpenter and Shop Manager; Nicole Stutzman-Forbes, Chair of Learning Initiatives and DMA League Director of Education; Joni Wilson-Bigornia, Exhibitions Manager; Rebecca Winti, Senior Graphic Designer; Tamara Wootton-Bonner, Associate Director of Collections and Exhibitions; Eric Zeidler, Publications Manager; and Jeff Zilm, Intellectual Property Manager.

Our outside partners also played a vital role in bringing the catalogue to fruition. These include Ellen Hirzy, editor; Chris Miller and Russell Stockman, translators; Brynn Warriner, proofreader; Ed Marquand, Jeff Wincapaw, Melissa Duffes, and Ryan Polich at Marquand Books, who designed and produced the catalogue; and Patricia Fidler and Madeleine Kloss at Yale University Press, who have once again proved to be exemplary partners in publication.

Finally, we owe special gratitude to Charlene and Tom Marsh for their generosity in underwriting the catalogue, ensuring that it would meet the high aspirations the co-curators had for it.

It is our hope that this exhibition and publication will realize an important step in fulfilling our commitment to advance the knowledge and understanding of all categories of art from the world's cultures, past and present.

Maxwell L. Anderson
The Eugene McDermott Director
Dallas Museum of Art

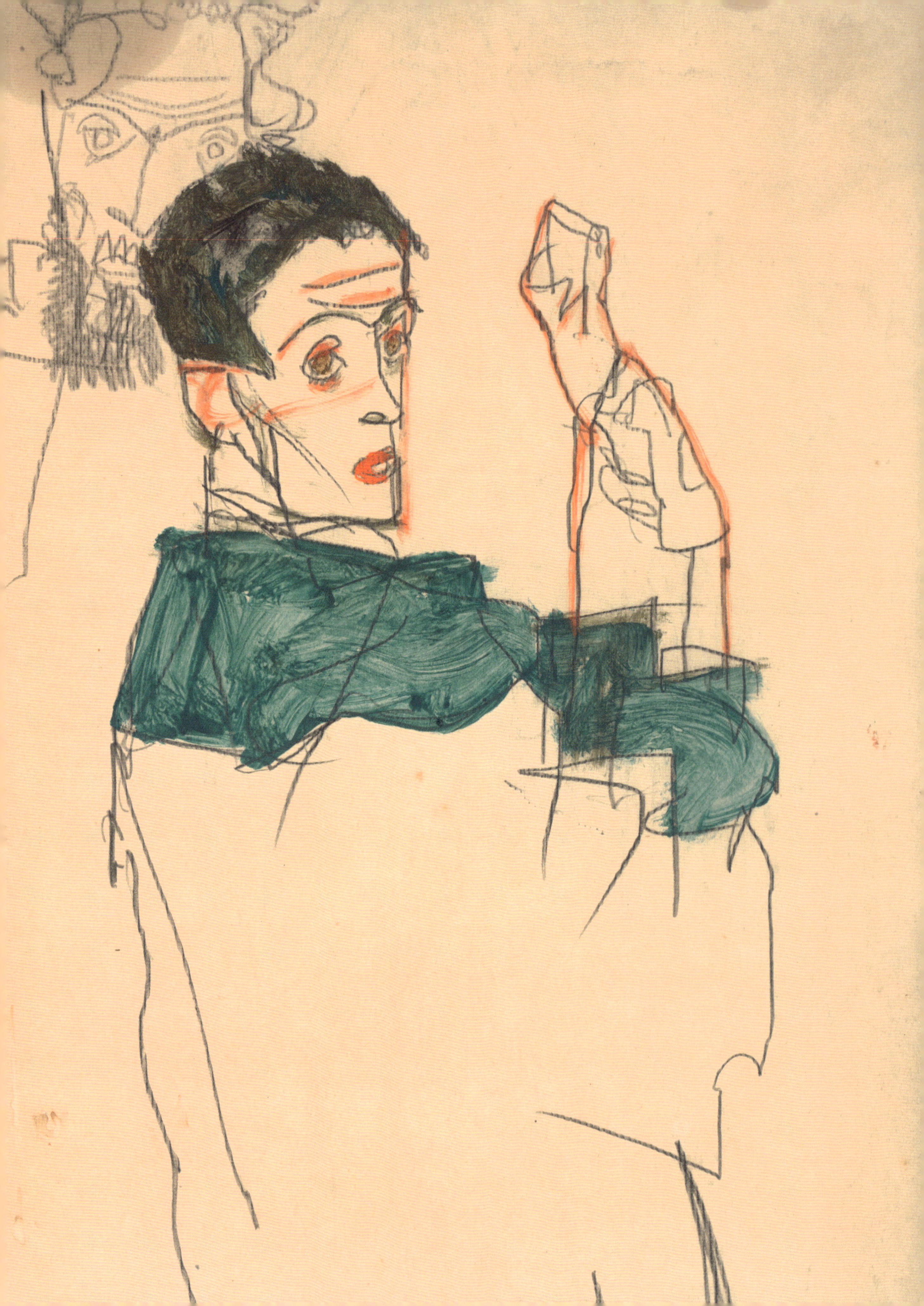

Curators' Preface

A wealthy man once asked a dealer who had offered him a beautiful drawing, "Why would I want a drawing when I could have a painting?" meaning really, "Why would I want a drawing when I can afford a painting?" It might be possible to answer that question in words. But since both of us—and most of the other contributors to this catalogue—have been lovers of drawings in one way or another for most of our lives, we have decided to try to answer it with this exhibition. This show—and this catalogue—are about the pleasures of collecting. They are made up of beloved objects that, for the most part, have been temporarily pried loose from people whose lives they enrich every day. The owners have made this sacrifice in the interest of answering the question above and finding out what kind of story we would be able to tell in the process. Alas, just as a personal collection is almost never "complete," there will be gaps in the story that in an ideal world would be filled by what is to be acquired next. But that is for later. For now, why drawings at all?

Almost all of us, as children, were draftsmen once, if only briefly. Given the chance, we were eager to set down our perceptions of the world, our wishes and fears. Those images made perfect sense to us and charmed our parents and others into saving them, but once early childhood had passed and our educations progressed, we mostly lost that ability—indeed, that urge—to think visually. Artists are those who retain it, and who despite their educations cannot fully express what is on their minds without recourse to images. Drawings are the natural outcome of that expression, and they have an irreducible character. Not all drawings serve the same purpose for the artist. Some—usually unself-conscious ones—are mere tools or steps in the process of visualization. Others—usually very finished or virtuosic ones—are ends in themselves. Still others can offer unique combinations of exhibitionism and secrecy, spontaneity and procrastination, elliptic or comprehensive attempts to describe the world. For artists, drawings can be the first faltering steps of an envisioned achievement or the most calculated summation of protracted invention; for collectors, they can be talismans by which to immerse oneself in the mind of a cherished genius, a lost past, a creative process. In almost every case, it is impossible to understand the visual artist without some recourse to his or her drawings.

Most collectors who start quite young to acquire works of art begin with things they can just manage to afford, and these are often prints and drawings. As time goes on, one learns to value these most intimate and direct expressions of an artist's inner musings, even in relation to finished paintings, which, after the labor of completing them, can often have lost some of the spark of life that animated their preparatory drawings and sketches. This sense of direct communication with the artist is the most attractive aspect of drawings, and therefore they can be, in their way, among the most precious objects that any museum possesses. As the Dallas Museum of Art prepares to increase its activity in the area of works on paper, it seemed desirable to carry out a fresh assessment of our own collection, as well as to assay the resources and level of interest within our own community that might complement those of the Museum. After learning what is here, it seemed appropriate that this show and its catalogue should focus on European art from the French Revolution in the late 18th century to the dawn of modernism in the early 20th century. Future exhibitions of works on paper in North Texas—equally rich—could just as advantageously concentrate on art between the two world wars, art after World War II, contemporary art, American art, or the entire field of prints, where local collections are surprisingly replete as well.

The graphic holdings of the DMA naturally parallel the personal tastes of the collectors who gravitated to the Museum throughout the 20th century. Among its European drawings, French art of the 19th and early 20th centuries predominates—especially impressionist and post-impressionist works acquired in the 1985 gift of the Wendy and Emery Reves Collection. We are fortunate to possess important drawings by some of the great French artists of that period: Pissarro, Manet, Renoir, Degas, Cézanne, Toulouse-Lautrec, and many more. But equally good news is that the private collections of North Texas complement these riches by embracing the art of earlier times and with a much greater geographic diversity. Not every work belonging to the Museum or to area private collections is a masterpiece; some are working drawings whose value lies in what they can tell us about an artist's mind and process. Thus, in addition to a very strong group of French drawings from the time of David and Robert up to and beyond the advent of impressionism, we are able to show an extraordinary variety of works from the rest of Europe as well. And just as one of the main accomplishments of modern scholarship has been to open the public's eyes to the worth of artists whose names have not been part of the traditional canon, collectors in North

Texas, like those elsewhere, have embraced quality where they found it, providing a view of art that more accurately reflects what was really happening in the academies, studios, and homes of a rapidly changing Europe.

We have tried in this volume to let the objects speak for themselves and to arrange the entries to allow a sense of historical flow and interaction, not according to an arbitrary thematic or stylistic scheme. And since one of the pleasures of collecting drawings is the research and speculation involved in knowing each work and relating it to the artist's overall oeuvre, we wanted each entry to reflect that train of thought. Fortunately, the diversity of drawings is such that we are able to consider many of the different ways that drawing can serve the artist's needs and illustrate them with examples by great draftsmen: how drawing is an essential learning exercise (David, Degas, Fortuny); how it can serve as a form of note taking, as exemplified by the *croquis,* or quick sketch (Robert, Wicar, Toulouse-Lautrec, Vuillard); how it is an indispensable tool of planning and development leading up to large or complex works (Delacroix, Barye, Puvis de Chavannes, Degas, Bonnard, Schiele); how it can be a vehicle for commentary, satirical or otherwise (Daumier, Gavarni, Guys); how it can serve as a vehicle for virtuosity (Robert, Henriquel-Dupont, Meissonier, Hirémy-Hirschl); or how it is a unique stage for aesthetic exploration (Cézanne, Degas, Seurat, Picasso, Mondrian, Gabo). All these dimensions of the art of drawing—and more—are illustrated by artists you will have heard of and artists who may be new to you. But each of these works has been, or still is, part of the mental furniture in the life of someone who has inhabited this community.

All true collectors are fascinated to know where the objects they own have been—who possessed them before they did. For this reason, we have researched the collection history of each drawing, when it could be determined. New information has been found, and it is discussed where relevant in the entries. Many of the works exhibited, as it happens, have belonged to distinguished collectors of earlier generations. Some are revered as masters of the art of collecting: Jean-Baptiste Faure, Étienne Moreau-Nélaton, Louis-Antoine and Véronique Prat, and Norton Simon; some represent dynasties of collectors, like the families Doria, Pourtalès, Vaudoyer, Delessert, or Rouart; some were art historians or artists, like Sir Kenneth Clark, Aristide Bruant, and Pierre Le-Tan; and some were artists and dealers, like Walther Halvorsen. All were lovers of drawings. But as interesting as such information can be, works of art are almost invariably not collected because of their provenance but rather because the images and the pictorial qualities of each resonate with the taste of the new owners. Thus, from a list like the one above—primarily of privileged Europeans—we move to another, which includes some of the founding families and committed supporters of the Dallas Museum of Art, who have already contributed to the Museum's core collection of works on paper and among whom we would like especially to acknowledge: Rozwell Sam Adams; Nona and Richard Barrett; Mr. and Mrs. Franklin B. Bartholow; Mr. and Mrs. Duncan Boeckman; Mr. and Mrs. Alfred L. Bromberg and the other members of the Bromberg family; Mr. and Mrs. James H. Clark; Dr. Alessandra Comini; Mr. I.C. Deal; Violet Hayden Dowell; Patsy Lacy Griffith; Nancy and Jake L. Hamon; Leon Harris; Henry Hawley III; the Mrs. Edwin B. Hopkins Fund; Mrs. Barron Kidd; Mrs. Arthur Kramer Sr.; Natalie H. (Schatzie) and George T. Lee Jr.; the Edward S. Marcus Fund; Mr. and Mrs. Eugene McDermott; Charlene and Tom Marsh; the Meadows Foundation, Inc.; the Munger Fund; Mrs. John W. O'Boyle; heirs of Lawrence and Hortense Pollock; Wendy and Emery Reves; Joanne Stroud; Denni Davis Washburn and Marie Scott Miegel; Mrs. Nora Wise; Lois and Howard B. Wolf; and A.E. Zonne.

The old and great American collections of works on paper benefited from the long-term curatorial leadership of great connoisseurs. At Harvard's Fogg Museum, for example, Paul J. Sachs and Agnes Mongan not only trained generations of American museum directors and curators but also worked with passionate collectors like Grenville Winthrop to build holdings that can tell the unfolding story of art in great detail. Institutions like the Metropolitan Museum of Art, the Morgan Library, the Art Institute of Chicago, and others in America's older population centers did the same thing, and still do, led by visionary curators and directors and supported by the collectors they educated and encouraged. Achievements of that magnitude cannot be duplicated today, but with adequate resources impressive collections can still be built in dynamic younger communities, as surely has been demonstrated by the J. Paul Getty Museum, only since 1981. We hope that in the future we can count on the continued support of those who have brought us this far.

We would like to express our gratitude to the colleagues around the world who have generously contributed their time and expertise toward the success of this catalogue. There could have been no greater pleasure than working with our team of scholars, whose names appear on the title page and who have made this book so much more than a mere record of what was exhibited. First among them, we must single out for special thanks Louis-Antoine Prat, the leading scholar and collector of French drawings today, for his enthusiastic embrace of the project and his generous participation not only in the formation of the loan list but also in the writing of the entries. Our friend and colleague George T. M. Shackelford also deserves our special thanks not only for his important contribution as a Degas scholar but also for his generous advice on the content of the show. And Richard R. Brettell has a deep knowledge of collections in North Texas and has generously shared his scholarship with us again on this occasion. The preservation and conservation of works on paper is a critical and specialized field, and one central to this undertaking. We were given invaluable assistance in this regard by the DMA's Chief Conservator, Mark Leonard, and by independent paper conservator Patricia Brewer, both of whom deserve our special thanks.

In addition to those already named, countless others have assisted us in specific ways. They include Jean-Luc Baroni, Claire Barry, Laura Bennett, Mark Brady, Robert Dean Brownlee, Hubert Duchemin, Laure de Margerie, Patrick Matthiesen, Jill Newhouse, Stephen Ongpin, Édouard Papet, Roger Ramsay, Philippe Thiébaut, and Cheryl and Kevin Vogel.

Finally, we want to express our personal thanks to the most important participants of all in this endeavor, the lenders who have agreed to share their beloved objects with us. We hope this project will be followed by many more that will continue to explore the subtler pleasures of collecting.

Olivier Meslay
William B. Jordan

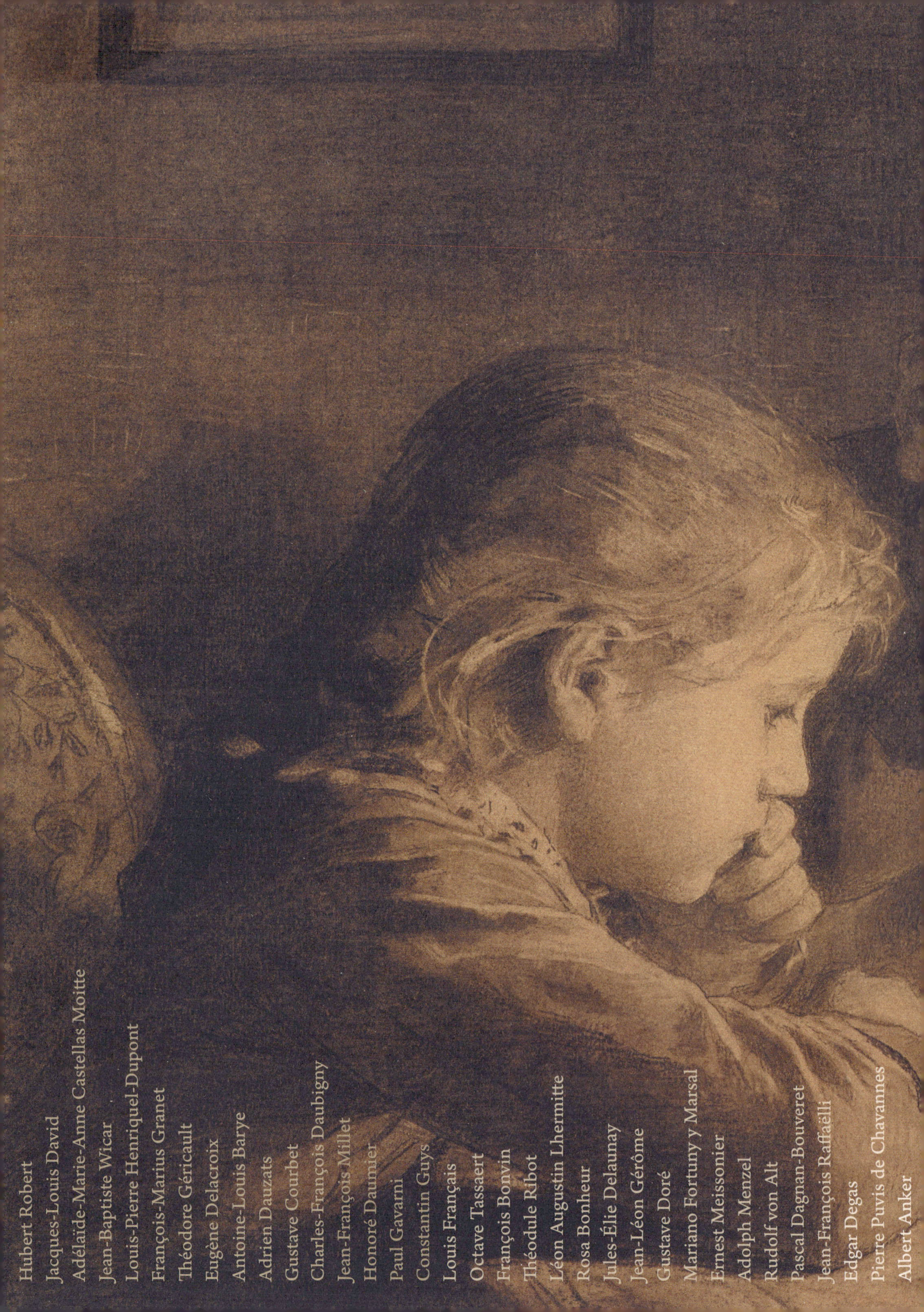

Hubert Robert
Jacques-Louis David
Adélaïde-Marie-Anne Castellas Moitte
Jean-Baptiste Wicar
Louis-Pierre Henriquel-Dupont
François-Marius Granet
Théodore Géricault
Eugène Delacroix
Antoine-Louis Barye
Adrien Dauzats
Gustave Courbet
Charles-François Daubigny
Jean-François Millet
Honoré Daumier
Paul Gavarni
Constantin Guys
Louis Français
Octave Tassaert
François Bonvin
Théodule Ribot
Léon Augustin Lhermitte
Rosa Bonheur
Jules-Élie Delaunay
Jean-Léon Gérôme
Gustave Doré
Mariano Fortuny y Marsal
Ernest Meissonier
Adolph Menzel
Rudolf von Alt
Pascal Dagnan-Bouveret
Jean-François Raffaëlli
Edgar Degas
Pierre Puvis de Chavannes
Albert Anker

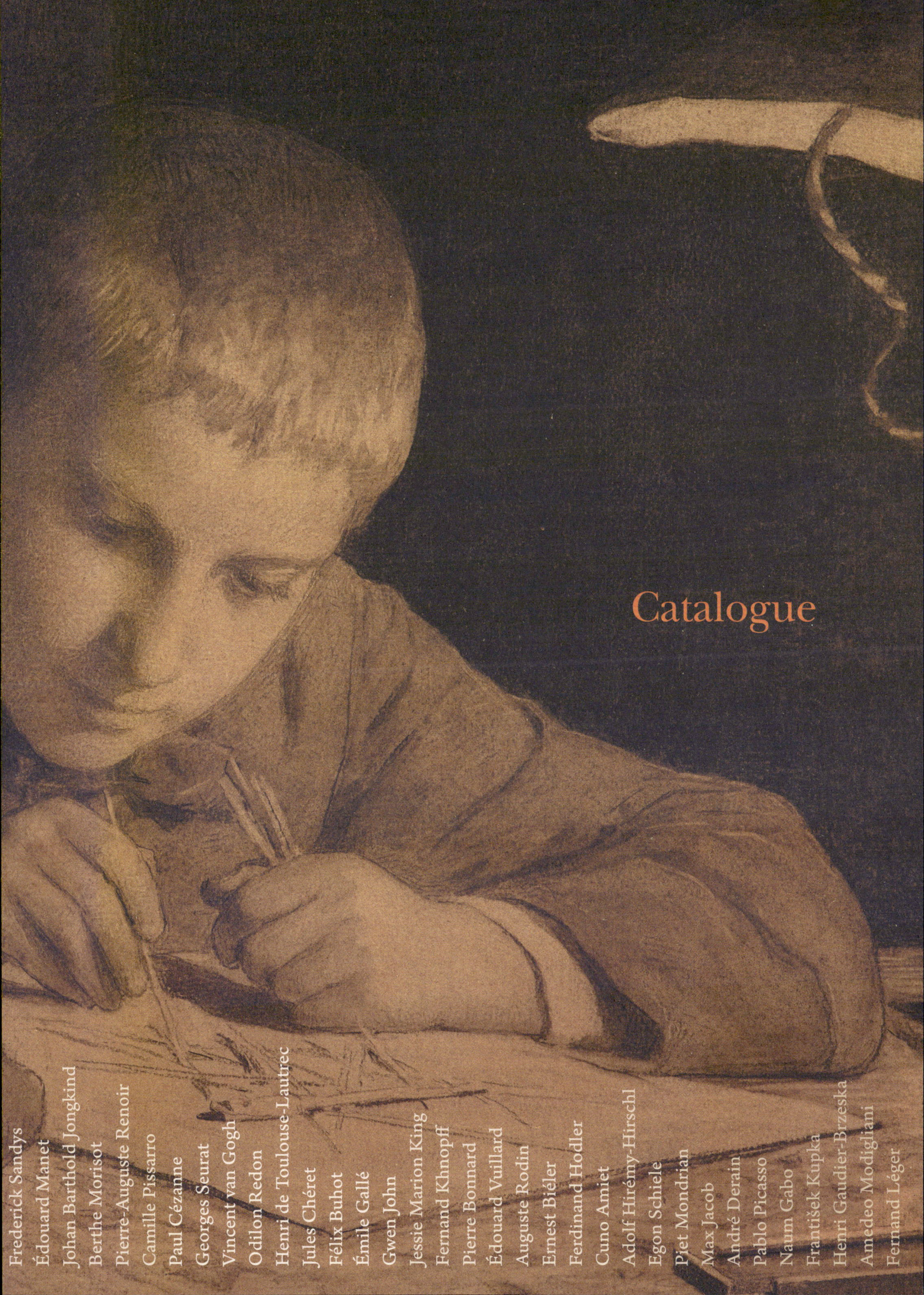

Catalogue

Frederick Sandys
Édouard Manet
Johan Barthold Jongkind
Berthe Morisot
Pierre-Auguste Renoir
Camille Pissarro
Paul Cézanne
Georges Seurat
Vincent van Gogh
Odilon Redon
Henri de Toulouse-Lautrec
Jules Chéret
Félix Buhot
Émile Gallé
Gwen John
Jessie Marion King
Fernand Khnopff
Pierre Bonnard
Édouard Vuillard
Auguste Rodin
Ernest Biéler
Ferdinand Hodler
Cuno Amiet
Adolf Hirémy-Hirschl
Egon Schiele
Piet Mondrian
Max Jacob
André Derain
Pablo Picasso
Naum Gabo
František Kupka
Henri Gaudier-Brzeska
Amedeo Modigliani
Fernand Léger

1

Hubert Robert French, 1733–1808

VIEW OF THE GARDENS AT THE VILLA MATTEI, *1761*

Red chalk on paper, 13¾ × 20⅝ in. (349 × 524 mm)
Inscribed lower left: *Villa Mattei*
Dallas Museum of Art, fractional gift of Charlene and Tom Marsh, 2006.17

PROVENANCE Georges Mülhbacher (d. 1906); sale, Paris, Hôtel Drouot, March 3, 1944, lot 12; where purchased by a member of the Hottinguer family, and by descent to Baron Hottinguer (1902–1985); sale, Christie's, Paris, *Ancienne Collection du Baron Hottinguer,* December 3, 2003, lot 512; where purchased by Flavia Ormond Fine Arts, Ltd., London; where purchased 2006 by Charlene and Tom Marsh; Dallas Museum of Art, fractional gift of Charlene and Tom Marsh.

BIBLIOGRAPHY Flavia Ormond Fine Arts 2005, cat.10 (entry by Victor Carlson).

The leading landscape artist in France during the final decades of the 18th century, Hubert Robert was a painter whose activity straddled the great divide represented by the French Revolution, and like a few others of such a long lifespan, he also managed in some ways to bridge the gap between neoclassicism and romanticism. A prolific draftsman and painter, his images of the ruined classical monuments of ancient Rome earned him the moniker "Robert des Ruines." When he returned to Paris, he brought with him this fascination with the derelict and obsolete structures of the past, observing (and sometimes imagining) the demolition of Paris's historic buildings. The two drawings catalogued here exemplify complementary aspects of Robert's graphic oeuvre: the finished studio drawing of a famous Italian monument and the on-site sketch of an actual event in modern Paris, which involved the destruction of the old to make room for the new.

The large and masterful red chalk drawing *View and Gardens at the Villa Mattei* (cat. 1, facing page) dates to the period when Robert was traveling in Italy with his fellow artist Jean-Honoré Fragonard and their patron, the wealthy connoisseur the Abbé Saint-Non. It represents the Villa Mattei, today known as the Villa Celimontana, built in the Roman countryside during the Renaissance era. Robert made at least three drawings of the Villa Mattei, of which this example is the only one known to survive. The others are recorded only by a counterproof (Musée des Beaux-Arts et d'Archéologie, Besançon) and by a print commissioned by Saint-Non after a lost drawing. The present drawing (unlike the second Robert drawing in this catalogue) is a fully developed studio drawing, no doubt based on sketches that Robert made at the site but intended as a finished, self-sufficient work of art rather than a study or preparatory sketch. Such drawings were much prized by 18th-century collectors.

The black chalk drawing *Ruins of the Church of the Saints-Innocents, Paris* (cat. 2, p. 23) records the destruction of the 13th-century Gothic church (just south of the Forum des Halles, near what is now the Centre Pompidou), whose much older, adjacent cemetery had become the primary burial place for Parisians. Concern for the public health hazard posed by the overflowing cemetery led to its closure in 1785 and the transfer of its bones to the catacombs on the edge of the city. In 1786–1787 the church, deemed unsafe, was razed as well. Robert witnessed the slow demolition of the Gothic edifice, recording it in at least one other drawing of the church interior filled with debris (Staatliche Kunsthalle, Karlsruhe). In the Salon of 1787, he exhibited a tiny painting of the subject (*Vue intérieure de l'église de Saints-Innocents au debut de sa demolition*) and, around the same time, painted the somewhat larger version now in the Pushkin Museum of Fine Arts, Moscow (fig. 1, p. 22), which uses the present drawing as its point of departure. The drawing shows the church occupied above and below, with workers methodically dismantling the roof and clearing the debris away at ground level, while other small figures observe the process or simply rest amid the ruins.

HMacD and WBJ

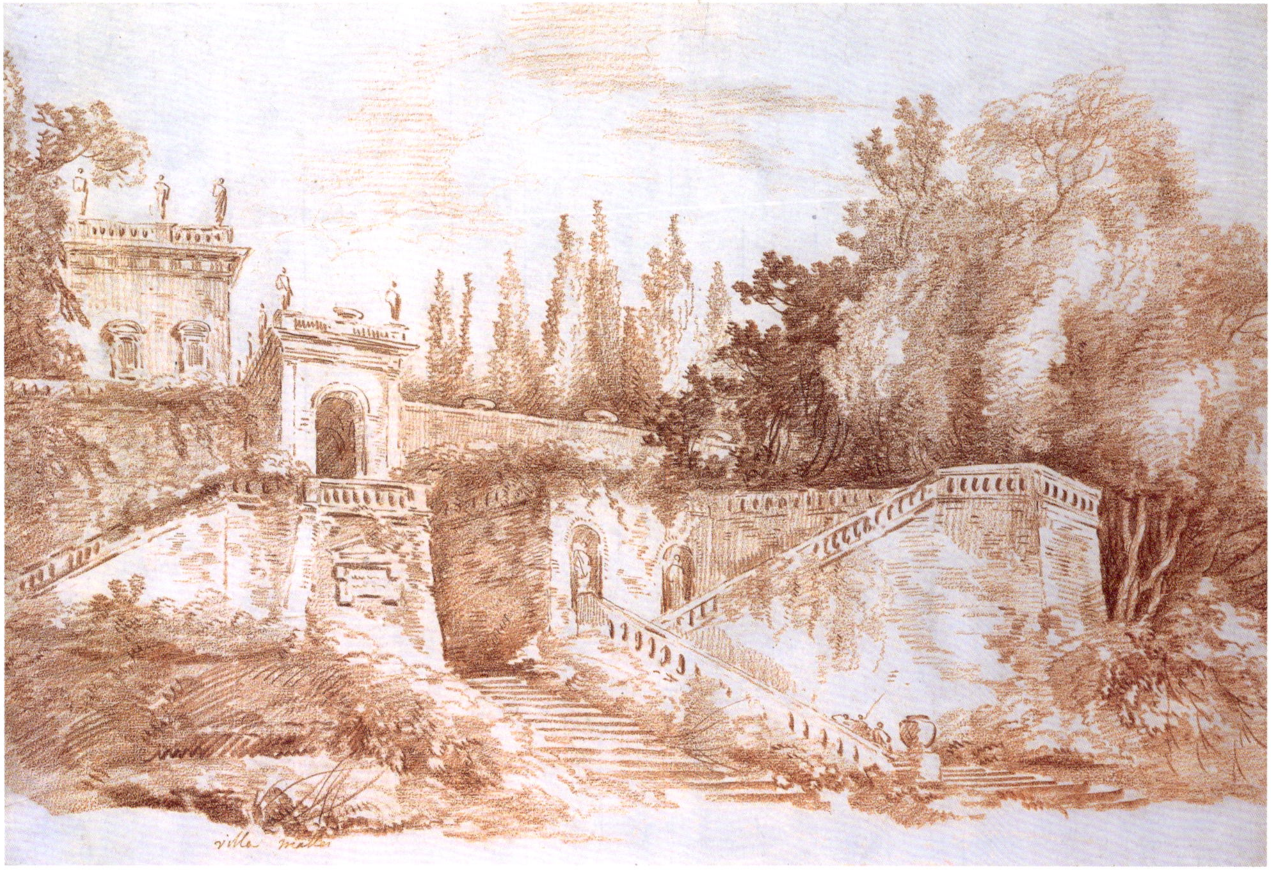
villa

2

Hubert Robert French, 1733–1808

RUINS OF THE CHURCH OF THE SAINTS-INNOCENTS, PARIS, C. *1786–1787*

Black chalk on paper, 16½ × 11⅛ in. (421 × 282 mm)
Private collection, Dallas

PROVENANCE Suzor Collection; Louis-Antoine and Veronique Prat, Paris (Lugt 3617); Artemis Fine Arts, S.A., Luxembourg-Geneva; where purchased 2003 by the current owner.

EXHIBITED C.G. Boerner, Inc. (subsidiary of Artemis Fine Arts), New York, *Old Master Drawings,* January 22–February 8, 2003, cat. 34.

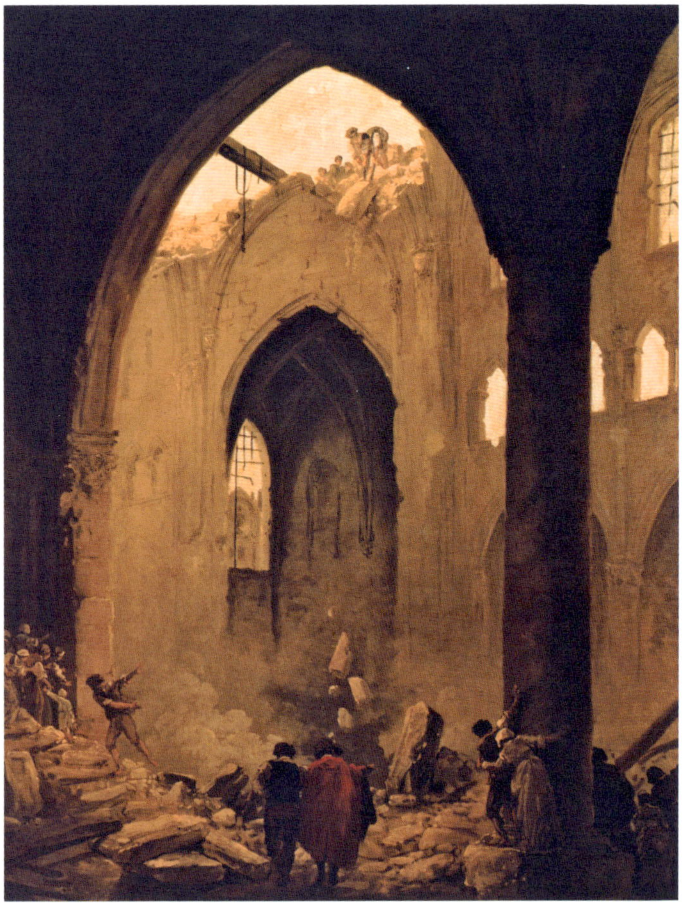

Fig. 1 Hubert Robert, *Demolition of a Church,* c. 1787. Oil on canvas. Moscow, Pushkin Museum of Fine Arts, inv. 1076.

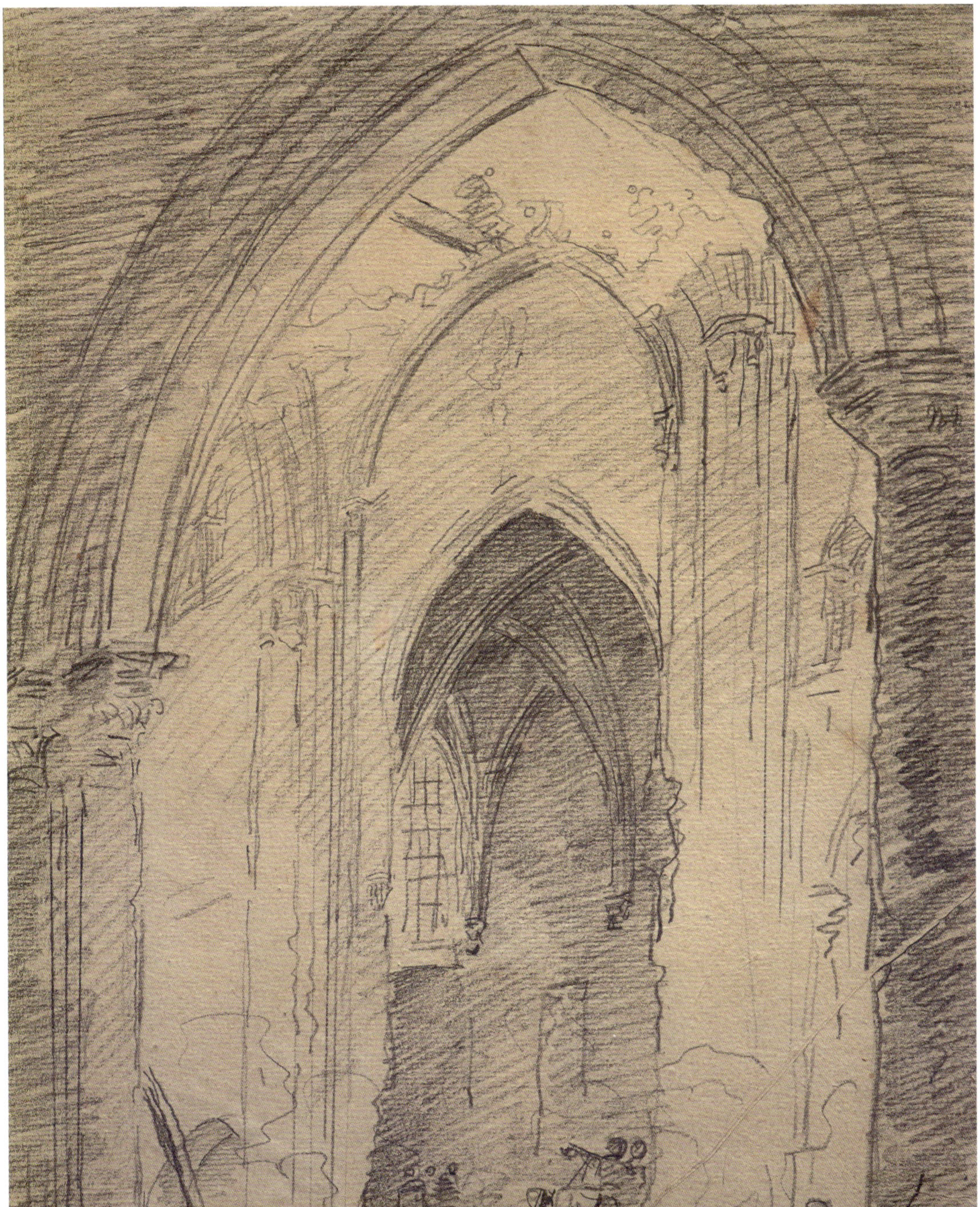

Jacques-Louis David French, 1748–1825

TWO STUDIES OF THE HEAD OF A YOUNG MAN CROWNED WITH A LAUREL (DEUX TÊTES DE JEUNE HOMME LAURÉ, VU DE PROFIL ET TOURNÉ VERS LA DROITE), *C. 1780*

Black chalk on laid paper, 4½ × 6⅞ in. (115 × 175 mm)
Inscription in pen and brown ink from the hand of Delécluze on a piece of paper to which the sheet drawing is pasted: *Ce croquis fait à Rome par L. David m'a été donné par lui en / 1813. E. J. Delécluze*
Private collection, Dallas

PROVENANCE Etienne-Jean Delécluze (1781–1863); Albert Vaudoyer (Hautecoeur 1954); Galerie J.-F. and Ph. Heim, Paris, 1990 (8, repr. 9); anonymous sale, Sotheby's, Monaco, December 5, 1992, lot 146, color repr.; anonymous sale, Sotheby's, New York, January 12, 1994, lot 212, repr.; where purchased by the current owner.

BIBLIOGRAPHY Delécluze 1855, 112 (reprint Mouilleseaux 1983, 460n17); Duguet 1899, 4; Saunier 1925, 13; Saunier 1929, 410; Baschet 1942, repr. opp. 272; Hautecoeur 1954, 43n27; Wildenstein and Wildenstein 1973, no. 1515; Nash 1973 (photocopied 1996), 121; Howard 1975, 16; Schnapper 1980, 45–46; Bordes 1979 (1981), 183, fig. 9 (Debret's lithograph); Néret 1989, 23; Sérullaz 1989–90, 68–69, fig. 35; Montagu 1994, 97–98, fig. 129; Rosenberg 2000, 61–62, 16, ill.; Rosenberg and Prat 2002, 38, no. 13, repr.; Prat 2011, 28–29, fig. 39.

In the graphic work of any great artist, certain sheets have a seminal character that immediately stands out. For Jacques-Louis David, this drawing clearly assumes that role, summing up both a doctrine and a practice. One of the best-documented examples among several hundred surviving drawings by David, it is also one of the most frequently cited, beginning with its first owner, Étienne-Jean Delécluze—the student of David, now known mainly for his *Souvenirs* of his experience in his master's studio—who wrote a celebrated paragraph about it.

Speaking in the third person, Delécluze presents himself as a studious and attentive young man. His teacher David combines the spoken word with a graphic example, placing an old drawing in his student's hands as a gift. According to Delécluze, the scene took place in 1807, but his handwritten inscription at the bottom of the drawing gives the date as 1813. We know in any case that he had joined the cohort of David's students (called "the 10,000" in reference to Xenophon's *Anabasis,* though in fact there were only a few hundred) in 1797. Delécluze describes the experience in this way:

> Among all the sketches of this period [David's first stay in Rome after the 1774 Prix de Rome, 1775–1780], one was given by David to Étienne and Étienne took special care of it not least because his master, when he handed it over, added a rather curious observation. It is a drawing of two heads. One is that of a young sacrificer wearing a laurel crown; faithfully copied after the antique, it bears the tranquil character that the ancients imparted to the faces of figures whose moral dignity they wish to emphasize. "You see, my friend," said David to Étienne, "this is what I then called *the raw antique.* When I had very carefully and with great pains copied this head, I went home and did the one that you see beside it. *I seasoned it with modern sauce,* as I used to say in those days. I made the brows frown a little bit, I highlighted the cheekbones, I opened the mouth slightly; in short, I gave it what the moderns call *expression,* and which I nowadays [this was in 1807] call a *grimace.* Do you understand, Étienne?"—"Yes."[1]

During David's first stay in Rome, his "cataract" was removed by the sight of antiquity after having proclaimed too quickly that he would not be seduced by it. On his wanderings through the Eternal City, he covered page after page of his small sketchbooks with copies after Hellenistic and Roman statues and low reliefs; he later combined the leaves of these sketchbooks thematically into two large albums that his heirs transformed in 1825 into 12 collections. These works are now for the most part in museum collections. We do not know whether the present sheet was originally part of one of these sketchbooks. The model that he copied on the left has nevertheless been identified by Carlo Gasparri. It is not, as Delécluze supposed, the head of a "young sacrificer," but a copy of a cameo in the Medici collection representing Augustus assimilated to Apollo (National Archaeological Museum, Florence, inv. 14521). Since David copied it reversed, he probably used a print or *calque* after the cameo.[2]

Notes

1. Delécluze 1855, 112.
2. The drawing's fame is attested by a copy traced in black chalk (135 × 198 mm), bearing underneath the drawing a handwritten inscription in pen and brown ink made by L. David in Rome in 1777, which went on sale in Paris, Hôtel Drouot, Piasa, November 21, 2001, no. 83. The original drawing was also engraved in reverse by Jean-Baptiste Debret on the occasion of the annual

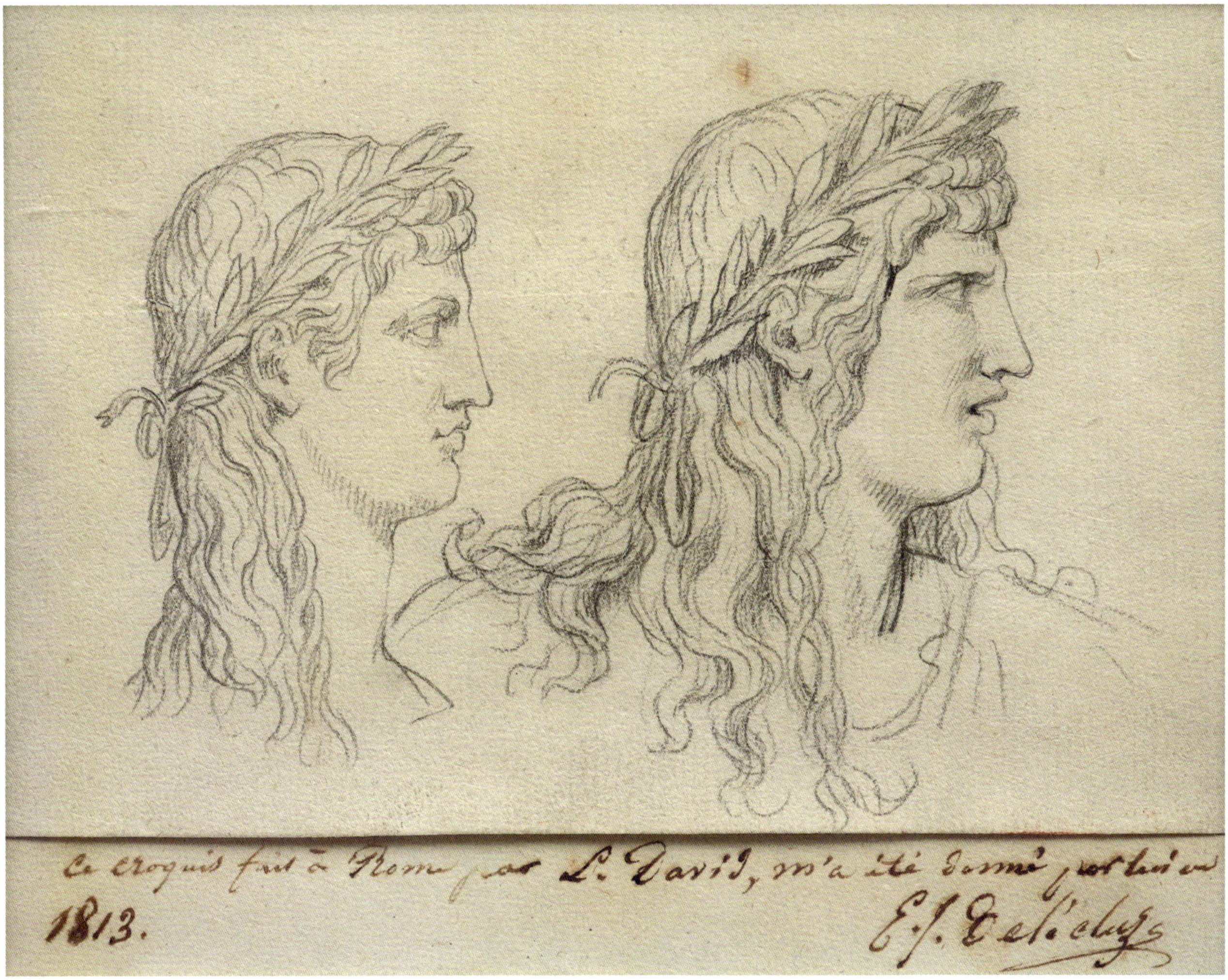

banquet for the students of David in 1845. The engraving bears the facsimile signature of David and the inscription: *L'expression d'un sentiment douloureux, inspiré des formes nobles du calme de l'antique.* One impression is conserved at the École nationale supérieure des Beaux-Arts in Paris and another in the album of Jean-Germain Drouais at the Musée de Rennes (inv. 74.73.410).

The transformation of this coldly classical head into a much more expressive face perfectly fits the aesthetic of dramatization that David cultivated in his paintings of the time, starting notably with his *Belisarius Begging for Alms* of 1781 (Palais des Beaux-Arts, Lille). His metaphor for the conversion from raw to seasoned has a symbolic value. His purpose was to bring antiquity back to life in a form imbued with greater sentiment and more accessible to his contemporaries. But whether David gave the drawing to Delécluze in 1807 when returning to the theme of *Leonidas at Thermopylae* (Musée du Louvre, Paris)—a composition in which he sought to attain an exclusively Greek classicism—or in 1813, when his manner had become stiffer, we must understand David's reported words as a sort of self-critique. The artist was reproaching himself with a tendency toward what he condemned as *grimace* but which we now prefer to celebrate in the name of dramatic expressivity.

LAP

4

•

Adélaïde-Marie-Anne Castellas Moitte French, 1747–1807

GIRLS PLAYING THE PIANO, C. *1795*

Pen and black ink on paper, 13⅛ × 6⅞ in. (335 × 175 mm)
Watermark, coat of arms with a star above a crown; inscribed in watermark: *G. DALA [. . .] ON / 1787*
Private collection, Dallas

PROVENANCE Galerie Charles et André Bailly, Paris, 1990; where purchased by the current owner.

BIBLIOGRAPHY Meslay 1989, 90, repr.

Painter and draftswoman Adélaïde-Marie-Anne Castellas was the pupil of Jean-Jacques Le Barbier. After she married the sculptor Jean Guillaume Moitte in 1781, she left painting as a profession, but she remained involved in the artistic circle of her time. At the beginning of the French Revolution, through her private generosity and personal effort, she launched a movement to resolve the French financial crisis. She wrote two pamphlets encouraging women artists to donate their jewels to save the nation and support the king.[1] She led a patriotic demonstration at the Assembly on September 7, 1789, joined by the wives of other artists, including Mmes. Jacques-Louis David, Jean-Honoré Fragonard, Antoine Vestier, and Joseph-Marie Vien. Other women's groups followed their example and challenged the new Assembly with their private initiatives. Her efforts inspired painters like Louis Gauffier, who painted a canvas on the subject now in the Musée Sainte-Croix, Poitiers. During the difficult moments of the French Revolution, she converted her home into a boardinghouse where children studied languages, writing, and piano. Her diary, published in 1932 by Paul Cottin, provides a fascinating insider's view of the artistic life in Paris during the Napoleonic years.

Moitte described in drawings the special atmosphere of her home. These drawings formed a small album, now disassembled, from which this sheet was taken. In her depictions of children and their hosts, lectures around the table, and piano or violin lessons, Moitte seems to relish the details of daily life and attitudes as she gives us a charming and unique perspective on her extraordinary time. With their tight series of lines—as in a chiseled print, often sinuous, sometime extremely busy, and often unfinished—her drawings are highly recognizable. She has an effective way of inviting us into close relationships with her models.

OM

Note

1. *L'Âme des romaines dans les femmes françaises* (Paris: Gueffier, 1789) and *Suite de l'Âme des romaines dans les femmes françaises* (Paris: Knapen, 1789).

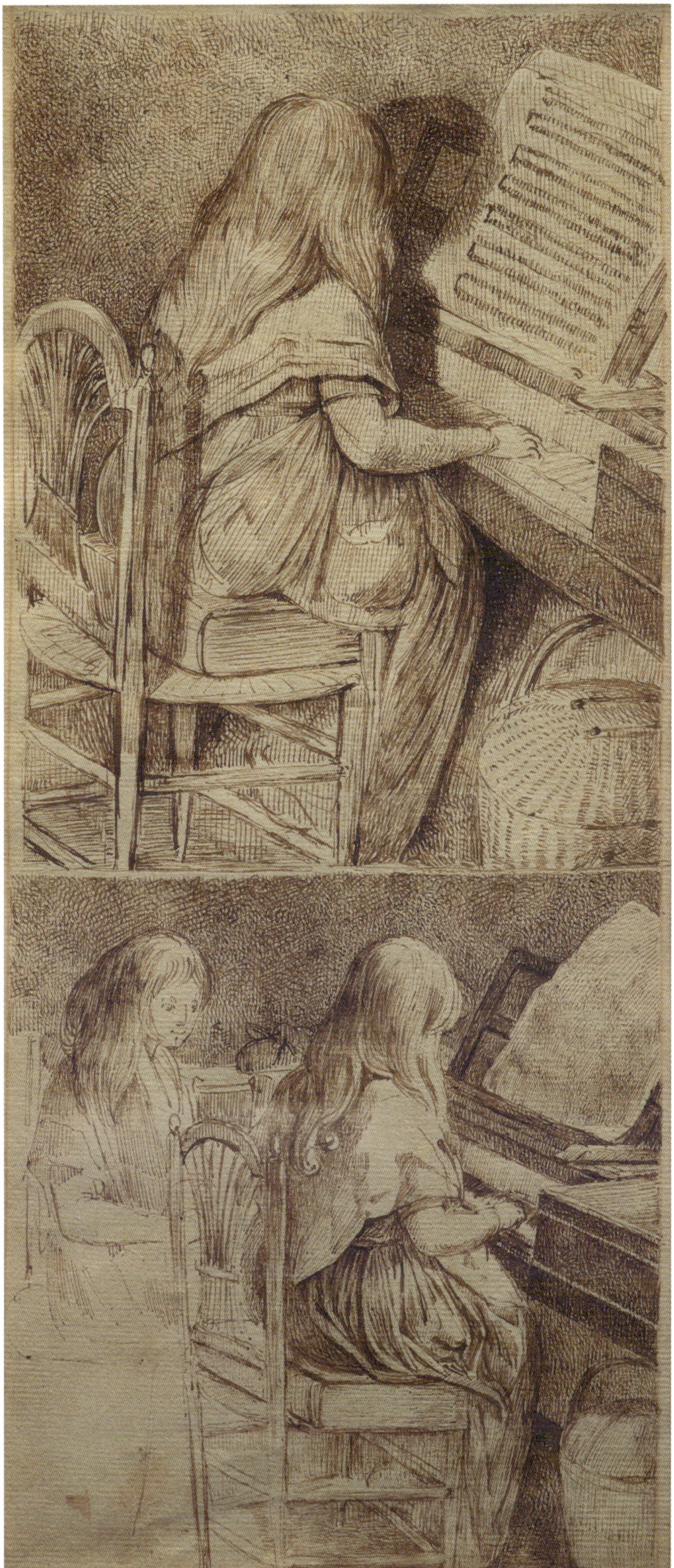

5

Jean-Baptiste Wicar French, 1762–1834

SEATED MAN IN A DRESSING GOWN (SELF-PORTRAIT?) (RECTO), *C. 1800;*
HORSES AND HANDLERS IN A LANDSCAPE WITH A BARKING DOG (VERSO), *N.D.*

Pencil on medium-weight cream wove paper, 9 × 6⅜ in. (229 × 162 mm)
On recto, inscribed lower left with iron gall ink (faded): *1824* or *1826* (?); inscribed along right margin in pencil in two lines (difficult to read): *Croquis d'après N*r [Nature] *huit*. . . . On verso, inscribed along right margin in pencil: *L336-F2*
Private collection, Dallas

PROVENANCE The Drawing Shop (later Shepherd Gallery), New York; where purchased 1963 by the current owner.

EXHIBITED The Drawing Shop, New York, *The Non-Dissenters (Second Exhibition): David through Meissonier,* March 5–April 19, 1963, cat. 12 (tentatively attributed to Théodore Chassériau), ill., pl. III.

RELATED BIBLIOGRAPHY Fumaroli et al. 1992, 23–26, 141–143; Gordon and Aldega 1995.

In the 50 years this drawing has been in the same collection, many eminent drawing specialists have looked at it. Only recently was a convincing attribution put forward, by Louis-Antoine Prat.[1] The double-sided sheet represents on the recto a full-length portrait sketch of a man in a dressing gown seated in an armchair, freely and quickly drawn, with no attempt to pause over details. Hatching around the shoulders and along the left side and the floor set the figure in space. Inscribed along the right margin is a notation in the artist's hand: *Croquis d'après N*r [Nature] *huit*... (Sketch from life, eight). Severely frontal in its pose, the figure gives the impression of someone looking at his reflection in a full-length dressing mirror. This could be the case, since the sitter, with his curly hair and broad face, strongly resembles the artist whose style coincides in every way with both sides of the sheet: Jean-Baptiste Wicar (fig. 2).

Wicar had two manners of drawing: one highly finished and the other vigorous and unabashedly sketchy. His male nude academies and finished portraits are so breathtakingly accomplished that David called his favorite pupil "le plus fameux dessinateur de France" (the most famous French draftsman). His private sketches, mostly in sketchbooks in the Musée des Beaux-Arts in Lille (his hometown museum, which he endowed upon his death), are sure-handed, rather schematic analyses of anatomy and figural groupings. The drawing on the verso of this sheet, depicting a group of handlers and a barking dog trying to control an unruly stallion (right), is a typical example of this purpose-driven style in which drawing was a tool of thought and planning rather than a finished product.

Tenacious and perhaps not a little opportunistic, Wicar rose from poverty to become not only an honored artist, but also one of the most important collectors and connoisseurs of his time. Protected and encouraged by his fellow Jacobin Jacques-Louis David, he was appointed curator of antiquities at the Louvre during the revolution and later became an important member of the commission that selected and

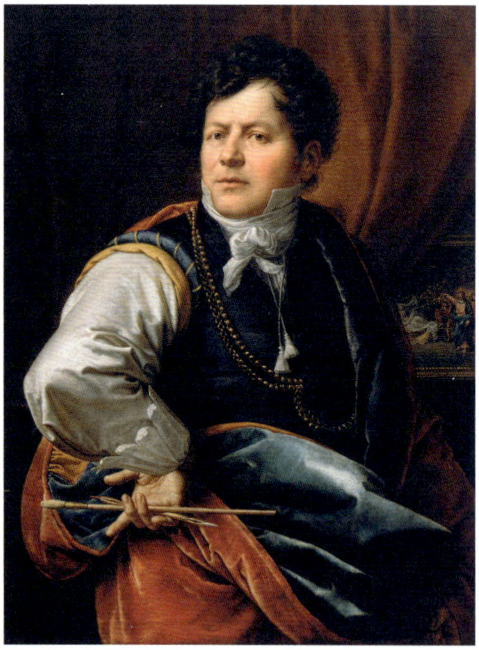

Fig. 2 Jean-Baptiste Wicar, *Self-Portrait in Fancy Dress,* after 1806. Oil on canvas. Palais des Beaux Arts, Lille, France, No. 887.

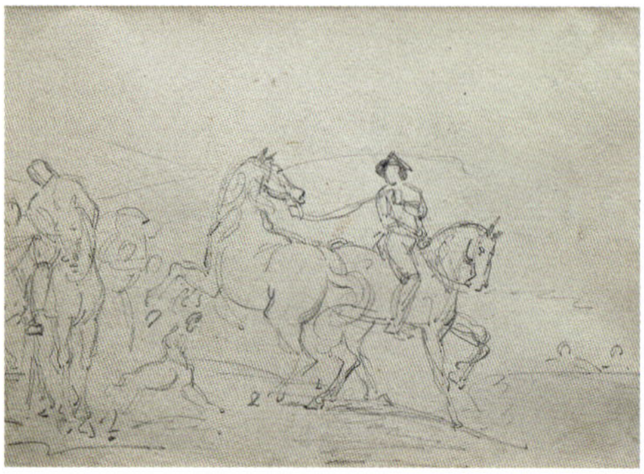

Cat. 5, verso.

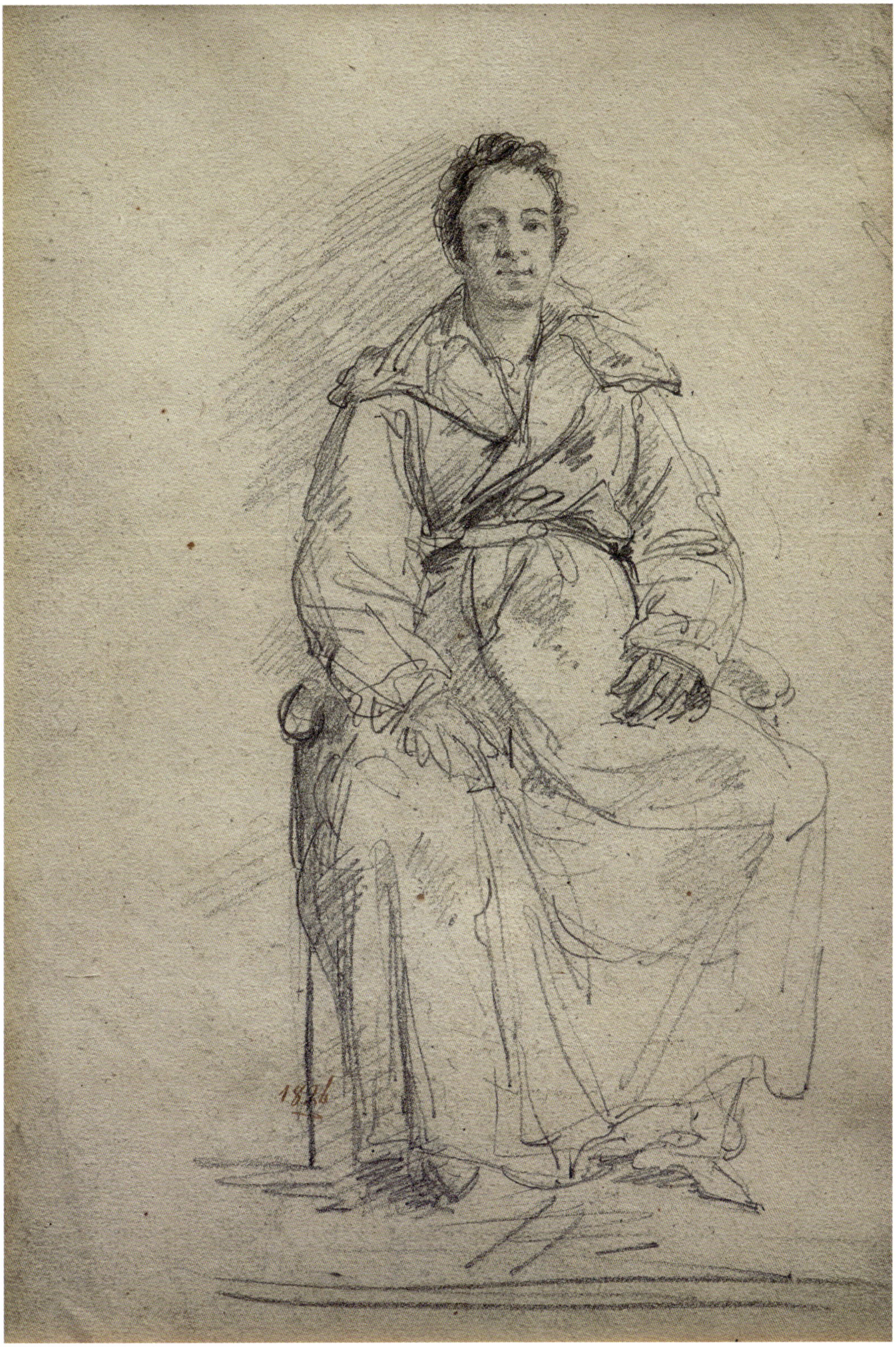

Cat. 5, recto.

Note
1. Personal communication, Louis-Antoine Prat. August 12, 2013

requisitioned Italian works of art to be sent to France during the Napoleonic years. In 1801 he settled permanently in Rome, where he built for himself the most important collection of Renaissance and baroque drawings of that era. Numbering in the thousands, these works today are among the greatest treasures of the drawing cabinets of the Musée du Louvre; the British Museum; the Ashmolean Museum, Oxford; and the Musée des Beaux-Arts, Lille.

WBJ

6

Louis-Pierre Henriquel-Dupont French, 1797–1892

PORTRAIT OF A WRITER, *1825*

Pencil and white gouache on paper, 10¾ × 8½ in. (272 × 216 mm)
Signed and dated lower right on the desk: *HDupont 1825*
Collection of George T. M. Shackelford

PROVENANCE Galerie Fischer-Kiener, Paris; from whom purchased 1989 by the current owner.

Louis-Pierre Henriquel-Dupont was probably the most important French engraver of the first half of the 19th century, and his influence lasted until the century's end. Two engravings in particular brought him acclaim. He worked for six years to reproduce Paul Delaroche's decoration *Hemicycle of the Fine Arts* at the École des Beaux-Arts, Paris. Théophile Gautier said that his engraving "made this beautiful composition so familiar to everyone that it is unnecessary to describe it. . . . But how greatly superior is the modified reduction to the original."[1] Henriquel-Dupont's other great success was the burin engraving of Ingres's famous portrait of M. Bertin, presented at the Salon of 1844. Since then this burin has been considered one of the finest examples of engraving of the entire 19th century. Henriquel-Dupont's friend the great romantic sculptor David d'Angers made a beautiful medallion portrait of him, which was edited in bronze.

Henriquel-Dupont engraved, drew, or painted many portraits of his contemporaries, like the one of Charles Normand (1827), the beautiful standing portrait of the violinist and collector Alexandre Sauvageot holding objects from his collection (1833), and the portrait of the architect Alexandre Brongniart (1840). *Portrait of a Writer* seems to be among the earliest known by the artist. The quill in the sitter's right hand could be the sign of a writer, while the imposing armchair with lion's heads could be associated with a statesman. Although one is tempted to compare these portraits to the best portrait drawings by Jean-Auguste-Dominique Ingres because of their benevolent spirit and their reliance on line more than chiaroscuro, there is still something of Jacques-Louis David in their acuteness and their graphic ambitions. Altogether, Henriquel-Dupont's portraits have a style all their own that deserves to be better known.

OM

Note
1. Théophile Gautier, *Complete Works*, vol. 3 (*The Romance of a Mummy* and *Portraits of the Day*), ed. and trans. F. C. de Sumichrast (London: Postlethwaite, Taylor & Knowles, Ltd., 1909), p. 257.

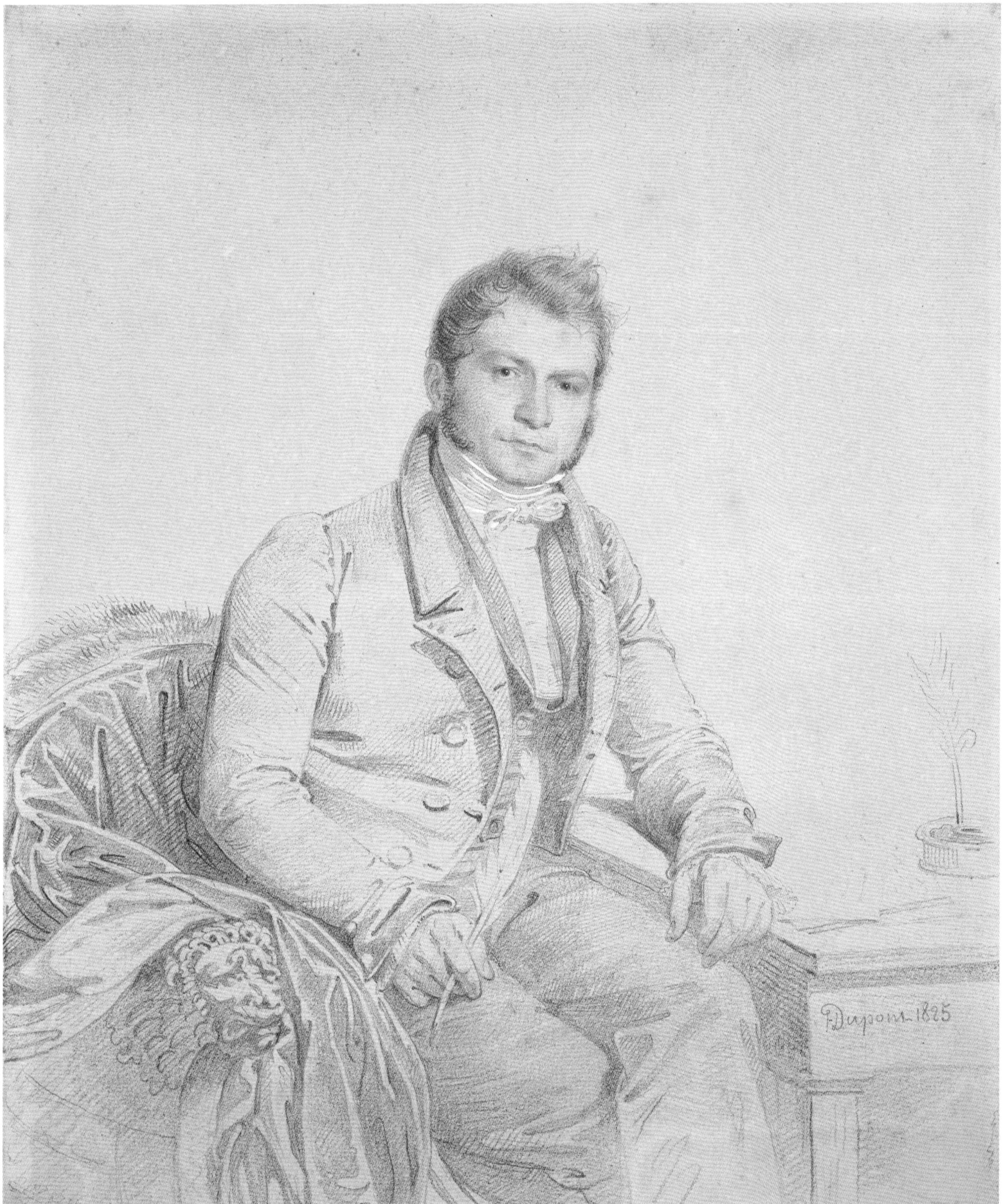
P. Dupont 1825

7

François-Marius Granet French, 1775–1849

CORNER OF A ROMAN CLOISTER, *N.D.*

Graphite and watercolor on paper, 4¾ × 7⅛ in. (120 × 180 mm)
Private collection, Dallas

PROVENANCE With Hubert Duchemin, Paris; Artemis Fine Arts Sarl., Paris; where purchased 2003 by the current owner.

The son of a mason, François-Marius Granet was born in the southeastern town of Aix-en-Provence. Aix was founded as a Roman city, and its southern sloping land sat at the crossroads of the well-traveled roads between northern France and Italy. Its warm sun and Italianate architecture may have predisposed Granet to become a lifelong Romanophile.[1]

At the encouragement of his childhood friend Comte Auguste de Forbin, Granet traveled from Aix to Paris in 1797 and was admitted to the atelier of Jacques-Louis David with Forbin's introduction. Granet excelled as a draftsman under David's rigorous tutelage, but the young artist was abruptly forced to stop his training for lack of funds. Unlike many of David's other students, Granet did not aspire to history painting in the grand manner. His Salon entry of 1799, *The Little Cloister of the Feuillants*, marks a different path. This critically praised interior of a monastery in the rue Saint-Honoré, Paris, points to his preference for real and imagined church interiors, cloisters, and ruins.

In 1802, Granet traveled with Forbin to Italy following a route through Siena, Florence, Pisa, Tivoli, and Naples. He maintained a primary residence in Rome for more than 20 years, and his deep appreciation for the city and its people became one of the central themes of his *Memoirs*. He writes: "Here I am at the height of my wishes: I see myself in this village founded by Romulus, in the most famous city of the world . . . with the thought of spending my life in this land, I search to better situate myself in the spirit of the Romans and conforming myself to their tastes and their ways."[2]

Granet made his living in Rome selling picturesque views of the ancient ruins as well as local crypts, catacombs, and church interiors. In his *Memoirs*, he refers to himself as an "Old Priest from Provence" and "This Capuchin,"[3] identifying with the religious order of the Franciscans, whose austerity was modeled on St. Francis. Granet was uninterested in religious iconography of the Old and New Testaments, preferring to picture the liturgical rituals of the local clergy. The present sheet is such an example, featuring two clerics performing their daily rituals in a simple though atmospheric cloister. As was his custom, Granet first established the composition in graphite and then went over his initial lines in sweeping strokes of transparent wash to evoke deep shadows and the dampness that only the cold stone of an ancient dwelling could provide in the harsh Roman sun. Though this sheet, like his many others, is composed largely with murky earth tones to evoke a somber interior, he adds subtle touches of color in the green leaves of the potted plant at center and in the hint of foliage behind the thick wall—inviting the viewer to imagine the Roman life that he so relished outside these walls.

EB

Notes
1. On Granet, see Olson 1989; Munhall 1988; and Coutagne 2008.
2. Quoted in Coutagne 2008, 105, 117.
3. Olson 1988, n. p.

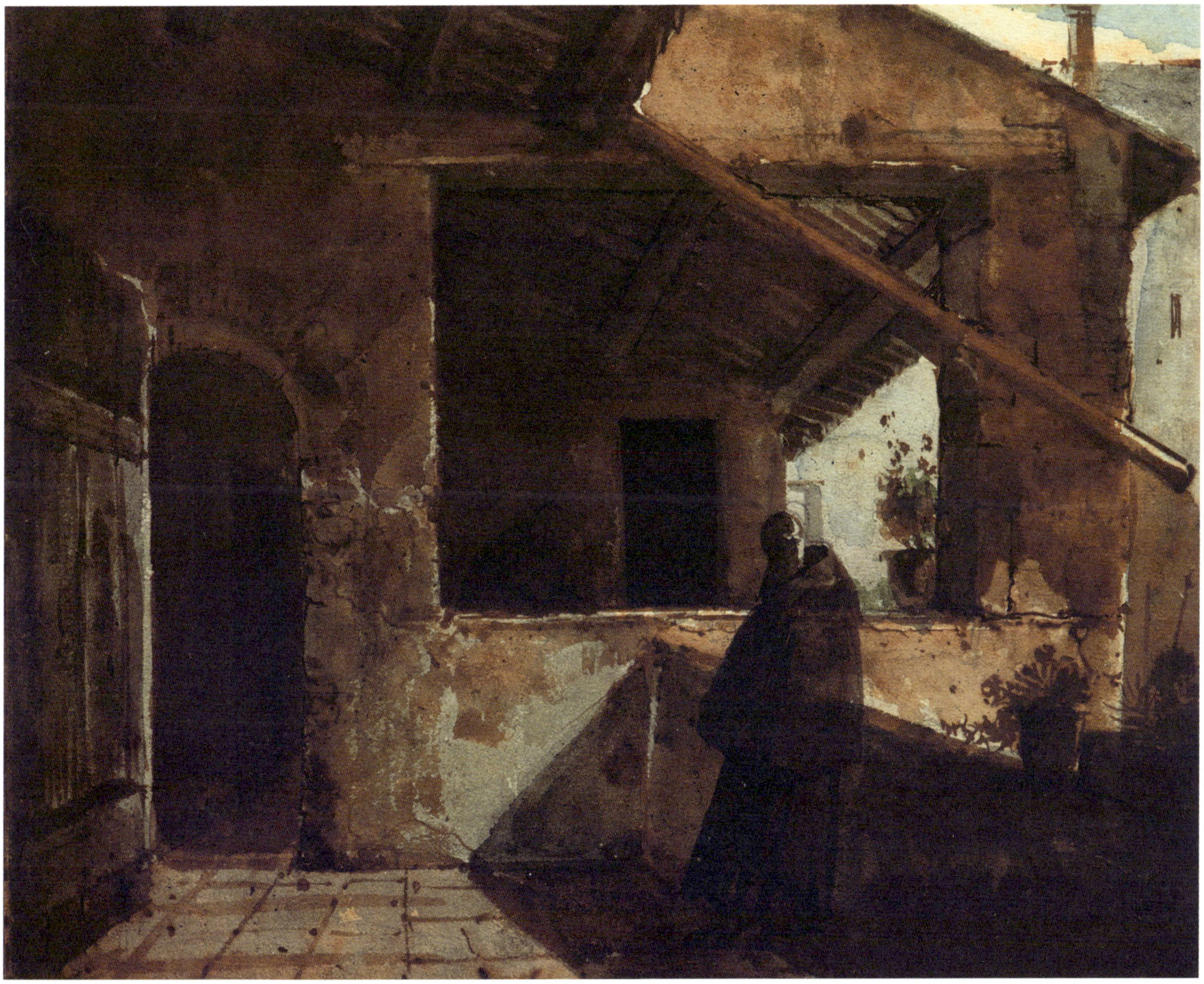

Théodore Géricault French, 1791–1824

A PENITENT PRESENTING THE BAISER DE PAIX TO TWO YOUNG CHILDREN, C. *1816–1817*

Black chalk, brown, yellow, and red wash, heightened with white on wove paper, mounted on a sheet, with Orfini arms watermark, 7⅝ × 5⅛ in. (195 × 131 mm)
Private collection, Dallas

PROVENANCE With Hubert Duchemin, Paris; Artemis Fine Arts Sarl., Paris; where purchased 2003 by the current owner.

EXHIBITED C.G. Boerner, Inc., New York, *Old Master Drawings*, January 22–February 8, 2003, no. 45, repr.

Although Théodore Géricault failed to win the Prix de Rome of 1816, he was determined to continue his artistic education. He financed his own trip to Italy in order to "observe and work," arriving in Florence in 1816 and soon after continuing on to Rome.[1] This lively drawing probably dates from Géricault's stay in Rome in 1816–1817. The poignant yet playful composition in black chalk and bright washes belongs to a group of studies illustrating the vibrant Roman street life. The looming cloaked figure is dressed in the costume of a penitent, perhaps on Maundy (or Holy) Thursday, the festival that commemorates the Eucharist on the Thursday before Easter, during which penitents are absolved from their mortal sins.

Géricault captures the moment when a penitent, most likely a well-born and devout Catholic, tenderly offers an unusual-looking object to a young girl, who gingerly leans forward to kiss it. This rectangular object, which has a handle on the back to make it easy to hold, is an osculatorium (tablet of peace), or, as the French say, *Baiser de Paix*. Since the 13th century, osculatoria—which usually bore low-relief images in ivory, metal, or wood of the Crucifixion, the Nativity, or some other suitable devotion—were a means of conveying the Kiss of Peace from the celebrant of the mass to the faithful about to receive communion. In this case, the man's hood and short cape likely indicate the color of his confraternity. Despite his masked face, the outline of his profile and the craning of his neck indicate a moment of tender affection.

One of the leading Roman artists during Géricault's stay in Italy was Bartolomeo Pinelli (1781–1835), who popularly chronicled daily life in a series of large print editions. Pinelli's images likely appealed to Géricault for their lively depictions of the decidedly "exotic" costumes and activities of the Roman people. Géricault's creation is stylistically and thematically similar to Pinelli's watercolor featuring a penitent frightening a young child in the Colosseum, signed and dated 1819 (Musée Condé, Chantilly, DE 178), a composition reminiscent of several scenes in Pinelli's *Nuova Raccolta di Cinquanta Costumi Pittoreschi* (1816), a compendium of illustrations with which Géricault presumably was familiar.

EB

Note
1. Eitner 1983, 99.

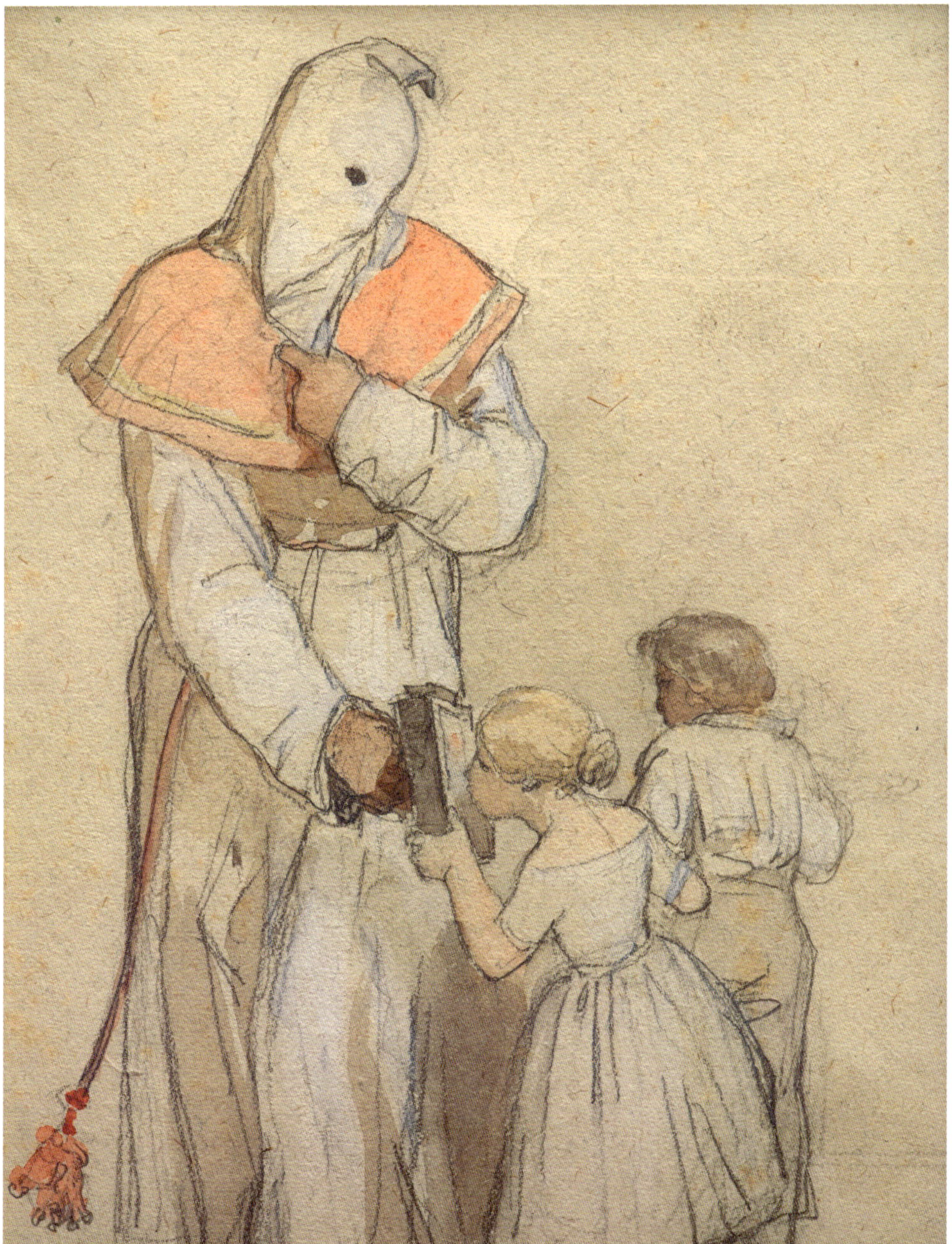

9

Théodore Géricault French, 1791–1824

A DEAD CAT, AND THREE STUDIES OF ITS HEAD, *C. 1819–1821*

Graphite, pen and brown ink, gray wash on paper, 11¾ × 16¼ in. (322 × 412 mm)
Stamped: *19–16*
Private collection

PROVENANCE Private collection; sale, Christie's, New York, *Old Master Drawings*, January 24, 2011, lot 133; where purchased by the current owner.

After his controversial entry in the Salon of 1819, *The Raft of the Medusa* (Musée du Louvre, Paris), Théodore Géricault traveled to London to exhibit his painting at a commercial gallery and charge a fee for admission. During his stay, he also sought to exploit the English taste for lithography, stating that his graphic projects could serve as an "advertisement. . . . As soon as the real connoisseurs have come to know me, they will use me for work worthier of myself."[1] Thus, he embarked on a compendium entitled *Various Subjects Drawn from Life and on Stone* (1821). London street life was of great interest to him, and he avidly sketched beggars, rabid street dogs, and even a public execution.

This study from life can be dated securely to Géricault's London period (1819–1821) because of a related drawing in the Musée Bonnat, Bayonne (inv. 787), which bears a tracing of two lithographs published in London: *Horses Going to the Fair* and *The Flemish Farrier*. Like other French artists from the late romantic period—such as Eugène Delacroix and Antoine-Louis Barye, who sketched the zoological collections, dead and alive, at the menagerie at Saint-Cloud and the Jardin des Plantes in Paris—Géricault studied animals and transformed their savage forms into compositional elements that were central to some of his dramatic scenes. This drawing, however, was likely made from investigations of the body of a dead animal. With its careful observation of the natural form and its deliberate and sharp hatching in ink, it studies with precision the cat's sharp fangs, buoyant whiskers, and glassy eyes, as well as the serpentine line of its lifeless body.

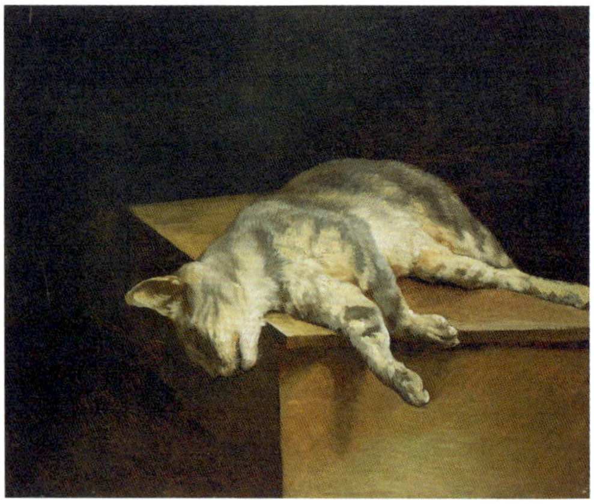

Fig. 3 Théodore Géricault, *Dead Cat*, 1821. Oil on canvas. Musée du Louvre, Paris, RF 2003–6.

Variations of the feline forms seen here, including the cat draped over the step or stone in the lower register, can be found in drawings in the Musée du Louvre, the Fogg Art Museum, and the Musée Bonnat.[2] A related painting in the Louvre (fig. 3), unknown until 2003 when its attribution changed from Jean-Baptiste-Siméon Chardin to Géricault, was listed in the artist's posthumous inventory as "after a dead cat."[3]

EB

Notes
1. Eitner 1983, 221.
2. Bazin 1997, vii, nos. 2366–68.
3. Laveissière 2003, 22.

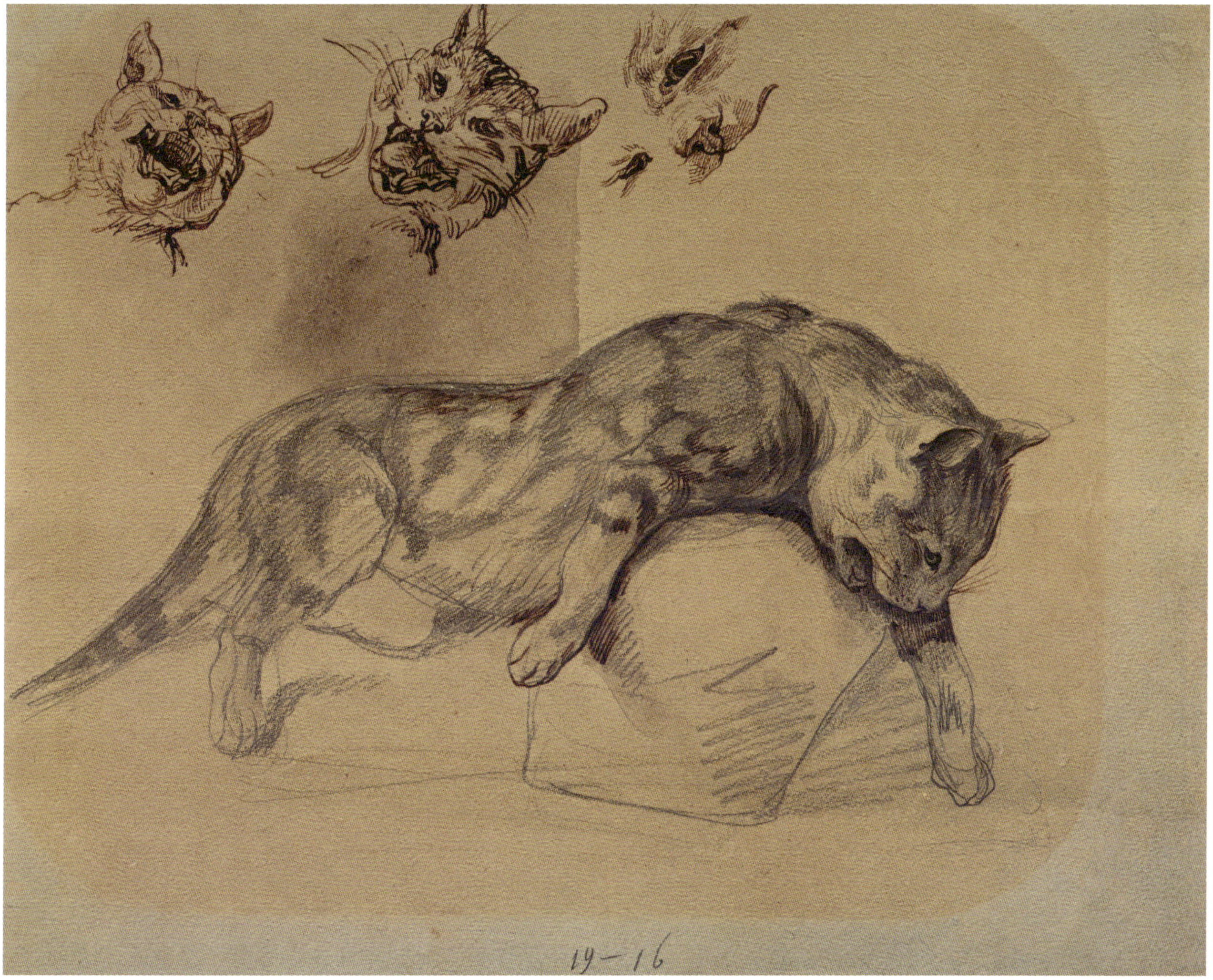
19 – 16

10

Eugène Delacroix French, 1798–1863

SHEET OF MOROCCAN STUDIES, *N.D.*

Iron gall ink on cream wove paper, 14⅛ × 8⅝ in. (358 × 219 mm);
sight size: 13¼ × 6⅝ (335 × 167 mm)
Inscribed in brown ink on verso: *par Eug. Delacroix / AR* (Alfred Robaut)
Collection of Mary Ralph Lowe, Fort Worth

PROVENANCE Brandt Dayton & Co., New York; from whom acquired 1990 by the current owner.

Eugène Delacroix looms over any discussion of art in 19th-century France. To a degree unparalleled by any of his contemporaries—even his arch-rival Jean-Auguste-Dominique Ingres—he personified the complete artist in the grand mode of the Old Masters, a protean talent capable of expressing the tenderest intimacy or the stagiest and most colossal grandiloquence. His imagination was drawn to the narrative challenges of literature, religion, and poetry and to the appetite of his time for the exotic, even the dangerous. From the very beginning of his prolific career, the well-born artist was the acknowledged leader of the French romantic movement. Famous for his avowed preference for color over line, he was nevertheless unmatched as a draftsman. He left many thousands of drawings, some of them mere notations of what he saw, made on the spot for possible later use; others that were studies for details in his complex historical works; still others that were complete compositional studies; and some that were finished works in their own right. Since his death in 1863, his works on paper—embracing the media of pen and ink, pencil, watercolor, pastel, and combinations of them—have been collected avidly and are now dispersed throughout the world.

Delacroix painted his first masterpieces of so-called orientalism—*The Massacre at Chios* (1824), *Greece on the Ruins of Missolonghi* (1826), and *The Death of Sardanapalus* (1827)—without ever having seen the Middle East. In 1832 he managed to join the diplomatic mission to Morocco conducted for King Louis-Philippe by the Comte de Mornay. The alien and exotic culture filled him with delight, which he likened to being surrounded by Greeks and Romans in their togas and robes. The drawings and studies he made on this trip served for the rest of his life as sources of inspiration and points of departure for paintings and drawings that continued to spring from this romance with the exotic. The present sheet is surely one of those later works inspired by visions Delacroix wanted never to forget. The drawing bears no estate stamp; thus it may be a work that the artist sold or gave away in his lifetime. This seems corroborated by the inscription on the verso of the sheet (*par Eug. Delacroix /AR*), which appears to be a connoisseur's attestation of the drawing's authenticity, the connoisseur being none other than Alfred Robaut, author of the first catalogue of Delacroix's works. Whether the drawing was among the many that belonged to Robaut himself has not been confirmed, but it could be one of those (*Têtes de Marocains et d'Arabes*), which he cited in several collections and dated to 1832.[1]

The elegant strokes of a pen with iron gall ink hover over this page like Japanese calligraphy on a scroll. Each figure has been captured, as if observed as an individual who might be recombined later into one of the fictive crowds that animate so many of the artist's Moroccan compositions. Figures have been caught in odd, unposed angles that offered the artist opportunities to study the elegant ways a burnoose can envelop the human form or frame a facial profile. Particularly audacious is the reclining figure at the top, leaning on his shoulder but seen from behind. Each gestural stroke of the pen has captured the contour and volume of the figure with an energy and utter economy of means that mark Delacroix as one of the great draftsmen of all time.

WBJ

Note
1. Robaut 1885, no. 1602.

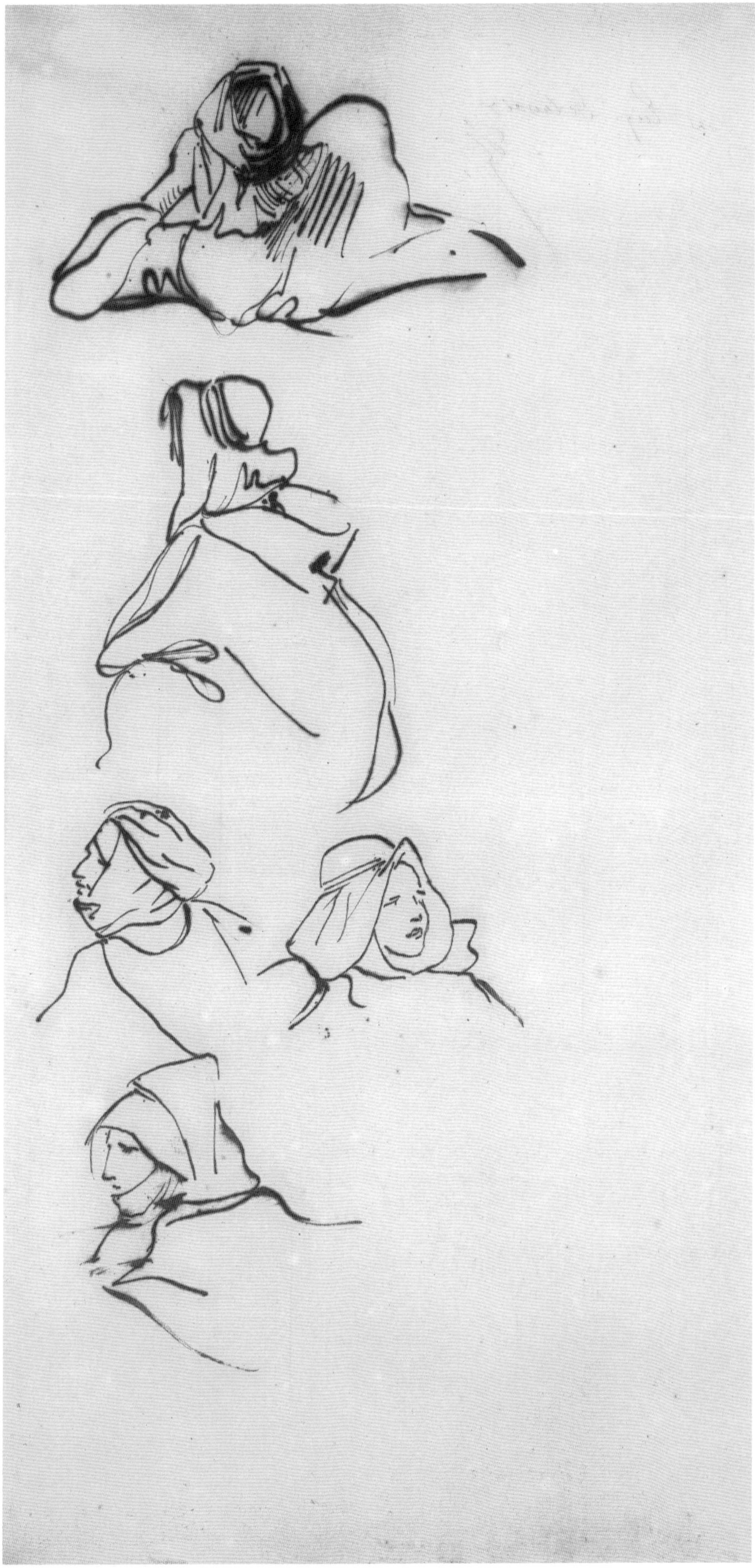

11

Eugène Delacroix French, 1789–1863

SHEET OF STUDIES FOR THE JUSTICE OF TRAJAN (FEUILLE D'ÉTUDES POUR LA JUSTICE DE TRAJAN), C. *1840*

Pencil on paper, 8⅝ x 13⅞ in. (220 x 352 mm)
Estate stamp lower right: *ED* (Lugt 838); inscribed lower left: *Félix Bernard rue de / la Tixaranderie no. 14*
Dallas Museum of Art, given in memory of Louie N. Bromberg and Mina Bromberg by their sister Essie Bromberg Joseph, 1982.40

PROVENANCE Private collection, Europe; Hazlitt, Gooden & Fox, London; where purchased 1982 by the Dallas Museum of Art, the Bromberg-Joseph Fund, given by Essie Bromberg Joseph.

EXHIBITED Hazlitt, Gooden & Fox, London, *Nineteenth-Century French Drawings,* June 10–July 8, 1982, cat. 31, pl. 23; Dallas Museum of Art, *Before Impressionism: French 19th-Century Art in the Dallas Museum of Art,* August 27, 2004–January 2, 2005.

BIBLIOGRAPHY Johnson 1986, 93 (under entry for cat. 271).

Exhibited at the Salon of 1840 and currently in the collection of the Musée des Beaux-Arts, Rouen, the monumental painting *The Justice of Trajan (La Justice de Trajan),* inspired by Canto X of Dante's *Purgatorio,* was the subject of several dozen preparatory drawings, the largest of which rehearse the composition as a whole. Some studies of details exist, including this example, whose three main motifs concern the young man seen from behind in the right foreground of the painting. Delacroix drew variants of his headdress with its characteristic headband. The feminine head and the hand seem to belong to two less prominent and somewhat overshadowed figures at the center of the composition. "I thought of putting a group of people climbing on columns," Delacroix wrote to Frédéric Villot while in the throes of composing his painting.[1] As a result, the figures observe the scene from between the columns.

LAP

Note

1. Delacroix to Villot, November 4, 1839, *Correspondance générale d'Eugène Delacroix* (Paris: Plon, 1937–45).

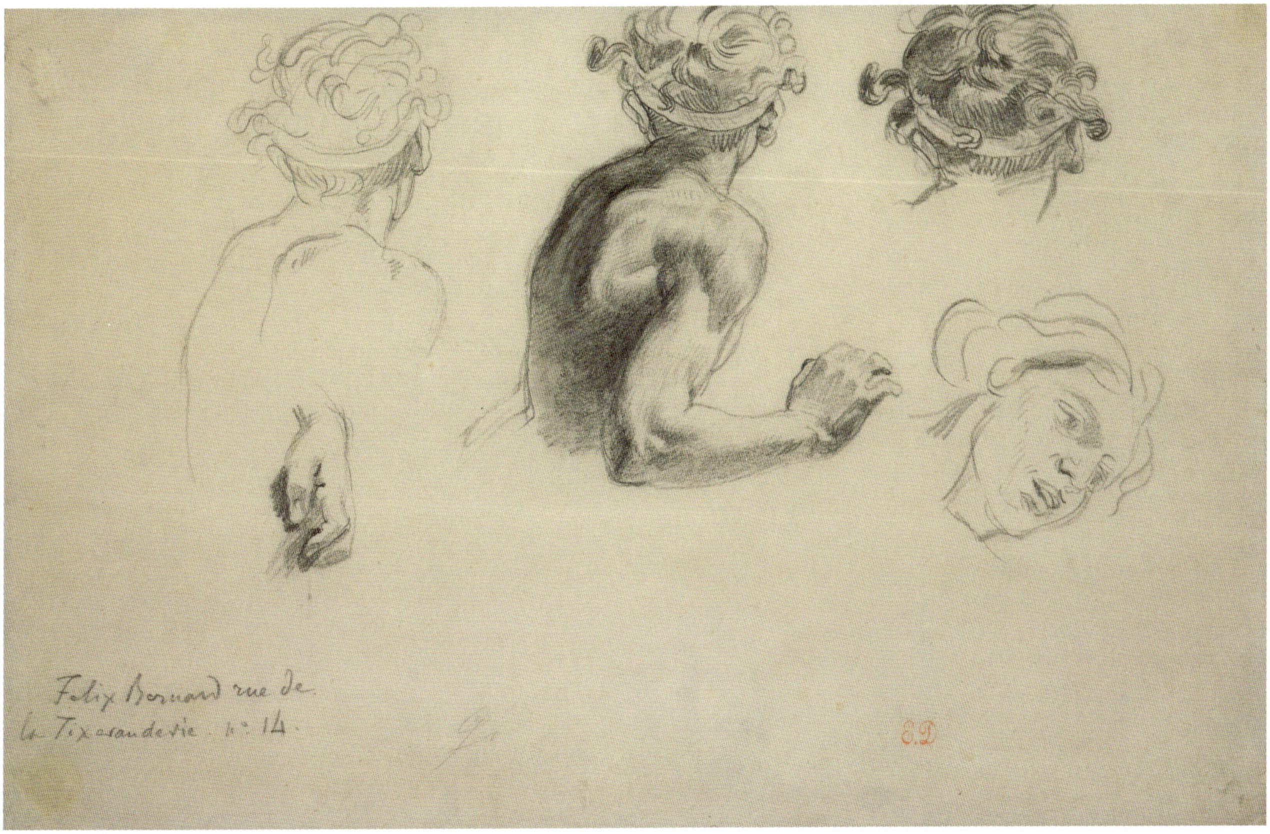
Felix Bernard rue de
la Tixeranderie n° 14.
E.D

12

Eugène Delacroix French, 1789–1863

SHEET OF STUDIES AFTER RUBENS (FEUILLE D'ÉTUDES D'APRÈS RUBENS), *1840*

Graphite on paper, 9⅞ × 14¾ in. (250 × 375 mm)
Graphite inscription lower right: *8bre 40*; with the estate stamp *ED*
Collection of Mr. and Mrs. Barron U. Kidd, Dallas

PROVENANCE Atelier Delacroix (Lugt 838a mark, lower right); Delacroix sale, Paris, Hôtel Drouot, February 22–27, 1864, part of lots 636 or 637, "Other Studies after Rubens, 97 drawings in pen or pencil"; where purchased by Messrs. Seligman, Rouillard, and Dieterle; the current owner.

BIBLIOGRAPHY Robaut 1885, part of no. 1958 or no. 1959.

Eugène Delacroix's fascination with—we might almost say addiction to—the work of Rubens is well known and confirmed by some dozen copies and more than 100 drawings and watercolors made after paintings in situ or that he knew through engravings, often reversed relative to the original. In his youth, Delacroix was influenced by Rubens and studied the enormous canvases of the *Life of Marie de' Medici* cycle after their transfer in 1816 from the Palais du Luxembourg to the Musée du Louvre. Several times he copied details or entire canvases. Among the holdings of the Graphic Arts Department of the Louvre, which include more than 20 leaves drawn after Rubens, is a beautiful graphite interpretation of *The Arrival of Marie de' Medici at Marseilles* (inv. RF 32249). Delacroix also made several studies of the group of naiads to the lower left of the painting, a group that later attracted Paul Cézanne. He also executed a remarkable wash in situ in 1850 after the *Lamentation (Christ on the Straw)* in the Koninklijk Museum, Antwerp (inv. RF 10484).

But Delacroix loved above all to rediscover the "fine exaggeration" of form that he so admired in Rubens's paintings.[1] Attracted by the "emphasis, . . . the exaggerated and loose [forms],"[2] he repeatedly copied the engravings by Pieter Soutman or Schelte a Bolswert of Rubens's various *Hunts,* which had a dynamism and vitality that thrilled him. Less frequently, he paid homage to Rubens through an intermediary, the woodcut printmaker Christophe Jegher, who interpreted some of Rubens's paintings from 1619–1620 on the ceiling of the nave of the Jesuit Church in Antwerp. The church was destroyed by fire in July 1718, and all that remains of the paintings today are sublimely energetic oil sketches. This drawing reproduces with scrupulous fidelity the detail of two engravings after the ceiling panels: the figure of Christ, upper center, and the hands of the devil, on the right, presenting an object, come from the engraving of *The Temptation of Christ.*[3] The rest of Delacroix's drawing—the leg (right, mid-height), Christ raising a crown, the feminine head (of the Virgin), above it the head of a bearded man (belonging to God the Father), and the upside-down hand (also belonging to God the Father)—are taken from Jegher's engraving after the panel of the *Coronation of the Virgin.*[4]

The quality of the layout of these different motifs, admirably arranged in the confined space of the leaf, is as striking as the use of graphite, here preferred to pen, which makes it possible through carefully modulated hatchings to reproduce with astonishing fidelity the nuances of Jegher's burin. A clear sensation of power emanates from the leaf as a whole: "I have words with him because of his heavy forms. . . . There is a man, anyway, who has the courage to be himself; he forces you to accept those so-called defects deriving from that force which sweeps along the man himself," noted Delacroix in his journal, seemingly intent on justifying his own stylistic exaggerations.[5]

Delacroix made two major trips to Belgium, in 1839 and 1850. During the first, he wrote to his friend Pierret that he considered Rubens "uneven, like everyone else . . . when he frees himself from his models, that is the great Rubens. I shall show you that in detail. I saw everything there is to see in Antwerp."[6] Though unable on that occasion to view the ceiling of the Jesuit Church, which had already burnt down, Delacroix may be said to have expressed in these few words the need that every great artist feels to be inspired by his predecessors while going beyond them. Difficult to date from the perspective of style, this beautiful sheet undoubtedly derives from this very ambitious manner of interpreting one's great predecessors.

LAP

Notes

1. Delacroix 1972, 132 (January 23, 1847).
2. Ibid., 155 (March 6, 1847).
3. Martin 1968, fig. 42.
4. Ibid., fig. 103.
5. Delacroix 1972, 687–88 (October 20, 1860).
6. Delacroix to Pierret, September 21, 1839, *Correspondance générale d'Eugène Delacroix* (Paris: Plon, 1937–45).

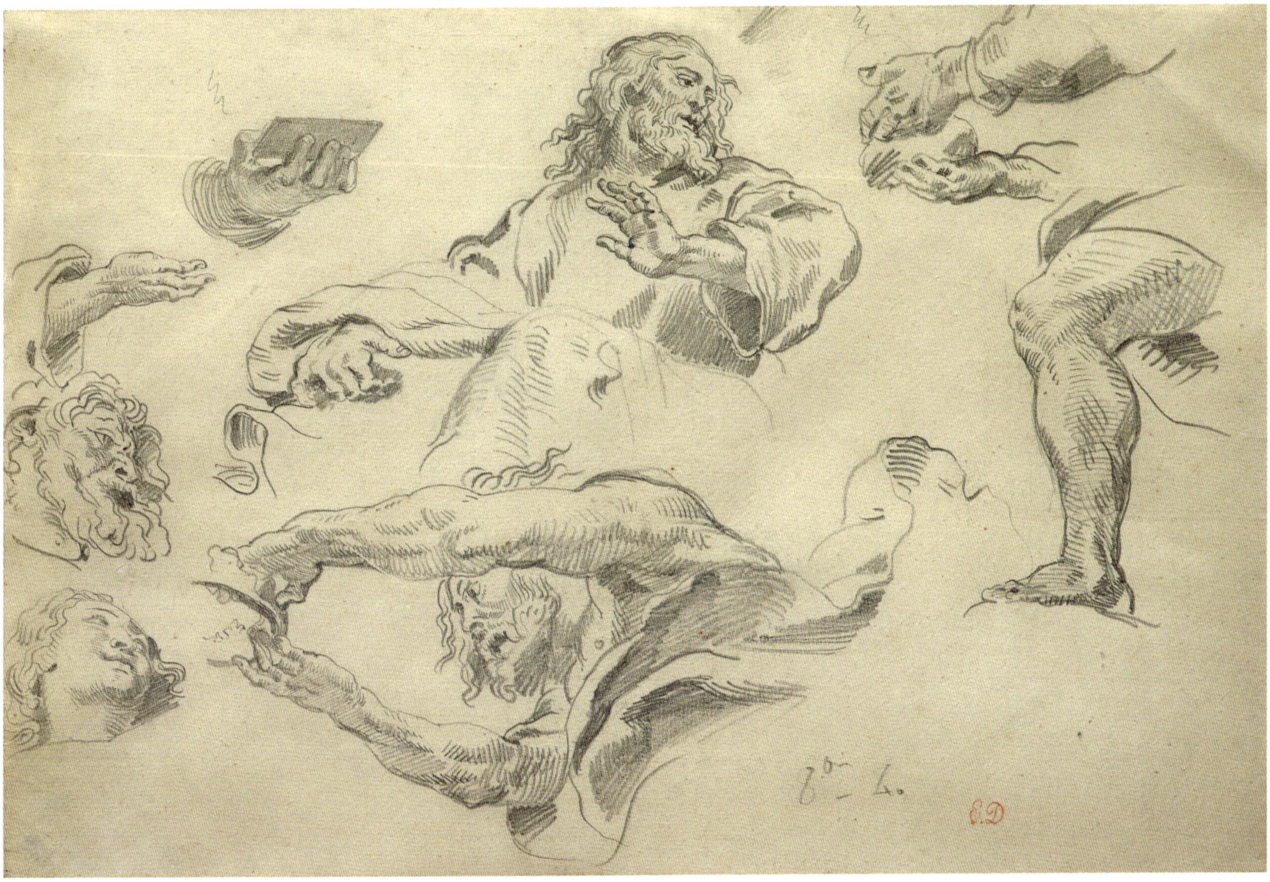

13

Eugène Delacroix French, 1789–1863

INDIAN SCALPING A FALLEN ADVERSARY (INDIEN SCALPANT UN ENNEMI À TERRE), *1845*

Pen and brown ink on laid paper, 7⅞ × 12⅜ in. (200 × 313 mm)
Private collection, Dallas

PROVENANCE Atelier Delacroix (Lugt 838a mark, lower right); Delacroix sale, Paris, Hôtel Drouot, February 22–27, 1864, no doubt part of lot 652 ("*Croquis d'après des sauvages Iowas* 1834 [*sic*]; 33 feuilles de dessins et croquis; en quatre lots à MM. Riesener, Barbet de Jouy, Sensier, Philippe Rousseau"); Philippe Rousseau, animal painter (1816–1887); Galerie Bernheim-Jeune, Paris; Etienne Moreau-Nélaton, Paris? (but not part of his donation to the Musées nationaux); Jean-Pierre Durand-Matthiesen, Geneva, in 1963; Thomas Le Claire Gallery, Hamburg, (*Handzeichnungen und Aquarelle 1500–1900*, 1987, 124, no. 63); Brandt Dayton Gallery, New York; where purchased 1988 by the current owner.

EXHIBITED Galerie Bernheim-Jeune, Paris, 1954, *Gros, Géricault, Delacroix*, no. 298; Musée du Louvre, Paris, *Exposition Eugène Delacroix à l'occasion du centenaire de la mort de l'artiste*, 1963, no. 354.

BIBLIOGRAPHY Robaut 1885, no doubt part of no. 1671; Sérullaz 1963, no. 351, repr. 260; Sérullaz et al. 1984, vol. 2, 99, no. 1514.

We know a great deal about the group of Ojibwa dancers who came to Paris in the autumn of 1845; Delacroix refers to them in letters to his pupil Planet (August 30, 1845) and to George Sand (September 1845). Delacroix made several known studies of Indians in situ, but most seem to have been made after paintings by the American artist George Catlin, which were exhibited that same year in 1845 in the Salle Valentino as *Galerie Indienne*. The Musée du Louvre already held one such study (inv. RF 9311),[1] and recently acquired a sketchbook containing several others. The principal subject of the sketchbook is the Pyrenean landscapes Delacroix made while staying at Eaux-Bonnes from July 22 to August 15, 1845.[2]

Catlin's paintings astonished his contemporaries with the fearsome scenes they presented. George Sand emphasized the hideous nature of the depictions of death, torture, and initiation into mysteries.[3] We should probably look for the scene reproduced here in one of those lost paintings (a different version of a scalping is at the Smithsonian American Art Museum);[4] it seems unlikely to derive from direct observation of the peaceful Iowa Indians who came to Paris.

LAP

Notes
1. Sérullaz et al. 1984, no. 1514.
2. Musée du Louvre, inv. RF 52997, folios 44 recto and verso, 45 recto and verso, 46 recto and verso, and 47 recto.
3. Sand, "Les sauvages de Paris" (The Savages of Paris), *Diable à Paris*, 1846, quoted in Beetem 1961, 130.
4. *Mandan Scalping an Enemy*, oil on canvas, 1835–1837, Smithsonian American Art Museum, gift of Mrs. Joseph Harrison Jr., 1985.66.498.

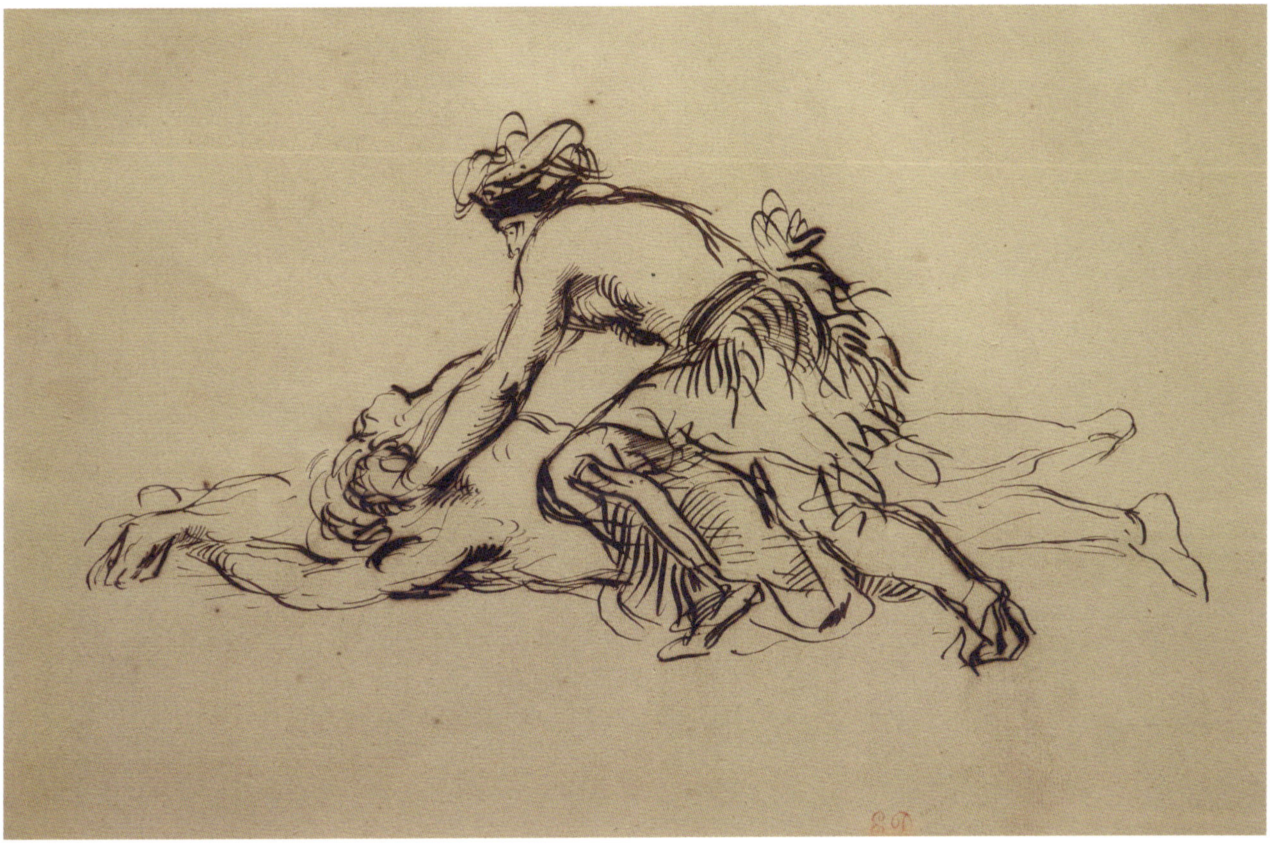

14

Eugène Delacroix French, 1789–1863

ARAB HORSEMAN AT THE GALLOP (CAVALIER ARABE AU GALOP), *1849*

Graphite on tracing paper, 12½ × 10⅛ in. (320 × 257 mm)
Private collection, Dallas

PROVENANCE Atelier Delacroix (Lugt 838a mark, lower left); Delacroix sale, Paris, Hôtel Drouot, February 22–27, 1864, part of lot 571 or 572; W. M. Brady Gallery, New York; where purchased 1996 by the current owner.

BIBLIOGRAPHY Robaut 1885, part of no. 1632.

The painting to which this drawing relates (formerly Alain Delon, Paris) has been dated by Lee Johnson to c. 1849, while Alfred Robaut placed it around 1856.[1] Johnson gave long consideration to the nature of the object concealed in the cactus, in the lower left of the painting, which so alarms the horseman: Is it a snake? a naked blade? In fact, nothing is clearly visible, and that motif has disappeared in this drawing, which faithfully reproduces the main group with the exception of the mountainous background, absent here. Is the drawing a sort of *ricordo* of the painted work, perhaps intended for reproduction as an illustration in a journal? The *calque* that serves as its support might suggest this. Or is it really a preparatory drawing, something that the freedom of its style might suggest? There are some differences in the horseman's burnoose. His expression is more dramatic but less perfectly captured in the drawing, in which the treatment of the horse's head seems, by contrast, highly characteristic.

LAP

Note
1. Johnson 1986, vol. 3, 194, no. 384; vol. 4, pl. 193; Robaut 1885, no. 1294.

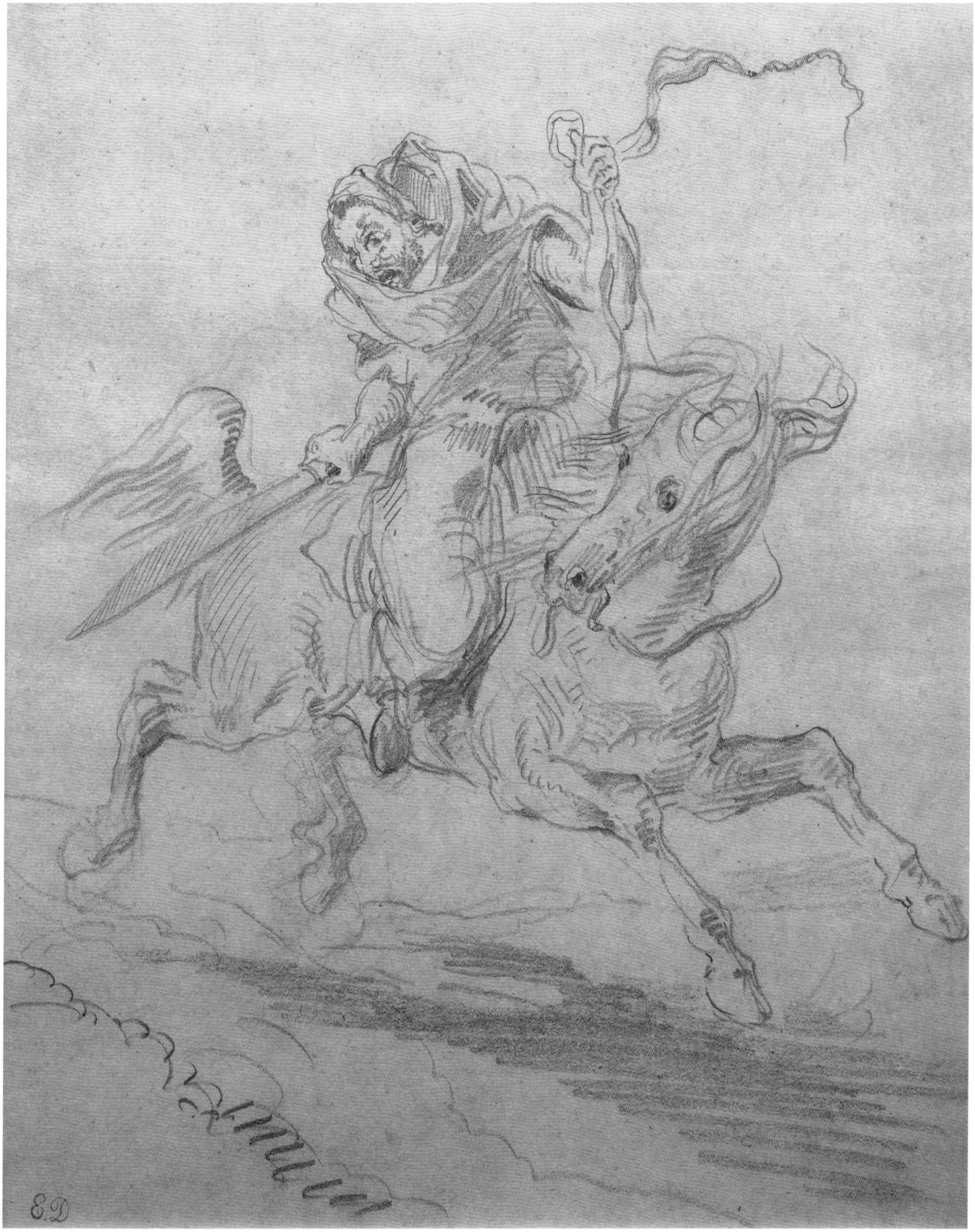
E.D

15

Antoine-Louis Barye French, 1795–1875

PYTHON COILED ON A BRANCH, *1850s–1860s*

Graphite on tracing paper laid down on cardboard, 7⅛ × 12 in. (180 × 305 mm)
Estate stamp lower left in red: *BARYE* (Lugt 220)
Private collection, Dallas

PROVENANCE Barye sale, Paris, Hôtel Drouot, February 7–12, 1876; Shepherd Gallery, New York; where purchased 1968 by the current owner.

EXHIBITED Shepherd Gallery, New York, *The Non-Dissenters: David through Puvis de Chavannes,* May–June 1968, cat. 40; Wildenstein & Co., New York, *The Wild Kingdom of Antoine-Louis Barye (1795–1875),* November 4–December 9, 1994 (catalogue by Joseph Baillio), 25, 130, cat. 130.

BIBLIOGRAPHY Baltimore Museum of Art and Walters Art Museum 2005, entry by Simon Kelly, 100; Johnston and Kelly 2006, entry by Simon Kelly, 212.

Antoine-Louis Barye built a great reputation in Europe and America by exploiting the allure of the "other"—the wild, irrational side of nature and human nature—that was central to the movement known as romanticism. A quiet man of modest manners, best known for his relatively small-scale sculptures and watercolors of wild animals, Barye was nevertheless one of the giants of the 19th century. The supremely confident superstar of that century's later decades, Auguste Rodin—who had studied briefly with him and was his opposite as a personality—referred to Barye as "the great man of our century" and stressed that "it is . . . from him that I've learned the most."[1] Such regard was shared by most of his contemporaries—including Eugène Delacroix, Jean-Baptiste-Camille Corot, Jean-François Millet, Henri Rousseau, Honoré Daumier, and Charles-François Daubigny—who were his friends and colleagues and most of whom owned his works.

In the 1820s, often accompanied by Delacroix, Barye frequented the animal exhibits in Paris's Jardin des Plantes, where he came to understand the anatomy and movement of wild beasts as no one before him had. He used this knowledge in creating small sculptures with a jewel-like finish that found huge favor with both the expanded collector base of the new middle class in Paris and the royalty and aristocracy of his time. Not content with such specialization, he also sought and obtained important government commissions for large-scale public monuments representing classical themes as well as the romantic animal subjects for which he was so well known.

In his lifetime, Barye's watercolors were even more highly valued than his sculptures, prized not only for their exotic subject matter but also for their often-unorthodox techniques. This powerful drawing is a *calque,* or artist's tracing, that formed an integral step in the creation of two such works purchased in the 1880s by the Baltimore collectors Henry Walters and George A. Lucas. As Simon Kelly has noted, Barye's fascination with snakes probably was encouraged by the two pythons from Java acquired by the Jardin des Plantes in 1838 and by the opening of the Reptile House thereafter.[2] The motif of the huge serpent coiled upon a branch is central to both the Baltimore watercolors, but in one the tree is barren of foliage and looms in a mountainous desert, while in the other the tree is in a dark and leafy forest (fig. 4). Both watercolors derive from a pencil drawing in the Musée du Louvre[3] once belonging to the painter Jean-Léon Gérôme, in which Barye was observing the python directly from life in the Jardin des Plantes. In the *calque,* using a sharp pencil on the nearly transparent paper, the artist copied and reinforced the contours of the Louvre drawing and the pattern of the serpent's skin, greatly clarifying the form. He then transferred the design in ink to the watercolor paper, where it could provide the armature for the painted image. The *calque* could thus be used again and again, much as plaster molds served the same function in the creation of sculptures.

WBJ

Notes
1. Quoted in Johnston 2006, xi nn. 8, 9.
2. Kelly, in Johnston 2006, 212.
3. Antoine-Louis Barye, *Python Coiled on a Tree Limb,* black and brown chalk on beige paper with brown wash, 8⅜ × 12½ in. (212 × 320 mm), Musée du Louvre, Département des Arts Graphiques, Paris, RF 4223.

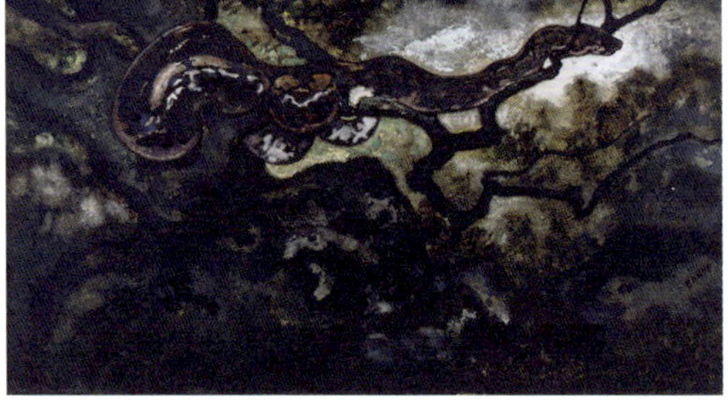

Fig. 4 Antoine-Louis Barye, *Python in a Tree,* c. 1850s–1860s. Watercolor with scraping and gum varnish on cream, thick wove paper. The Walters Art Museum, Acquired by William T. Walters, 1883, 37.817.

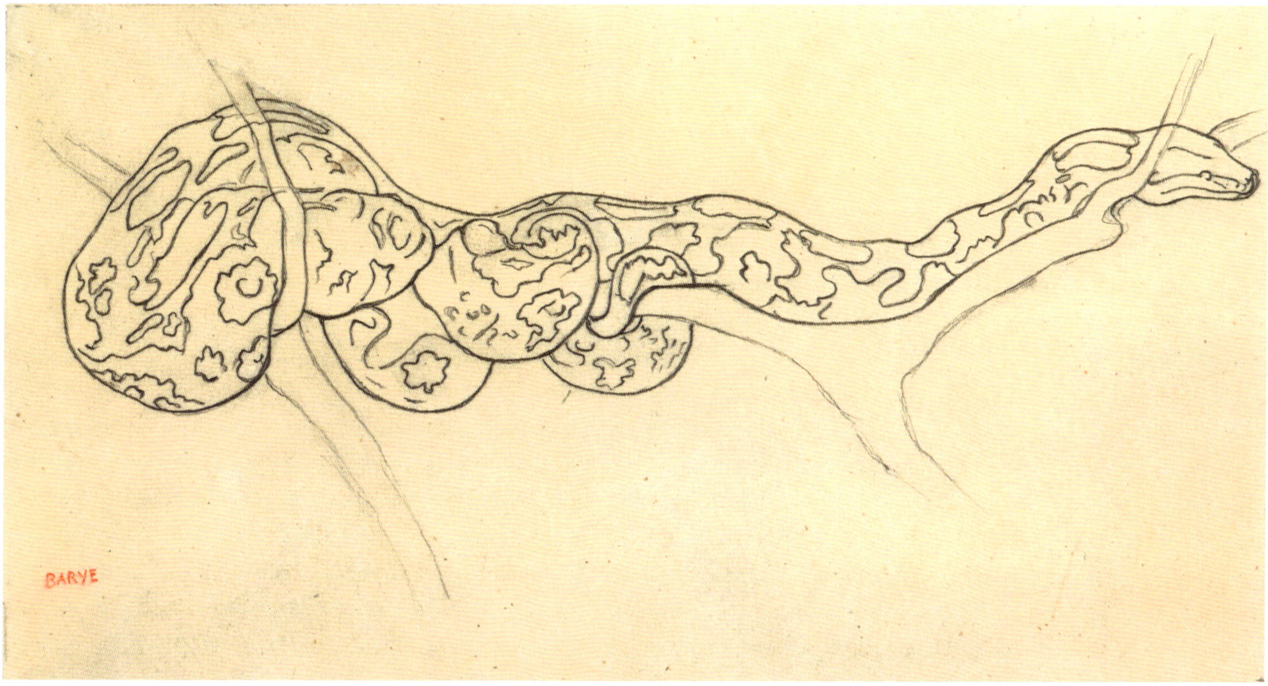
BARYE

16

Adrien Dauzats French, 1804–1868

RECLINING ZOUAVE (?) (RECTO), *1839;*
VILLAGE WITH STEEPLE (VERSO), *1840*

Graphite on wove paper, 7½ × 10¼ in. (190 × 260 mm)
On recto: Watermark at lower left, *W*; inscribed and dated in graphite, upper left: *Vendredi 12 avril 1839 (4e in J . . . d'Armes)*
On verso: Watercolor over graphite
Private collection, Dallas

PROVENANCE Shepherd Gallery, New York; Martin L. H. Reymert, New York; from whom purchased September 30, 1989, by the current owner.

EXHIBITED Shepherd Gallery, New York, *French Nineteenth-Century Drawings, Watercolors, Paintings, and Sculpture,* spring 1987, no. 55, repr.

Adrien Dauzats began his career as a painter of stage scenery, first in his native Bordeaux and then in Paris, where he arrived in 1824. After furthering his artistic training in the studio of Julien Michel Gué, Dauzats met theater enthusiast and editor Baron Isidore-Justin-Séverin Taylor. Baron Taylor was the editor of the multivolume *Voyages pittoresques et romantiques dans l'ancienne France* (1828–1870), and he hired artists like Dauzats to supply him with images of the French countryside and its monuments. Satisfied with his illustrations of Champagne, Dauphiné, and Languedoc, Taylor invited Dauzats—whom he called "le peintre voyageur"—on an expedition to Egypt, Judea, Palestine, Syria, and Spain in 1830.[1] Taylor had been sent to Luxor to oversee the transport to Paris of the obelisk that now stands in the Place de la Concorde. He published a two-volume account of the journey in *La Syrie, L'Egypte, La Palestine, et la Judée* (1839) with illustrations by Dauzats.

Dauzats's success as an itinerant illustrator of the Middle East led the duc d'Orléans to select him, with Auguste Raffet and Alexandre-Gabriel Decamps, to document another long voyage, this time to Algeria in September 1839. The Portes de Fer expedition was one of the great military successes of the Algerian military campaign commanded by the oldest son of Louis-Philippe I.

While the military costume in this drawing cannot be identified with certainty, it might depict someone Dauzats encountered just before he embarked on his voyage. While vaguely Zouave in manner, the man's slippers and the absence of a belt to carry a sword or bayonet show that the dress is not a standard military uniform.[2] Rather than a study from life, the drawing might be explained more accurately as a sketch made by conflating a model reclining in the artist's Parisian studio or an acquaintance at a social gathering with an imagined soldier he expected to encounter on his journey. Dauzats had recorded the modern military costume in his illustrations for *La Syrie, L'Egypte, La Palestine, et la Judée.* The vagaries or inaccuracies in the costume depicted in the present drawing reveal something important about Dauzats: he was not a slave to scientific documentation but rather a romantic.[3]

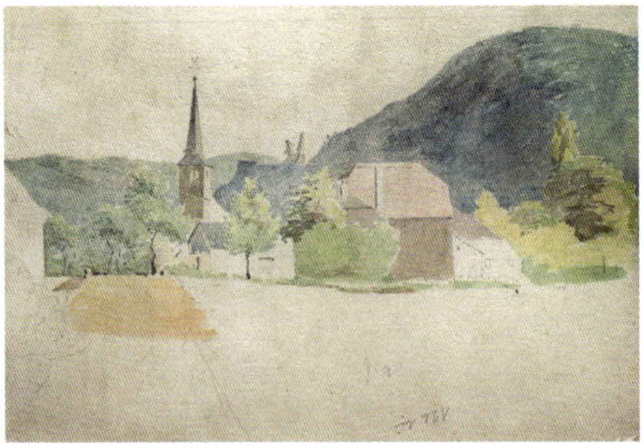

Cat. 16, verso.

The scene on the verso from the following year (above) may be from the village of Buisson in Artonne, where Dauzats retreated in 1840 after the expedition to Portes de Fer. The church steeple and the architecture of the simple structures resemble those seen in this Provençale village; a similar composition, though lacking the steeple, can be seen in the painting *La ferme des Boissons* (Musée Magnin, Dijon, inv. 233).[4]

EB

Notes
1. Plessier 1990.
2. Emilie Robbe, conservator, Musée de l'Armée, Paris, written correspondence, September 27, 2013.
3. The author wishes to thank William B. Jordan for his observations.
4. Plessier 1990, 137.

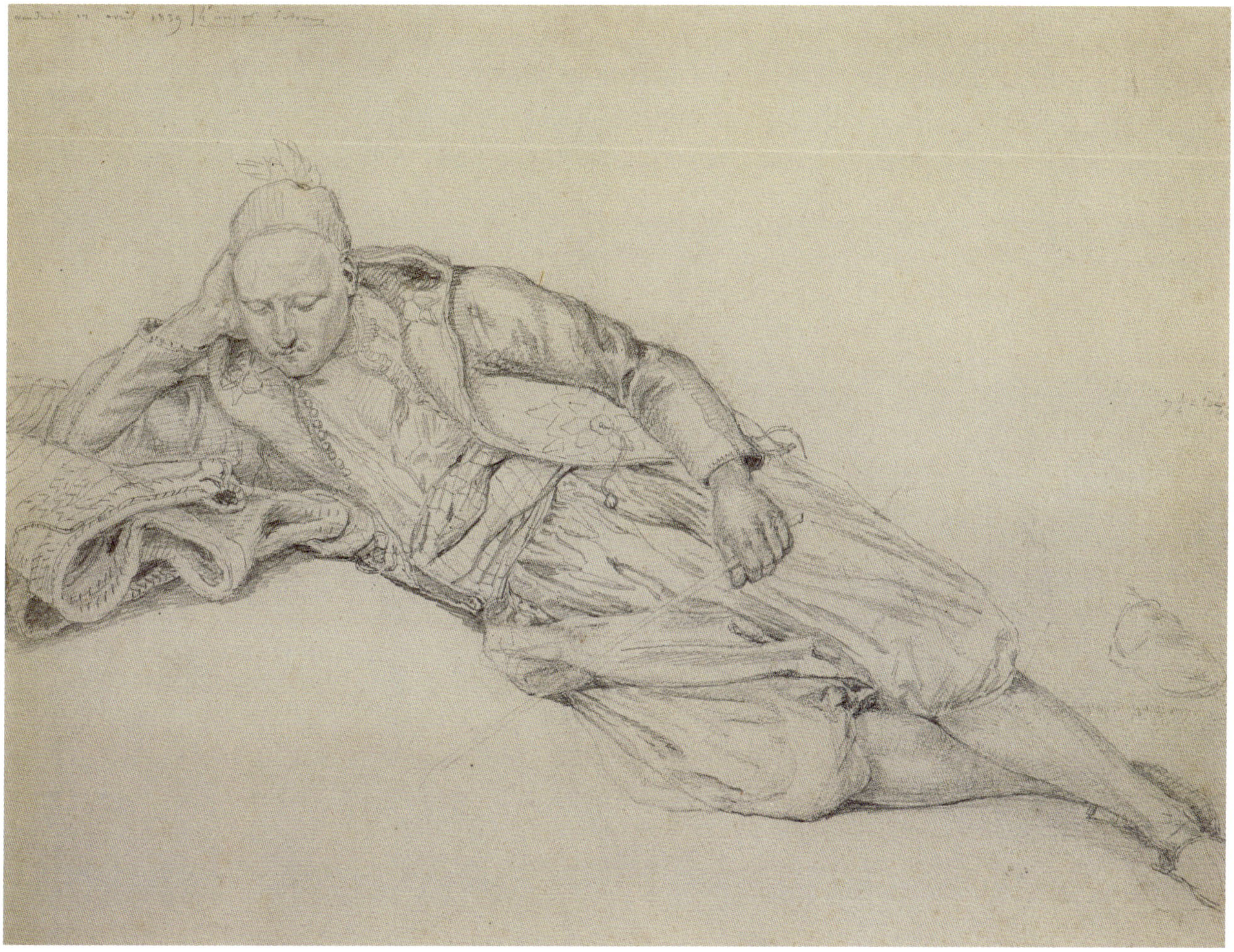

Cat. 16, recto.

17

Gustave Courbet French, 1819–1877

PORTRAIT OF A YOUNG WOMAN (PROBABLY THE ARTIST'S SISTER ZOÉ COURBET), C. *1846–1847*

Black chalk on beige paper, 22½ × 17 in. (570 × 435 mm)
Oval estate stamp lower left: *ATELIER / Gustave COURBET* (Lugt 463b)
Private collection

PROVENANCE Estate of the artist; *Vente Tableaux modernes,* Versailles, Me. Paul Martin, February 16, 1969, lot 143; where purchased by Alfred Daber, Paris; private collection; *Vente Tableaux et dessins anciens et du XIXe siècle,* Sotheby's, Paris, June 27, 2013, lot 89; where purchased by the current owner.

EXHIBITED École nationale des Beaux-Arts, Paris, *Exposition des oeuvres de Gustave Courbet,* 1882, no. 144.

Complex and self-obsessed, Gustave Courbet grew up in the rural Franche-Comté, the son of a well-to-do landowner and farmer, with an idealistic passion to make a difference in the world. Largely through the force of will and self-study, he succeeded by his 30s in becoming the leading force in the realist movement in France, a painter with strong utopian political leanings who relished provocation and by his engaged and committed life offered himself as an enduring role model for every rebellious, anti-establishment artist who followed. As Robert Fernier has noted, Courbet is not an artist best known for his drawings, yet he was an extraordinary and very original draftsman.[1] As a young man, his favorite model for both his paintings and his drawings was himself, followed by other members of his immediate family—particularly his father and his three sisters, Zélie, Zoé, and Juliette. Especially in the 1840s, he made countless self-portraits in various role-playing guises, taking a narcissistic delight in his sensuous good looks. And he portrayed his sisters not only in individual portraits but, after they had grown up, also used them as models in some of his most ambitious early works.

This portrait drawing is one of Courbet's best early works on paper. Its confident yet sparing use of line—complemented by dense areas of hatching and, in the face, richly modeled shading of the features with black chalk—is a technique he employed throughout the 1840s but never again brought to such a perfect balance. Simultaneously, and predominantly later on, his drawings were executed in charcoal and have a much softer, more atmospheric character.

It has been suggested that the sitter of this drawing could be Virginie Binet, his lover and model, with whom he had a 10-year relationship and fathered an illegitimate son.[2] But on examination the idea is not convincing. Virginie is presumed to be the woman depicted in several of Courbet's fanciful self-portraits (such as *Lovers in the Country,* Musée des Beaux-Arts, Lyon), yet there is not a strong resemblance to the sitter here. There is a compelling similarity, however, between this rather plain but pretty young woman seated in a kitchen chair, dressed in simple country clothing and wearing an apron, and the artist's sister Zoé, who, with her roundish face, button nose, and similar coiffure, is depicted on the left in the painting *Courbet's Three Sisters: The Stories of Grandmother Salvan,* painted about 1846–1847 (fig. 5). Furthermore, in the painting she is portrayed wearing virtually the same thing, except that she has added a broad-brimmed hat. All three sisters were depicted again in *A Burial at Ornans* (1850, Musée d'Orsay, Paris) and again in *Young Ladies of the Village* (1851–1852,

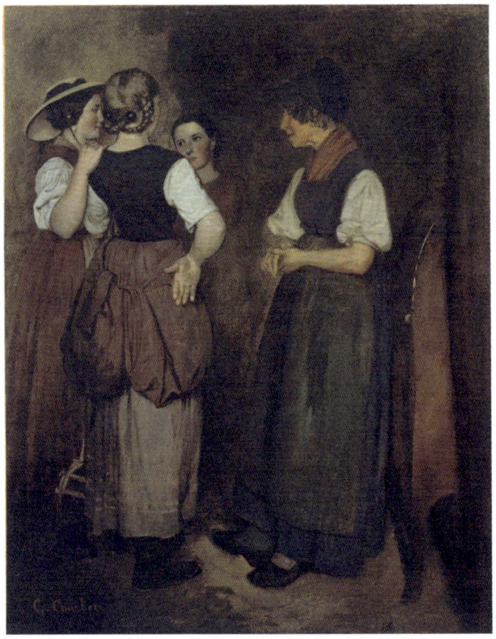

Fig. 5 Gustave Courbet, *Courbet's Three Sisters: The Stories of Grandmother Salvan,* 1846–1847. Oil on canvas. Curtis Galleries, Minneapolis, Minnesota.

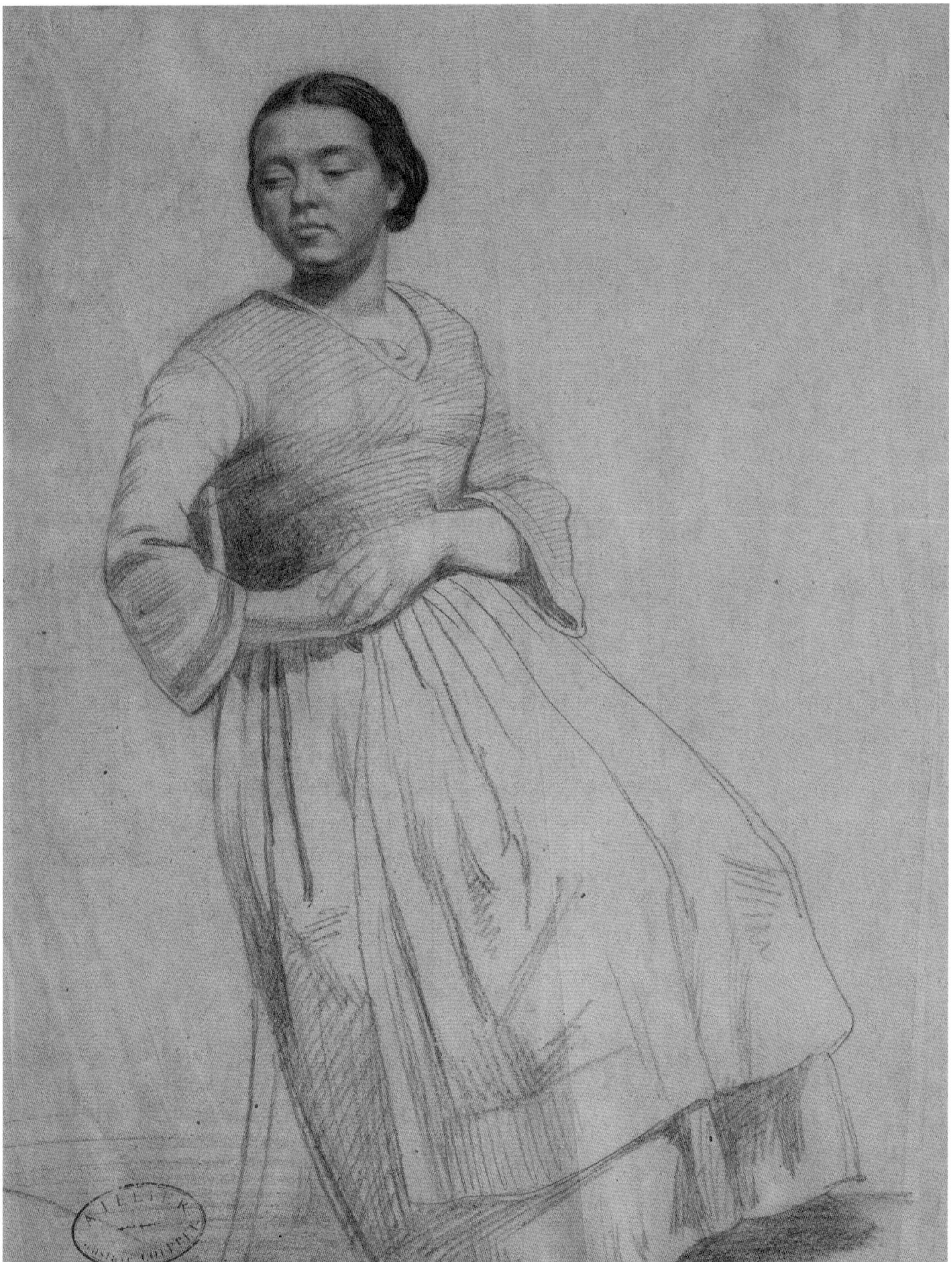

Notes
1. Fernier 1978.
2. *Vente tableaux et dessins anciens et du XIXe siècle*, Sotheby's, Paris, June 27, 2013, lot 89.
3. Galitz, in De Font-Reaulx et al. 2007, 133, cat. 23.

Metropolitan Museum of Art, New York). And several years later, in 1855, Zoé was the model for the central figure in *The Grain Sifters* (Musée des Beaux-Arts, Nantes), where her coiffure and country clothing are again similar. As Kathryn Calley Galitz observed, the Courbet sisters and their domestic setting are reflected in Champfleury's novel *Les Demoiselles Tourangeau* (1864), inspired by the author's visit to the Courbet family at Ornans in 1856.[3] There the "impetuous and rebellious" Zoé provided the inspiration for the character Émelina, with "a head muddled up with silly books" and "an incredible volubility." Not primarily known as a portraitist, Courbet gives us a glimpse in this drawing of the seldom-seen depths of his talent.

WBJ

18

Charles-François Daubigny French, 1817–1878

THE TOMB OF JEAN-JACQUES ROUSSEAU IN THE ÎLE DES PEUPLIERS, ERMENONVILLE (LE TOMBEAU DE JEAN-JACQUES ROUSSEAU À ERMENONVILLE), *1866*

Charcoal on laid paper, 19½ × 13 in. (495 × 330 mm)
Estate stamp, lower left and lower right (Lugt 518)
Private collection, Dallas

PROVENANCE Daubigny sale, Paris, May 6–11, 1878 (estate stamp, lower left and lower right, L.518); Alfred Robaut, notary's paraph on original backing (Lugt suppl. 2140d); sale, Libert and Castor, Paris, April 16, 1999, lot 23; with Concorde Fine Arts (Neil Fiertag, Paris and New York); where purchased 1999 by the current owner.

At the invitation of the Marquis de Girardon, the writer and philosopher Jean-Jacques Rousseau spent the last weeks of his life at Ermenonville in the Oise. He died suddenly on July 2, 1778, and was buried in the evening two days later by the light of torches on the Île des Peupliers in the castle park. It was the ideal resting place for this contemplative and solitary man, who loved to "revel at length in the charms of nature."[1]

Jacques-Philippe Le Sueur built a tomb based on designs by Hubert Robert that remained even after the philosopher's body had been transported to the Panthéon in Paris. This site soon became a pilgrimage destination for Rousseau's admirers and a picturesque motif for painters. Robert himself painted the Île des Peupliers several times, and other artists imitated him. It is therefore not surprising that Charles-François Daubigny—that "marvellous and truthful painter of the banks of the Seine and the Oise," as Émile Zola called him in his "Letter from Paris" of 1876—also depicted it. He probably did so near dusk one day in October 1866. This sheet and another of the artist's sheets with the same date bear witness to the fact.

The tall, spindle-shaped poplars with which the little island is planted surround the philosopher's cenotaph and are reflected on the surface of the water, which offers an image of "the instability of the things of this world," as Rousseau wrote in the Fifth Promenade in his *Rêveries du promeneur solitaire.*[2] This rapid sketch is characteristic of Daubigny, who famously loved depicting the undulating surface of water and the reflections inhabiting it. Daubigny enjoyed a brilliant career as a landscape artist under the Second Empire. In 1866, he was a member of the Salon jury alongside his friend Jean-Baptiste-Camille Corot and exhibited *Morning Effect on the Oise* and *Banks of the Oise, near La Bonneville.* From 1857, Daubigny tirelessly painted landscapes on the banks of the Oise, which he navigated aboard his studio-boat.

The other sheet, in the collection of the Dublin City Art Gallery,[2] is in landscape format and shows a more panoramic representation, which suggests that this drawing was sketched from the opposite bank or from a boat.

Recognized as one of the Barbizon School, Daubigny is also considered a precursor of impressionism thanks to his virtuosity in capturing the fleeting sensations of nature. That ability, along with the inherent poetry of this small sketch, probably seduced the collector to whom it belonged: Alfred Robaut, the artist, art historian, and biographer of Delacroix and Corot.

LL

Notes

1. Jean-Jacques Rousseau, *Rêveries du promeneur solitaire: cinquième promenade,* 1782 posthumous.
2. Ibid.
3. *Le tombeau de Jean-Jacques Rousseau à Ermenonville,* 1866, black chalk on paper, 13¼ × 19½ in. (336 × 495 mm), Dublin City Gallery The Hugh Lane, reg. 1215.

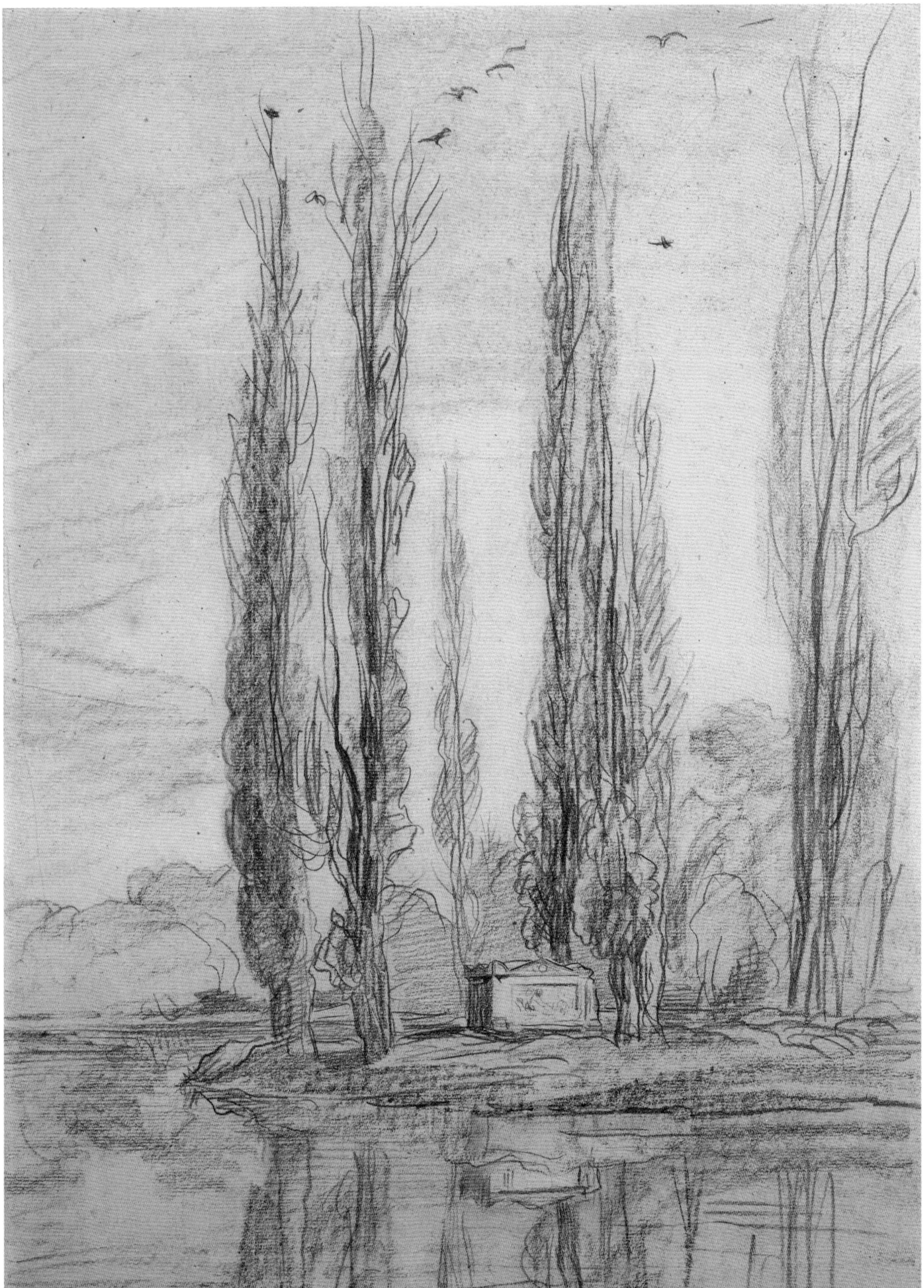

19

Jean-François Millet French, 1814–1875

STUDY OF AN OLD PERSON'S THROAT AND CHIN, C. *1847–1850*

Black and sanguine conté crayon on buff paper,
10⅜ x 7½ in. (264 x 191 mm)
Estate stamp, left, below center: *.J.F.M* (Lugt 1460)
Private collection, Dallas

PROVENANCE Shepherd Gallery, New York; where purchased late 1960s by the current owner.

Modern scholarship is providing an understanding of the true stature of Jean-François Millet, which for much of the 20th century was obscured by the great fame of his scenes of peasant life and the negative associations attached to them in the century of modern criticism. A leader of the Barbizon School of painters, Millet was one of the greatest artists of his time, however, and cannot be pigeonholed so easily. Born into a modest farming family in Normandy, he had a natural talent for drawing encouraged by his mother, who saw to it that he received every opportunity to develop it, which he did in Paris in the late 1830s. With his naturally voracious intellect and passion for reading, he also became what Robert Herbert has called "the most erudite artist of his generation."[1] From his earliest portraits and sensual figure studies, through his depictions of what it was to be a working man or woman in his time, to his prescient landscapes prefiguring the concerns of the impressionists, he left 3,000 drawings, watercolors, and pastels—works admired and collected by artists like Edgar Degas, Odilon Redon, and Georges Seurat as well as by the collector-magnates of London, Boston, and New York. Rooted in tradition yet brimming with technical and aesthetic innovation, his works also communicated a sense of authentic humanity unequaled in his century. In this respect Vincent van Gogh felt indebted to him above all others: "Millet is *father* Millet, counselor and mentor in *everything* for young artists."[2]

The drawing catalogued here is an early work executed in what was Millet's preferred medium, conté crayon, which was capable in his hands of an incredible tonal range. Unlike his familiar scenes of rural life, which invite identification with the subject, this drawing is a pure visual study, focusing close up on the folds of flesh in an old person's throat. Such a detailed view of only a part of the human form, with no context, makes the drawing difficult to read at first, but once oriented, the viewer can appreciate the amazing richness of the form, in which the blank paper, graded hatching, and delicate line all add up to a palpable image that inspires respect from anyone who has ever tried to draw. The drawing could either have been preparatory to an early portrait or it could even have been a study after an old master painting done purely to develop his skill.

WBJ

Notes
1. Quoted in Murphy 1999, 5.
2. Van Gogh, letter to Theo van Gogh, quoted in Murphy 1999, 2.

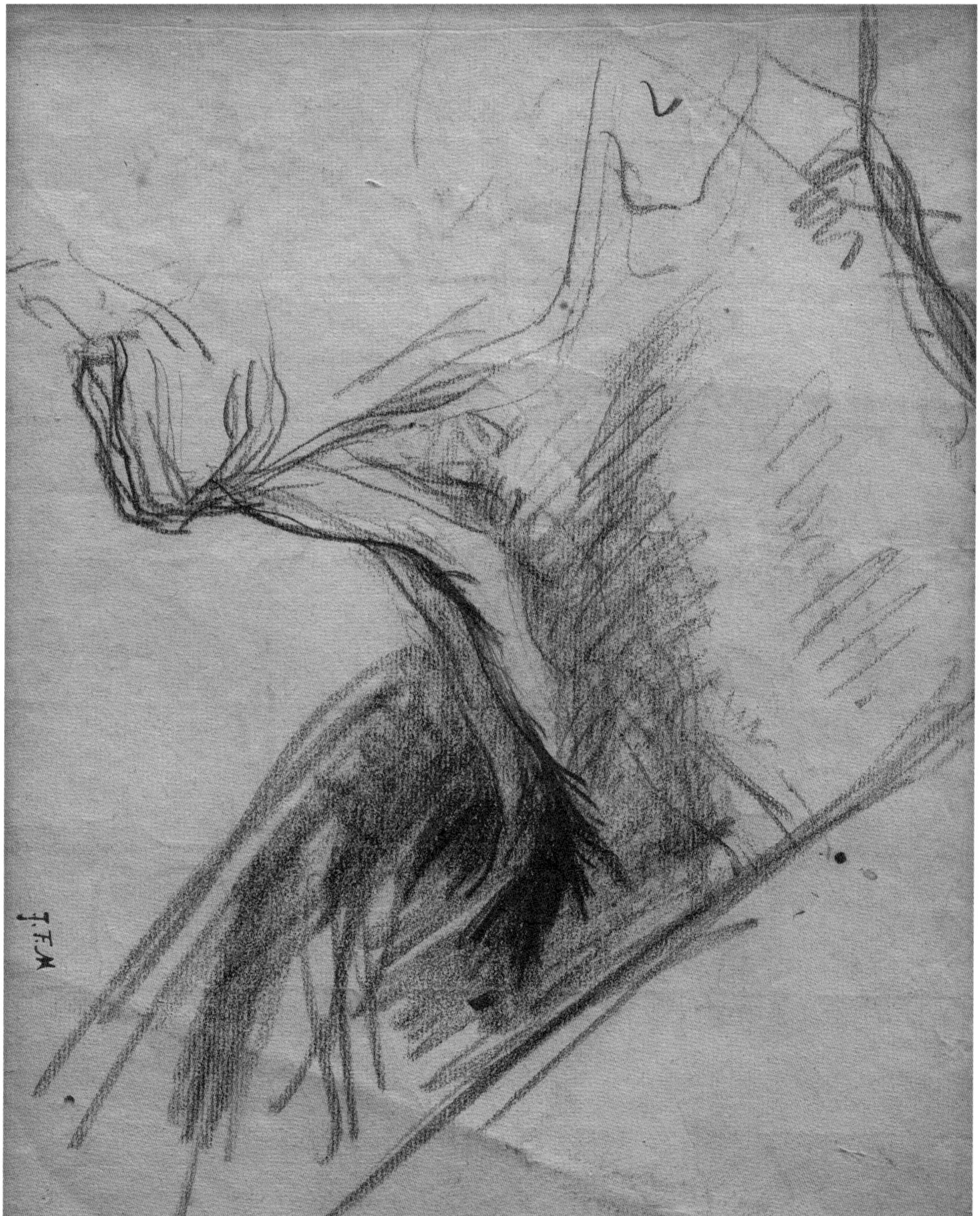
J.F.M

20

Honoré Daumier French, 1808–1879

THE SMOKER AND THE READER (LE FUMEUR ET LE LECTEUR), C. *1860–1865*

Pen and ink over charcoal on paper, 5 × 7⅞ in. (125 × 200 mm)
Collection of Mr. and Mrs. Barron U. Kidd, Dallas

PROVENANCE Paul Gallimard, Paris; Hector Brame, Paris; Edwin C. Vogel, New York; sale, Sotheby's, New York, *Important Paintings and Drawings from the Collection of the Late Edwin C. Vogel,* October 17, 1973, no. 16; Acquavella Galleries, New York; from whom purchased by the current owner.

EXHIBITED Tate Gallery, London, *Daumier: Paintings and Drawings,* June 14–July 30, 1961, no. 124; Metropolitan Museum of Art, New York, loan, summer 1968.

BIBLIOGRAPHY Maison 1968, vol. 2, no. 317, pl. 88.

Honoré Daumier was a tireless chronicler of life in Paris, particularly the comings and goings of the bourgeoisie and working class, to whom he felt a close affinity. In this quick and insightful sketch he portrayed two men seated at a table, one reading intently from a newspaper or journal, the other, cigarette in hand, leaning on his elbow and looking up out of the picture. Although the two figures are turned from each other, the impression is that the man with the cigarette is listening raptly to his companion, who appears to be reading aloud. The subject of the text that appears to engross them is left unclear: Is it political, scandalous, or amusing? Daumier's caricatures are filled with such intense moments of daily discourse; one illustration, from the series *Les bons bourgeois* (1846) shows two men poring over newspapers above the caption, "Ce que le bourgeois est convenu de nommer une petite distraction" (What the middle class calls a little entertainment).[1]

As always, Daumier's pen work is straightforwardly simple yet convincingly descriptive, capturing the postures and expressions of the two men with ease and brilliance. The ink lines were drawn over a preliminary drawing made in charcoal, indicating that Daumier first composed the scene with the lighter chalk lines, which he then overdrew in pen, not always following his initial sketch. The style of drawing and characterization of the figures are similar to the technique used in Daumier's caricatures. Yet the motif was one he often portrayed in his paintings as well. The dynamic between the smoker and the reader in this drawing is very much in the same spirit as the small oil *The Beer Drinkers (The Smoker),* dated by Maison to 1860–1863 (Fritz Nathan Collection, Zurich).[2] The divide between Daumier's caricatures and what he would have considered his more serious fine art is not as great as is usually thought.

RR

Notes
1. Delteil 1902, 1490.
2. Maison 1968, vol. 1, no. I-155.

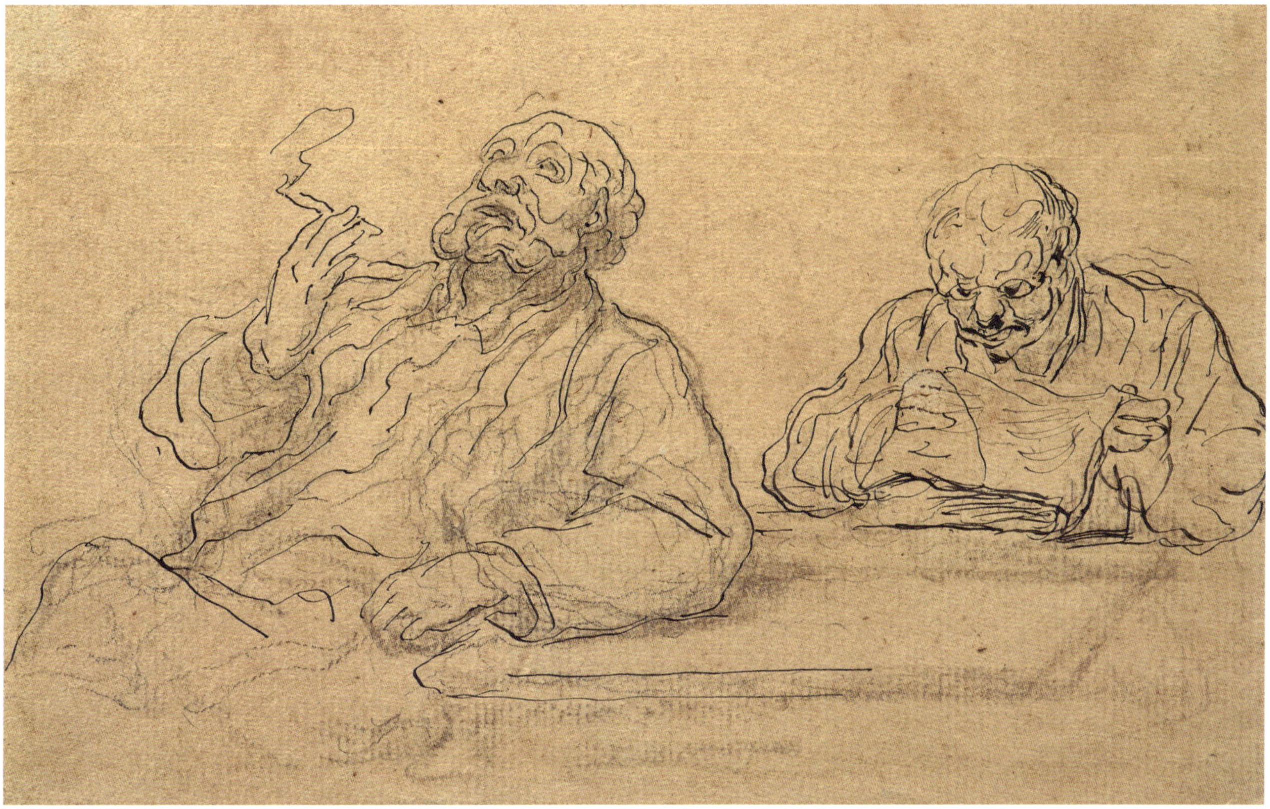

21

Honoré Daumier French, 1808–1879

THE SIDESHOW (LA PARADE), C. *1864–1865*

Red chalk and brown wash on laid paper, 15½ × 11 in. (394 × 279 mm)
Collection of Mary Ralph Lowe, Fort Worth

PROVENANCE Count Armand Doria, Paris, by 1878; Doria sale, Galerie Georges Petit, Paris, May 8–9, 1899, lot 378; Georges Viau, Paris; Viau sale, Paris, March 4? and March 21–22, 1907?, lot 106; (Libaude?); J. W. Boehler; Paul Cassirer, Berlin; Eduard Fuchs, Berlin-Zehlendorf; Galerie Huguette Berès, Paris, by 1988; where purchased by the current owner.

EXHIBITED Durand-Ruel, Paris, *Exposition des peintures et dessins de Honoré Daumier,* April 17–June 15, 1878, no. 166 (*Parade de saltimbanques*); École des Beaux-Arts, Paris, *Exposition Daumier, par le Syndicat de la presse artistique,* May 1901, no. 291; Paul Cassirer, Berlin, *Ein Jahrhundert Französischer Zeichnung,* 1929–1930, no. 21; Museum of Fine Arts, Houston, *Selected Works from Collections of Friends of the Museum of Fine Arts, Houston,* June 11–August 13, 1989; Städtische Galerie, Frankfurt, *Honoré Daumier Zeichnungen,* November 12, 1992–January 17, 1993; Metropolitan Museum of Art, New York, *Honoré Daumier Drawings,* February 26–May 2, 1993, no. 100; National Gallery of Canada, Ottawa, June 11–September 6, 1999, Galeries nationales du Grand Palais, Paris, October 5, 1999–January 3, 2000, and Phillips Collection, Washington, February 19–May 14, 2000, *Daumier,* no. 318 (*Parade de saltimbanques*).

BIBLIOGRAPHY Alexandre 1888, 377; Klossowski 1923, 187; Meier-Graefe 1930, 12; Maison 1968, no. 551.

This impressive drawing was featured in the retrospective exhibition organized by the dealer Durand-Ruel in Paris in 1878 with the title *Parade de saltimbanques*—that is, a sideshow of mountebanks. These entertainers stood outside the main exhibits at fairs, enticing spectators to pay for the show. This large sheet is boldly drawn with red chalk to which Honoré Daumier added brown wash, primarily to create the shadows of the principal central figures and to shade the foreground spectators. The artist focused on several stock carnival characters: Hercules—the strongman in the center—who menaces the cringing buffoon (known as *le jocrisse,* or the simpleton) with a stick, and the clown-drummer at left who captures the crowd's attention. The odd design on the painted backdrop represents, as is identifiable from other drawings by the artist,[1] a crocodile snapping at a fleeing man, a hint at the exotic spectacle available to paying customers. Daumier's nervous graphic technique adds to the energy of the scene.

Depictions of street performances, carnival characters, and itinerant musicians abound in Daumier's art, both in his early caricatures and then, beginning in the 1850s, in his drawings, watercolors, and oil paintings. He certainly witnessed such scenes on numerous occasions, but he produced these drawings from memory in the studio, distilling what he saw into complex and expressive works of art. It has been argued that such marginal, even subversive, popular street characters held political meaning for Daumier.[2] The present composition can be compared to a number of drawings datable to the early and mid-1860s, in particular the verso of a sheet in the Musée du Louvre, Paris, in which he sketched in black chalk a nearly identical interaction between strongman and buffoon.[3] The Louvre drawing is more cursorily rendered and may be considered a true sketch that Daumier developed more fully in this drawing, which he considered finished enough to sell. By 1878 it belonged to the noted collector Count Armand Doria, who owned no fewer than 28 drawings by Daumier.

RR

Notes
1. For example, Maison 1968, vol. 2, no. 556.
2. Harper 1976.
3. Maison 1968, vol. 2, no. 524.

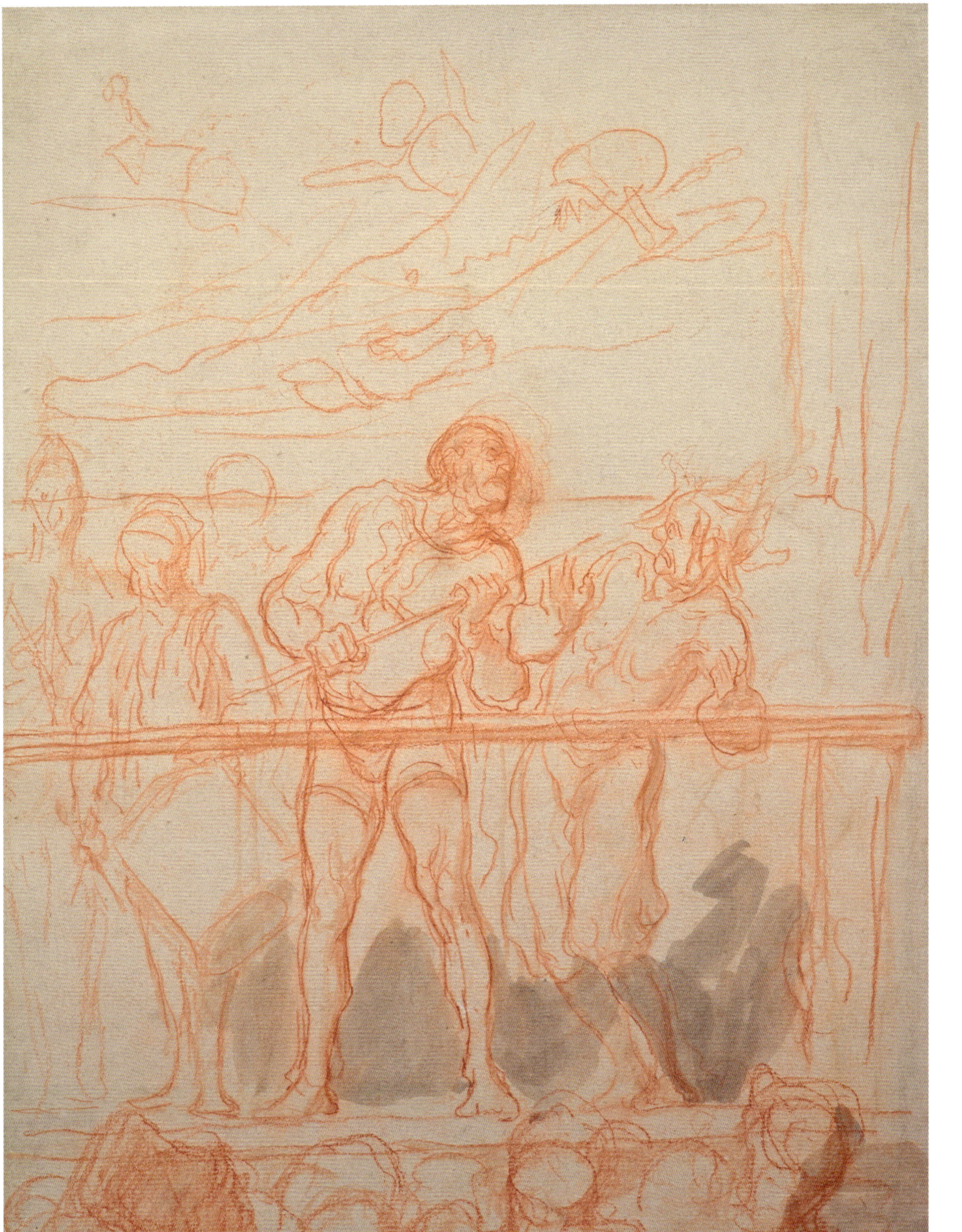

Honoré Daumier French, 1808–1879

AN ACTOR, C. *1865*

Pen, ink, and wash on paper, 9¾ × 6⅝ in. (248 × 168 mm)
Dallas Museum of Art, The Wendy and Emery Reves Collection, 1985.R.23

PROVENANCE "Lousada"; K. E. Maison; Dr. Peter Nathan, Zurich; from whom purchased 1954 by Emery Reves; given to the Dallas Museum of Art, The Wendy and Emery Reves Collection, 1985.

EXHIBITED Whitechapel Art Gallery, London, *French Exhibition,* 1932; Musée d'art et d'histoire, Geneva, *De Watteau à Cézanne,* 1951, no. 106, pl. xiv, ill.; Tate Gallery, London, *Daumier: Paintings and Drawings,* 1961, no. 166, pl. 28c, ill.; Dallas Museum of Art, *Impressionist and Modern Masters in Dallas: Monet to Mondrian,* September 3–October 22, 1989, 78, no. 20, ill.; Dallas Museum of Art, *All the World's a Stage: Celebrating Performance in the Visual Arts,* August 30, 2009–February 28, 2010.

BIBLIOGRAPHY Daulte 1953, no. 21, ill.; Maison 1961, no. 93, ill.; Maison 1968, vol. 2, no. 450; Nathan 1972, no. 43, ill.; Dallas Museum of Art 1985b, 88–89, ill.; Brettell 1995, 24–25, ill.

This bold drawing constitutes one of Honoré Daumier's most striking representations of a single figure. It was drawn with a very fine pen, the spidery marks tracing and retracing the contours of the short, stout man as he leans back, looking up with his hands splayed expressively. To these fine lines Daumier added bold washes of gray ink to define the shadows that throw the figure into stark relief. The exaggerated pose and accentuated facial features bring to mind the best qualities of Daumier's caricatures, yet the economy of means and powerful, nearly abstract forms are fully in keeping with the "fine art" to which he increasingly turned in the 1850s and 1860s.

There are precious few details to identify this dramatically posed man, but he is usually taken to represent an actor on stage, a perfectly reasonable assumption given his rhetorical stance and the sharp lighting indicative of footlights. Daumier was fascinated by actors, particularly the popular characters of the *commedia dell'arte* and the ubiquitous Paris street performers of the mid-19th century. This figure's face, with its prominent nose and bushy mustache, is close to the small painting called *Head of Pasquin,* also in the Reves Collection.[1] Nevertheless, the drawing relates more readily to Daumier's depictions of scenes from the plays of Molière, which he rendered in drawings, watercolors, and oil paintings in the early and mid-1860s. The figure's pose and the scratchy pen work are similar to those found in several drawings associated with Molière's comedies.[2] Charles Baudelaire had in fact compared Daumier's art to that of the great French playwright: "Like him, he goes straight to the point. . . . You only have to look to understand."[3] Before it was acquired by Wendy and Emery Reves, this wonderful drawing was owned by K. E. Maison, the great expert and cataloguer of Daumier's oeuvre.

RR

Notes
1. Maison 1968, vol. 1, no. I–156. See also Brettell 1995, 28–29.
2. See, for example, Maison 1968, nos. 483, 484.
3. Quoted in Laughton 1996, 87.

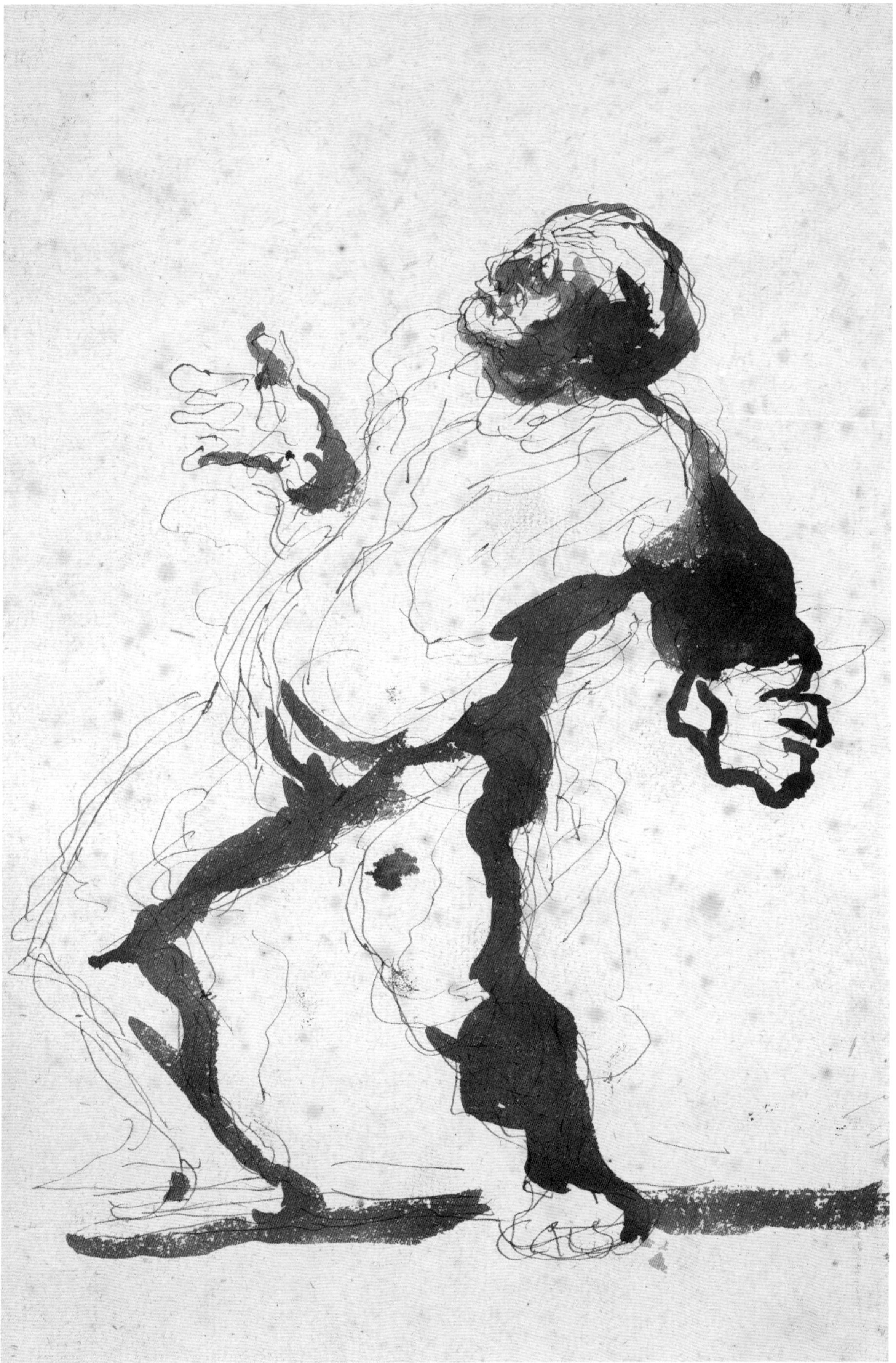

23

Paul Gavarni (Sulpice Guillaume Chevalier)

French, 1804–1866

I HAD PLAYED A WOMAN (J'AVAIS FAIT UNE FEMME), C. *1855*

Watercolor with gouache highlights on paper, 13 × 8¼ in. (330 × 210 mm)
Signed lower left: *Gavarni*; inscribed lower right: *Mon cher j'avais fait une femme, et . . . / T'as été refait (My dear, I had played a woman, then . . . / You have been had!)*
Private collection, Dallas

PROVENANCE Collection of Mme de Maljean, née Olry-Roederer; Galerie Antoine Laurentin, Paris, by 2000; where purchased 2000 by the current owner.

BIBLIOGRAPHY Lemoisne 1928, 255.

EXHIBITED École des Beaux Arts, Paris, *Des Maîtres français de la caricature et de la peinture de moeurs au XIXème siècle,* 1888, no. 200 (incorrect height).

"After so many works, an oeuvre of ten thousand pieces, where one finds for the first time in the history of art the talent of an artist united with that of a writer, after his exhausting research as a mathematician, a scholar and an inventor, he lies beside us, in the Auteuil graveyard. There he sleeps the big sleep, underneath the granite, image of the solidity of his fame and the immortality of his name; the simple and proud inscription on his grave: GAVARNI."[1] With these words, Edmond and Jules de Goncourt ended their admiring book about Paul Gavarni. And the Goncourts were not easy to please.

Along with Daumier, Gavarni was the most famous caricaturist and cartoonist of the mid-19th century in France during the reigns of Louis-Philippe and Napoléon III. Focusing on Parisian personality types more than on politics, he practically shaped the reputation of the city with his albums about women—like *Les Lorettes* (young and witty Parisian working-class women and occasional courtesans), *Les Actrices,* and *Les Débardeurs* (female transvestites during the carnival)—or young men, like *Les Fashionables.* Working for the newspaper *Le Charivari* and directing a successful magazine, *Les Gens du Monde,* Gavarni was extremely popular. He illustrated books by Eugène Sue and Honoré de Balzac, contributing to their successes, and later in his life he examined bourgeois family life. While tenderly poking fun at people, he was never mean-spirited.

Gavarni was a keen observer of nightlife and the world of the theater in Paris. In this drawing, he shows us actors who have played walk-on parts. The one seen from the back starts to explain that because he had previously played a woman, he has been asked to play one in this new Scottish play; the other, wearing a kilt, is telling him that he has been had. Their long, skinny legs and ill-fitting costumes signal a second-rank theater, poor actors accepting all sorts of roles just to survive. The drawing is among the best made by the artist: its crisp lines drawn in ink, the shadows indicated by luscious washes, and the actors' gestures cleverly observed demonstrate Gavarni's genius, his ability to capture the humanity of his characters and the highs and lows of their lives. The drawing's provenance (Madame Olry-Roederer) adds to its interest, as it comes from one of the most important collections of Gavarni's drawings in the 19th century.

OM

Note

1. "Après tant de travaux, un Oeuvre de dix mille pièces, où se trouve pour la première fois dans l'histoire de l'art, le talent de l'artiste réuni au talent de l'écrivain, après les épuisantes recherches du mathématicien, du savant et de l'inventeur, il repose à côté de nous, au cimetière d'Auteuil. Il dort là le grand sommeil, sous une dalle de granit, image de la solidité de sa gloire et la survie de ce nom: simple et fière inscription de sa tombe: GAVARNI." Goncourt 1925.

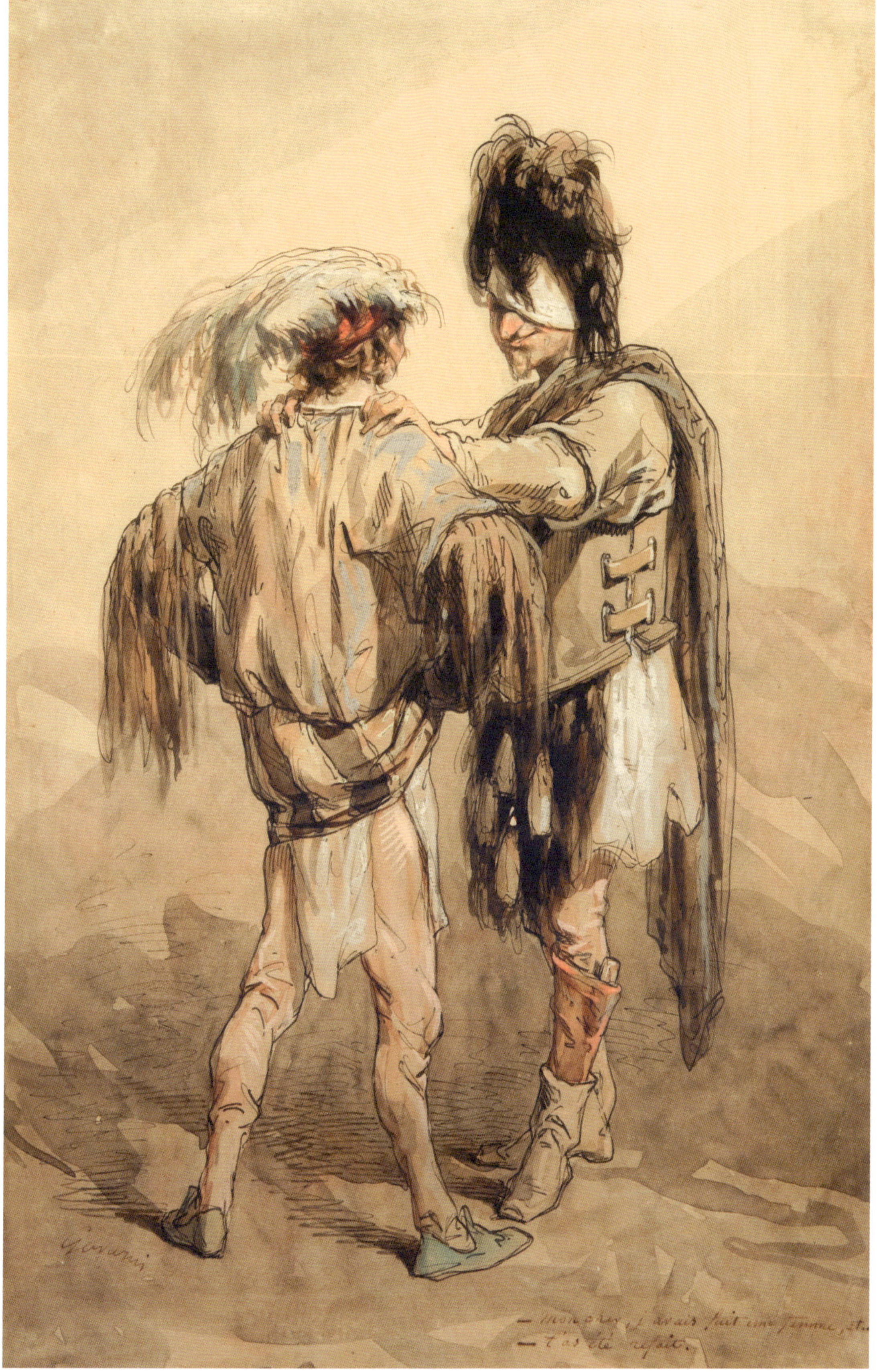
Gavarni
— mon cher, j'avais fait une femme, et…
— t'as été refait.

24

Constantin Guys French, 1802–1892

THE BALL (LE BAL PUBLIC), C. *1860s*

Pencil, brown wash, and watercolor on paper,
11⅞ × 9⅛ in. (300 × 230 mm)
Private collection, Dallas

PROVENANCE Charles Saglio, Paris; Annamaria Edelstein (Succi Ltd.), London; where purchased 1991 by the current owner.

EXHIBITED Musée des arts decoratifs, Paris, *Un peintre de la vie au XIX siècle: Constantin Guys, 1802–1892*, January–February 1937, no. 67.

Dutch-born Frenchman Constantin Guys represented something new on the European scene, and something essentially modern. Unconcerned with academies and Salons, he was a professional observer of the world around him—an illustrator. The first of the great illustrated journals—the *Illustrated London News* and *Punch*—were revolutionizing journalism, and throughout the 1840s and 1850s Guys was among the first artists to work for them in London, traveling throughout Europe and to Egypt, Greece, Turkey, Bulgaria, and anywhere else needed, covering the Crimean War and other momentous events of the time. His quick sketches in wash and watercolor were engraved to serve the function that photojournalism does today, but in their own right they had a profound impact on other artists and their subject matter. A great many of Guys's drawings, given by the artist himself, are preserved in the Musée Carnavalet, Paris.

Leaving wars behind, from the late 1850s on Guys settled in Paris, where he became a visual chronicler of Parisian society. Just as he had trained himself to do on the battlefront and in foreign capitals, it was not his aim to comment satirically or politically on what he saw—as contemporaries like Honoré Daumier or Paul Gavarni, to whom he was particularly close, might do—but simply to take note in vibrant sketches. He resembled no one so much as his 18th-century counterpart, the brilliant Gabriel de Saint-Aubin (1724–1780). Gentle, shy, and self-effacing, and an indefatigable *flâneur*, Guys recorded the daytime and nighttime activities of fashionable society as well as the middle class: promenading in the Bois de Boulogne, dancing at balls, or riding through busy streets in carriages. He missed little—not even in the earthier venues of dance halls and brothels, which were favorite haunts. In a long and extremely influential essay titled "The Painter of Modern Life," published in *Le Figaro* in 1863, Charles Baudelaire, who owned more than 100 of Guys's drawings, championed him as the quintessential modern artist.[1] The critics Théophile Gautier and Champfleury both collected his works, as did the painter Édouard Manet, who owned more than 60 of them and executed an unforgettable pastel portrait of the old man (Shelburne Museum, Vermont). By far the largest collection, however, was that of the photographer Nadar, formed over many years during which he photographed the artist in several magnificent portraits.[2] For a younger generation that ranged from Henri de Toulouse-Lautrec to Pablo Picasso, much of their work would have been unthinkable without his example.[3]

This brilliant watercolor highlights the 1860s fashion craze for dressing in the 18th-century style. One cannot help but compare it to the engraved fashion plates after drawings by artists like Augustin de Saint-Aubin, brother of Gabriel, that appeared in *Galerie des modes et costumes français* (1778–1787). Yet for all the static costume detail in the fashion plates, here the sense of motion is overwhelming: the female dancer swishes her crinolines, layered skirts, and plumes as she lunges onto the dance floor to take the hand of her unseen partner, while a chorus of onlooking heads is frozen in rapt attention.

Appropriately, the drawing's first recorded owner, Charles Saglio, who lent it the Guys exhibition in Paris in 1937, was since 1905 owner and publisher of the hugely successful weekly *La Vie Parisienne*.

WBJ

Notes
1. Hiddleston 1995, 603–21.
2. For the principal collections of Guys's drawings, see Jérôme Dufilho, "Les collections de dessins de Guys," in Paris-Musées 2002, 29.
3. John Richardson, "Constantin Guys, Baudelaire et Picasso," in Paris-Musées 2002, 45–50.

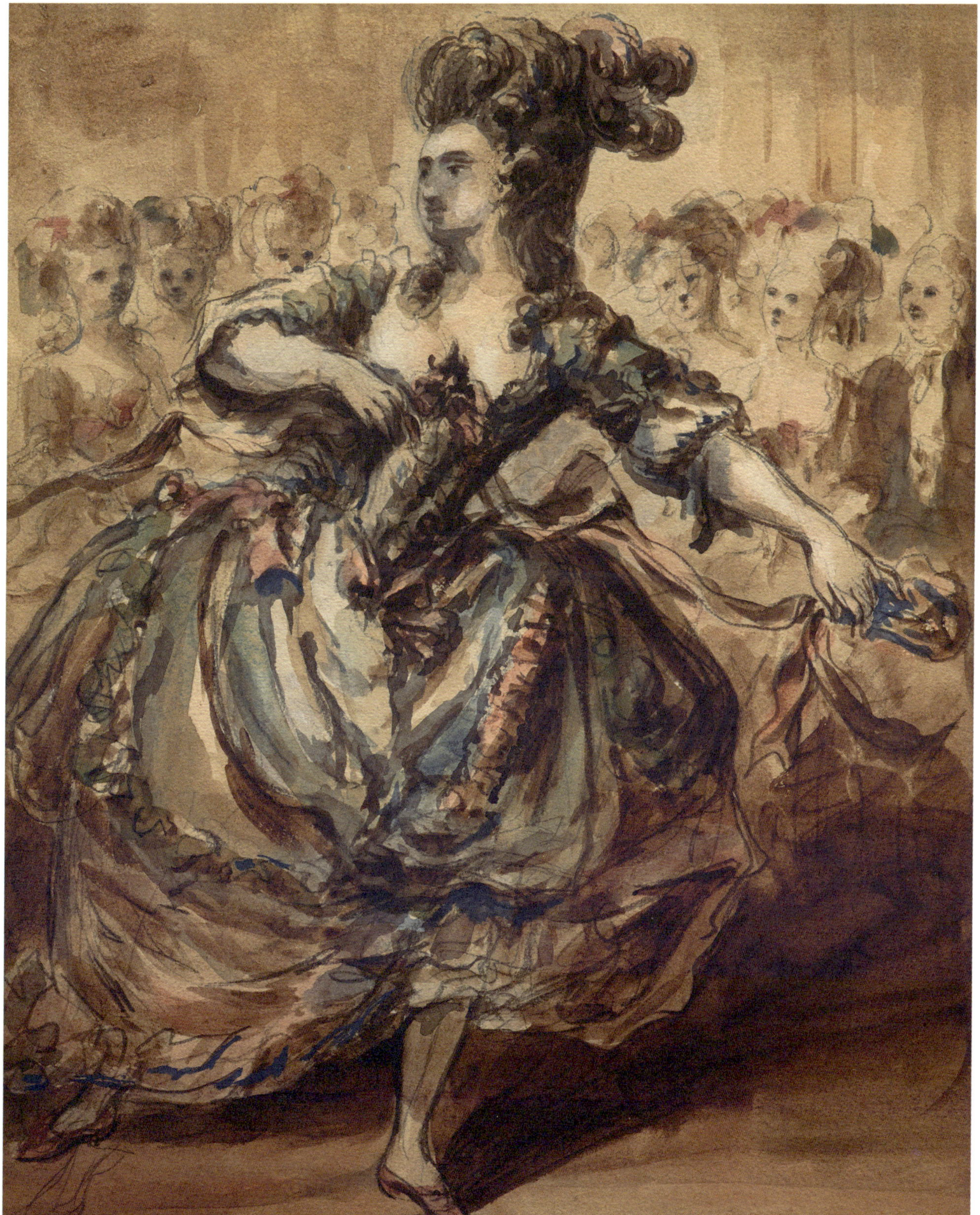

25

Louis Français French, 1814–1897

GIAMBOLOGNA'S FOUNTAIN IN THE BOBOLI GARDENS, FLORENCE (LA FONTAINE DE JEAN DE BOLOGNE DANS LES JARDINS DU BOBOLI À FLORENCE), *1858*

Pen and black ink, black wash on paper, 11¼ × 8¾ in. (286 × 213 mm) (sight)
Inscribed upper center: *qui trop en brosse / mal les peints* (who brushes in too much / paint[s] them badly); upper right: *Boboli, 17 avril 1858*; signed *Français Boboli*
Private collection, Dallas

PROVENANCE Alfred Hartmann, Munster, c. 1858; by descent to the current owner.

EXHIBITED Musée Louis Français, Plombières-les-Bains, France, *Louis Français: Exposition du Centenaire*, 1997.

BIBLIOGRAPHY Conilleau 1997, 74, repr.

In his own time, Louis Français's talent as a landscape artist won him many honors. Charles Baudelaire wrote in his observations about the Salon of 1846: "Monsieur Français is one of our most distinguished landscape-painters. He knows how to study nature, and how to blend it with a romantic perfume of the purest essence."[1] Those qualities are present in his depiction of the broad Piazzale del Isolotto and the steep slope of the Viottolone, an avenue planted with ancient cypresses and hornbeam hedges in the Boboli Gardens in Florence. The central island in the foreground is surrounded by a stone balustrade and vases containing lemon trees and aromatic plants. Giambologna's Ocean Fountain rises in the middle of the island. In the mid-ground, a gate and twin colonnettes surmounted by capricorns are visible. This beautifully organized landscape is animated by small figures harmoniously arranged as if at the hour of the traditional evening walk. The manner of Louis Français is evident in this elegant, virtuoso landscape. Precise use of the pen, highlighted by black wash, faithfully transcribes the charm of the place and meticulously describes Giambologna's white marble. With its statue of Ocean with a group of three rivers seated at his feet—the Nile, the Euphrates, and the Ganges—above an immense basin on a pedestal, this sculpture, made around 1575–1576 for Francesco I de' Medici, has been a source of inspiration for generations of artists.

The beautiful rendition of the landscape testifies to the artist's experience as an illustrator with Jean Gigoux and to his sensitivity to light, gained as a pupil of Jean-Baptiste-Camille Corot. Beginning with Français's first Italian voyage in 1846, the Boboli Gardens inspired many studies, including a drawing in the Musée du Louvre (fig. 6). He returned to Italy several times, occasionally in the company of the great collector Alfred Hartmann (1826–1898), a faithful admirer of the artist who had acquired many of his works and to whom this drawing belonged. Dated April 17, 1858, the landscape is related to a woodcut by Adolphe François Pannemaker (1822–1890), one of the illustrations for Arthur Mangin's book, *Les Jardins* (1867).[2] Français also made a painting of this landscape, in the Musée Louis Français in Plombières-les-Bains in the southern Vosges (no. 116).

LL

Notes
1. "The Salon of 1846," in Baudelaire 1965, 107.
2. Mangin 1867, repr. betw. 112 and 113.

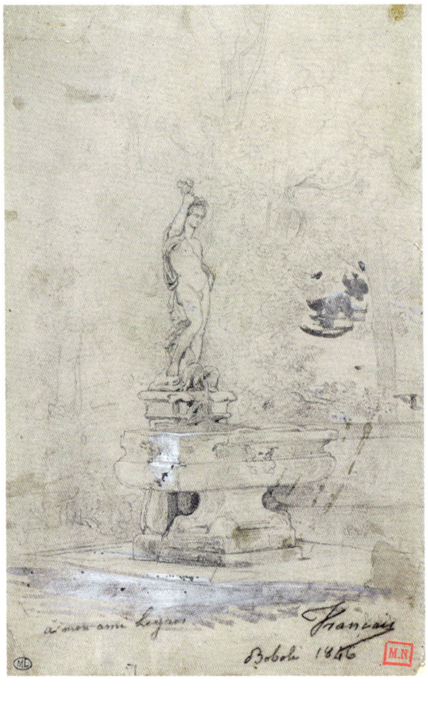

Fig. 6 Louis Français, *A Fountain in the Boboli Gardens*, 1846. Lead pencil with white heightening on paper. Musée du Louvre, Paris, RF 15656 (recto).

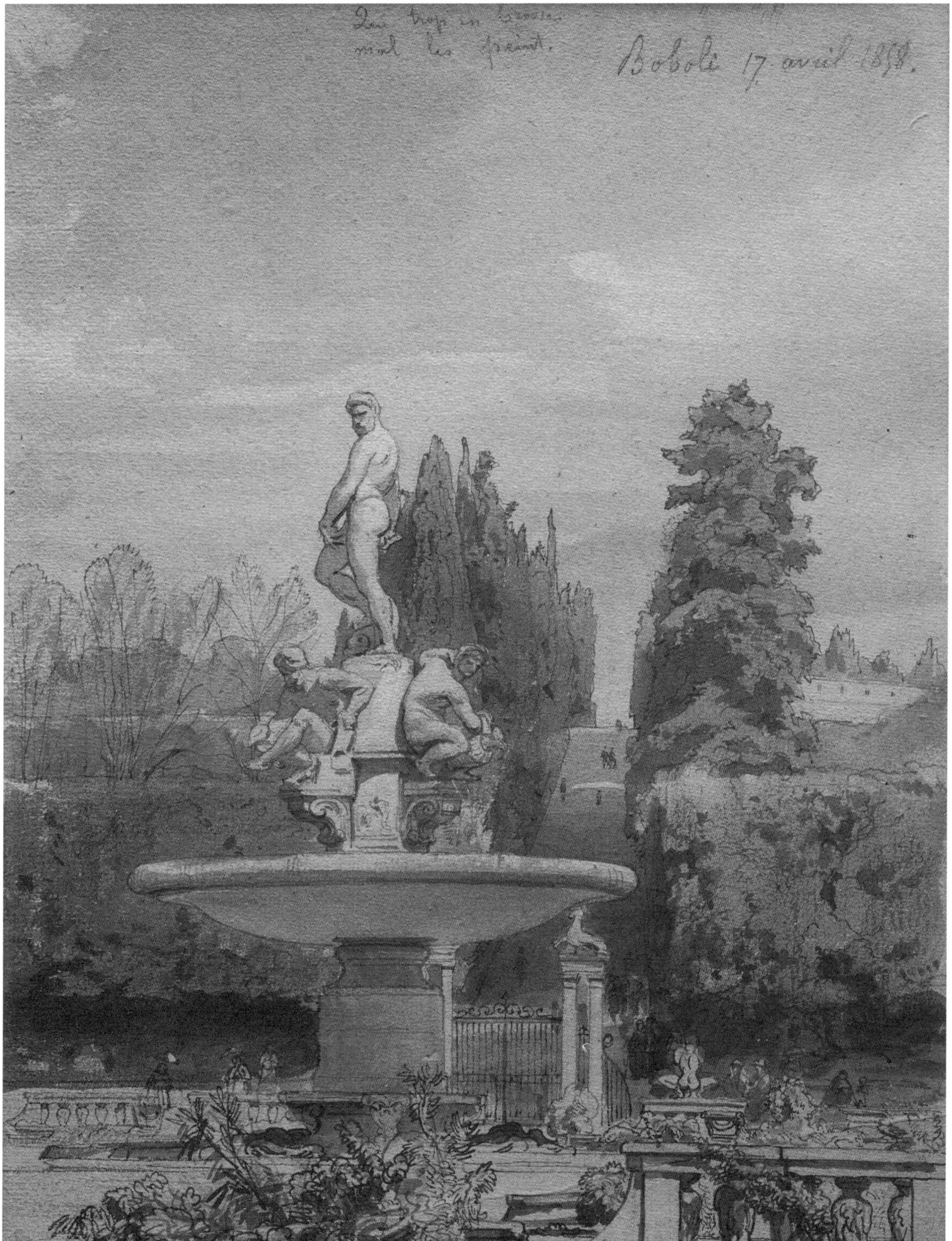
Boboli 17 avril 1858.

26

Louis Français French, 1814–1897

TREE LEANING OVER LAKE NEMI, *N.D.*

Pen, brown ink, and brown wash, 17¾ × 23¼ in. (450 × 590 mm)
Signed lower right: *Français*
Collection of Jeremy and Wendy Strick, Dallas

PROVENANCE Français estate; sale, Me Tual, Paris, Hôtel Drouot, March 14–15, 1898, no. 245; sale, Me Libert, Paris, Nouveau Drouot, April 27, 1983, no. 1, repr.

BIBLIOGRAPHY École des Beaux-Arts 1898; Bethune and Milès 1913; Conilleau 1997.

A large, ancient tree—an oak or white willow to judge by its form—plunges its branches into a glittering lake. A pensive and melancholic boy is seated, shaded by foliage, on one of the principal branches, which stretches out over the water. Together, child, foliage, and contorted branches are reflected in the crystalline surface of the water, which is bordered in the foreground by rocks, brambles, and low brush. Like his master Jean-Baptiste-Camille Corot, who was 18 years his elder, Louis Français left several views of Lake Nemi. This famous volcanic site some 15 miles east of Rome was visited by most French landscape painters who traveled to Italy. Beginning in 1848, it inspired him to produce a number of canvases, watercolors, and drawings exhibited at the Salon. Some of these compositions also appeared in the memorial exhibition of his work in 1898 at the École des Beaux-Arts in Paris.[1]

This drawing is almost identical to a composition entitled *Leaning Tree: Lake Nemi,* formerly in the collection of Alfred Beurdeley.[2] In that work, however, a nymph, not a boy, lies on the same branch above the reflection in the water. Watercolor touches moreover replace the brown wash in the Beurdeley drawing, which was sold as no. 148 in the post-mortem sale of Français on March 14 and 15, 1898, under the title *Arbre penché (lac de Nemi) (Leaning Tree [Lake Nemi]).* This makes it likely that no. 245 of the same sale, listed as *L'Arbre couché (lac de Nemi). Signé à droite. Lavis / Fallen Tree (Lake Nemi) Signed right. Wash,* referred to the present drawing. In the catalogue of works left by Louis Français to his native town, a further composition is also mentioned: *Tree Leaning over Lake Nemi: Study for a Tapestry.*[3] No doubt the two earlier drawings were also preparatory studies for this project. Several tapestries were made after works by Français, such as the Beauvais *Four Seasons* and the Gobelins *Daphnis and Chloe.* The latter was based on the picture exhibited at the 1872 Salon, now in the Musée des Beaux-Arts, Strasbourg. That large, poetic landscape also follows a mode of composition close to the heart of Français: one or more small meditative figures placed at the center of a wooded or aquatic landscape. The format can be understood as Français's debt to Corot's spiritualist conceptions, to which he added a touch of the poetic and ideal, introduced as an homage to the peaceful, idyllic, or melancholy landscapes of Claude Lorrain and his followers. The great love of Français's artistic life was landscape. Late in his life in 1883, he wrote to Édouard Charton: "If I had to live my life over again, I should choose to be a landscape painter."[4]

LL

Notes
1. Paris 1898, nos. 22, 130, 160, 204, 210, 211, 229, 273.
2. Paris, Galerie G. Petit, June 2–4, 1920, no. 154, repr.
3. Plombières-les-Bains 1913.
4. Français to Charton, in E. Charton (dir), *Le magasin pittoresque,* 1883, 138.

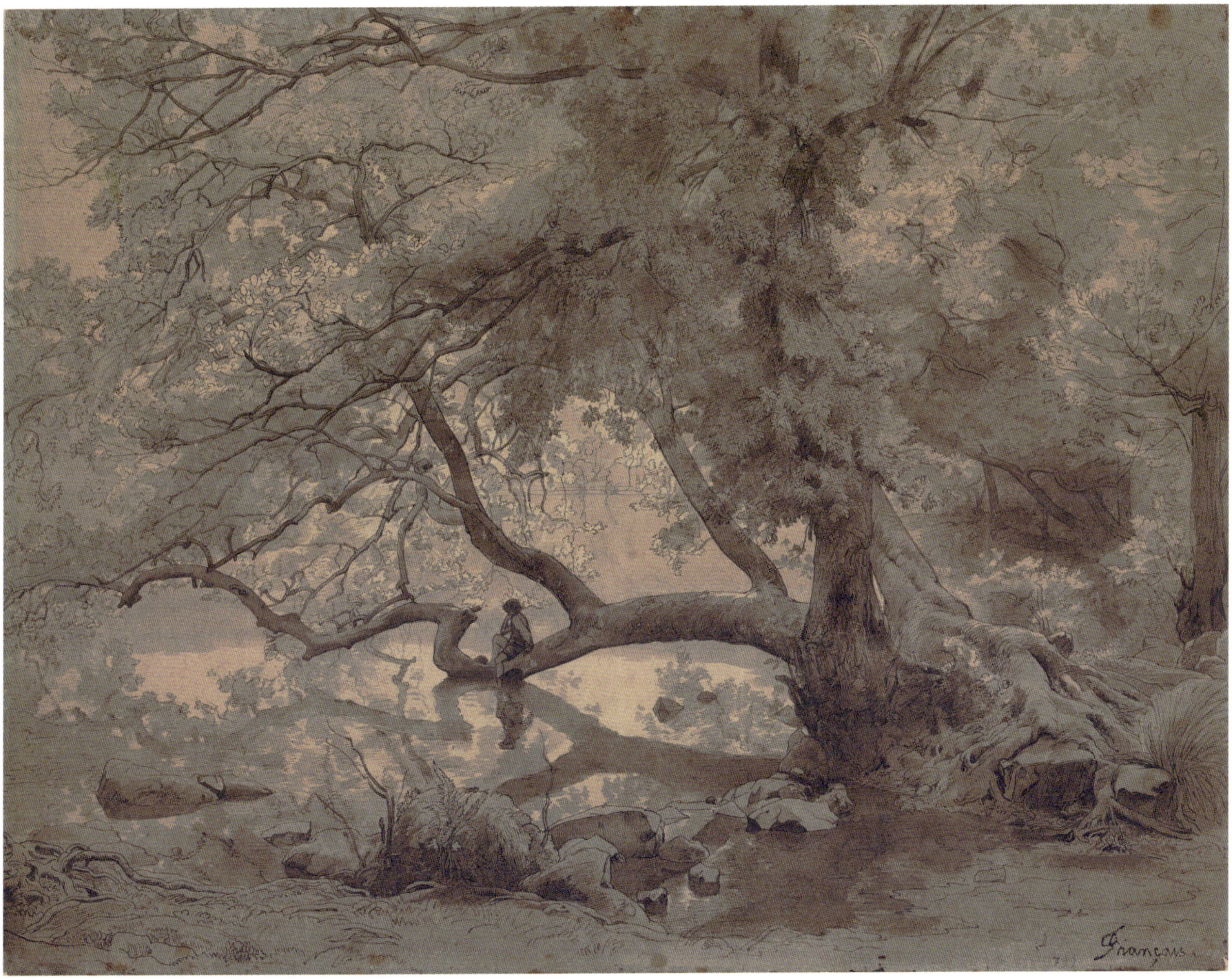
François

27

Octave Tassaert French, 1800–1874

THE FALLEN BIRD NESTER (FORMERLY LE DÉNICHEUR D'OISEAUX ENDORMI) (RECTO), C. *1859*; THE DREAM OF THE PASHA (LE RÊVE DU PACHA) (VERSO), *N.D.*

Pen and brown ink with brown wash on paper (recto);
black chalk on paper (verso), 11 × 14⅝ in. (280 × 370 mm)
Collection of Mary Ralph Lowe, Fort Worth

PROVENANCE Hazlitt, Gooden & Fox, London; sale, Sotheby's, Monaco, *Importants Tableaux Anciens et du XIXe Siècle,* June 19, 1992, lot 497; W. M. Brady & Co., Inc., New York; from whom purchased 1993 by the current owner.

EXHIBITED Museum of Fine Arts, Houston, December 10, 1992–April 22, 1994.

The life of Octave Tassaert can be seen as an archetype of the impoverished romantic artist's destiny. With almost no formal education beyond instruction from his father and older brother, he enrolled in the École des Beaux-Arts, where he studied under Guillaume Guillon-Lethière from 1817 to 1825. Despite winning several awards, he never succeeded enough in the highly competitive Parisian art world to earn a comfortable living. He often worked for publishers, providing drawings to be lithographed or erotic paintings to be sold discreetly through dealers. At the Salons, his paintings often dealt with the social themes associated with the realist movement, as in the case of his most famous painting, *An Unfortunate Family (The Suicide),* 1852 (Musée Fabre, Montpellier); his *Interior of a Studio,* 1845 (Musée du Louvre, Paris); or *Woman and Her Child,* 1855 (Musée Sandelin, Saint-Omer). Though Tassaert was more popular with the public than with critics, several discriminating collectors—including Alfred Bruyas and Alexandre Dumas fils—did acquire his works. During the 1850s, his health and financial condition started to deteriorate. He stopped submitting work to the Salons and eventually gave up painting altogether. Struggling with poverty and alcoholism for the rest of his life, he committed suicide in 1874.

This highly accomplished wash drawing displays Tassaert's skills at their fullest, showing his ability to evoke feeling through the masterful manipulation of his medium—in this case, almost a network of stains. Although it has been described as representing a sleeping bird nester, the drawing actually depicts a boy who has fallen from a tree while trying to gather eggs from a nest. A painting (location unknown) of the same subject and of almost the same composition, though vertical, was reproduced in the *Galerie contemporaine* (Paris: Baschet, 1877) under the title *Petit dénicheur d'oiseaux* (*Young Bird Nester*). In the article accompanying the reproduction, the painting is cited as the *Dead Bird Nester* and dated 1859. In the painting, a broken branch, the fallen nest, and dead baby birds are clues to the drama.

A preparatory oil sketch over black chalk and traces of pencil belonged to the great collector and art historian Baron Portalis.[1] The present drawing is probably a first thought for the painting.

OM

Note
1. His sale, Paris, Drouot, February 2–3, 1911, lot 185; then sold at Christie's, New York, October 29, 1986, lot 314. It resurfaced, attributed to Tassaert and without provenance, in Rennes, France, March 15, 2009, lot 26.

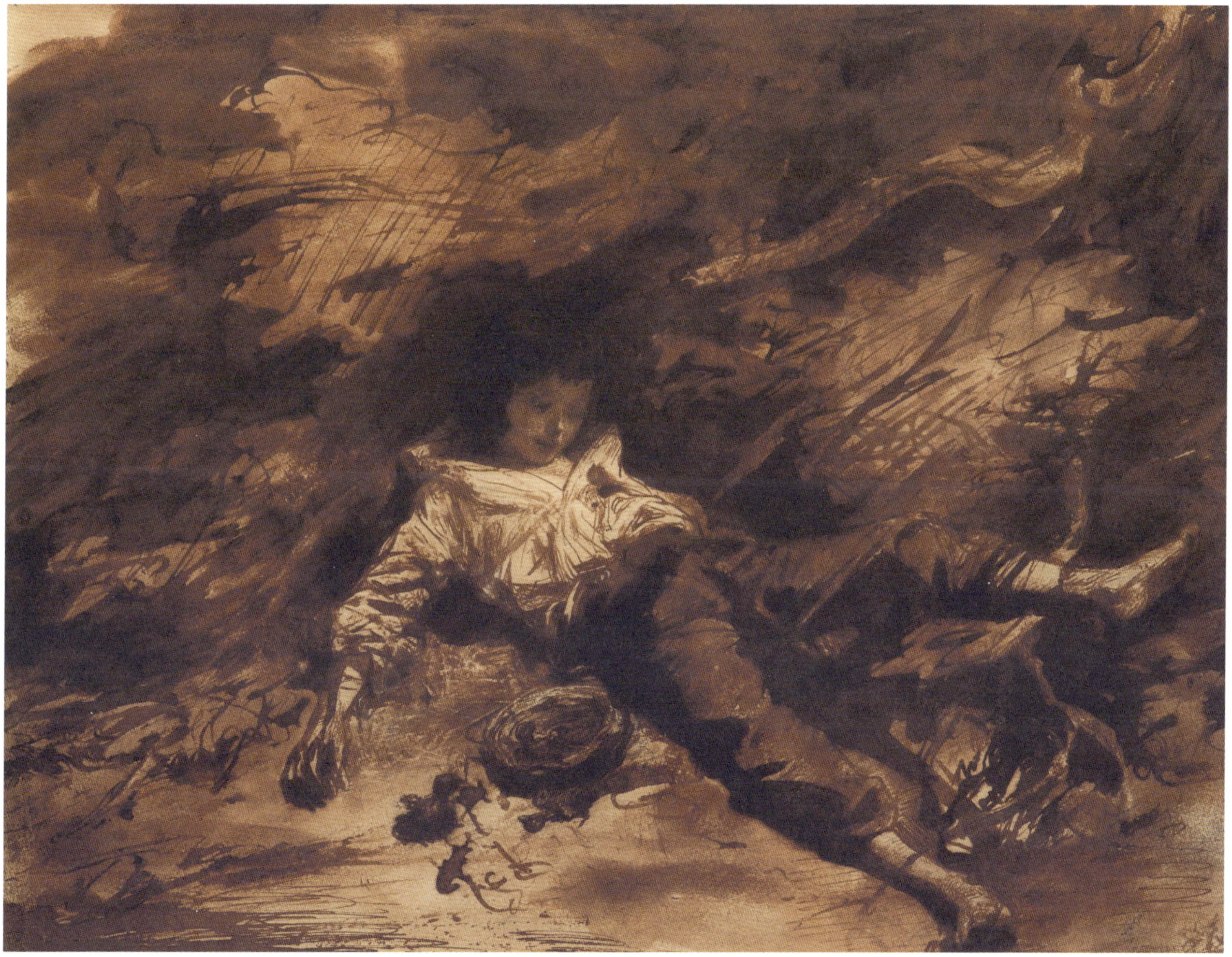

28

François Bonvin French, 1817–1887

BLACKSMITH AT REST SMOKING A PIPE (FORGERON AU REPOS, FUMANT LA PIPE), *1857*

Conté, crayon, charcoal, and stumping on paper, 16½ × 12¼ in. (420 × 310 mm)
Signed and dated center left: *F. Bonvin / 1857*
Collection of Mary Ralph Lowe, Fort Worth

PROVENANCE Sale, Tajan, Paris, *Dessins Anciens*, November 26, 1996, lot 19; Galerie Berès, Paris, by 1998; from whom purchased 1999 by the current owner.

EXHIBITED Galerie D. Rothschild, Paris, *Exposition de tableaux et dessins par François Bonvin*, May 10–31, 1886, 7; Galerie Berès, Paris, November 19, 1998–January 9, 1999, and Frick Art and Historical Center, Pittsburgh, February 5–April 11, 1999, *François Bonvin (1817–1887)*, 42.

BIBLIOGRAPHY Moreau-Nélaton 1927, fig. 28 (painting); Weisberg 1973; Weisberg 1979, 171, cat. 21 (painting).

Among the realist painters who began their careers at the end of the 1840s, François Bonvin is certainly the one who remained truest to the artistic principles of his youth until the end. A lifelong friend of Gustave Courbet, he nevertheless avoided the controversies associated with Courbet, following his own path of hard work, meticulous process, and a discreet, quiet life. His art is often compared to that of Jean-Baptiste-Siméon Chardin, with whom he shared an affinity for simple life, humble work, and modest surroundings. And in this regard, his single-figure compositions also reflect the influence of Edme Bouchardon's *Cris de Paris* prints depicting street workers of the 18th century.

This drawing is related to the painting *The Blacksmith's Shop, Remembrance of Le Tréport* of 1857 (Musée des Augustins, Toulouse), which Bonvin exhibited the same year at the Paris Salon. Almost the same bearded model is depicted, with the same hammer and the same large bucket. Bonvin started to work on this subject in 1852, as we can see in a watercolor in the Musée des Beaux-Arts, Dijon. In the painting, the blacksmith is in his busy shop with his two young assistants, surrounded by work implements, with a wooden staircase in the background. In the drawing, the blacksmith, wearing his leather apron, is resting and smoking his pipe, his hammer leaning against a block of stone. The atmosphere of the studio is boldly yet sensitively evoked through a careful contrasting of the deep, almost black, shadow and the nearly white background of the paper, achieving a structural integrity that is characteristic of Bonvin's work.

This drawing is closely related, in composition and attention to details, to Bonvin's best drawings, representing single figures carefully designed and composed.

OM

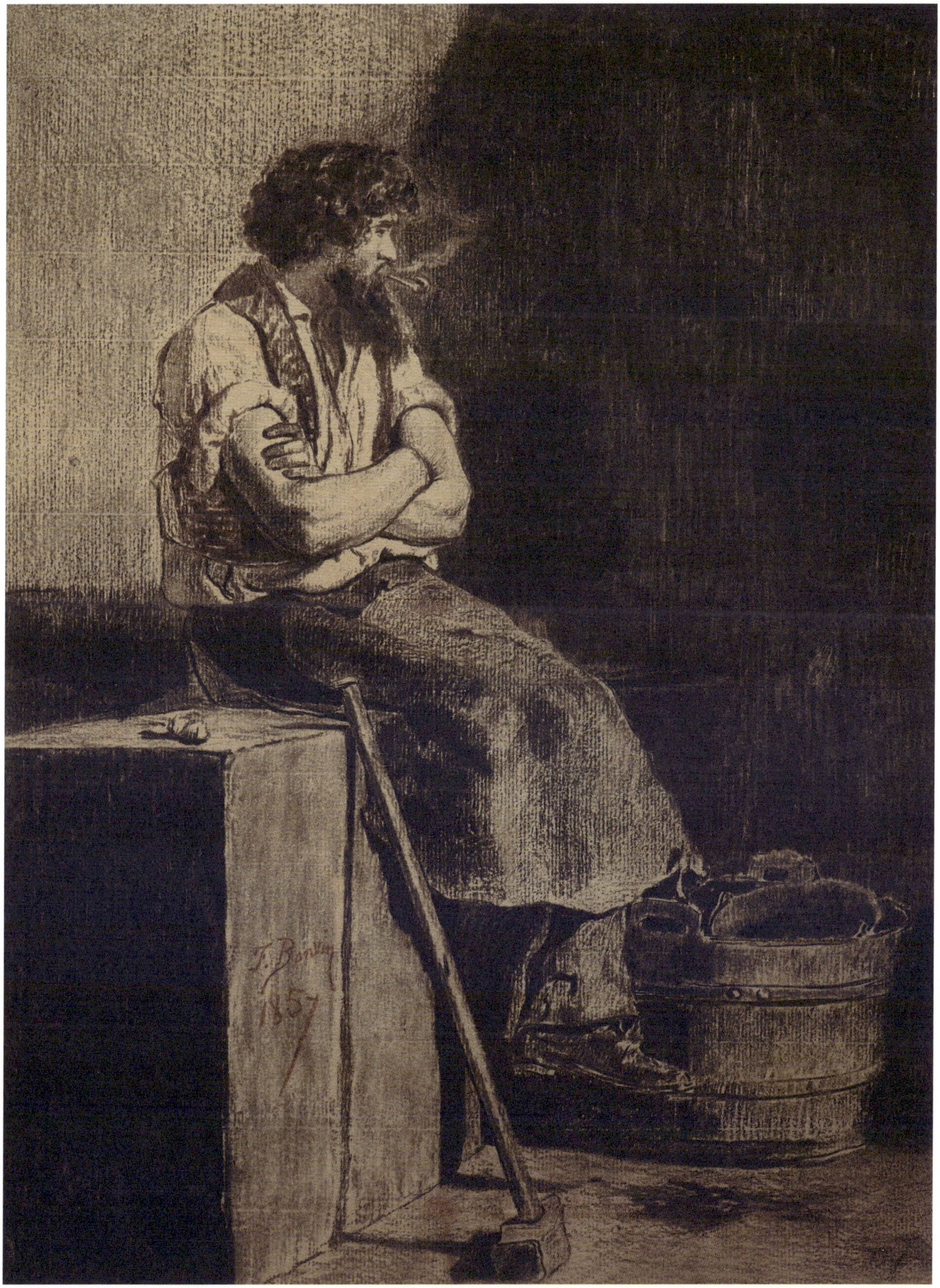
F. Bonvin
1857

29

Théodule Ribot French, 1823–1891

HEAD OF AN OLD MAN WITH BEARD AND A CAP, *1866*

Ink, black chalk, and white pigment on paper, 4⅜ × 5⅛ in. (108 × 105 mm)
Signed and dated lower right: *T. Ribot / 1866*
Dallas Museum of Art, gift of Henry Hawley, 2005.87.15

PROVENANCE Henry H. Hawley, Cleveland; given to the Dallas Museum of Art, 2005.

A self-taught artist, Théodule Ribot began as a decorator of gilded frames, a copyist of old masters, and a sign painter. After he was refused at the Salon in 1859, he exhibited in the studio of his friend François Bonvin with Henri Fantin-Latour, Antoine Vollon, Alphonse Legros, and James Abbott McNeill Whistler. He was accepted by the Salon of 1861, where he received considerable acclaim. Ribot was well respected by his fellow artists. He painted not only religious subjects like the *Saint Sebastian, Martyr*, which the French government bought in 1865, but also still-lifes, genre paintings, and history paintings. Inspired by old masters like Rembrandt, Frans Hals, and Jean-Baptiste Siméon Chardin, his most profound influence came from the Spanish painter Jusepe de Ribera, whom he discovered in the late 1840s at the Musée du Louvre in King Louis-Philippe's celebrated Galerie Espagnole. Ribot was fascinated by chiaroscuro and used muted tones and dark colors to make dramatic compositions. His drawings were highly regarded during his lifetime and were exhibited in galleries such as Bernheim-Jeune and in his posthumous exhibition at the École des Beaux-Arts in 1892.

This study of a man's head seems to have been reused in different paintings. Variations of the strong, bearded man wearing a cap can be found in *The Good Samaritan*, 1870 (Musée des Beaux-Arts, Pau) and *Oyster and Clients*, 1869 (Musée des Beaux-Arts, Caen), but the closest figure is Cimabue in the unlocated painting representing *Cimabue Teaching Giotto.*[1]

OM

Note
1. Sold Sotheby's Amsterdam, April 19, 2005, no. 128.

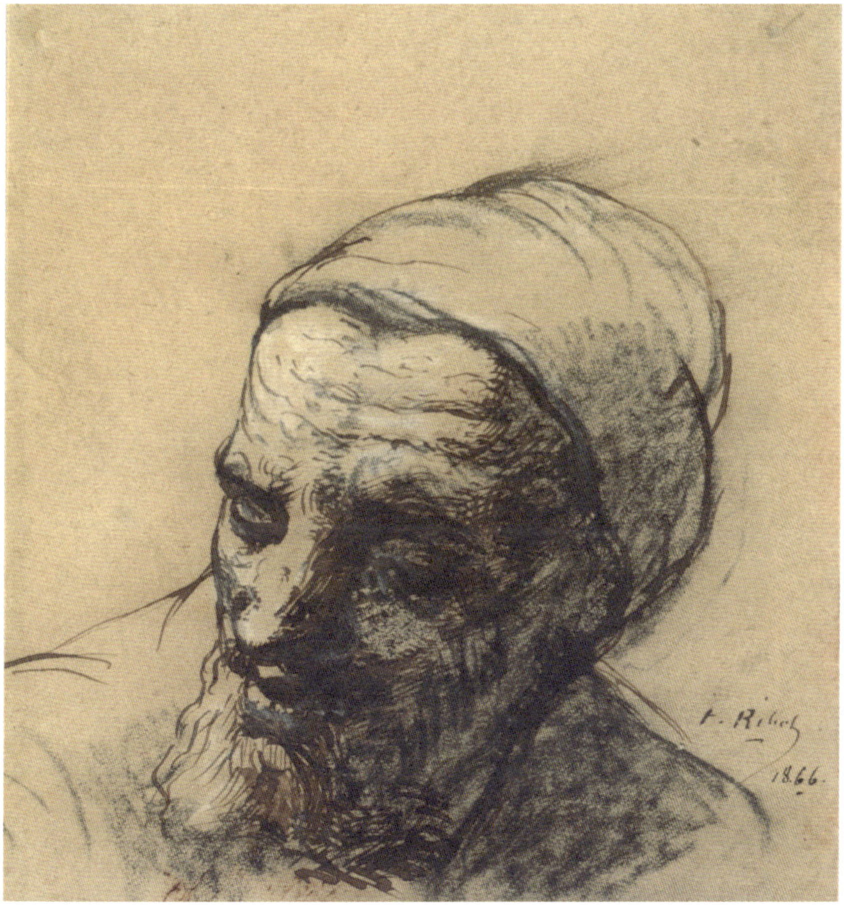
1866.

30

Léon-Augustin Lhermitte French, 1844–1925

WOMEN HARVESTING POTATOES (LES RAMASSEUSES DE POMMES DE TERRE), *1884*

Charcoal on paper, 11¾ × 18¾ in. (300 × 480 mm)
Signed lower right: *L. Lhermitte*
Private collection, Dallas

PROVENANCE Collection Paul Dalloz, December 1884; sale, Sotheby's, London, March 26, 1981; (Possibly sale, Thierry de Maigret, Paris, December 10, 2004, no. 17 [*Les rammasseuses de pommes de terre*, charcoal and stump drawing, signed lower right, 31 × 48 cm]); current owner.

BIBLIOGRAPHY Le Pelley Fonteny 1991, no. 743, repr.

Léon-Augustin Lhermitte's drawings and paintings were admired for their honest portrayal of scenes taken from daily life. The famous *Paying the Harvesters (Paye des moissonneurs)* (Musée d'Orsay, Paris), acquired by the government on the opening day of the Paris Salon of 1882, confirmed him, alongside Jules Breton, as the principal representative of "peasant painting" in the Third Republic.

In 1884, Lhermitte contracted with Paul Dalloz, editor of *Le Monde illustré,* to deliver 12 charcoal drawings illustrating "the rural months"; he was to be paid 500 francs for each drawing, which were to be engraved by Clément Edouard Bellanger. For October (this drawing), he chose to represent the potato harvest, renewing the tradition of depicting months with their corresponding activities, adjusted to the tastes of the time. But this subject also interested him throughout his long career. At Paris Salons, he exhibited *Potato Harvesters* in 1868 and *Potato Harvest,* a charcoal drawing, in 1872; the latter served as a study for an etching of the same subject (1873), in which the influence of Millet is clear. He returned to the subject in 1898 and again in 1913, this time in pastels, a technique that he favored from the second half of the 1880s. The drawing shown here was made in 1884 in his native village of Mont-Saint-Père in the Aisne. Lhermitte was the son of the village schoolteacher and spent his youth there. An acute observer of the rural world, his depictions of men and women bent over their work in the unremitting tasks of agricultural labor—as in the painting *The Harvest,* 1874, or straightening up in anxious scrutiny of the sky, as in the pastel *Wheatfield,* 1890—are very realistic.

The virtuosity, compassion, and accuracy of the artist's depictions of peasant reality are particularly evident in his black and white drawings, which have always enjoyed success in France, Great Britain, and the United States. But the most telling index of their merit is the admiration felt by Vincent van Gogh, who discovered Lhermitte's work in 1883 and thereafter actively sought out reproductions of his work. In a letter to his brother Theo, he makes a request: "If *Le Monde Illustré* prints compositions by him every month—this is part of a series of 'Rural months'—it would give me mighty great pleasure to collect this whole series, and I'd really like you to send them every time."[1] After receiving the print evoking the month of October, he was already inquiring about the next: "I have also found OCTOBER by Lhermitte, women in a potato field in the evening. Magnificent. Not yet November though. Have you kept up to date with that, by any chance?"[2] What struck him about the series was its strength and contemporaneity, as he told Theo: "When I think about Millet or about Lhermitte then I find modern art as great as Michelangelo and Rembrandt."[3]

Further evidence of Lhermitte's success came in 1884 with the first acquisition of one of his works by an American dealer, William Schaus. *The Grape Harvest* was exhibited at the 1884 Salon (no. 1538) and donated three years later to the Metropolitan Museum of Art, New York.

LL

Notes
1. Van Gogh to Theo van Gogh, March 2, 1885, in *Vincent van Gogh: The Letters,* http://vangoghletters.org/vg/letters/let484/letter.html (accessed November 20, 2013).
2. The drawing appeared in the supplement to no. 1495 of *Le Monde illustré*. Van Gogh to Theo van Gogh, November 28, 1885, in *Vincent van Gogh: The Letters,* http://vangoghletters.org/vg/letters/let545/letter.html (accessed November 20, 2013).
3. Van Gogh to Theo van Gogh, September 2, 1885, in *Vincent van Gogh: The Letters,* http://vangoghletters.org/vg/letters/let531/letter.html (accessed November 20, 2013).

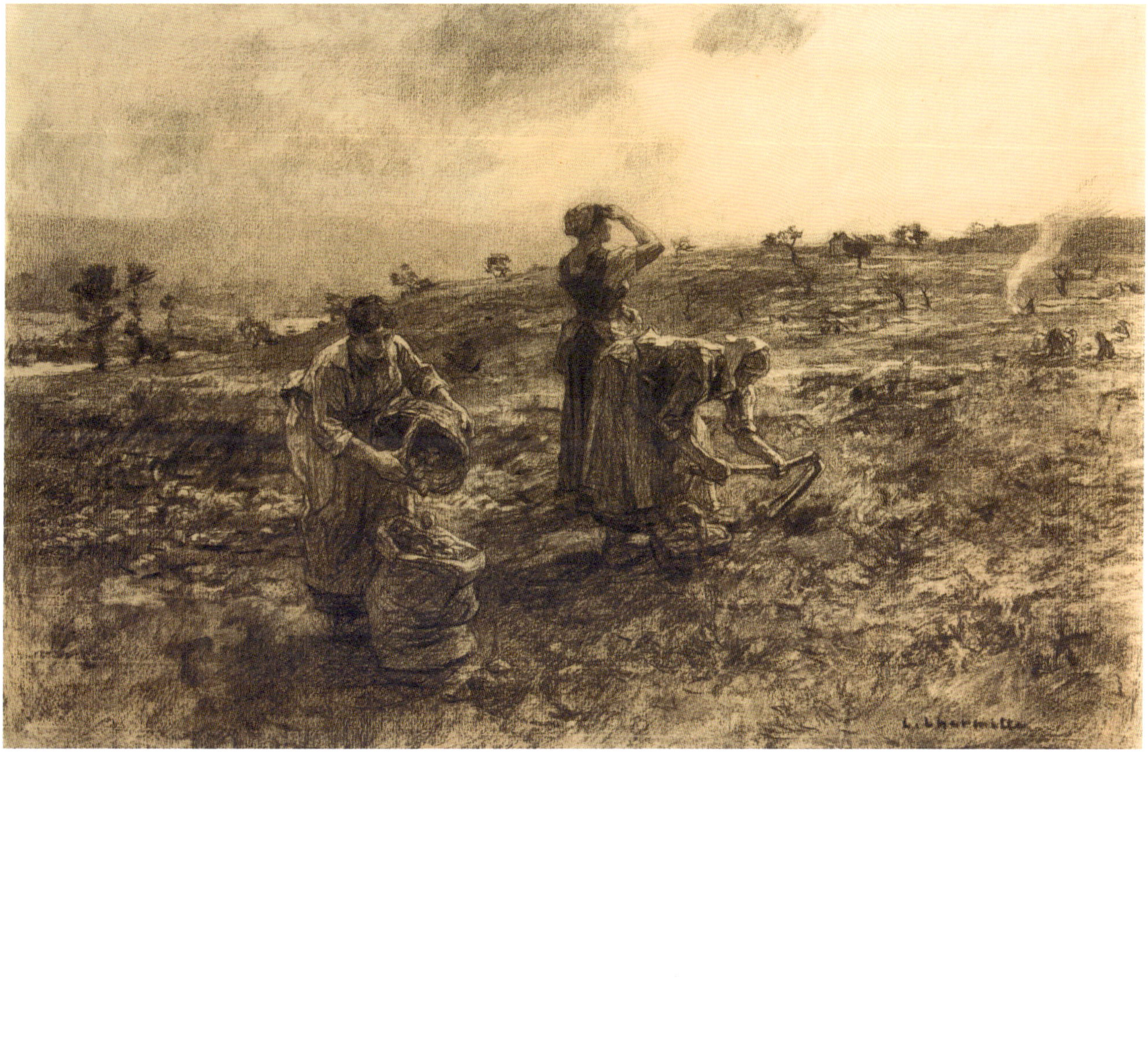

31

Léon-Augustin Lhermitte French, 1844–1925

THE CARPENTER'S WORKSHOP (L'ATELIER DE MENUISERIE), *1884*

Charcoal on tinted paper, 14½ × 21⅝ in. (370 × 550 mm)
Signed and dated lower right: *L. Lhermitte / 1884*
Collection of Mary Ralph Lowe, Fort Worth

PROVENANCE Allou Collection; Stoppenbach and Delestre, London, 1989; David Daniels, New York; Sandorval and Co., New York; from whom purchased 1996 by the current owner.

BIBLIOGRAPHY Le Pelley Fonteny 1991, 485, no. 990, repr.

From 1863 to 1897, Léon-Augustin Lhermitte listed and described his works in a notebook.[1] Concerning this drawing, he wrote in 1884: "Rampenault and his son busy themselves each at his own bench, one seen from the back, the other in three-quarter profile. In the background, their mother works by one of two windows with latticed panes." This carefully composed drawing was made in Lhermitte's native village of Mont-Saint-Père. As in so many of his scenes of rural and craft life, the drawing represents real inhabitants of the village. The artist uses charcoal here—as he often did in the 1880s—to depict this indoor scene with powerful realism and complete mastery. A virtuoso of black and white, he meticulously orders these figures as they are illuminated by the light coming from the latticed panes of the high windows, in a clear reference to the silent painting of the Dutch Golden Age. This kind of composition, with men going about their trade and seated women absorbed in their needlework, can be found in several other drawings made during the early 1880s: *The Cobblers* (1880, exhibited at the Hazlitt, Gooden, and Fox Gallery in 1990), *The Tool Grinder at Mont-Saint-Père* (1882, private collection, Belgium), and *The Little Bag-Seamstress* (1884, Smith College Museum of Art, also known as *Woman Sewing by a Window*). Almost all these descriptions of the manual trades—cobblers, weavers, blacksmiths, turners, spinners, and seamstresses—convey a similar impression of calm and concentration, slightly moralizing in tone. Lhermitte establishes himself as the scrupulous chronicler of a world that is surely coming to an end and whose existence he must document with a photographic eye.

Though we cannot know for sure whether this charcoal was intended as one, we do know that 1884 was a significant year for Lhermitte's illustrations. In that year he made eight charcoal drawings on the subject of Christmas for the special number of *Le Monde illustré* and later delivered to the same weekly 12 charcoals symbolizing the months of the year and illustrating rural life (see cat. 30). The latter series elicited considerable interest on the part of Vincent van Gogh, a great admirer of Lhermitte's work. On receiving two of these illustrations, van Gogh wrote: "He's a master of the figure. He's able to do what he likes with it—conceiving the whole neither from the colour nor from the local tone, but rather proceeding from the light—as Rembrandt did—there's something astonishingly masterly in everything he does—in modelling, above all things, he utterly satisfies the demands of honesty."[2]

LL

Notes

1. *Catalogue of the Works—Paintings, Drawings, Watercolors, and Pastels—Executed by Monsieur Léon-Augustin Lhermitte (Catalogue des ouvrages en peinture, dessin, aquarelle ou pastel exécutés par M. Léon-Augustin Lhermitte).*
2. Van Gogh to Theo van Gogh, September 2, 1885, in *Vincent van Gogh: The Letters*, http://vangoghletters.org/vg/letters/let531/letter.html (accessed November 13, 2013).

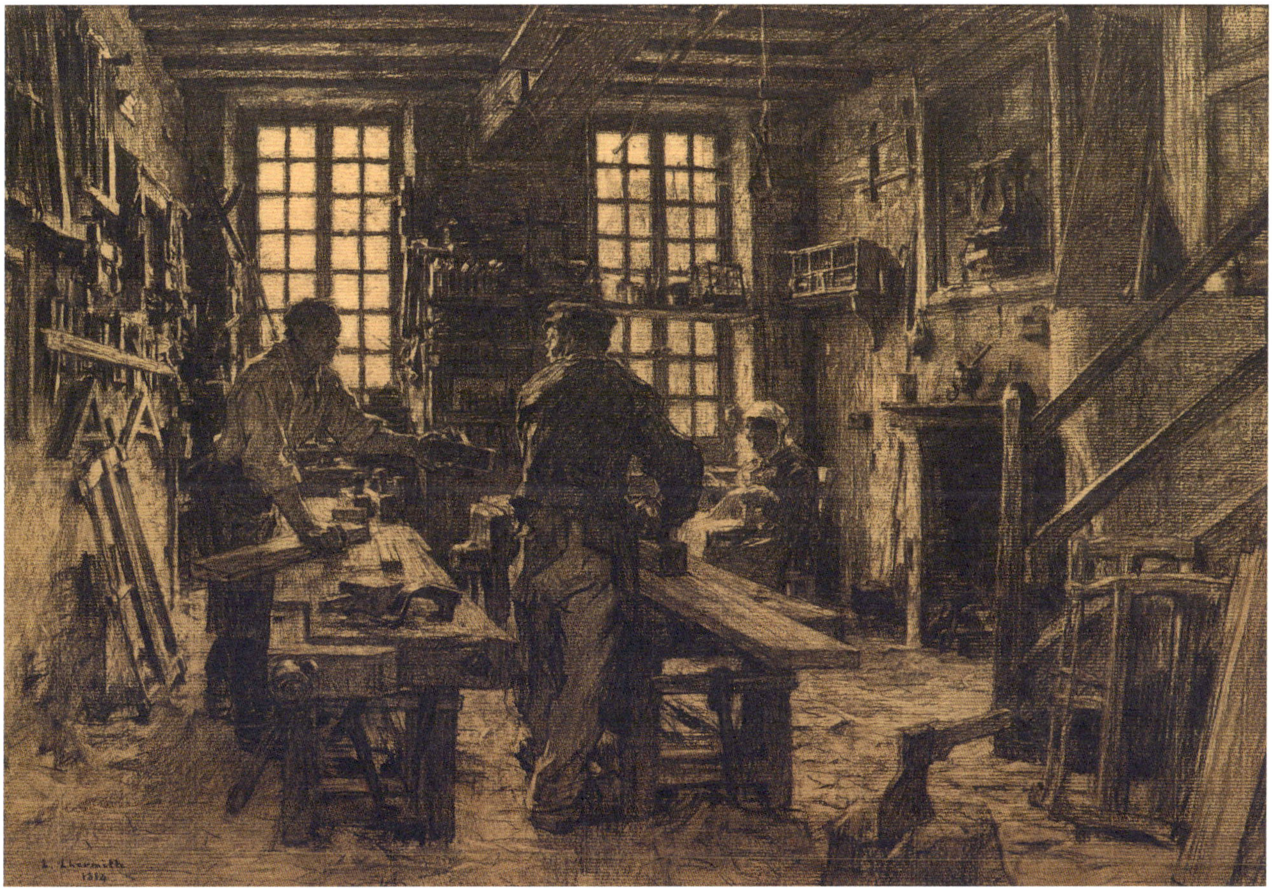

32

Rosa Bonheur French, 1822–1899

LION'S HEAD, CA. *1880–1885*

Pencil heightened with white on paper, 16 × 11 in. (406 × 280 mm)
Estate stamp, lower right: *Rosa Bonheur* (Lugt 275); red wax seal of the estate sale: *VENTE ROSA BONHEUR/1990* (Lugt 276) on back of original mounting
Collection of Mr. and Mrs. Thomas C. Campbell, Dallas

PROVENANCE Rosa Bonheur sale, Paris, G. Petit et Tedesco frères, June 5–8, 1900 (probably lot 1146: "*Lion's Head*. Front view, head thrown back, mouth open, look raised, jaws threatening. Pencil drawing, touched up with white"); Thomas Mabry Cranfill (1913–1995), Austin, Texas; by whom given c. 1985 to his nephew, the current owner.

Not many artists of the 19th century achieved anything like the celebrity status and financial security that Rosa Bonheur enjoyed throughout her long career. Born into a family of artists in Bordeaux, the strong-willed, highly independent Bonheur pursued most things in life—indeed, life itself—in her own way. Unruly as a student, she was instructed mostly by her father and her own self-study, adopting as if by nature the specialty of animal painting. Inspired by 17th-century masters, she developed a phenomenal facility for the handling of paint, and her realist style—unallied with any "ism" of its time—strongly appealed to conservative taste. Receiving a Gold Medal in the Paris Salon of 1848 from a jury that included Léon Cogniet, Eugène Delacroix, Ernest Meissonier, and Jean-Baptiste-Camille Corot, she was commissioned at age 26 to paint one of her most iconic works, *Plowing in the Nivernais* (1849), which depicts six pairs of oxen plowing through a muddy field. It was acquired by the state and resides today in the Musée d'Orsay, Paris. This painting and the monumental *Horse Fair* (first exhibited at the Paris Salon of 1853 and given by Cornelius Vanderbilt to the newly founded Metropolitan Museum of Art, New York, in 1887) were showpieces of animal flesh, movement, and painterly virtuosity. Works like these and the prints after them made Bonheur a well-off and hugely famous person, and this notoriety was in no small way augmented by her unabashed lifestyle of cross-dressing, cigarette smoking, and outspoken opinion. In 1859 she purchased a chateau on the edge of the Fontainebleau Forest, where, with her lifelong companion Nathalie Micas, she kept a menagerie of domestic and wild animals and received a steady stream of doting pilgrims, including not a few crowned heads of state and even the American William F. "Buffalo Bill" Cody.

In 1880 Bonheur's dealer Ernest Gambart presented her with the first two of her lions, a lioness and a handsome, four-year-old male named Nero. The animals were allowed a certain degree of freedom to walk about while Bonheur sketched them. Nero became very attached to his mistress but began to go blind and was given to the Jardin des Plantes in Paris, where he soon died. Gambart then found another pair in 1885, including an ill-natured male named Sultan, whom the artist managed to tame somewhat. But after keeping these lions long enough to make many studies of them, she felt compelled to offer them as well to the Jardin des Plantes. Later that year, a pair of tiny cubs arrived, one of which, Fatma, a crippled lioness, became like a favorite child until her own death from her congenital abnormalities.

Of the nearly 2,000 lots offered in Bonheur's estate sale in 1900, there were 76 paintings and 221 drawings of wild cats, most of them lions. Some of these drawings were dated in the 1860s and 1870s, but most were either working studies made in the 1880s or finished drawings made continually to address an important aspect of her market from then on. *Fore-paws of a Lion* (cat. 33, p. 85) is clearly a study for a major painting titled *The King of the Desert* (fig. 7, p. 84). Its sensuous grasp of the animal's powerful sinews and supple joints exemplifies Bonheur's virtuosity at its peak. *Lion's Head* (cat. 32, facing page) repeats the design of a painting of the same subject and was one of several more or less similarly described drawings in the sale. It is clearly not a study but rather a fully developed work made for the market. The almost audible roar and terrifying ferocity of the lion's glaring eyes go a long way to explain why the public was so crazy about this famous artist.

WBJ

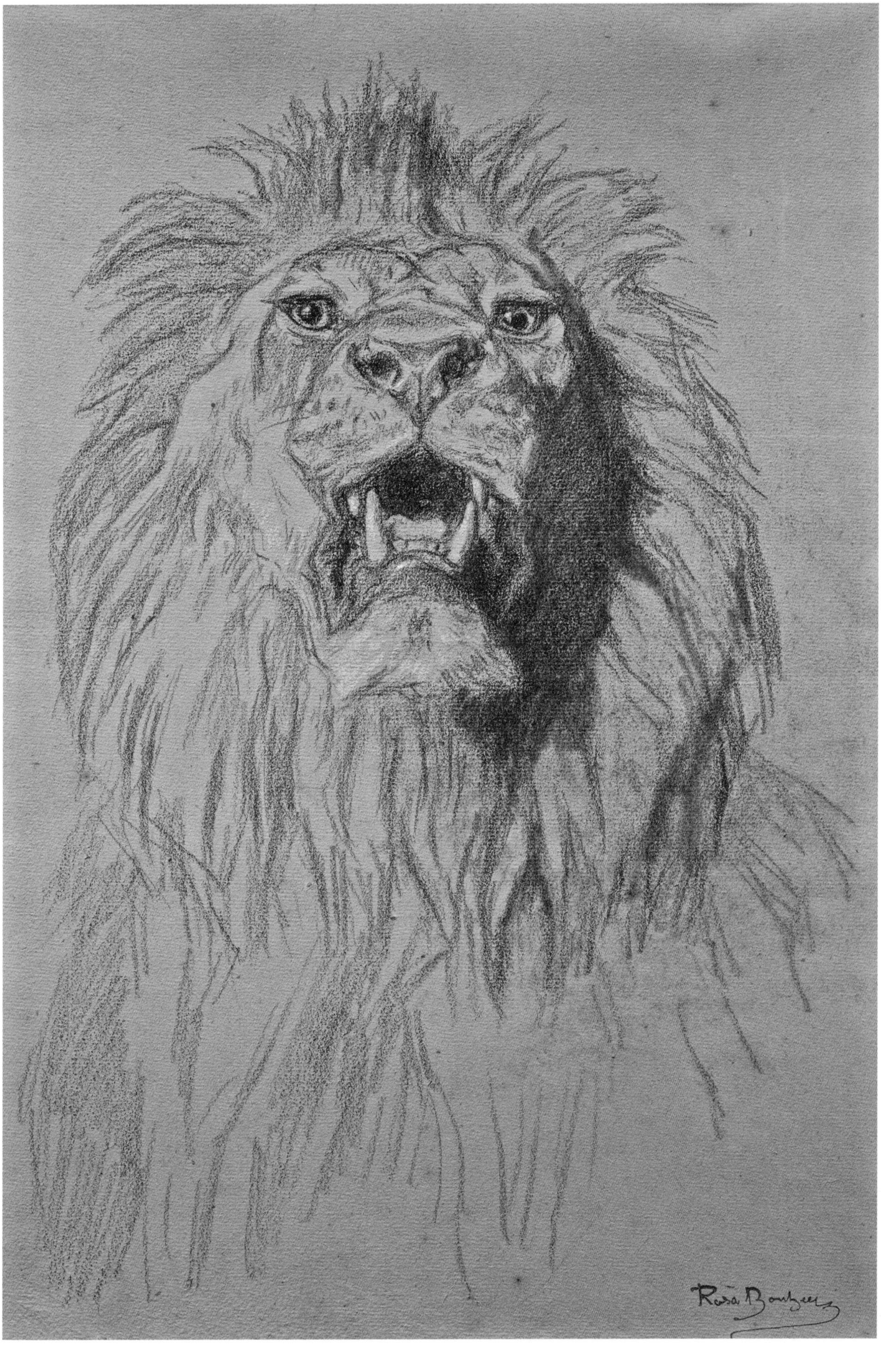
Rosa Bonheur

33

Rosa Bonheur French, 1822–1899

FORE-PAWS OF A LION (PATTES DE LION), CA. *1880–1885*

Black crayon on medium-weight wove paper with stumping,
25½ × 19¾ in. (648 × 505 mm)
Estate stamp lower left: *Rosa Bonheur* (Lugt 275); red wax seal of the estate sale: *VENTE ROSA BONHEUR / 1900* (Lugt 276), on original mounting board, removed in conservation
Private collection, Dallas

PROVENANCE Rosa Bonheur sale, Paris, G. Petit et Tedesco frères, June 5–8, 1900, lot 1096; private collection, Paris; with Hubert Duchemin, Paris; from whom purchased 2011 by the current owner.

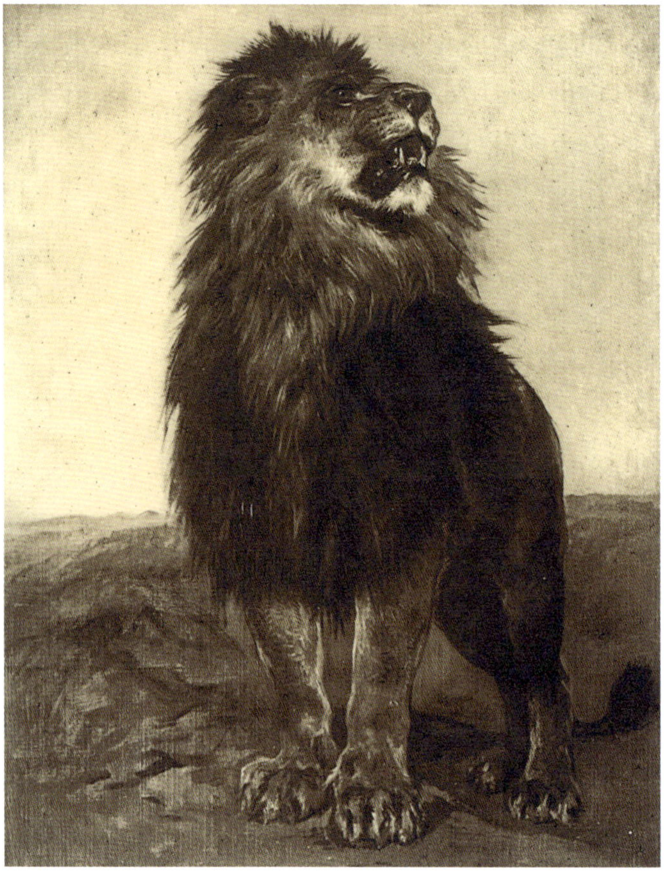

Fig. 7 Rosa Bonheur, *Le roi du désert (The King of the Desert)*, n.d. Oil on canvas. Location unknown.

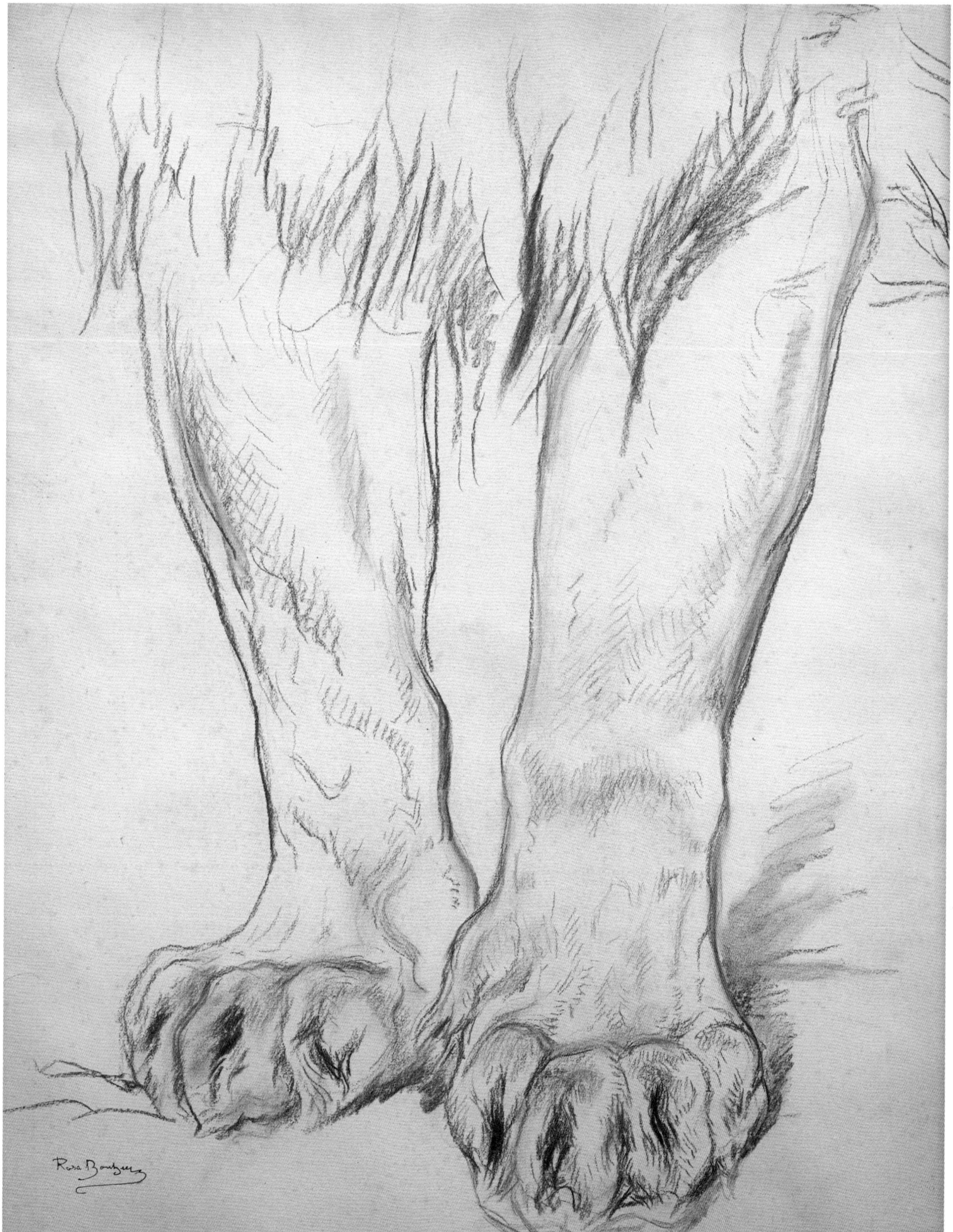

34

Jules-Élie Delaunay French, 1828–1891

STUDY FOR THE OATH OF BRUTUS (LE SERMENT DE BRUTUS), C. *1861*

Charcoal and black chalk on beige paper, 11¾ × 9½ in. (300 × 239 mm)
Signed and inscribed in brown ink across the bottom of the sheet: *E. Delaunay. Étude pour le tableau de la mort de Lucrèce ou le serment de Brutus qui est au Musée de Tours*
Collection of Mary Ralph Lowe, Fort Worth

PROVENANCE Frederick J. Cummings, Inc., New York; from whom purchased 1990 by the current owner.

A pupil of Hippolyte Flandrin, himself a devotee of Jean-Auguste-Dominique Ingres, Jules-Élie Delaunay was one of the most successful academic artists of his time. He received prestigious commissions for murals, including examples at the Opéra, the Hôtel de Ville, and the Palais-Royal in Paris. His beautiful portraits were praised for their accomplished technique and psychological acuteness.

This sheet is a preparatory drawing for one of Delaunay's most important history paintings, *The Oath of Brutus,* his last *envoi* from Rome in 1861—a requirement of the French Academy at the end of an artist's stay at the Villa Medici. Delaunay obtained the Grand Prix de Rome quite late, in 1856, when he was nearly 40 years old.

The subject of the oath of Brutus is taken from the Roman historian Livy's *Books from the Foundation of the City.* In the first book, Livy describes the reign of Tarquinius, king of Rome, and its violent end. After having been abused by Tarquinius's son Sextus, Lucretia, a relative of the king, committed suicide. Brutus, her cousin, took the bloody dagger from Lucretia's hands and swore upon it to overthrow the king. Brutus and his brothers summoned the people of Rome to banish the tyrant Tarquinius and his family. Thus the oath of Brutus is commemorated as the founding moment of the Roman Republic.

As he always did, Delaunay studied the composition carefully. Drawing was an integral part of his creative process, and he recorded each step in the process in a drawing. As his thinking evolved, the composition was transformed from a complex and indistinct grouping into a simple and eloquent visual opposition between Lucretia, on the left supported by two men, and Junius Brutus, on the right (not visible in this study). This drawing is probably one of the last in the series, as Delaunay seems to have found a definitive element of his composition. Many other studies for the painting are in the Musée des Beaux-Arts, Tours, where the finished work is also displayed. Others are in the Musée des Beaux-Arts, Nantes, the artist's hometown; four more are in the Musée du Louvre. This sheet for his *Brutus,* with its careful execution, is among the last in the conceptual process for one of Delaunay's most ambitious projects.

OM

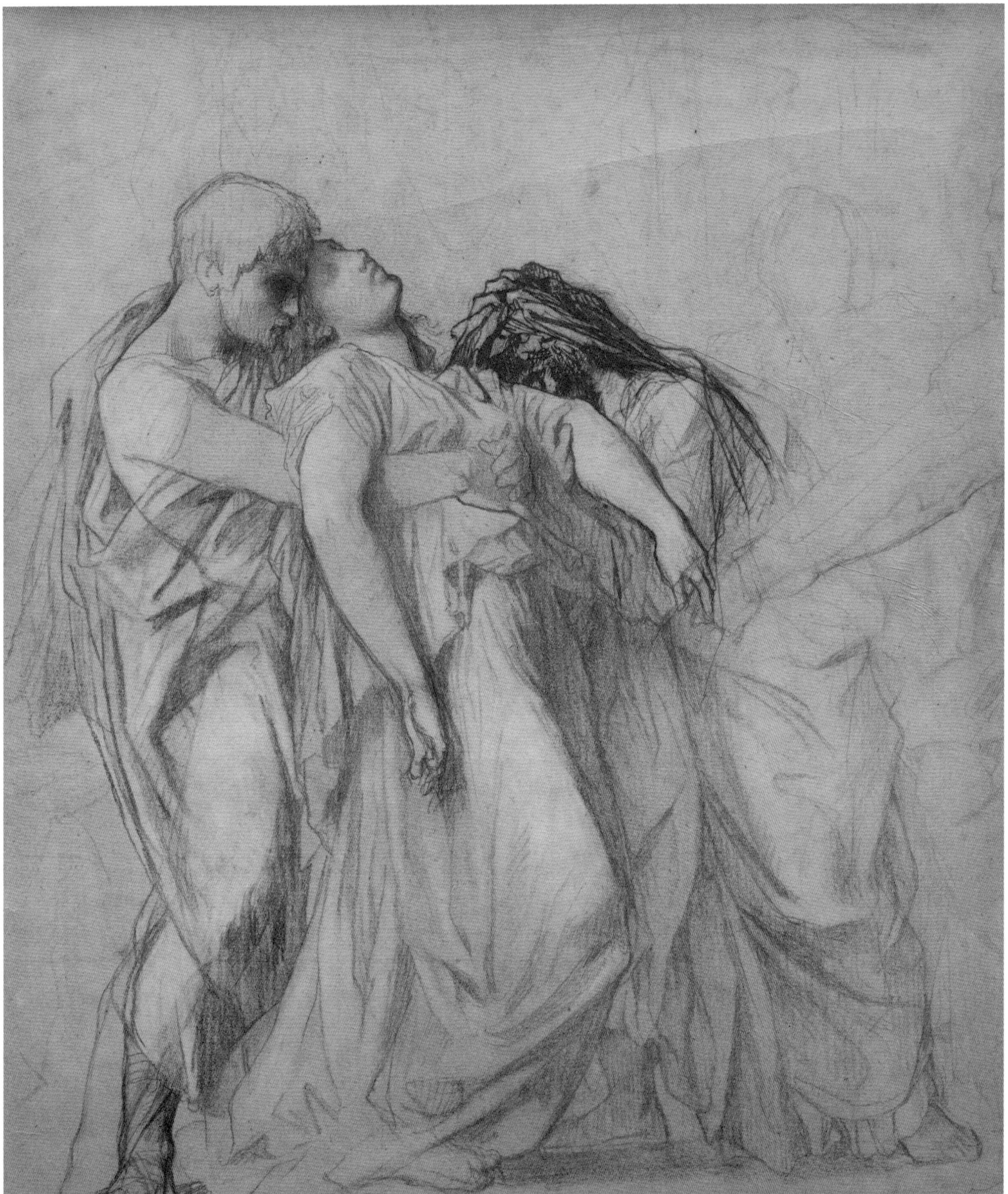

35

Jean-Léon Gérôme French, 1824–1904

OMPHALE, C. *1884–1885*

Pencil on paper, 13½ × 8½ in. (344.5 × 217.5 mm)
Dallas Museum of Art, Gift of Henry Hawley, 2005.87.7

PROVENANCE Henry H. Hawley, Cleveland; given to the Dallas Museum of Art, 2005.
BIBLIOGRAPHY Dallas Museum of Art 2007.

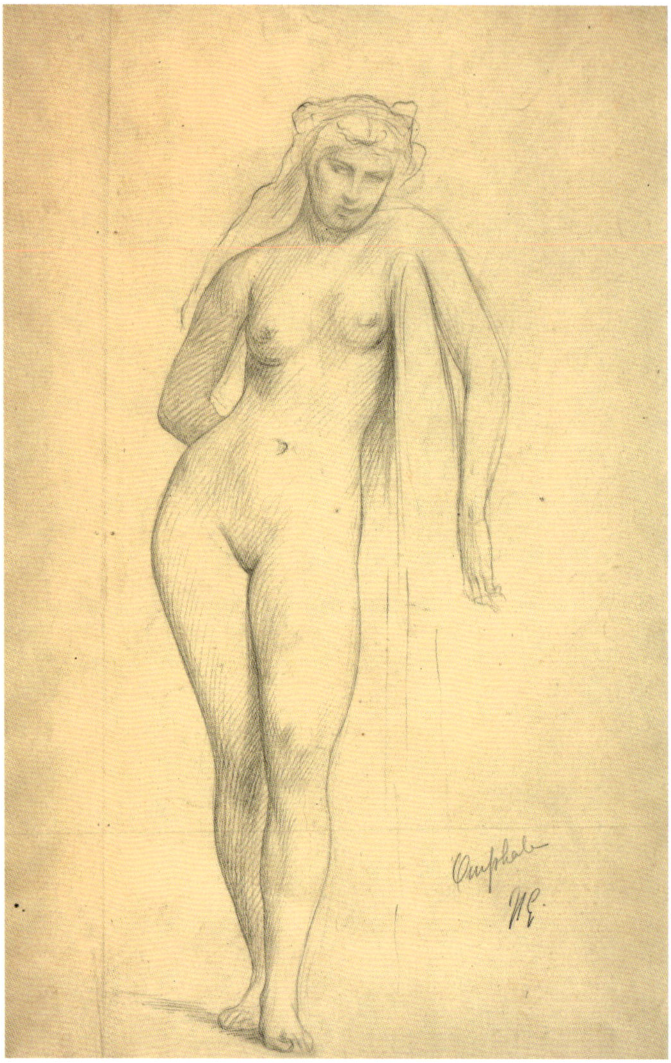

Jean-Léon Gérôme was among the most famous and most reproduced artists during the second half of the 19th century. His history paintings, which focused on themes of antiquity, European history, or orientalism, were admired by large crowds every year at the Salon. Gérôme married the daughter of the Paris dealer and art publisher Adolphe Goupil, who established a successful branch of his gallery in New York in 1846. Through his father-in-law, and thanks to the sales of reproductive prints, Gérôme achieved great renown in France and the United States, but after his death, in the climate of budding modernism, his fame vanished. Over the past 20 years, his influence on other artists has been revealed, along with his early knowledge and use of photography and the impact of his vision on the early history of film. Gérôme's sculptures—with his use of polychromy, mixing realism and the ideal—are now considered among his most fascinating works.

This drawing is a preparatory sketch for the sculpture *Omphale* that Gérôme completed in 1885 and exhibited at the Salon of 1887. The drawing differs from the plaster,[1] formerly in the Musée George Garret, Vesoul, and known through Louis Bonnard's photographs, and the marble,[2] currently in the same museum. The differences are especially noticeable in the position of Omphale's left arm and hand and in the lion's skin, which is no longer on her head. Gérôme's works on paper are often finished drawings that reflect or record the paintings rather than anticipate them. But in this case, the drawing seems to be a true attempt to find the right pose.

In late Greek mythology, Omphale, queen of Lydia, was the wife of Hercules. Before marrying her, Hercules was her slave, and in an ironic twist that the ancients loved, she obliged him to give her the famous lion skin and the club while wearing women's clothes. In this drawing, Omphale is wearing Hercules's lion skin on her head, leaning on the club placed under her armpit. The entire composition is taken from the famous antique marble known as the Farnese Hercules. This inspiration can be considered as a visual pun: Omphale fooled Hercules and forced him to dress as a woman while she wore his attributes, here even borrowing his most famous pose.

OM

Notes
1. Ackerman 1986, S.12P.
2. Ibid., S.12M.

36

Jean-Léon Gérôme French, 1824–1904

NYSSIA, C. *1857–1858*

Pencil on paper, 13¾ × 9 in. (349 × 229 mm)
Signed and inscribed center right: *JL Gérôme Dessin du tableau de Candaule*
Collection of Lon Elliott Leva

PROVENANCE Lucien Goldschmidt, Inc., New York; Cass Canfield (1897–1986), Bedford, New York; F.A.R. Gallery, New York, by 1975; Valley House Gallery, Dallas; where purchased by the current owner.

EXHIBITED *The Cass Canfield Collection at the F.A.R. Gallery*, New York; Valley House Gallery, Dallas, *Cass Canfield: Drawing Collection*, February 1976.

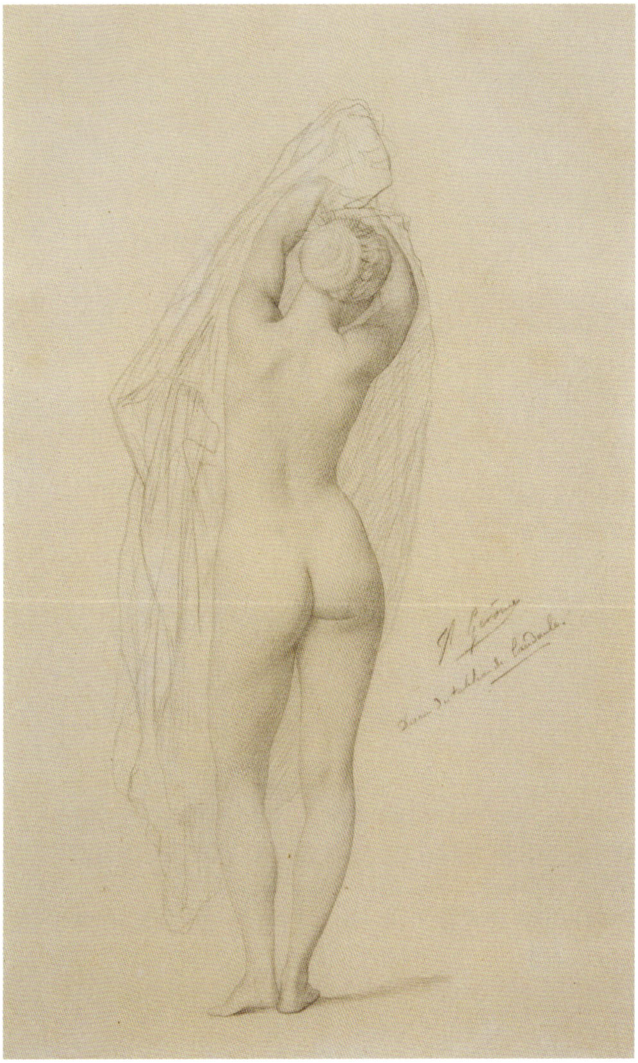

This drawing is a preparatory study for the central figure of Nyssia in the painting *King Candaules,* now in the Pushkin Museum, Moscow.[1] Nyssia's figure differs from the first version, exhibited at the Paris Salon of 1859 and now in the Museo de Arte Ponce, Puerto Rico,[2] in that she is standing on the other leg and has a different arm movement. Such subtle changes conformed to Gérôme's practice of painting slightly different versions of a same subject to fulfill his clients' desires to have an original composition. The two versions have both been reproduced in prints.

The story of King Candaules, an Asian ruler, was first told by Herodotus, but Gérôme found his inspiration through a short story published by Théophile Gautier in 1844. The king was so proud of his modest wife Nyssia that he wanted to share her beauty with Gyges, one of his guards. Upset by her husband's impudence, Nyssia asked Gyges to kill the king and then marry her himself. The drawing shows the moment when she unveils her body to enter the king's bed, realizing that Gyges, at the king's request, is peeping into the room. The entire painting focuses on Nyssia's body.

OM

Notes
1. Ackerman 1986, no. 112.
2. Ibid., no. 111.

37

Gustave Doré French, 1832–1883

MEDIEVAL CONCERT IN A FOREST, *N.D.*

Watercolor on paper, 15 × 10⅞ in. (380 × 275 mm)
Signed lower right: *Gve Doré*
Private collection, Dallas

PROVENANCE Caroline Delessert (1814–1880), baronne Henri Hottinguer; Rodolphe Hottinguer (1835–1920); Maurice Hottinguer (1872–1969); by descent to Suzanne Vernes (1908–1997); by descent to the current owner.

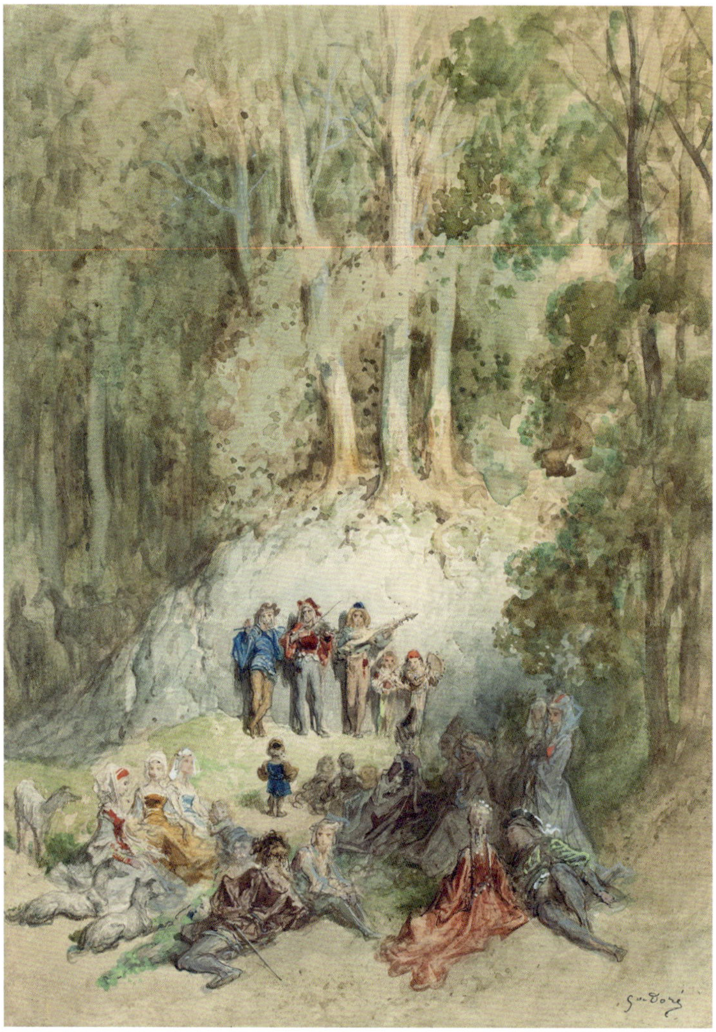

Painter, illustrator, and sculptor Gustave Doré was one of the most famous French artists of the 19th century. His ability to draw worlds of fantasy and to re-create the past, as well as to describe the destitute of the new industrial Europe, gave him a demiurgic power. He was able to bring to life fantastic worlds for the avid readers of his time, taking them where they were not able to go—into the past, the far away, the underworld, or the land of dreams and nightmares. His book illustrations brought him fame and wealth. His most famous illustrated books were the Bible, Dante's *Divine Comedy*, and John Milton's *Paradise Lost*.

This sensitive watercolor is a perfect example of Doré's style. In the heart of an old forest, five musicians are playing for a group of elegant people lying on the grass or standing to listen to the concert. Greyhounds and beautiful dresses take us to an aristocratic and refined medieval world where troubadours are singing about courtly love. Mysterious, the endless depth of the forest is made even more sublime by the point of view. Through his poetic elaboration of nature and his mingling of dream and reality, accurate details, and a sense of the epic, Doré found his own way of visualizing the imagination of some of the world's greatest authors.

This watercolor shows visual links to some well-known Doré engravings. One is the first plate of the Henry Wadsworth Longfellow translation of Dante's *Inferno*, which illustrates the following lines: "Midway upon the journey of our life / I found myself within a forest dark / For the straightforward pathway had been lost." Also related are two illustrations he made for *Hop-o'-My-Thumb*, a fairy tale by Charles Perrault, which depict the same deep forest, the same foreground, and a steep bank going under the trees. In this drawing, there is no drama, no fear as in Dante or *Hop-o'-My-Thumb*, only some musicians from a fabled age playing in the forest for an elegant party.

OM

38

Mariano Fortuny y Marsal Spanish, 1838–1874

MALE NUDE SEEN FROM BEHIND, AND OTHER STUDIES, *C. 1858–1860*

India ink wash, gouache, and pencil on heavy, buff paper, 16⅜ × 11⅜ in. (415 × 290 mm)
Estate stamp lower right in red: *Fortuny* (Lugt 942)
Private collection, Dallas

PROVENANCE Atelier de Fortuny, Ch. Pillet et M. Féral, Paris, Hôtel Drouot, April 26, 1875; Guillermo de Osma, Madrid; from whom purchased 1992 by the current owner.

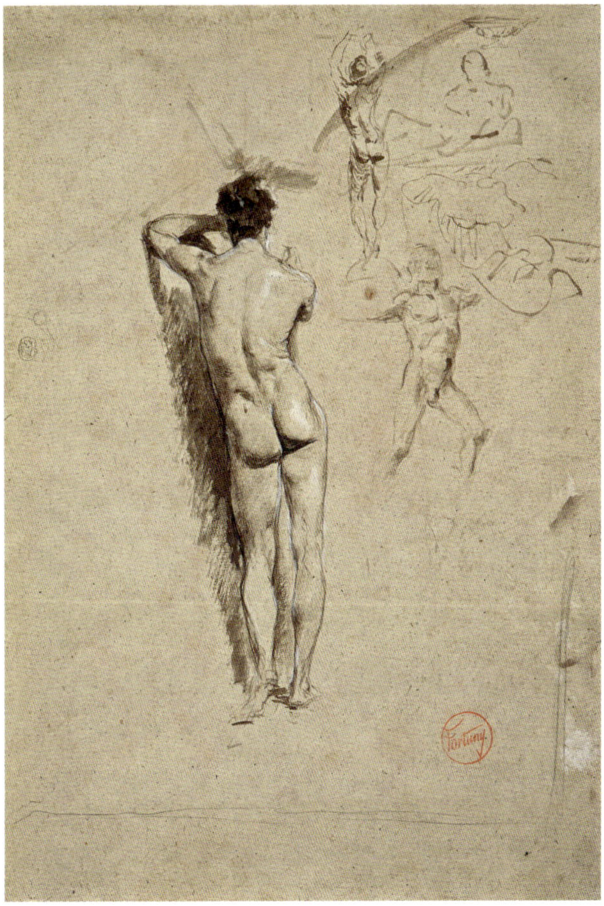

In the span of his tragically brief life, the Catalan painter Mariano Fortuny achieved greater renown than any Spanish artist between Goya and Picasso. At the height of his fame—a decade after his death—his works could command many times the price of a Manet or a Renoir. Whether addressing the era's taste for genre scenes like Ernest Meissonier's, orientalist subjects like Jean-Léon Gérôme's, panoramic battle scenes, or exotic landscapes, Fortuny captured the essence of 19th-century style with an elegance and concision that completely avoided the academic pomposity and occasional silliness of the time. Prodigiously talented and given the best instruction, he received a fellowship to study in Rome at age 20. Three years later he was a fully formed artistic personality, winning accolades and important commissions and producing paintings and watercolors of technical brilliance. Introduced to Federico de Madrazo, scion of Spain's leading artistic dynasty and director of the Museo del Prado, he soon married his daughter Cecilia, and from this union was born Mariano Fortuny y Madrazo (1871–1949), who became a seminal fashion and textile designer in the 20th century and whose creations, like those of his older contemporary Louis Comfort Tiffany, have always been in style. Through Fortuny's powerful dealer in Paris, Adolphe Goupil, his art was sought by robber-baron collectors from North America, tycoons from Latin America, and aristocrats from Spain. As a kind of artist's artist, his style transcended the enthusiasm for things Spanish that was raging in Paris and America, but he certainly contributed to it through his personal prestige and celebrity.

While a young man in Rome, Fortuny was an indefatigable copyist of Renaissance and baroque masters and antique sculpture, and while attending life drawing sessions at the Academia Giggi in the via Margutta, he produced a large number of male nude figure studies by which he honed his drawing skills. This sheet, which surely was executed early in this period, exemplifies the force of Fortuny's innate originality. In a genre where one academic nude is apt to look pretty much like the next, he manages to stand out as distinct. A large number of these drawings, belonging to the Real Academia de Bellas Artes de San Jorge, Barcelona, were executed in conté crayon, graphite pencil, or charcoal, but a few, like this one, were wash drawings done with a brush. Some of them depict this same model. Another group of drawings, executed about 1858–1860 and on larger sheets of paper as in the present case, once formed part of an album inherited from Rosario Falcó, daughter of the Duke of Fernán Núñez and an intimate friend of the artist's wife Cecilia.[1]

WBJ

Note
1. González López and Martí Ayxelà 1989, vol. 2, nos. AC–2.03.58/60, AC–2.01.59/60.

39

Ernest Meissonier French, 1815–1891

THE SMOKER (A MAN OF THE FIRST EMPIRE) (LE FUMEUR), *1873*

Watercolor and gouache on paper, 13⅞ × 8⅝ in. (352 × 219 mm)
Signed and dated lower right: *EMeissonier 1873*
Collection of Mary Ralph Lowe, Fort Worth

PROVENANCE Atelier Meissonier sale, Paris, Galerie Georges Petit (*Deuxième vente: aquarelles et dessin*), May 18, 19, and 20, 1893, lot 420 (*Étude de figure*); Mr. Raphael (probably Édouard Raphael, banker in Paris), 1897; private collection, England, 1988; Sandorval & Co., Inc., New York; from whom purchased 1990 by the current owner.

EXHIBITED Taft Museum, Cincinnati, June 25–August 16, 1992, Corcoran Gallery of Art, Washington, September 19–November 15, 1992, and Arnot Art Museum, Elmira, N.Y., November 21, 1992–January 17, 1993, *Cavaliers and Cardinals: Nineteenth-Century French Anecdotal Paintings*, cat. 84.

BIBLIOGRAPHY Gréard 1897, 213, ill. (*The Smoker*), 384 (described as "1873. *A Man of the First Empire* [(h. 34½; w. 0,20)]. Standing, in soft leather boots, and a long riding coat, one hand in his pocket, the other holding a pipe"); Zafran 1992, cat. 84.

It could be said that Ernest Meissonier achieved the distinction of being at once the most honored and the most vilified artist of his time. To a greater degree than any of his peers, he embodied both tradition and modernity, and the problem came with how one defined both things. Largely self-taught, he was not a product of the École des Beaux-Arts and its focus on classicism. Drawn by his own taste to the painters of 17th-century Holland and Flanders, he was basically a realist with a keen sense of the actuality of life. Uninterested in the lofty mythological and literary subjects that appealed to the official crowd, he perfected a unique type of genre painting, usually depicting individuals dressed in period costume engaged in perfectly ordinary but pleasurable activities like reading or writing, playing music or looking at pictures. These usually quite small works did not convey any moral or sentimental significance; they were just vibrant evocations of daily life, so acutely observed and brilliantly executed that they often left the viewer astonished. In addition, he pioneered a strain of obsessive historicism—not unlike that adopted in the 20th century by film director Luchino Visconti—which resulted in prodigious historical paintings treating mostly the glories of Napoleonic battle. No less ravishing than the films of Visconti, Meissonier's paintings found huge success among wealthy middle-class collectors, making him without question one of the richest, most famous, and most influential painters in the world. The fame evaporated after his death, however, when his meticulous, studied approach—misunderstood by his successors—came to be regarded as the antithesis of everything the avant garde stood for. Only later did Salvador Dalí, with a certain sense of self-serving irony, champion him as the greatest artist of the 19th century.

In addition to the countless pencil sketches and oil studies that Meissonier made in the course of creating his deeply researched paintings, he also made fully resolved and deliciously accomplished drawings and watercolors for the market. This superb watercolor, *The Smoker*, is a perfect example. We don't know the story of this man with so little to do that he can lounge about on the street and smoke his pipe, but because of the hyperrealism with which the artist has rendered his physiognomy, his stance, his clothing, and his hygiene, we are left to wonder. As a feat of image making, of evoking life on a page, it is hard to imagine anything more vivid. The fashion for such images did not last, but aesthetic fashions are more like tides than currents; they don't just flow in one direction, and there is again something attractively "modern" about Meissonier's obsessions.

WBJ

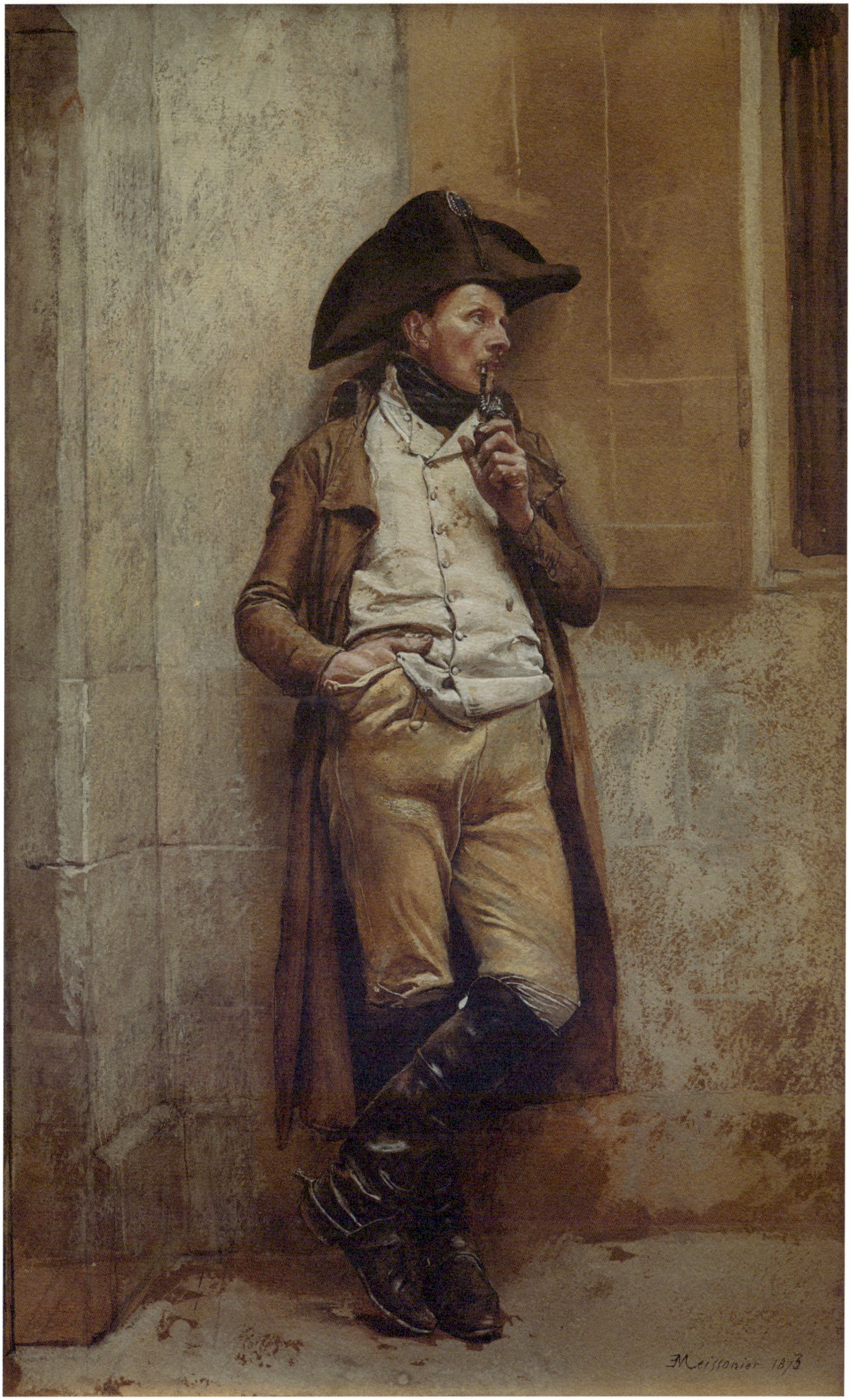
EMeissonier 1873

40

Adolph Menzel German, 1815–1905

STUDIES OF A YOUNG BOY, *1871*

Graphite and red and gray watercolor on paper, 7½ × 4¾ in. (190 × 120 mm)
Signed with initials and dated lower right: *AM / 71*
Collection of Mary Ralph Lowe, Fort Worth

PROVENANCE Private collection, Europe, since 1920s and by descent to previous owner; Jill Newhouse, New York, by 1996; from whom purchased 1996 by the current owner.

41

STUDIES OF THREE MEN (MANN MIT MANTEL), *1892*

Graphite on paper, 5⅛ × 8¼ in. (130 × 210 mm)
Signed with initials and dated lower right: *AM / 92*
Collection of Mary Ralph Lowe, Fort Worth

PROVENANCE Jill Newhouse, New York; from whom purchased 1990 by the current owner.
EXHIBITED Museum of Fine Arts, Houston, *Adolph Menzel 1815–1915: Master Drawings from Berlin*, December 1, 1990–January 27, 1991.

Adolph Menzel's graphic work is unmatched in Germany in the 19th century in both quality and quantity. His painting is distinguished by a representation of atmosphere and visible reality achieved by purely painterly means. Aside from brief attendance at the Berlin Academy in 1833, Menzel was self-taught. He began his training in 1830 in his father's lithography shop in Berlin, which he continued to run after his father's death in 1832. Between 1834 and 1857 he produced graphic works on Prussian history. In the 1840s he began painting pre-impressionist landscapes, interiors, and portraits that were not exhibited until the early 20th century. Most of his society and court pictures were produced after 1862, and in 1875 he painted the highly realistic *Iron Rolling Mill in Königshütte* (Staatliche Museen zu Berlin). He traveled frequently within Germany, Austria, and Bohemia, and in 1855, 1867, and 1868 visited Paris, where he made contact with Gustave Courbet. He became a member of the Königliche Akademie der Künste, Berlin, in 1853 and was ennobled in 1898. While Menzel was actively collected and discussed even in France and the United States during his lifetime, his work is now known abroad only by art historians.

With his earnest gaze, parted hair, and coat buttoned up high, a child is represented from three different angles in *Studies of a Young Boy* (cat. 40). His identity is unknown. The overlappings and abrupt changes of pose in the renderings of the child produce a gliding effect that characterizes a number of Menzel's drawings. From the *en face* portrait in the upper left, the viewer's gaze sweeps clockwise to the almost complete figure and to the head at the bottom edge looking out of the picture to the left. The artist deliberately manipulates the viewer's eye movement in this way, a point that has been made repeatedly in the literature. The combined pictures provide a sequence of different perceptual experiences that come together in a single image, giving these drawings a virtually cinematic quality.

Famous for constantly drawing his surroundings, Menzel asserted in 1891 that "one can draw when there is neither time nor space for painting. And draw everything, whether for a specific purpose or not. Then simply for the exercise. Moreover, for the artist it should not be only a sideline."[1] He was mainly interested in everyday and somewhat incidental situations that artists rarely recorded. In *Studies of Three Men* (cat. 41), Menzel depicts a man being helped into his coat. The drawing captures a single moment in the sequence of movements. It is clear that the artist was interested in the man's cramped pose and the play of light on the wrinkled garment in its everyday banality. The subject is seen a bit from below, perhaps because of the artist's short stature. There are two related studies that again picture the two main figures. The officer on the left is seen from a slightly angled perspective from below, the focus on his face. In the upper right corner of the picture the profile of a fourth man is only suggested. The drawing is related to the study *Man Putting on His Coat Seen from the Back (Mantelanziehender Mann in Rückenansicht)* in Berlin's Kupferstichkabinett (inv. N 3662), which presumably depicts the same subject and action from a different point of view.[2] Studies such as these gave Menzel an opportunity to observe the expressiveness of his figures more closely in advance before transferring them to canvas.

FK

Notes
1. Menzel, letter to Lucie Wolter-Sigora, September 1891, quoted in Menzel 2009.
2. The drawing also relates, in the positioning of the figures, to an 1856 gouache called *Voltaire in His Dressing Gown* (Lempertz sale, November 15, 1995).

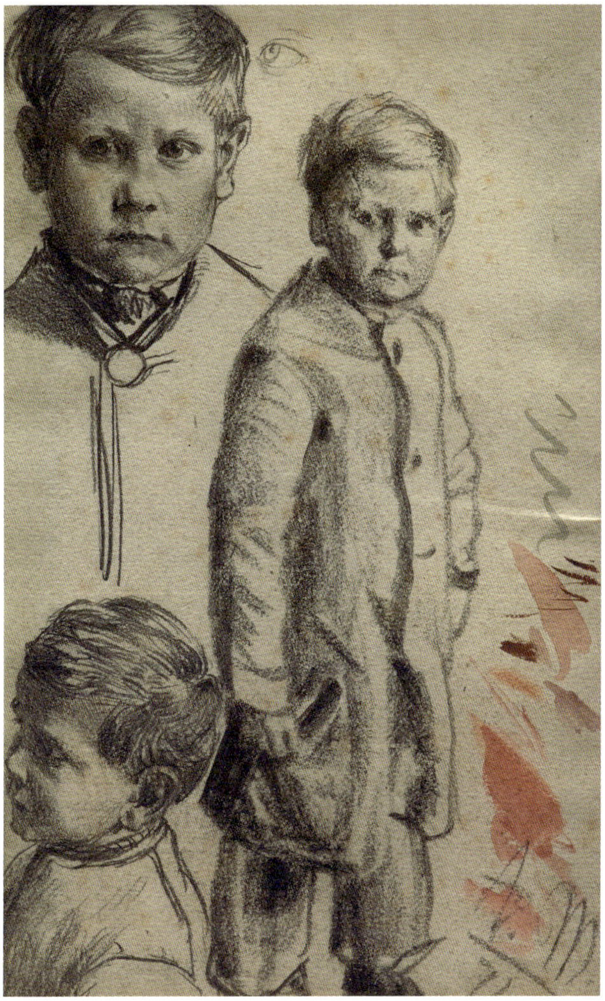

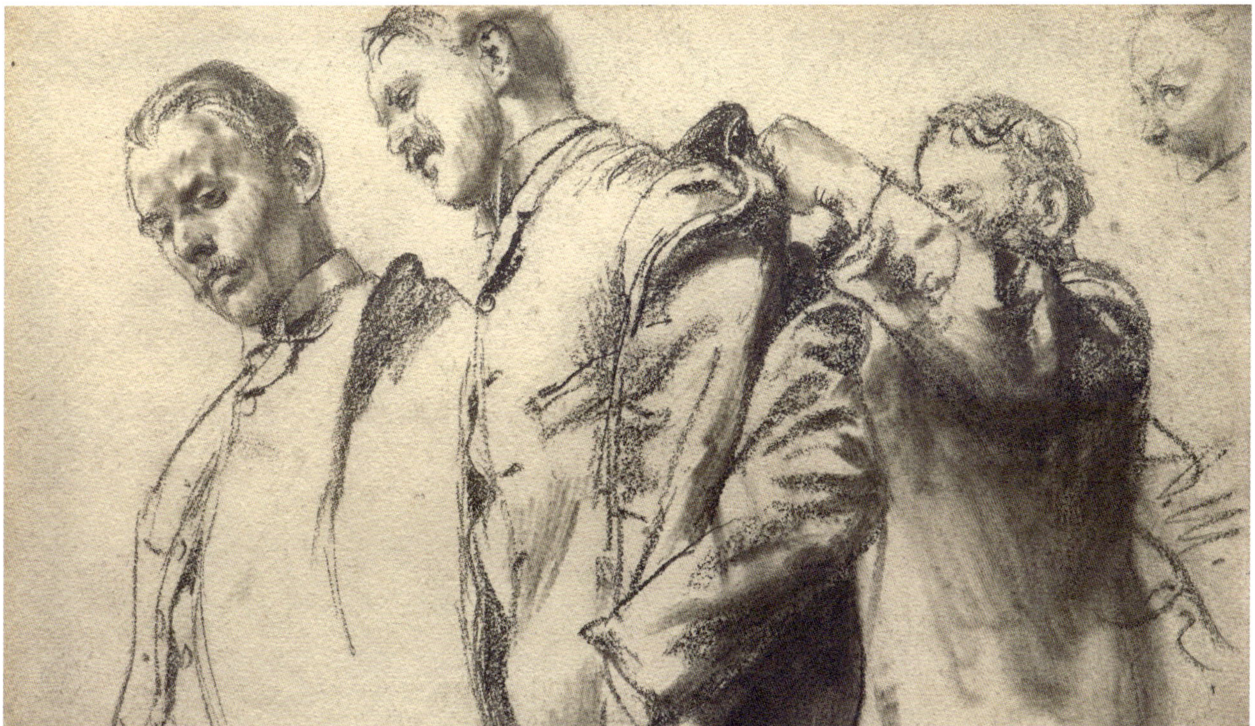

42

Rudolf von Alt Austrian, 1812–1905

LANDSCAPE, C. *1867*

Watercolor on two pieces of paper joined by a strip of paper glued to the back, 10⅝ x 9¼ in. (270 x 236 mm)
Signed lower center: *R. Alt*
Dowell Family Collection, Dallas

One of the most interesting Austrian artists of his age, Vienna-born Rudolf von Alt gives us throughout his long career an unusually vivid picture of life in his time. Alt was a painter interested in both nature and the urban landscape, but that landscape for him included both the world out of doors and the interior world of elegant society. His brilliant, minutely descriptive images of his native city, as well as his views of the many places he visited during his long life, are among the best evocations we have of the 19th century. Precise but never dry, his architectural landscapes are accurate and beautiful at the same time, full of details but also atmospheric, almost fragrant, to a degree rarely found in topographically reliable views. His interest in nature and in the countryside developed through his long hikes all over the Habsburg Empire, from Crimea to Dalmatia. His love for Italy led him often to Venice and northern Italy, sometimes to Naples, and once to Sicily, in 1867. One of the leading artists during the Emperor Franz Josef's reign, he gained nobility in 1889, giving him the right to be addressed as Ritter (Knight) von Alt. A particularly rich collection of his drawings is preserved in the Albertina in Vienna, which organized an important exhibition of his work in 2005–2006.

Alt probably made this quick watercolor sketch in Sicily. The presence of a palm tree on the left and aloe plants on the right offers comparison to other watercolors the artist did in Ragusa. He sometimes left drawings unfinished, as is the case here, but their spontaneity makes them as vibrant and beautiful as the completed compositions. The way Alt tightens his work around a single point and leaves the rest of the paper empty—not even trying to build a net of perspectives—is typical of his process, and very seductive.

OM

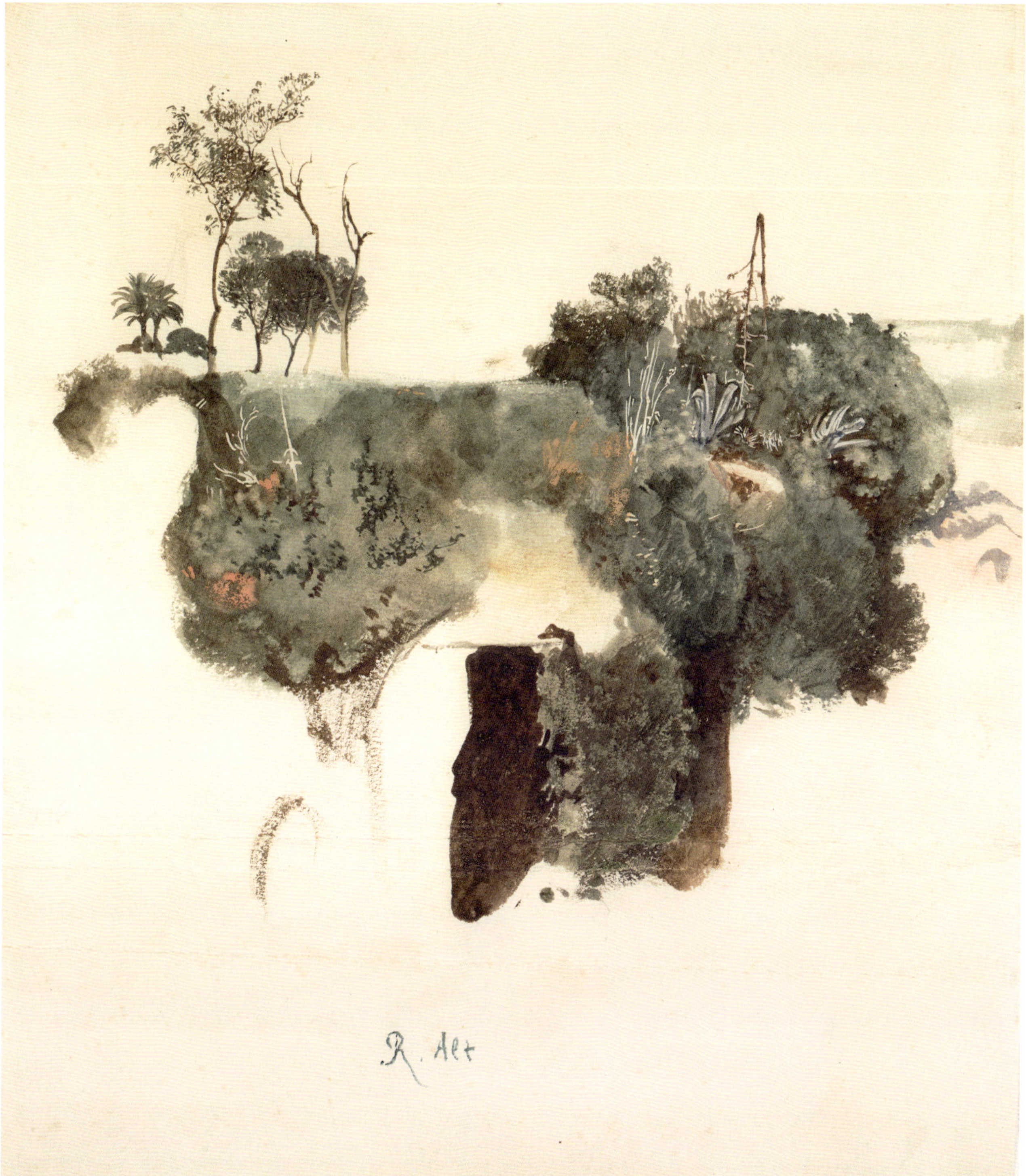
R. Alt

43

Pascal Dagnan-Bouveret French, 1852–1929

PORTRAIT OF GUSTAVE COURTOIS, *1873*

Black chalk on paper, 11½ × 8⅜ in. (290 × 212 mm)
Signed, dated, and inscribed at right: *A mon ami G. Courtois / P.A.J. Dagnan. / Mai 1873*
Collection of George T. M. Shackelford

PROVENANCE Gift of the artist to Gustave Courtois; sale, Me De Maigret, Paris, Hôtel Drouot, June 18, 2009, lot 128; Pierre Le-Tan, Paris; Galerie Nicolas Schwed, Paris; where purchased by the current owner.

EXHIBITED Galerie Nicolas Schwed, Paris, *Dessins Français,* 2013, no. 34.

Pascal Dagnan-Bouveret, like his friend Gustave Courtois, who posed for this portrait, was a pupil of Jean-Léon Gérôme at the École des Beaux-Arts in Paris. Known mainly for his descriptions of rural life—especially in Brittany and in the Franche-Comté—he became a highly popular artist with the public while also receiving frequent government commissions for work that promoted rural traditions and values and raised social issues. For many years, his paintings were chosen to illustrate textbooks; examples include *Ex Voto* (Musée des Beaux-Arts, Rouen), *Blessing before the Wedding* (Pushkin Museum, Moscow), *An Accident* (Walters Art Museum, Baltimore), and *Brittany Pardon* (Metropolitan Museum of Art, New York). One of the champions of the "new realism," as Gabriel P. Weisberg called it in his monograph on the artist,[1] Dagnan-Bouveret was part of a movement that became important at the end of the 19th century with painters like Jules Bastien-Lepage, Jules Adler, and Jean-François Raffaelli. Their attention to social issues was sustained by an extraordinary amount of visual detail, which was intended to lend a certain irrefutability to their arguments. Dagnan-Bouveret was also among the early painters to use photography as a tool.

This portrait is an early and moving testimony to the lifelong personal partnership between Dagnan-Bouveret and his companion Gustave Courtois (1852–1923). The date of its execution, 1873, was the first year of their life together in a shared studio in Paris. Later Dagnan married Courtois's cousin, and the three of them lived in the same house in the suburbs of Paris. Courtois, who had his own career as a painter, did many portraits, among them a fascinating portrait of Madame Gautreau (1891)—the same sitter who, as Madame X, caused such a scandal for John Singer Sargent at the Paris Salon of 1884.

In this superb early drawing, Dagnan-Bouveret has produced a work still influenced by—and quite worthy of—his master Gérôme.

OM

Note
1. Weisberg 2002.

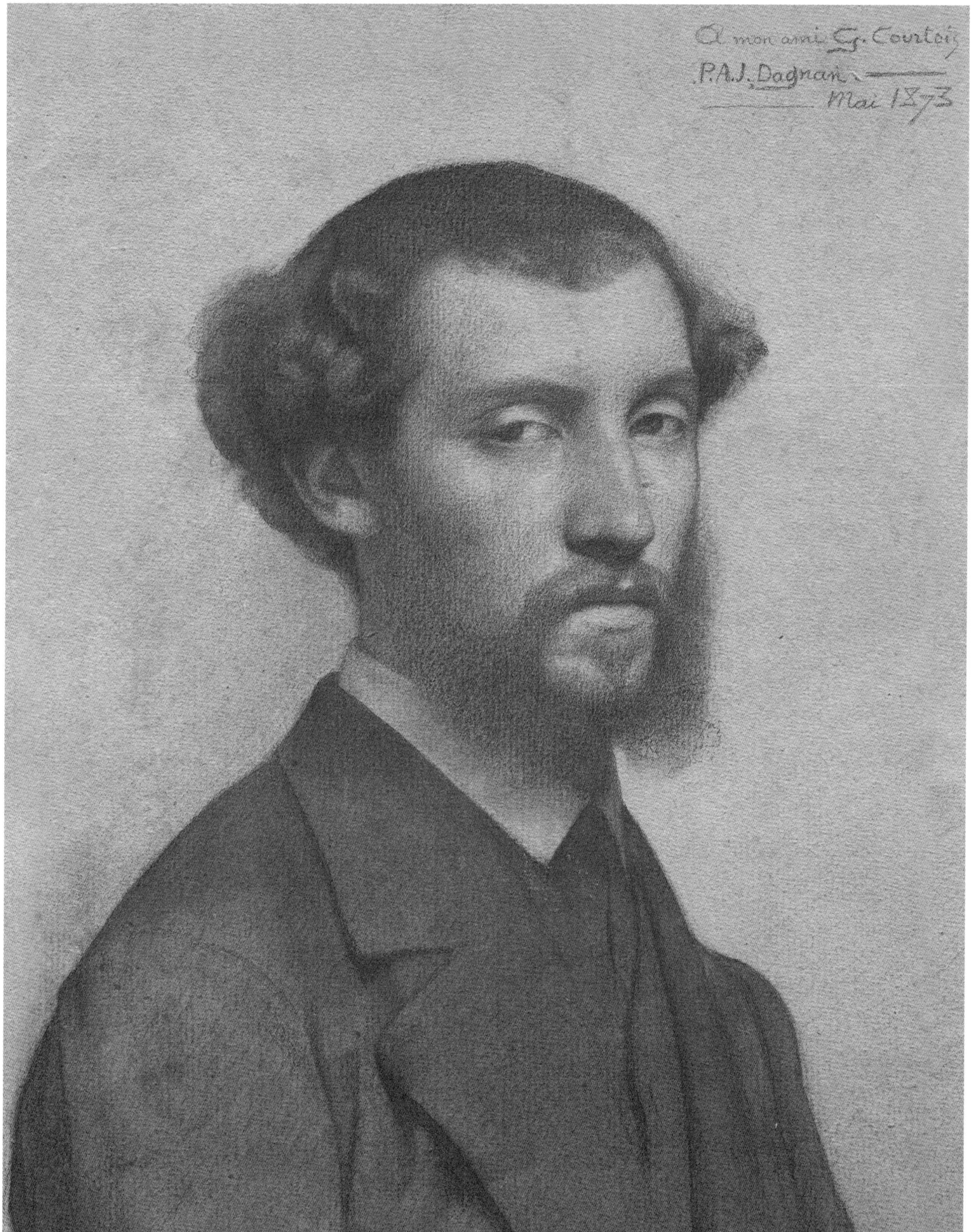
A mon ami G. Courtois
P.A.J. Dagnan
Mai 1873

44

Jean-François Raffaëlli French, 1850–1924

PORTRAIT OF ALBERT BARTHOLOMÉ WITH A TOP HAT ON HIS CANE, C. *1885*

Oil and charcoal on board, 22½ × 14¼ in. (572 × 362 mm)
Collection of Mary Ralph Lowe, Fort Worth

PROVENANCE David and Constance Yates Fine Drawings and Works of Art, New York; from whom purchased 1995 by the current owner.

This elegant portrait, showing a seated man with his legs crossed balancing his top hat on the tip of his cane, is a study for the famous painting *Clemenceau Giving an Electoral Speech at the Cirque Fernando* (Musée National du Château de Versailles). Jean-François Raffaëlli used only the head in the painting, but we can recognize the sitter, Albert Bartholomé, on the third row from the top of the group depicted in the audience (the penultimate on the left). Bartholomé was himself a painter until the death of his first wife Prospérie de Fleury in 1887. Following his friend Edgar Degas's advice, he turned to sculpture in order to make her tomb, and the project evolved into a much larger monument dedicated to the forgotten dead. Built at the Père Lachaise Cemetery in Paris, *Monument aux Morts* was unveiled on All Saints Day in 1899. With almost 60,000 visitors on that day alone, the monument and its creator became instantly famous. Bartholomé was probably Degas's closest friend, and many photographs of the painter were taken in Bartholomé's house and studio. It was Bartholomé who took care of Degas's sculptures after his death.

Painter, sculptor, and printmaker, Raffaëlli is known for his vivid descriptions of Paris and its suburbs. His portrayals of the poor and the working classes won him the sympathy of naturalist authors like J. K. Huysmans and the critic Gustave Geffroy, as well as Degas, but he also embraced the bustle of urban life in all its variety. Degas invited him to participate in the fifth and sixth impressionist exhibitions in 1880 and 1881. The *Catalogue illustré des œuvres de Jean-François Raffaëlli,* which illustrates his exhibition on the avenue de l'Opéra in 1884, exemplifies the rich variety of his art, with Parisian scenes of every sort, seascapes, portraits, and sculptures.[1]

Raffaëlli portrayed other sculptors, such as Jules Dalou and Auguste Rodin, as well as writers like Georges Rodenbach, Alphonse Daudet, and Edmond de Goncourt. This portrait study is by all standards among the most elegant he produced. Raffaëlli gives Bartholomé a relaxed, somewhat stylish pose, which reminds us that before the long, white beard of his old age, he was, like his friend Degas, something of a dandy. On a practical note, the curule chair is found in many other portraits by Raffaëlli, including the one of Jean Ajalbert,[2] and in the portrait of an old sculptor.[3] It was Raffaëlli's own studio chair, as we can see in an anonymous photograph showing the artist at his easel (documentation, Musée d'Orsay).

OM

Notes
1. Raffaëlli 1884.
2. Geffroy *Les hommes d'aujourd'hui* 8, no. 374, ill. front cover.
3. Paris, Drouot, Galerie George Petit, Salle 1, December 15, 1933, no. 105.

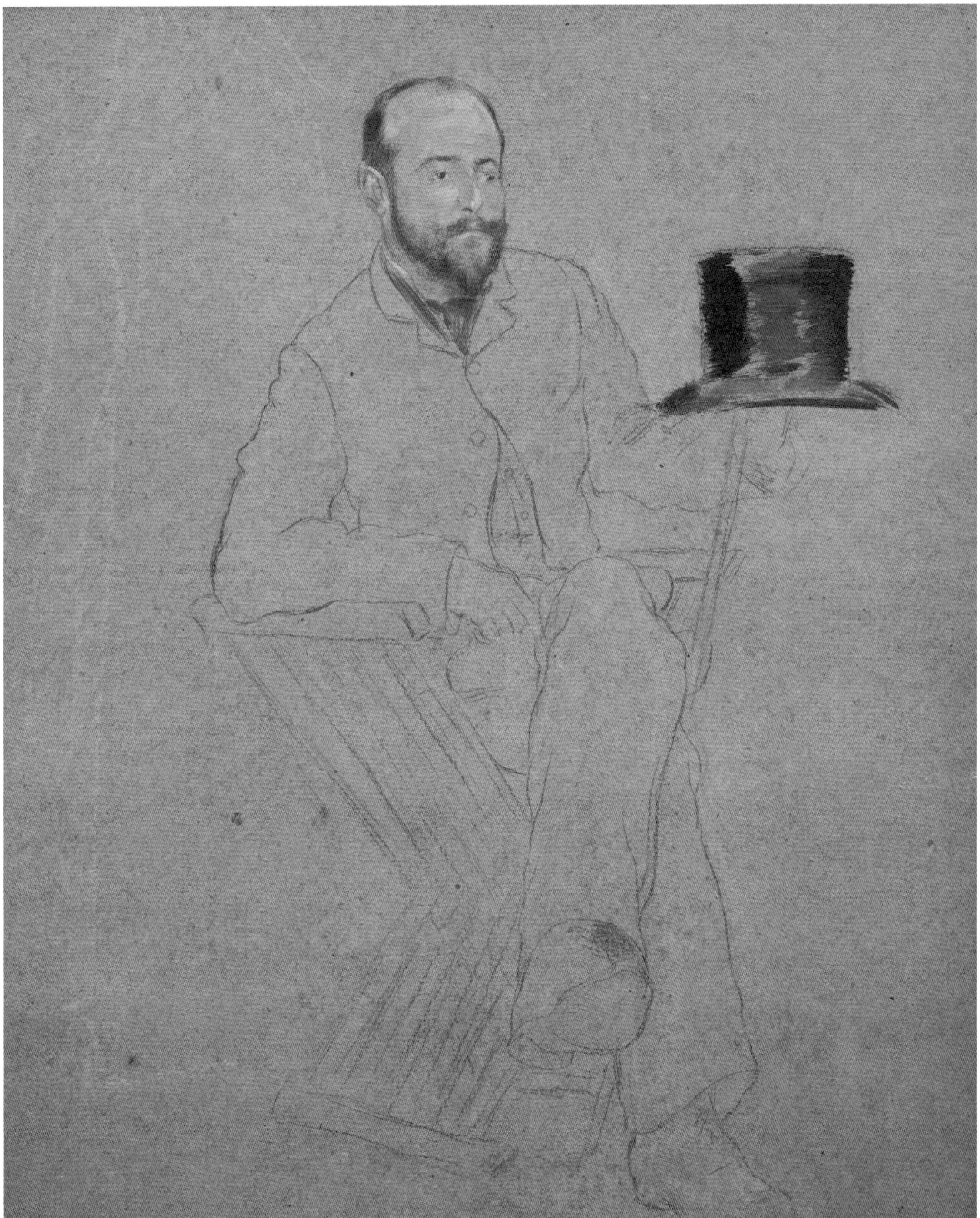

45

Edgar Degas French, 1834–1917

SEATED MALE NUDE (RECTO), *1856–1858*; KNEELING MALE NUDE SEEN FROM BEHIND (VERSO), *1856–1858*

Pencil on paper, 14½ x 10¾ in. (363 x 272 mm)
Recto, inscribed twice, lower right, *Rome*
Private collection, Dallas

PROVENANCE Owned by the artist's niece, Mlle Jeanne Fevre; sale, Galerie Jean Charpentier, Paris, Collection of Mlle J. Fevre, June 12, 1934, lot 31 (given as no. 5 in 1937 catalogue); sale, Paris, Hotel Drouot, May 5, 1937, lot 24; private collection; W. M. Brady, New York; from whom purchased January 2011 by the current owner.

Edgar Degas, whose father was a well-to-do Parisian banker born in Naples and whose mother was a beauty raised in New Orleans, was one of the best educated and best traveled of the Impressionists. His first lessons in drawing were part of his training at the distinguished Parisian École Louis-le-Grand, where he was a student from 1845 to 1853. Leaving school, he began drawing copies after the art of the past at the Musée du Louvre and the imperial library before he embarked briefly on the study of law. In due course, he was admitted to the École des Beaux-Arts, then generally considered the finest art academy in the world. Though he followed the courses of the École through 1855 and early 1856, it was really in Italy, where he traveled between the summer of 1856 and 1858, that Degas learned how to draw.

He did so without a formal tutor, both by continuing to copy the works of artists he admired in museums and churches and by drawing, in time-honored tradition, from live models. At the Villa Medici, the seat of the French Academy in Rome, models were made available in informal drawing sessions to artists whose Roman stays were sponsored by the state and also to independent students like Degas. Among the artists working alongside Degas in Italy were Jules-Élie Delaunay (see cat. 34), whom he had first met at the École des Beaux-Arts, and Gustave Moreau (1826–1898).

This careful study of a seated man is undoubtedly one of the drawings that Degas made in the company of other artists, gathered around a model posing beneath a light source—a lantern or a window high on a wall. The man looks up toward the light, throwing parts of his thin but muscled body into shadow. Establishing the contour of shoulders, arms, and torso, Degas sculpts the figure on the page with the tip of his pencil, employing distinct contrasts of bright light and deep, uniform shadow. Sometimes these contrasts are almost schematic, as on the figure's arm at right or on his outstretched leg, where Degas sketches in a series of vertical lines from upper thigh to kneecap to instep, dividing light—the bare paper at left—from dark—the hatched shadows at right. As he studies the figure's torso, however, Degas uses fine hatching to create a more nuanced modeling, defining the muscles and underlying bones of the man's chest and neck with loving attention.

On the other side of the paper, the artist used the same technique to study the fall of light on the back and legs of a kneeling model who rests his weight on a posing block at right. Double and even triple lines suggest that Degas was carefully adjusting the contour of the figure's torso and legs before firmly establishing a final line. This study may have predated a more fully rendered example of this pose, known on another sheet.

GTMS

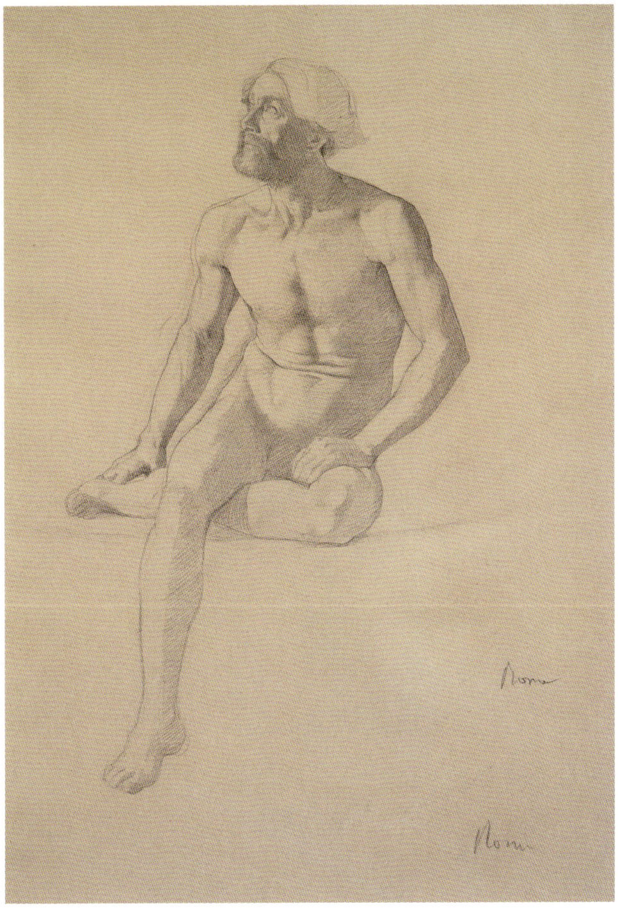

Cat. 45, recto.

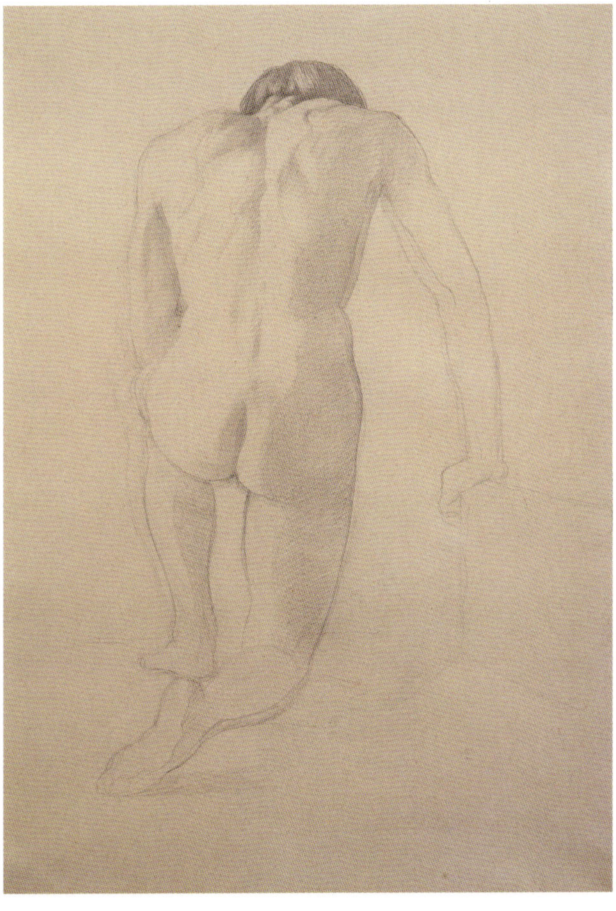

Cat. 45, verso.

46

Edgar Degas French, 1834–1917

RUNNING YOUTH, STUDY FOR THE DAUGHTER OF JEPHTHAH, C. *1859*

Black chalk on paper, 11¾ × 8⅝ in. (285 × 220 mm)
Stamped lower right: *ATELIER / ED. DEGAS* (Lugt 657, quite faded); *Degas* (Lugt 658)
Collection of Mary Ralph Lowe, Fort Worth

PROVENANCE Atelier Degas, sale, Paris, Georges Petit, May 6, 1918, no. 6b (unsold); July 2–4, 1919, no. 117 (sold with three other studies); Brandt Dayton & Co., New York; from whom purchased 1990 by the current owner.

EXHIBITED Museum of Fine Arts, Houston, short-term loan, November 15, 1990–February 1, 1991.

When Degas returned to Paris from Italy in 1859, he was frankly unsure of what course his art would take. Although he had pursued the kind of artistic education that would prepare him for a career as a history painter in the classical manner, his temperament led him in a more romantic direction. He began to work on *The Daughter of Jephthah*, an ambitious subject drawn from the Old Testament: the tragic story of the warrior Jephthah, forced by a vow to sacrifice his daughter to God. Degas said that he wanted to combine in the painting "the spirit and love of Mantegna"—the early Renaissance painter known for his rational, balanced compositions—with "the verve and color of Veronese"—the Venetian master known for his brilliant brushwork.

The painting, now in the collection of the Smith College Museum of Art, was never finished, and exactly how it was prepared is difficult to know. It seems likely, though, that Degas began to work on this first major multifigure composition as he was to work for the rest of his life—by drawing a host of studies of figures in attitudes that he might find useful, based on a general idea of where he was going. Once he had assembled a large body of studies, he would put them together to compose the final tableau.

One of those studies is the drawing exhibited here, showing a running youth with his arms raised as if to support a banner. The artist has captured the movement deftly by emphasizing the contours of the young man's back and extended right leg, at the same time seemingly granting the following left leg—drawn and redrawn—greater latitude of movement. Animated movement, in fact, is what the artist has sought to pin down: the man's torso and legs, with their sharp outlines, give the impression of vibrating in space because of the many nervous lines that flow along and around the contours.

This figure did not, in the end, appear as one of the characters in the painting—at least not one visible to our eyes today. The drawing was among the many preparatory studies for *Jephthah* found in Degas's studio at the time of his death. It was sold, along with three other drawings relating to the painting, in one of the auctions of Degas's estate in 1919—which explains both the faint numbers along the bottom of the sheet (a record of the photograph taken of the drawing) and the red stamped "signature" at lower right, applied to all the works by Degas that appeared in the sale.

GTMS

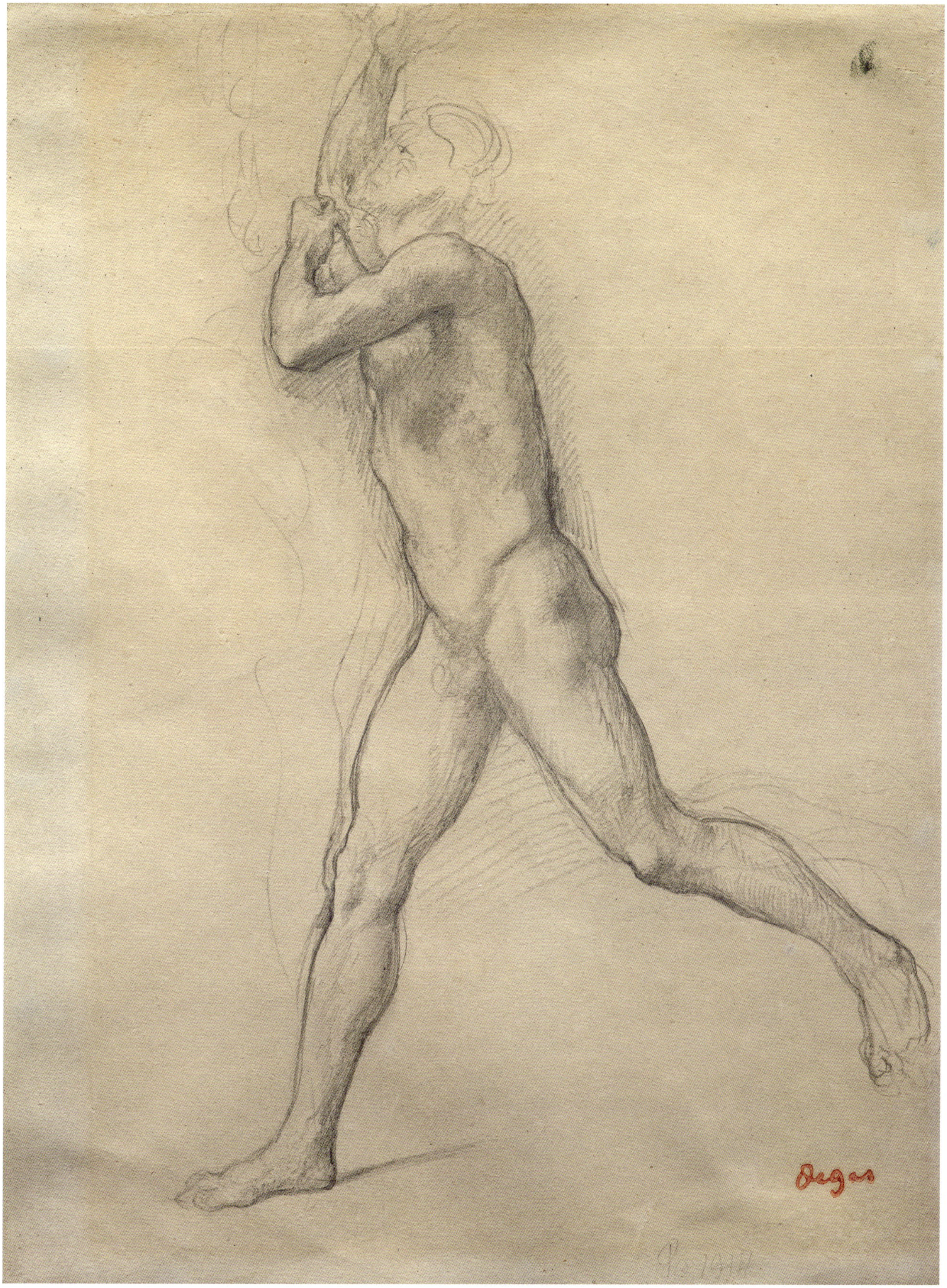
Degas

47

Edgar Degas French, 1834–1917

A RACEHORSE, WITH A STUDY OF A RIDER, *1867–1870*

Pencil on tracing paper mounted on wove paper,
7⅝ x 11⅛ in. (194 x 283 mm)
Stamped, lower left, *Atelier Ed. Degas* (Lugt 657, faded)
Private collection, Dallas

PROVENANCE Baron de Chollet, Fribourg; sale, Christie's, New York, November 15, 1990, lot 00105 (*Cheval selle et étude de cavalier*); private collection; sale, Christie's, New York, February 7, 2002; where purchased by the current owner.

EXHIBITED Berner Kunstmuseum, Bern, *Degas à Berne*, November 1951–January 1952, no. 134; Wildenstein & Co., New York, *Degas' Racing World*, 1968.

Years after he first exhibited a painting of a racehorse, Degas confessed that he started painting equestrian subjects without understanding much about how a horse acted. "You are probably unaware," he told a journalist, "that about 1866 I perpetrated a *Scène de steeplechase*, the first and for long after the only one of my pictures inspired by the racecourse. Even though I was quite familiar with 'the noblest conquest ever made by man,' even though I had had the opportunity to mount a horse quite often, even though I could distinguish a thoroughbred from a half-breed without too much difficulty, even though I had a fairly good understanding of the animal's anatomy and myology, having studied one of those plaster models found in all the caster's shops, I was completely ignorant of the mechanism of its movements."

In fact, in the years around the 1867 exhibition of his steeplechase canvas, Degas set about to learn a great deal about how horses were put together, how they walked and stood, and how their coats behaved in sunlight. He had already shown horses in such large historical compositions as *The Daughter of Jepthah* and in depictions of a queen of Babylon and of war in medieval France. But around 1865, his goals shifted, and he determined to paint subjects from modern life, among them the life of the turf and the track. Racing scenes, along with ballet dancers and laundresses, would be fitting themes for an observant young man to depict, novel themes that would single him out from his contemporaries.

With an eye to the modern, Degas looked for sources in a wide variety of places, turning as often to printed material as to paintings. Newly imported Japanese prints were appealing, as were comic lithographs and caricatures. Among the plethora of materials at his disposal were photographs, including, it seems clear, photographs of racehorses.

This drawing, finely executed in pencil on smooth, thin tracing paper, is related to photographs taken by the Parisian practitioner Louis-Jean Delton (1807–1891?), who had an open-air studio near the Bois de Boulogne where he took equestrian portraits and views of the racing world of his day. It is known that Degas made a tracing of one of Delton's photographs, and in this sheet he may well have referred to Delton's portrayal of a horse called "Shang Hai," winner of the 1866 Grand Prix of the Société Hippique Française (fig. 8). It may be that Degas actually traced parts of this sheet—the head and neck, for instance—from a print of the photograph, as he had done before. Perhaps inspired by still other photographs, he drew a saddle on the horse's back, and below the animal's neck, at left, faintly indicated the position of a jockey on that saddle. The artist's turn to the static model of a photographed horse gave him the time to achieve the extreme precision of line and shade that he demonstrates here. The purpose of the drawing was to teach the artist a lesson in contour and modeling—this horse never appears in a painting by Degas.

GTMS

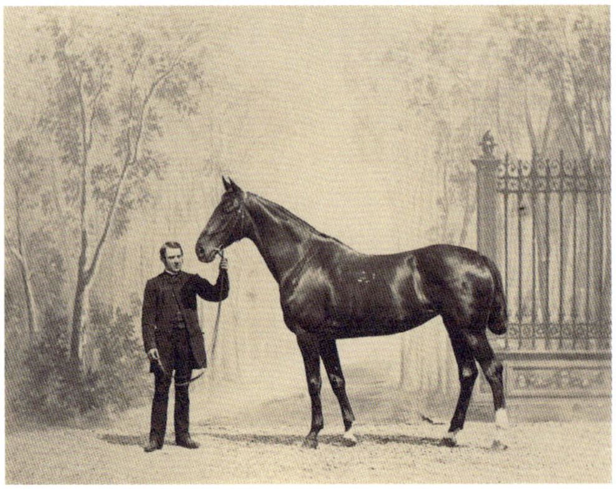

Fig. 8 Louis-Jean Delton, *Shang Hai, Normand d'attelage, premier Grand Prix, Société Hippique Française*, c. 1867. Albumen silver print. Philadelphia Museum of Art, 125th Anniversary Acquisition. The Lynne and Harold Honickman Gift of the Julien Levy Collection, 2001.

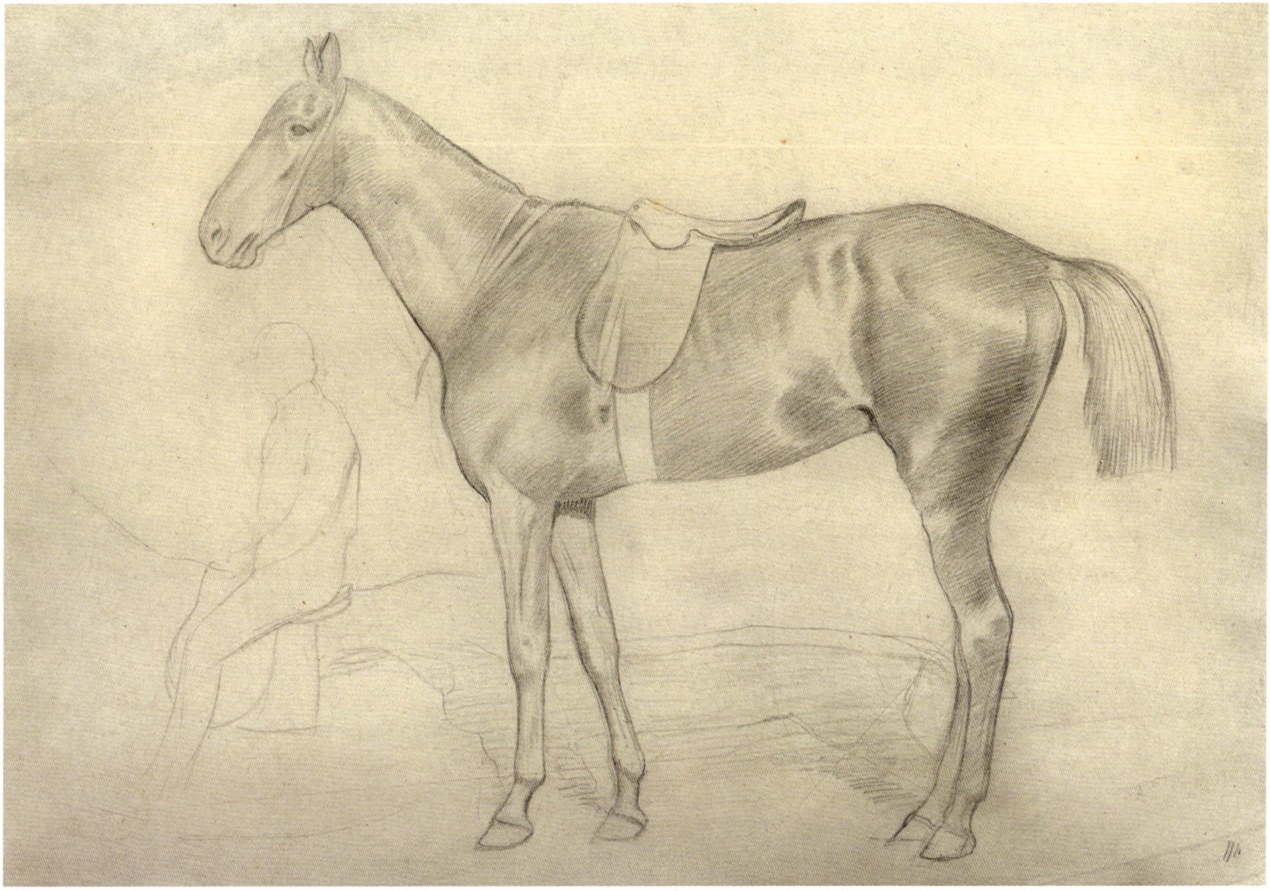

Pierre Puvis de Chavannes French, 1824–1898

STUDY FOR MASSILIA, GREEK COLONY: FOUR MALE NUDES IN THE ACT OF LEVERING A HEAVY OBJECT, *1868/1869*

Pencil with pale brown wash on paper, 31⅜ × 39 in. (798 × 990 mm)
Inscribed in pencil by the artist on verso: *groupe des constructeurs tirant sur l'echelle*
Private collection, Dallas

PROVENANCE Estate of the artist (with red wax seal of atelier on old canvas backing, removed in conservation and saved); possibly the work referred to by Maître Delapalme, unpublished MS inventory of the estate of Pierre Puvis de Chavannes, dated November 14, 1898, as no. 15 ("Un dessin, Marseille. 150 francs"); by descent to Louis de Vaugelas (according to inscription on stretcher of previous backing canvas); Mme Puvis de Chavannes, La Maison de Cuiseaux, near Lyon; from whom purchased by the family of the penultimate owner; Jean-Luc Baroni, Ltd.; from whom purchased 1999 by the current owner.

EXHIBITED Colnaghi, New York, *Master Drawings,* May 7–30, 1998, cat. 46; Colnaghi, New York (at Adam Williams Fine Art, Ltd.), *Master Drawings,* May 6–28, 1999, cat. 46.

BIBLIOGRAPHY Price 2010, vol. 2, 142, cat. 165 (under "Related Works").

A latecomer to art and a slow starter, Pierre Puvis de Chavannes was not really interested in the graphic refinements taught by the academies, and he never found a comfortable fit in a traditional drawing class. Nevertheless he eventually developed his own accomplished and highly personal way of drawing, which was at the core of his art. Many hundreds of works on paper by Puvis survive, almost all of them working drawings done in preparation for his highly ambitious and often enormous paintings. Those paintings were often conceived as monumental decorations in the vast public buildings erected throughout France during the Second Empire and early Third Republic. The idealistic artist believed in the ethical purpose of these murals, whose civic-minded themes, poetic, Arcadian style, and muted coloration were aimed at a harmonious wedding of art and architecture. Many critics did not understand the antirealist thrust of his art at first, but some—like Jules Castagnary—changed their minds, and others—like Théophile Gautier—became huge champions, to the extent that eventually Puvis became that rarest of things: a painter celebrated equally by the artistic establishment and the avant garde. Fin-de-siècle artists like Paul Gauguin, Vincent van Gogh, Maurice Denis, and Georges Seurat acknowledged their debt to him, and Aristide Maillol spoke for all when he said: "Puvis! To him we owed the greatest feeling for art in our youth: his fine composition, his beautiful drawing filled us with an impression of poetry."[1] By 1893 his fame was such that he was invited to America to execute a series of decorations for the Boston Public Library.

This large drawing is an actual-size cartoon for a small detail in one of Puvis de Chavannes's important early murals, *Massalia, Greek Colony,* which together with its pendant *Marseille, Gateway to the Orient,* was commissioned in 1867 to decorate the newly constructed Palais Longchamp in Marseilles (Musées des Beaux-Arts, Marseilles). Installed in August 1869 after being exhibited in the Paris Salon of that year, the work measures approximately 14 by 18 feet. A perfect example of the artist's Arcadian style, the painting depicts the Greek settlers of Marseilles going about their peaceful daily lives, while in the background workmen are building the Temple of Diana, which was initially intended to be the principal subject of the mural. The four youths in this drawing are working in tandem to lever a heavy stone intended for use in the temple. Two drawings among 73 given to the Marseilles museum by the artist's nephew following his death are preliminary studies for three of the four figures in the finished cartoon.[2] In the latter, the youths' adolescent bodies are modeled more finely in Puvis's familiar, idealized style that appealed so much to Seurat, to the young Picasso of the Blue Period, and to others of that generation.

The most time-consuming part of Puvis de Chavannes's work on a commission of this type was the planning process, during which many drawings would be executed. The actual execution of the painting could then proceed rather quickly. By the time he made this painting, the artist had decided to invert the image of the four youths, so the drawing is punched with tiny pinpricks along every contour so that it could be transferred to the canvas in the inverse direction. After use in this process, it was mounted on its own canvas by the artist and framed, then kept in the studio until his death, when it appears to have been catalogued as a separate item from all the other drawings grouped in large lots and stamped on the back with the wax seal of his estate.

WBJ

Notes
1. Quoted in Price 1994, 22–23.
2. Colnaghi 1998, cat. 46, figs. 3, 4.

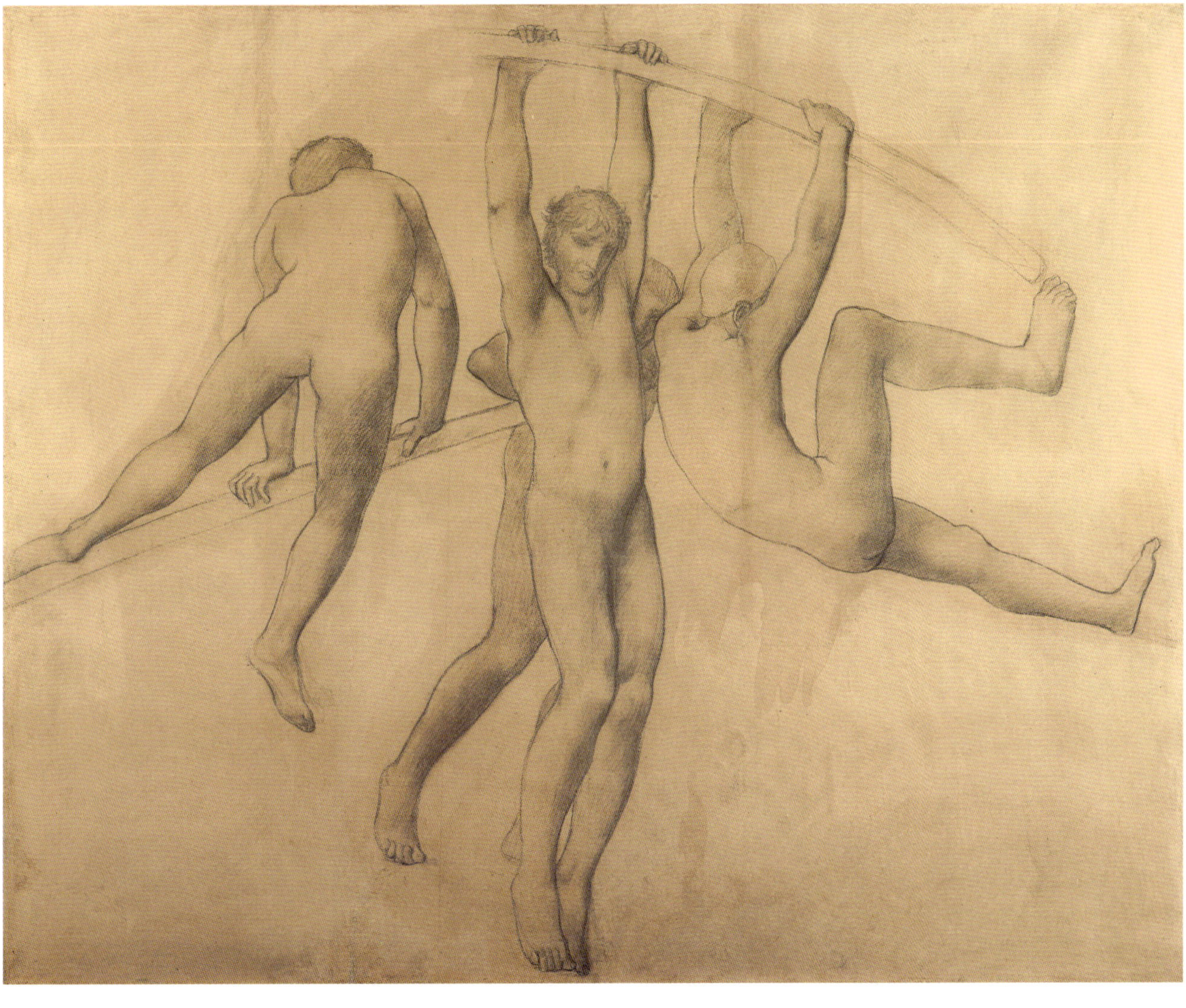

49

•

Albert Anker Swiss, 1831–1910

GIRL AND BOY WITH PICK-A-STICK GAME
(MÄDCHEN UND KNABE BEIM MIKADO-SPIEL), *N.D.*

Charcoal on paper, 14½ × 19¾ in. (370 × 500 mm)
Nona and Richard Barrett Collection, Dallas

BIBLIOGRAPHY Lüthy 1989, S.72, ill.

The painter Albert Anker enjoyed a substantial reputation in his native Switzerland and throughout Europe in the 19th century. He divided his work and life between the village of Anet (near Berne) and Paris, where he stayed regularly between 1860 and 1890. His specialty was genre painting inspired by domestic scenes from traditional Swiss peasant and bourgeois life. A special place in his work is reserved for the world of childhood, of which he was—as this drawing testifies—an attentive and respectful observer.

Anker shows us a little girl and boy wholly absorbed in their game. The theme and the sober atmosphere are reminiscent of Jean-Baptiste-Siméon Chardin, the French 18th-century painter whose work found fresh relevance in the 19th century. Reacting to the fashion of that period, Anker also painted children playing in 18th-century costumes. In this drawing, he seeks to translate his protagonists' intense absorption. Typical of interiors of the time, the oil lamp at far right enhances this effect by the play of its light, which emphasizes the seated children's faces while the framing cuts off their lower bodies.

This reminds us that Anker's art was admired as much for its realism as for its meticulous sense of detail. He practiced drawing throughout his life, alternating between preparatory studies and autonomous works. In the absence of any painting known to relate to this drawing, it is difficult to know to which of these categories it belongs.[1] A more summary drawing in pencil and ink, dated 1881, represents the artist's daughters and favorite models, Louise and Marie Anker, in a similar fashion.[2]

As so often with Anker, this everyday scene of bourgeois family life has its own moral implications. Before becoming a painter, he contemplated the Protestant priesthood. For him, childhood embodied an ideal of purity and innocence, and simplicity was a virtue in itself. The subtle treatment of faces and expressions in this drawing also reflects Anker's explicit taste for psychology—"a little remnant of my theology," as he said— and the profound humanity of his approach to the human face. Late in his life he declared, "It has always seemed to me that a picture loses much of its power if it is devoid of any psychological interest. . . . People are interested in people and they will always be the best models."

SP

Notes
1. See Kuthy and Bhattacharya-Settler 1995.
2. Gianadda Foundation 2003, 224, no. 101.

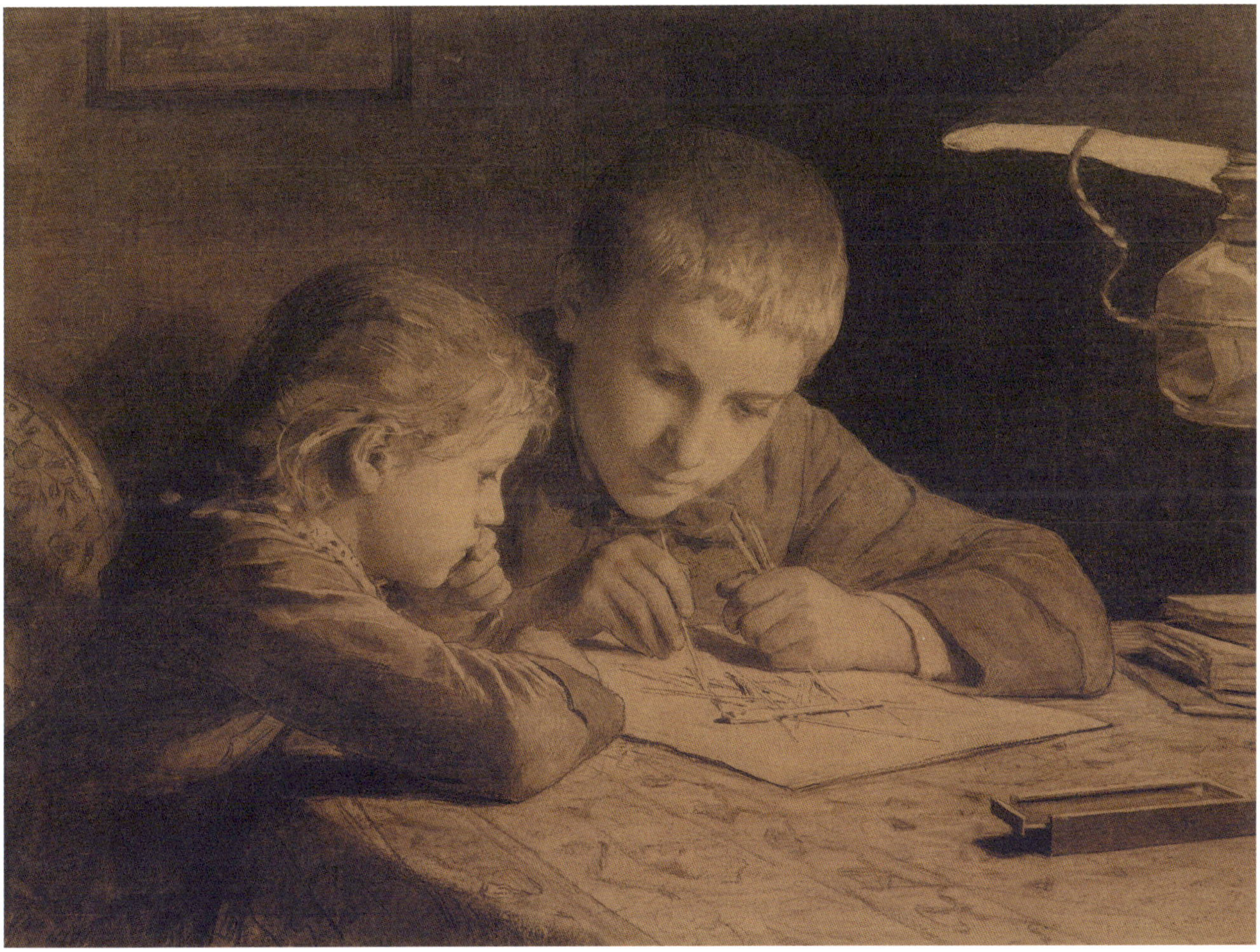

50

Sir Edward Coley Burne-Jones British, 1833–1898

HEAD OF A WOMAN, *1890*

Red, black, and white chalks on buff paper, 12 3/8 × 9 1/4 in. (314 × 235 mm)
Signed and dated lower right: *EBJ / 1890*; inscribed bottom edge: *TO FERNAND KHNOPFF from EDWARD BURNE-JONES 1894*
Collection of Mary Ralph Lowe, Fort Worth

PROVENANCE Edward Burne-Jones; gift to Fernand Khnopff, 1894; Thibaut de Maisières' Family, Seneffe; sale, Christie's, London, *Fine Victorian Drawings and Watercolors,* November 5, 1993, lot 127; from whom purchased by the current owner.

EXHIBITED Musée des arts décoratifs, Paris, October 10–December 31, 1979, Musées royaux des Beaux-Arts de Belgique, Brussels, January 18–April 13, 1980, and Kunsthalle, Hamburg, April 25–June 16, 1980, *Fernand Khnopff: 1858–1921,* no. 92; Bunkamura Museum, Tokyo, June 8–July 8, 1990, Himeji City Museum of Art, Japan, July 14–August 12, 1990, Nagoya City Museum, Japan, August 18–September 30, 1990, and Yamanashi Prefectural Museum of Art, Japan, October 7–November 11, 1990, *Fernand Khnopff,* 133, no. 129, color ill.; Museum of Fine Arts, Houston, short-term loan in conjunction with the exhibition *Visions of Love and Life: Pre-Raphaelite Art from the Birmingham Collection, England,* November 5, 1995–January 2, 1996; Dallas Museum of Art, *The Pilgrim at the Gate of Idleness,* December 15, 1996–February 16, 1997; Tate Gallery, London, October 16, 1997–January 4, 1998, Haus der Kunst, Munich, January 30–April 26, 1998, and Van Gogh Museum, Amsterdam, May 15–August 30, 1998, *The Age of Rossetti, Burne-Jones, and Watts: Symbolism in Britain 1860–1910,* 229, no. 96, color ill.; Europalia International, Brussels, *Crossroads of Cultures Exhibit,* August 29, 2000–November 5, 2000.

BIBLIOGRAPHY Delevoy et al. 1987, 59–60, color ill.; Busine 1962, 61, ill.; Wilton 1997, 241; des Cars 1998 (French ed.), 33, 35, fig. 32; des Cars 1999 (English ed.), 33, 35, fig. 32.

This drawing is a tangible and famous testimony of the mutual admiration between Edward Burne-Jones and the Belgian artist Fernand Khnopff (see cat. 85). The English artist gave this drawing in 1894 to Khnopff, who responded in 1896 with a drawing of his own, also representing a head of a woman. This exchange illustrates the rich and complex interconnections among European symbolists, and it demonstrates the influence of Burne-Jones on the European scene. Exhibited at the Universal Exposition in Paris in 1878 and again in 1889, his paintings caused a sensation among artists, including Khnopff, as well as critics and the general public.

A pre-Raphaelite painter but also considered a European symbolist, Burne-Jones was the most influential British artist of his generation. From his twenties, with his lifelong friend the designer and craftsman William Morris, he had a profound influence on the way educated Englishmen viewed their world. He received lessons from Dante Gabriel Rossetti and became a friend of John Ruskin. His first large exhibition, in 1877 at the Grosvenor Gallery, was very well received. In addition to his paintings and drawings, Burne-Jones was also active as a book illustrator and a designer of tapestries and other decorative works. Like other 19th-century artists, he experimented a great deal with technique, often employing complex combinations of media, such as gouache, pencil, colored chalk, and gold paint. He also frequently used colored papers—red, as in the case of this drawing, but also green, gray, or brown.

OM

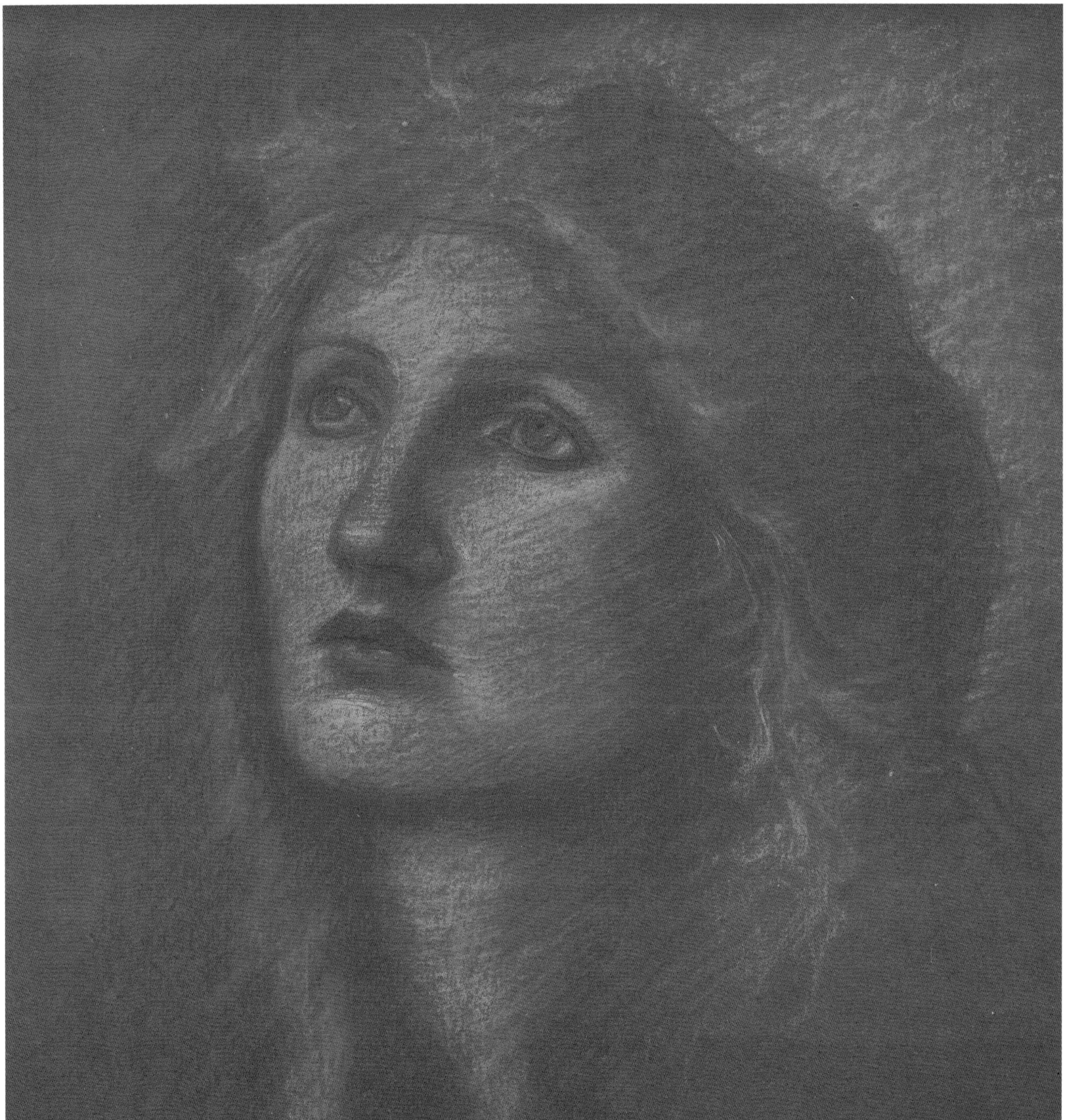

51

Simeon Solomon British, 1840–1905

THE UNAPPEASED DESIRE, *1887*

Colored chalks on paper, 14¼ × 11½ in. (362 × 292 mm)
Monogrammed and dated *SS 1887*; inscribed as a title, *The Unnappeased Desire*
Private collection, Dallas

PROVENANCE Lublin Galleries, New York; from whom purchased by the current owner.

In 1887, the same year this piece was created, the poet Arthur Symons used the words "a shipwreck of a genius" to describe Simeon Solomon's final years. Solomon started his life and his career under the best auspices. Born to a successful factory owner, the youngest of eight children, Simeon was admitted to the Royal Academy Schools in 1856. During his life, he befriended many artists and poets, among them Dante Gabriel Rossetti, Albert Moore, Algernon Charles Swinburne, Oscar Wilde, and William Burges. His work is strongly related to that of the second generation of pre-Raphaelites, but with an even more pronounced sense of eroticism and decadence. Exhibiting at the Royal Academy, traveling to Italy, illustrating books, or making designs for stained glass, Solomon was enjoying success and prosperity when he suddenly disappeared from public view after being arrested in 1873 for indecent exposure; he was subsequently sentenced to prison. The following years were marked by slow but irreversible decay. Other arrests, for alcohol and vagrancy, led him to workhouses. In his final years, while still exhibiting at the Royal Academy and among peers in various places, Simeon Solomon survived by selling drawings "for a few shillings." He collapsed on a street in May 1905 and died in St. Giles's Workhouse some days later.

This drawing is one of a series on a recurrent and obsessive visual theme of an ambiguous head of Medusa combined with the wings of the god Mercury. Very similar later versions are titled *The Tormented Conscience,* 1889 (private collection) and *Corruptio Optimi Pessima,* 1893 (private collection). The desperate sadness of the face suggests a shrill and useless call for help. The theme of Medusa, a woman petrifying men through her hideous and deadly appearance, most notably snakes sprouting like hair, was a favorite of other artists, including Rossetti, Edward Burne-Jones, Gustave Moreau, and Arnold Böcklin.

OM

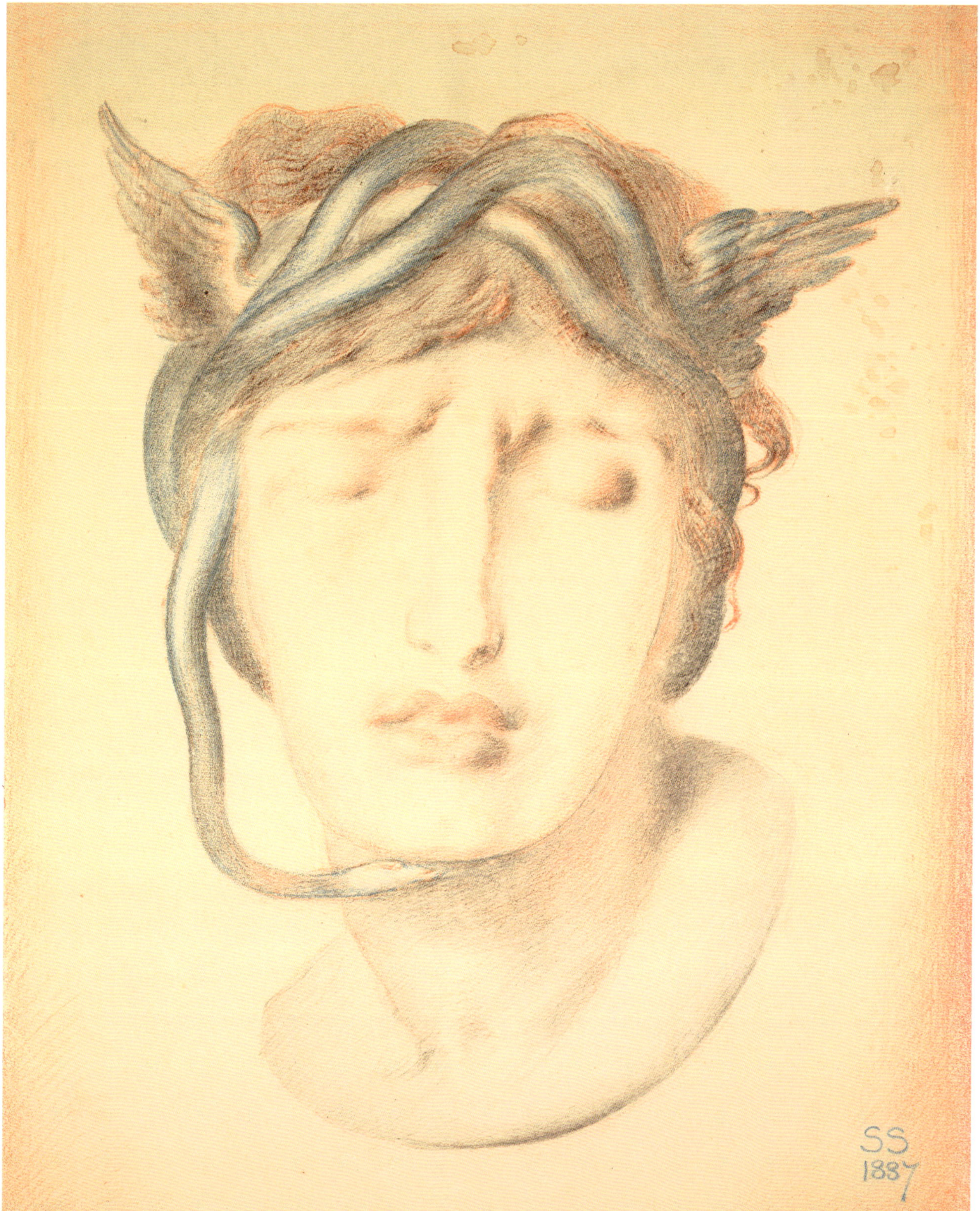
SS
1887
The Unappeased Desire

52

Frederick Sandys British, 1829–1904

PROUD MAISIE, VI, *1893*

Pencil and red chalk on paper, 15 × 11 in. (380 × 280 mm)
Dated, verso: *February 13th 1893*
Collection of Mary Ralph Lowe, Fort Worth

PROVENANCE Purchased from P. & D. Colnaghi, London, 1925; estate of a family in Norfolk, sold by Phillips, April 15, 1985, lot 158; purchased by Peter Nahum, Ltd., London; from whom purchased 1991 by the current owner.

EXHIBITED Brighton Museum and Art Gallery, May 7–July 14, 1974, and Mappin Art Gallery, Sheffield, July 2–August 25, 1974, *Frederick Sandys, 1809–1904*, no. 158, pl. 117; Peter Nahum, Ltd., London, *Second Exhibited: Master Drawings of the Nineteenth and Twentieth Centuries*, 1985, no. 6; Museum of Fine Arts, Houston, short-term loan, February 8, 1991–April 16, 1991; Museum of Fine Arts, Houston, short-term loan in conjunction with the exhibition *Visions of Love and Life: Pre-Raphaelite Art from the Birmingham Collection, England*, November 5, 1995–January 2, 1996.

BIBLIOGRAPHY Elzea 2001, 193–94, no. 2.A.116.

Frederick Sandys was born in Norwich and studied at the Norwich School of Design. Even though he first gained notoriety through a print parodying John Everett Millais's painting *Sir Isumbra at the Ford* (1857, Lady Lever Art Gallery, Liverpool), he later joined the Pre-Raphaelite Brotherhood. He even shared for a year the studio of his close friend Dante Gabriel Rossetti on Cheyne Walk. Mostly known as a draftsman, Sandys produced illustrations for magazines and drawings that were readily saleable to collectors. He also portrayed noteworthy figures like Vivien and Morgan le Fay of Arthurian legend.

The features of *Proud Maisie* are those of Mary Emma Jones, Sandys's companion for more than 40 years and the mother of their 10 children. Mary was Sandys's muse and model, but she also had a career as an actress known as Miss Clive. The title of the drawing is taken from Sir Walter Scott's poem "Proud Maisie," in *The Heart of Midlothian*, first published in 1818. A young girl sitting in the woods asks a robin about her future and her wedding. She is too proud to understand the bird's prediction: that she will die and be put into the grave.

Sandys did not associate this composition with Scott's poem until he produced the third version of the drawing in 1868. Until then the composition was just known as *Study of a Head*. It was so hugely successful that nine autograph versions are known today, each differing in slight details and all testifying to its fame. It is hard to imagine a more apt description of its sensual appeal than that of Sandys's great admirer Algernon Charles Swinburne, who declared it one of the artist's "most solid and splendid designs; a woman of rich, ripe, angry beauty, she draws one warm long lock of curling hair through her full and moulded lips, biting it with bared bright teeth, which add something of a tiger's charm to the sleepy and couching [*sic*] passion of her fair face."

OM

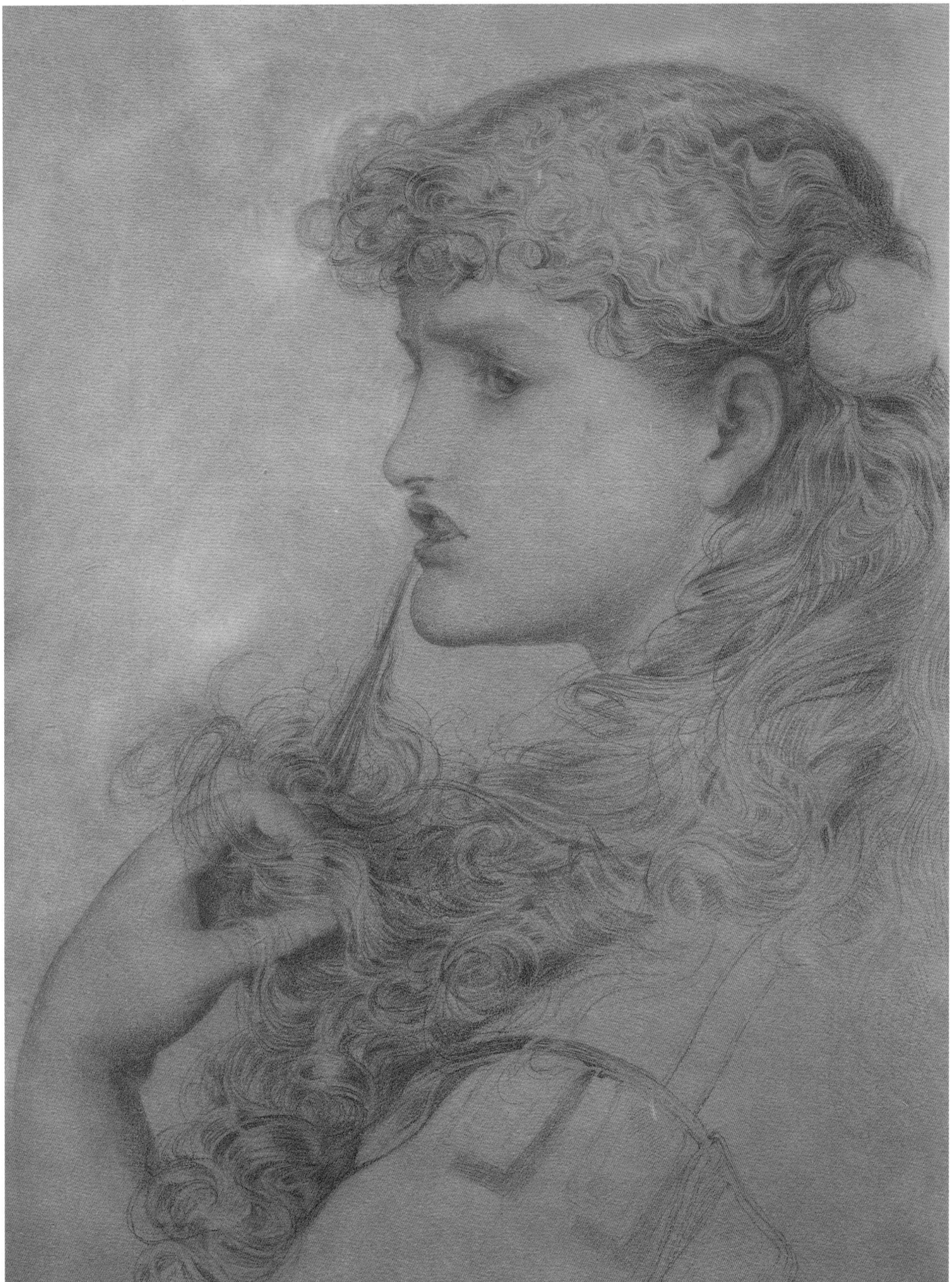

53

Édouard Manet French, 1832–1883

THE SPANISH SINGER, C. *1861*

Watercolor, gouache, and graphite on laid paper, 11 × 8¾ in. (280 × 222 mm)
Signed lower left: *Manet*
Dallas Museum of Art, The Wendy and Emery Reves Collection, 1985.R.33

PROVENANCE Antonin Proust, Paris, 1864; Jean-Baptiste Faure, France, by 1906; Durand-Ruel, Paris, March 13, 1907; M. Miethke, June 28, 1910; Dr. Eissler, Vienna, 1922–at least 1958; Esther Hunt Slater Kerrigan, New York, Washington, and Palm Beach; Captain Hunt Kerrigan and Anthony Kerrigan, New York, until November 11, 1960; Hirschl & Adler Galleries, New York, November 18, 1960–February 11, 1961; Wendy and Emery Reves, France, February 11, 1961–1985; given to the Dallas Museum of Art, The Wendy and Emery Reves Collection, 1985.

EXHIBITED École des Beaux-Arts, Paris, *Exposition Posthume Manet,* 1884, 117; *Universal Exposition of 1889,* Paris, 399; Durand-Ruel, Paris, *Exposition de 24 Tableaux et Aquarelles par Manet,* March 1–31, 1906, 8 *(Le Chanteur Espagnol)*; Dallas Museum of Art, *Impressionist and Modern Masters,* September 3–October 22, 1989, 48 *(The Spanish Singer)*; Dallas Museum of Art, *Impressions from the Riviera,* November 5, 1995–February 4, 1996; Dallas Museum of Art, *All the World's a Stage: Celebrating Performance in the Visual Arts,* August 30, 2009–February 28, 2010.

BIBLIOGRAPHY Faure 1902, 19, ill.; Glaser 1922, no. 1; Jamot and Wildenstein 1932, 119; Tabarant 1947, 102, 512; Richardson 1958, 118, ill.; Courthion 1962, 64; Hanson 1966, 68; Daulte 1969, 68, 69, color ill.; de Leiris 1969, 10, 11, 105, ill.; Isaacson 1969, 27; Guerin 1969, no. 16; Harris 1970, 51, ill.; Rouart and Wildenstein 1975, no. 459, ill.; Metropolitan Museum of Art 1983, 69; Dallas Museum of Art 1985b, 90–91, color ill.; Brettell 1995, 26–27, color ill.

Édouard Manet was the dean of avant-garde French painters from the early 1860s until his premature death in 1883. Although known almost universally as a painter, he made important contributions to the graphic arts and left a small but distinguished body of drawings in watercolor, ink wash, chalk, pencil, and pastel and prints in both intaglio and lithographic mediums. *The Spanish Singer* is among his earliest masterpieces in watercolor. It relates directly to a major painting of the same title, now in the Metropolitan Museum of Art, New York, which was exhibited to considerable acclaim at the Salon of 1861 under the title *Spaniard Playing the Guitar.* Unlike many earlier French painters, Manet seems not to have used a graphic preparatory process for the painting, preferring to work directly from the model and making his numerous adjustments to the composition on the painting itself. This major watercolor is a reduction of the painting rather than a preliminary study, probably made at the request of Manet's friend and the first owner of the work, Antonin Proust, after the success of the painting at the Salon. It may also have served Manet as he translated the painting into the graphic medium of etching. *The Spanish Singer* was etched by Manet in 1861 and printed in five states between 1861 and 1863.

Manet's process of translation from painting to print has been extensively studied by Juliet Wilson Bareau, who notes that the drawings and prints stemming from the Metropolitan's *Spanish Singer* created a pattern of work that Manet was to use throughout much of his life.[1] It seems that Manet started the process with a photograph of the painting, which he then traced and used as the basis for both the watercolor and the subsequent print. The Reves *Spanish Singer* and its print both describe a slightly smaller pictorial field than does the painting, and certain details (the right shoe, the onions, the cigarette smoke, the shirtfront, and the scarf) have been adapted to the reduced scale of the format.

We can speculate that Manet used watercolor because he wanted to translate the entire work, color and all, to a small scale before translating again into the black-and-white medium of etching. Most of his watercolors after paintings have the characteristics of miniature paintings, and collectively they tend to be quite faithful to the original except in tonality. Evidently because of the reduction in scale, Manet generally suffused the smaller versions with greater light and space, allowing them to operate independently of the paintings to which they relate. In *The Spanish Singer* the background is both lighter and, of course, more transparent than in the oil version, and the floor recedes more dramatically.

For all its brio and life, *The Spanish Singer* has many of the oddities that mark Manet's mature style. The

Note
1. Bareau 1986.

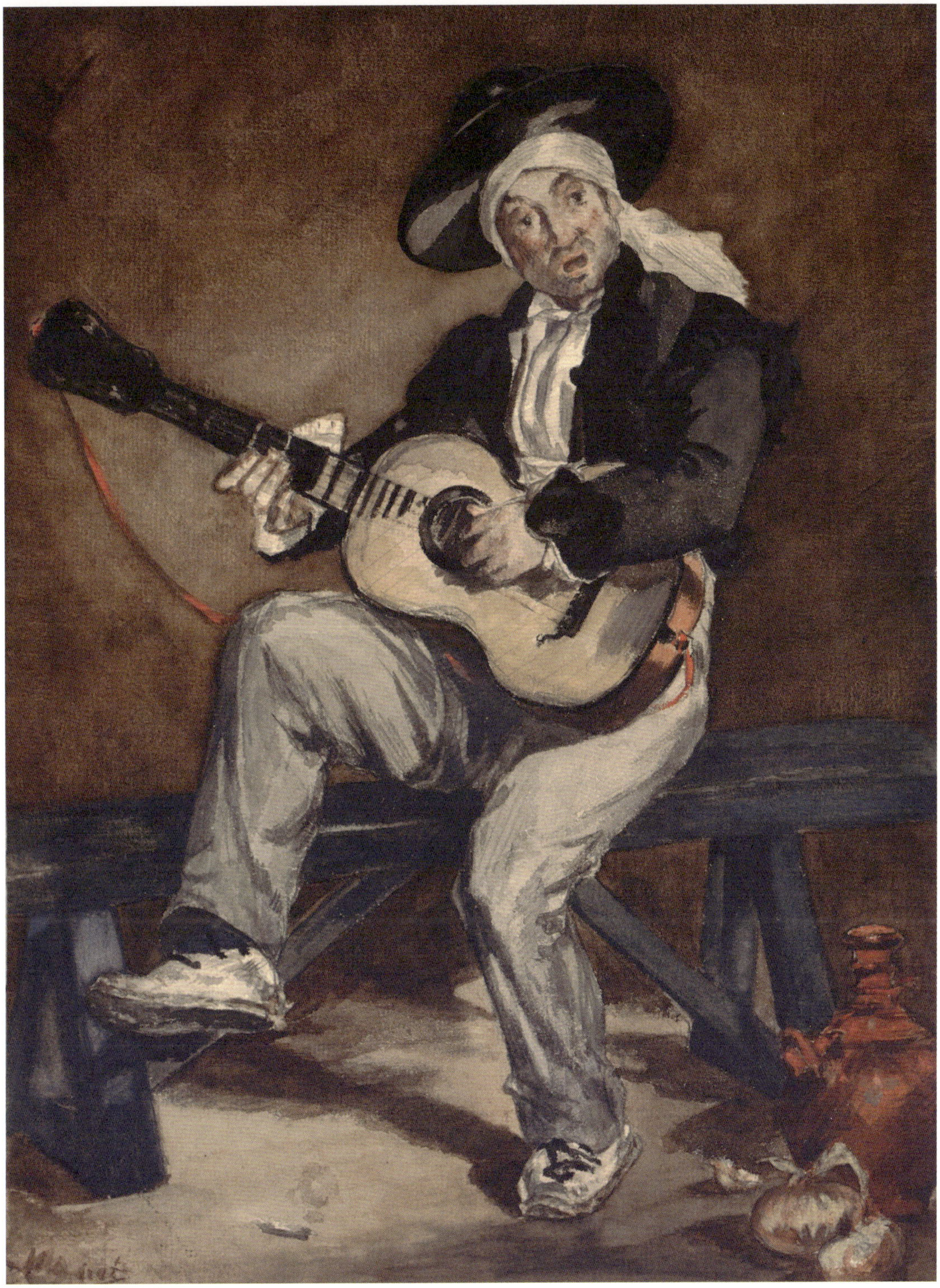

singer's pose is inexplicably unstable, as if he is tapping his foot while playing and singing. His mouth is also ambiguously painted in both the oil and watercolor versions, making his status as a singer questionable. Many Manet scholars have searched in the art of Francisco Goya, Bartolomé Esteban Murillo, and Diego Velázquez for sources, while others have concentrated on French influences in the painting of Jean-Baptiste Greuze and Gustave Courbet. Yet, as always, Manet eludes his scholarly hunters by combining elements of many sources, heightening some and disguising others. He was also resolute in making his "Spanish" singer French. In fact, early commentators identified the singer's jacket as coming from Marseilles, and his pants must be from Montmartre!

RRB

Édouard Manet French, 1832–1883

THE TAVERN (LE BOUCHON), *1878*

Ink and pencil on laid paper, 8¼ × 11⅛ in. (210 × 283 mm)
Stamped lower right: *AB* [coinjoined in a circle]
Dallas Museum of Art, The Wendy and Emery Reves Collection, 1985.R.35

PROVENANCE Cachet Atelier Manet; A. Barrion until 1904; Barrion sale, 1904; Alexis Rouart, Paris; Emery Reves, France, by 1962 and until 1985; given to the Dallas Museum of Art, The Wendy and Emery Reves Collection, 1985.

EXHIBITED M. Guiot Gallery, Paris, *Les Deux Ecritures de Goya à Lautrec,* 1953, no. 62; Dallas Museum of Art, *Impressionist and Modern Masters in Dallas,* September 3–October 22, 1989, 80, no. 50.

BIBLIOGRAPHY Duret 1910, 177; Waldmann 1923, 41; Courthion 1962, no. 69, 38; de Leiris 1969, 78–79, no. 501, fig. 379; Rouart and Wildenstein 1975, no. 510; Brettell 1995, 66–67; Brettell 2000, 92, fig. 50.

This brilliant brush drawing was made about 1878 as part of Édouard Manet's effort to capture all aspects of the urban café. It belongs to a small family of closely related works in a variety of mediums, including two pencil drawings and a freely painted oil in the Pushkin Museum, Moscow. In fact, it appears to have been made directly in preparation for the unsigned and undated Pushkin painting, which seems to have been sold in Manet's lifetime to the collector Tavernier.

Like many of Manet's brush drawings, this one owes a considerable debt to Asian traditions of painting. Using several brushes that were either "dry" or filled with india ink of various strengths, Manet defined the central figure of a worker seated alone at an outdoor café. This figure is shown next to a slumped-over, presumably drunk female, and both are seen behind a prominent tree trunk, which indicates that they are in an outdoor café. There have been attempts to identify the setting as either a café in the city on place Moncey or along the Barrière de Clichy at the edge of Paris. The latter theory seems more likely and has won widespread acceptance. Scholars have also argued over the relationship between this group of works and Émile Zola's novel *The Dram Shop (L'Assommoir),* published serially to enormous acclaim—and controversy—in 1876–1877. No doubt a real similarity of subject exists between Manet's visual investigation of working-class drunkenness and Zola's literary one, but it would be wrong to interpret Manet's painting as an illustration of any particular passage in the novel. While Zola treated the world of working-class alcoholism with a grim determinism, relishing its most sordid smells, textures, and sounds, Manet remained aloof. The artist seems to feel an odd respect for the independence of this worker and his snoozing companion. They exist completely in their own world, unaware of the painter / viewer. While Zola's image of drunkenness is noisy and disgusting, Manet's is silent.

Manet never came as close to a proletarian subject as he did in this drawing and its related painting. Neither has played a prominent role in the interpretation of Manet's café subjects, possibly because the painting has been relatively inaccessible; it left France early in the century. Both it and this splendid preparatory drawing deserve to be better known.

RRB

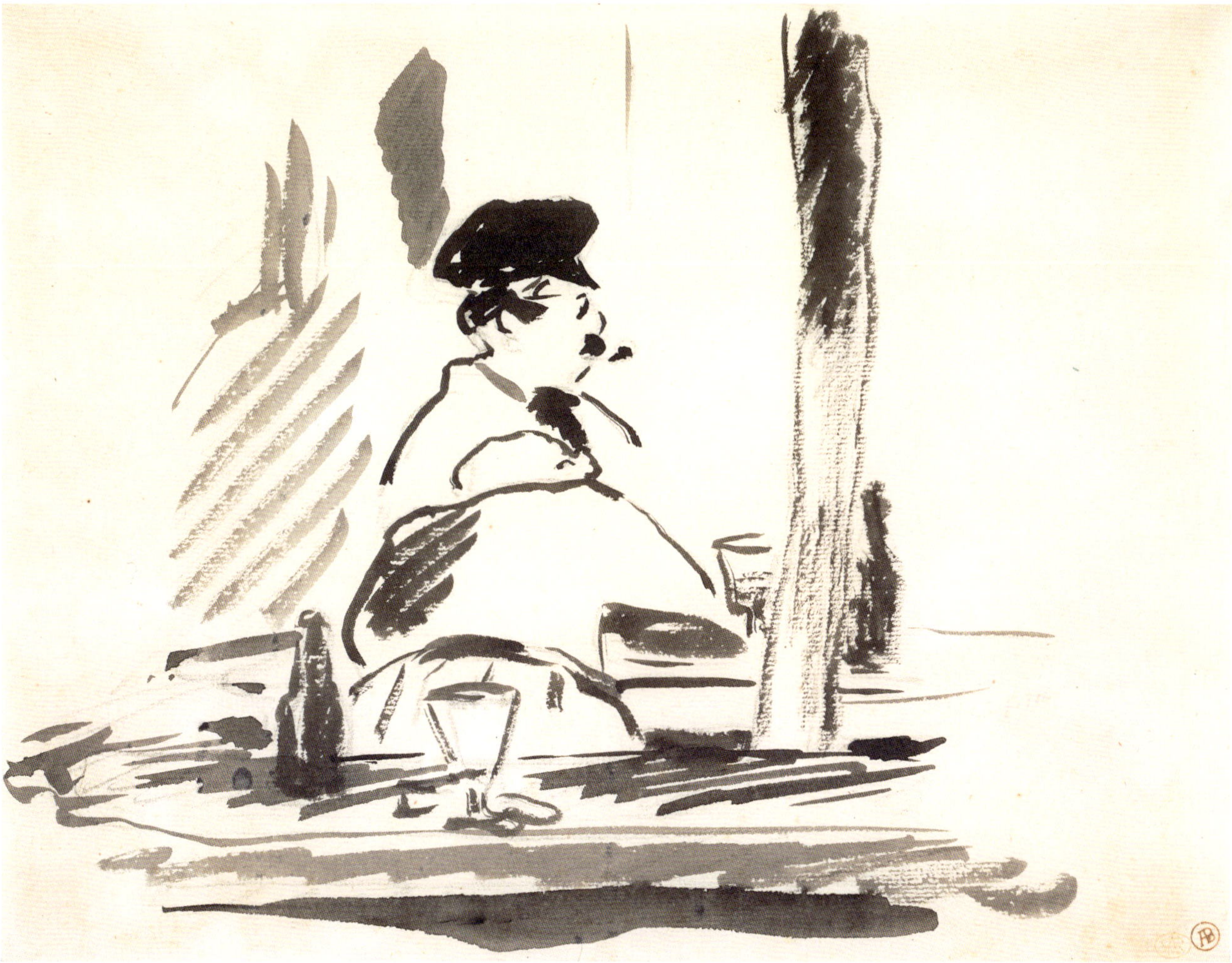

55

Johan Barthold Jongkind Dutch, 1819–1891

ROUEN, *1863*

Watercolor and charcoal on laid paper, 13 × 20¾ in. (330 × 527 mm)
Signed, dated, and inscribed lower right: *a [sic] mon ami Jean Rousseau / Paris, 11 mars 1864 J. B. Jongkind*
Dallas Museum of Art, The Wendy and Emery Reves Collection, 1985.R.30

PROVENANCE Acquired from the artist, through gift or purchase, by Jean Rousseau, March 11, 1864; Emery Reves, France, 1953; given to the Dallas Museum of Art, The Wendy and Emery Reves Collection, 1985.

EXHIBITED Galerie Alfred Daber, Paris, *Jongkind Pientres et Aquarelles,* May–June 1960; Institut Néerlandais, Paris, *L'Aquarelle Néerlandaise au siècle dernier,* February–March 1963; Galerie Robert Schmit, Paris, *The Impressionists and Their Precursors,* May–June 1966; Institut Néerlandais, Paris, *Watercolor Exhibit,* January–March 1971; Dallas Museum of Art, *Impressionist and Modern Masters in Dallas,* September 3–October 22, 1989, 80, no. 39.

BIBLIOGRAPHY Paris 1946; Brettell 1995, 30–31, color ill.

The Dutch painter Johan Barthold Jongkind was of secondary importance as an artist, but he exerted a powerful influence on the development of impressionism and can be called one of the three or four crucial mentors of the young painters who joined together as "independent" artists in 1874. Jongkind was known as a virtuoso watercolorist and landscape painter in both his native Holland and the region around Paris. This watercolor is among his most accomplished and mature. If its inscription was made at the same moment as the drawing itself, it dates from the spring of 1864. It is more likely that the watercolor was retrieved from a sketchbook or from a large stack of works already completed by the artist and inscribed to its recipient. The watercolor seems to have been made in the summer months, when the foliage was fully developed, and can plausibly be dated to the previous summer of 1863.

For his motif, Jongkind chose a spot on the towing path along the Seine River just north of Rouen. The principal inland port in France, Rouen was also a medieval ecclesiastical capital of great importance, and the spires of its famous cathedral rise from the alluvial plain of the Seine at the center of Jongkind's landscape. Yet, despite the centrality of the spires, they are overwhelmed in scale and pictorial importance by the foreground and middle-ground trees and by the *péniche à vapeur,* or motorized barge, that plies the river, steaming to the port of Le Havre. For Jongkind, painting was an easy, direct, and apparently unfettered act of transcription in which modernity was more important than history. The sheer simplicity and directness of his paintings in watercolor and oil gave strength to the young impressionists who sought to bring their world firmly forward and anchor it in vivid representation.

RRB

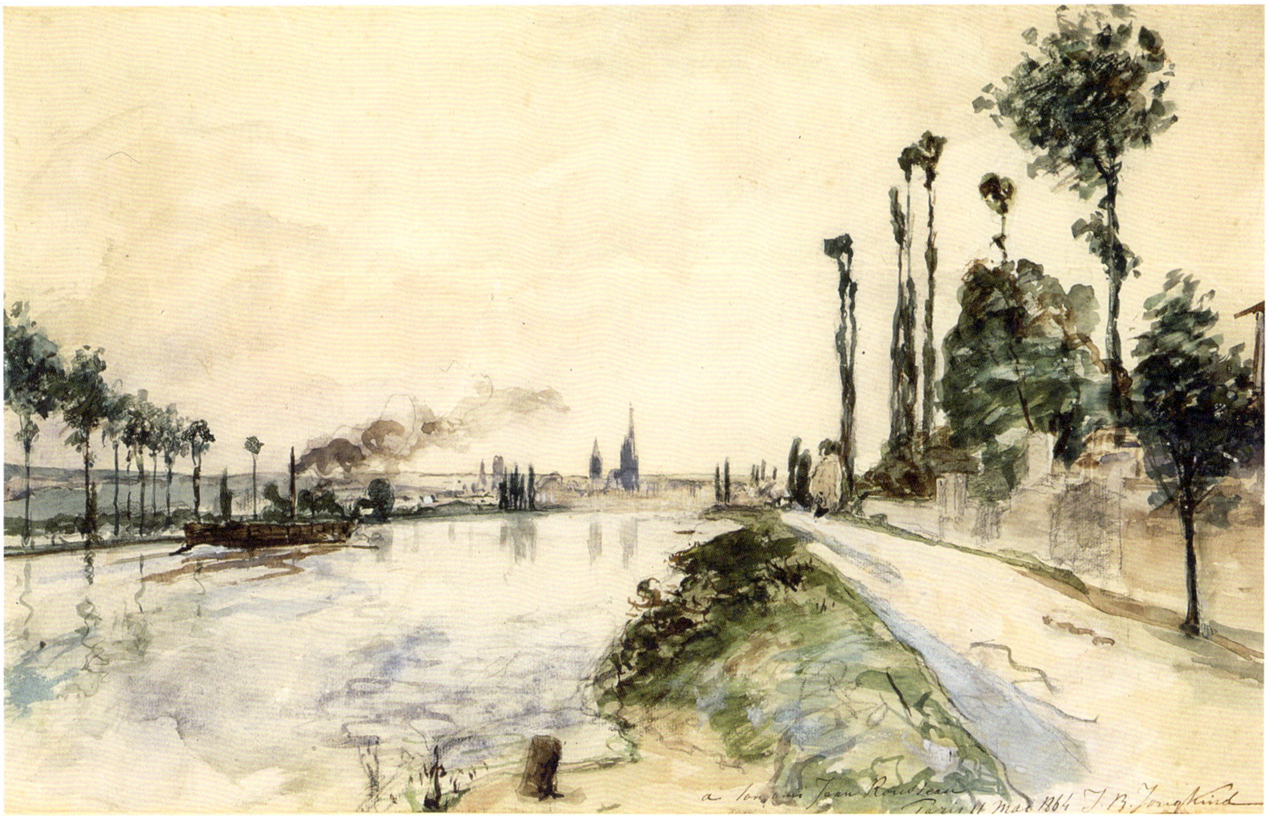
a son ami Jean Rousseau
Paris 11 mai 1864 J.B. Jongkind

56

Berthe Morisot French, 1841–1895

HARBOR SCENE (MARINE), *1880*

Pencil and watercolor on cream wove paper, 8⅛ × 5¾ in. (207 × 148 mm)
Signed lower left: *Berthe Morisot*
Private collection, Dallas

PROVENANCE By descent from the artist to Yves Rouart; from whom purchased 2000 by the current owner through Galerie Hopkins-Thomas-Custot, Paris.

Berthe Morisot was, after her friend Camille Pissarro, the second in fidelity to the impressionist exhibitions, sending her work in all mediums to seven of the eight exhibitions organized by the loose coalition of artists between 1874 and 1886. The pampered daughter of a wealthy family, Morisot was fiercely independent and maintained a career as an artist quite separate from her duties as a daughter, sister, wife, and mother. She maintained her own name as an artist, perhaps because her husband, Eugène Manet, was the younger brother of the great painter. Her only child, Julie Manet, became one of the most documented of the impressionist children, eventually married into the even wealthier Rouart family, and wrote her memoirs late in life. Morisot's painting style was often linked to watercolor practice in its delicacy, transparency, and pale pastel hues. In fact, she painted watercolors throughout her life, although they have never been catalogued, as have her oil paintings.

Morisot painted two major groups of "marines" or boat-filled harbor scenes—one on the Isle of Wight in 1875 and the other in Nice in 1880. Although it is tempting to identify this signed watercolor with a work in the same medium exhibited as number 179 at the impressionist exhibition of 1876 and entitled *Avant d'un Yacht,* the buildings of West Cowes on the Isle of Wight do not conform to those in the present work. Indeed, it is clearly part of the latter group and represents boats in the protected harbor of Nice, which is surrounded by multistory hotels and apartment buildings and dominated on the inland side by the Church of the Immaculate Conception, whose tower we see rising above the black boat in the present work. The harbor was called Le Port Lympia in the 19th century and was part of the old town of Nice, some distance from the fashionable Promenade des Anglais with its luxury hotels, restaurants, and shops. Nice, the birthplace of Garibaldi, the founder of modern Italy, had become French only in 1860, when it was ceded to France from the former kingdom of Savoy as payment for Napoleon III's military aid to Italy.

This wonderful fluid watercolor was painted relatively quickly on a sheet of paper from a small promontory on the Quai des Emmanuels. Its deftness is matched by Morisot's exactly contemporary oil studies of the same subject, two of which were included in the 1882 impressionist exhibition and one of which is now in the Wendy and Emery Reves Collection, Dallas Museum of Art (1985.R.40).

RRB

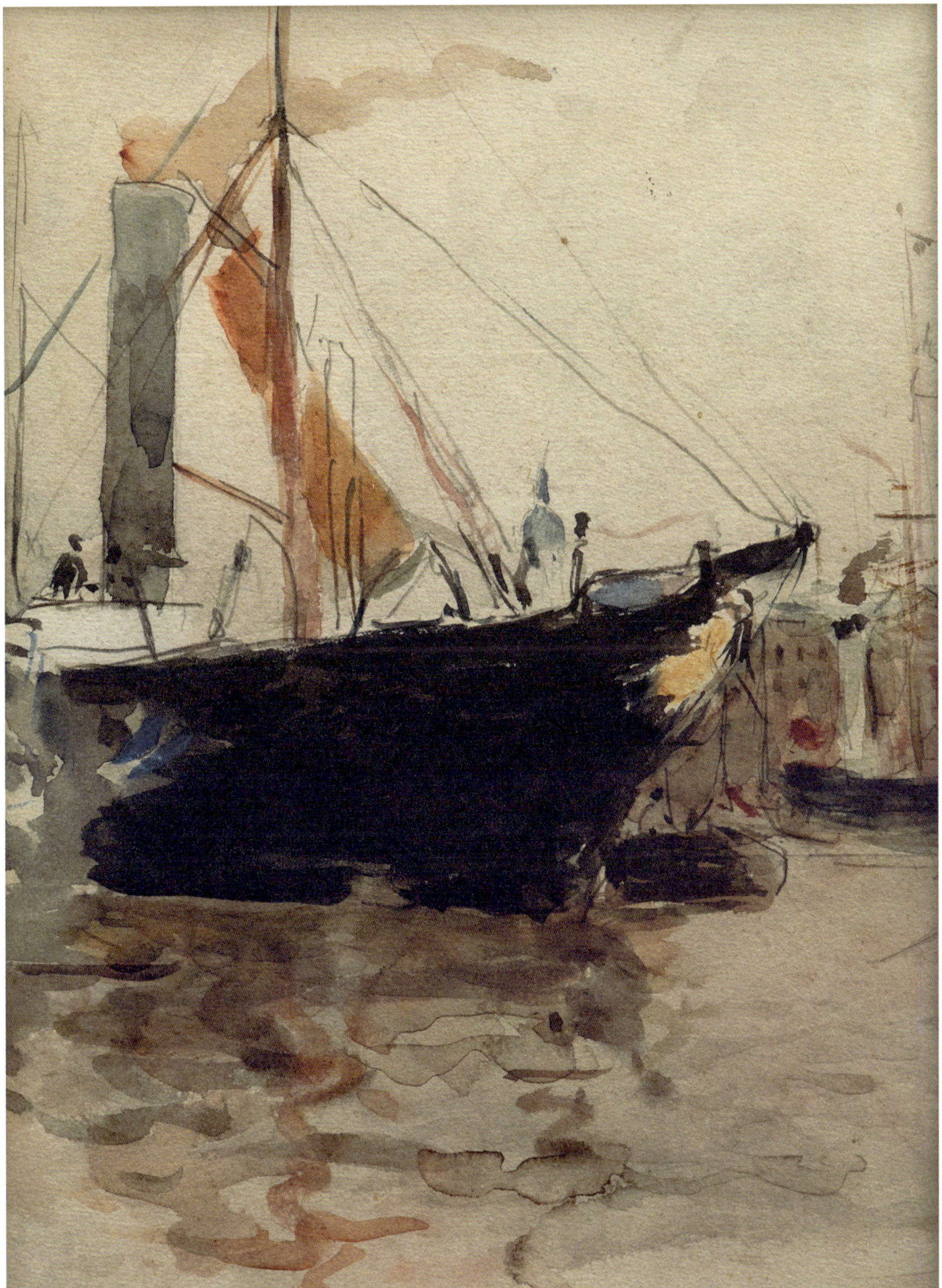
Berthe Morisot

57

Edgar Degas French, 1834–1917

ARIA AFTER THE BALLET, *1879*

Pastel and gouache over monotype (?) on thick wove paper, 23½ × 29½ in. (597 × 750 mm)
Signed lower right: *Degas*
Dallas Museum of Art, the Wendy and Emery Reves Collection, 1985.R.26

PROVENANCE Andre Pillot; Durand-Ruel, Paris, 1907; Durand-Ruel, New York, until at least 1946; Emery Reves, France, c. 1946; given to the Dallas Museum of Art, The Wendy and Emery Reves Collection, 1985.

EXHIBITED *Exposition des Impressionistes,* Paris, 1879, no. 73 (*Grand Air, Après un Ballet*); Knoedler and Co., New York, *Masterpieces by Old and Modern Painters,* 1915; Durand-Ruel, Paris, *Exhibition of Manet to Degas,* April 1916, no. 18; Durand-Ruel, New York, *Degas,* January 1918, no. 5; Durand-Ruel, New York, *Degas,* February 1928, no. 22; Palais national des Beaux-Arts, Paris, *Exposition des Chefs-d'Oeuvres de l'art Français,* 1937, no. 309; Durand-Ruel, Paris, *19th- and 20th-Century Works from Private Collections,* May 1945, no. 12; Durand-Ruel, Paris, *The Painters of Music,* May 1948, no. 20; Smith College Museum of Art, Northampton, Mass., April 1951–December 1952 (*L'Air Après le Ballet*); Dallas Museum of Art, *Impressionist and Modern Masters in Dallas,* September 3–October 22, 1989, 78, no. 23 (*Aria after the Ballet*); Dallas Museum of Art, *Impressions from the Riviera,* November 5, 1995–February 4, 1996 (*Aria after a Ballet*); Dallas Museum of Art, *Passion for Art: 100 Treasures 100 Years,* October 12, 2003–March 14, 2004; Dallas Museum of Art, *All the World's a Stage: Celebrating Performance in the Visual Arts,* August 30, 2009–February 28, 2010.

BIBLIOGRAPHY Rouart 1945, 18, 72; Lemoisne 1946, vol. 1, 243–44, vol. 2, viii, 292–93; Russoli and Minervino 1970, 120, 121; Dallas Museum of Art 1985b, 114–15; Tinterow 1987; Loyrette 1988; Kendall 1993, 137; Brettell 1995, 70–71; Dallas Museum of Art 1997, 107; DeVonyar and Kendall 2002, 188, no. 209; MacDonald 2013, 76–79, 81.

The scene Degas presents is bewildering, even unsettling. A vast mountain range rises up into the clouds in the distance. At left, lit from below, a strangely clad woman gestures histrionically, her mouth open in what must be song but could be a dramatic address. Beside her, a group of ballet dancers scuttles away, their arms and legs a confused jumble. Then, as if from nowhere, like menacing great serpents arching to attack, appear the necks of two bass violins, emerging threateningly from the bottom of the picture at right, just above the artist's jaunty signature.

The viewer can rest easy, for most of these mysteries can be explained. As Jill DeVonyar and Richard Kendall have discovered, the landscape is in fact the set of Gounod's *Faust,* in which some of the singers wore toga-like draped and caped costumes similar to the one Degas places on his lady.[1] The visual cacophony of forms can be explained as a cunning exaggeration of the real view the artist might have had when sitting just beside the orchestra, looking sharply up at the performers at the edge of the stage, his view of the action blocked in part by musical instruments. The picture's title, *Aria after the Ballet,* further helps the unfamiliar viewer to understand its subject. This title was given by the artist, who showed the work at the fourth exhibition of the impressionists in 1879. It is assumed, at least, that he showed it there, but not a single writer mentions it in the many reviews of the exhibition that were printed at the time, and that fact is bewildering. Perhaps, as on other occasions, Degas planned to send the work to the exhibition, then held it back in the end. For how could a reviewer have missed the opportunity to point out the radical nature—radical genius or radical effrontery, depending on the author's aesthetic viewpoint—of this magnificent work?

Precedents for the composition can be found in the art of Honoré Daumier (see cats. 20–22)—one of Degas's heroes—who similarly depicted the stage as seen from the orchestra pit in lithographic cartoons published in the 1850s. In Degas's own work, paintings of orchestra musicians at work had included glimpses of the performances they accompanied. All these precedents were careful to show the edge of the stage, but in *Aria after the Ballet* Degas changes the boundaries of his vision slightly. By moving his frame upward toward the distant mountaintop, he "loses" the orchestra itself and the floor of the stage, taking away the anchoring elements that would have explained the space depicted and would have given order to the sudden and startling juxtaposition of singer, dancers, and musical instruments.

As he worked on *Aria after the Ballet,* one of his most daring compositions, Degas took evident delight in his mastery of painting and pastel. The picture has traditionally been thought to have as its base one of Degas's monotype prints—a drawing executed with the brush and greasy black ink on a metal plate, then printed in reverse onto a sheet of paper.[2] If a

Notes

1. DeVonyar and Kendall 2002, 188–89.
2. In the past, observers have interpreted the square indentation found at varying ranges from 1 to 2.5 cm from the edge of the paper as a plate mark—made when the paper was run through a press with a sheet of metal. In 1987, paper conservator Jacqueline Gilliam proposed that the indentation was, instead, a deformation of the paper resulting from the pressure of paper tape that had been adhered to the back of the sheet at its margins. Recent examination of the sheet by curators and conservators under magnification has not resolved the question.

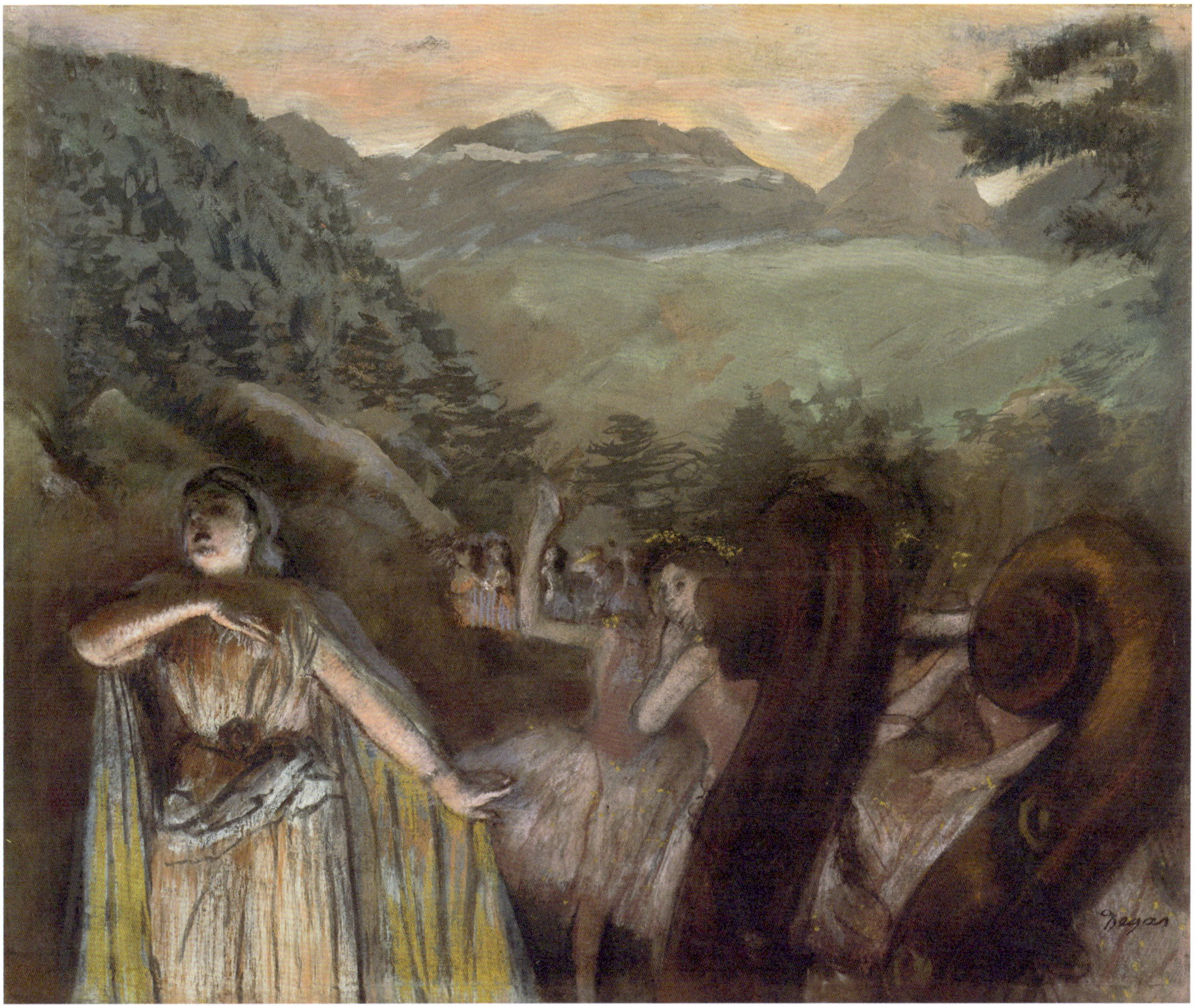

monotype lies below the present image, it is invisible: the artist applied rich, liquid passages of gouache, opaque and sometimes surprisingly thick, to fill the background. On top of this brushed-on landscape, he drew vigorously in pastel color, applying skeins of strokes to define the singer's pleated robe, patches of pink, red, and blue to bring out the tutus of the dancers, and long, gestural strokes of red-brown and black, enhanced with orange and ocher, to conjure up the bass violins. Degas's gestural bravura, his technical sleight-of-hand, was, in fact, perfectly in keeping with the measure of his ambition to arouse and to amuse his audience.

GTMS

Edgar Degas French, 1834–1917

DANCER WITH A FAN, C. *1879*

Pastel on paper, 17¾ × 11⅜ in. (450 × 290 mm)
Signed upper left: *Degas*
Private collection

PROVENANCE Henri Rouart; Ernest Rouart; Denis Rouart; purchased December 1, 1965 by the current owner.

EXHIBITED Galeries Georges Petit, Paris, *Exposition Degas,* April 12–May 2, 1924, 66, no. 122; Hôtel Jean Charpentier, Paris, *Exposition de la Jeunesse vus par les maîtres français et étrangers du XVI au XIX siècle,* June 1–30, 1928, 29, no. 96; Musée de l'Orangerie des Tuileries, Paris, *Degas,* March–April, 1937, 80, no. 97; Galerie Gazette des Beaux-Arts, Paris, *Degas dans les collections françaises,* 1955, 45, no. 84; Durand-Ruel, Paris, *Edgar Degas,* June 9–October 1, 1960, no. 25; City Art Museum, St. Louis, January 20–February 26, 1967, Philadelphia Museum of Art, March 10–April 30, 1967, and Minneapolis Society of Fine Arts, May 18–June 25, 1967, *Drawings by Degas,* 148, no. 93; Philbrook Art Center, Tulsa, *French and American Impressionism,* October 2–November 26, 1967, no. 3; Dallas Museum of Art, *Dallas Collects: Impressionist and Early Modern Masters,* January 24–February 26, 1978, no. 11; Dallas Museum of Art, *Impressionist and Early Modern Masters in Dallas,* September 3–October 22, 1989, 25, pl. 27, no. 27; Joslyn Art Museum, Omaha, February 7–May 3, 1998, Sterling and Francine Clark Art Institute, Williamstown, Mass., May 30–September 8, 1998, and Baltimore Museum of Art, October 4, 1998–January 3, 1999, *Degas and the Little Dancer,* no. 27; Dallas Museum of Art, *All the World's a Stage: Celebrating Performance in the Visual Arts,* August 30, 2009–February 28, 2010.

BIBLIOGRAPHY Galerie Manzi-Joyoant 1912, 21, no. 75; Alexandre 1912, 130; Rouart 1945, 22; Lemoisne 1946, vol. 2, 203, no. 545; Cabanne 1958, 42, 98, 108; Cabanne 1960, 35, pl. 16.

Edgar Degas is most famous for his images of the dance, in particular the ballet of the Paris Opera. His first paintings of dancers showed them in performance, glimpsed above the heads of musicians in the orchestra pit, but by 1871 he had painted the first of his many pictures of dancers in rehearsal in the practice rooms of the opera. From then on, whether shown in practice or in performance, alone or in groups, the ballet dancer interested him passionately and became the subject of paintings, drawings, pastels, and prints of varying degrees of complexity and finish, right up to the last years of his working life.

By the late 1870s, when he completed *Dancer with a Fan,* Degas showed a recurring interest in depicting a certain type of dancer. His models were often young, even teenagers, long-limbed and generally thin, with pronounced bone structure, frequently showing bony shoulders, elbows, wrists, or knee and ankle joints. The most famous of his models was a young dancer from the opera ballet named Marie van Goethem, who posed for him repeatedly around 1878–1880 and on whose form and face he modeled his most famous sculpture, *Little Dancer, Aged Fourteen,* which premiered at the impressionist exhibition of 1881.

Presumably around the same time, Degas wrote a sonnet about a young student of the Paris ballet. The sonnet has often been linked to his sculpture, but it might apply equally to all the youthful dancers the artist depicted in these years—young women, that is, like *Dancer with a Fan*:

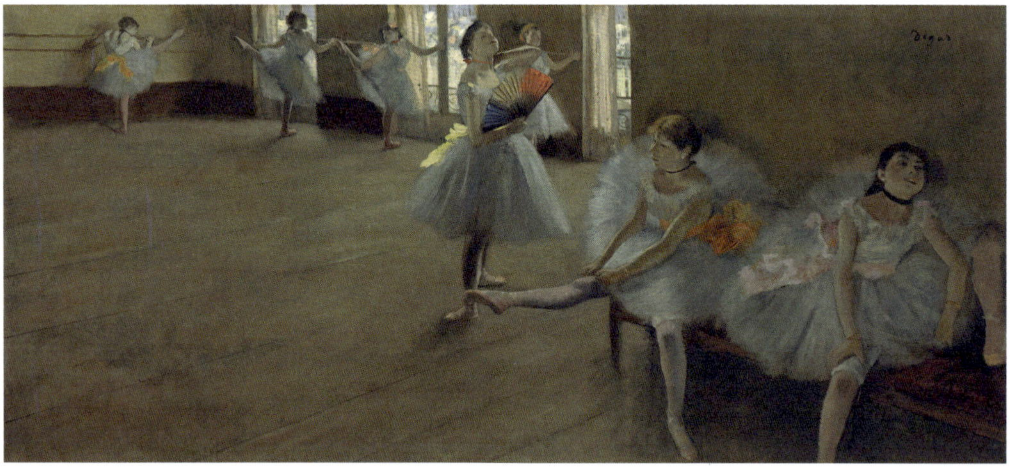

Fig. 9 Edgar Degas, *Dancers in a Classroom,* c. 1880. Oil on canvas. Sterling and Francine Clark Art Institute, Williamstown, Massachusetts.

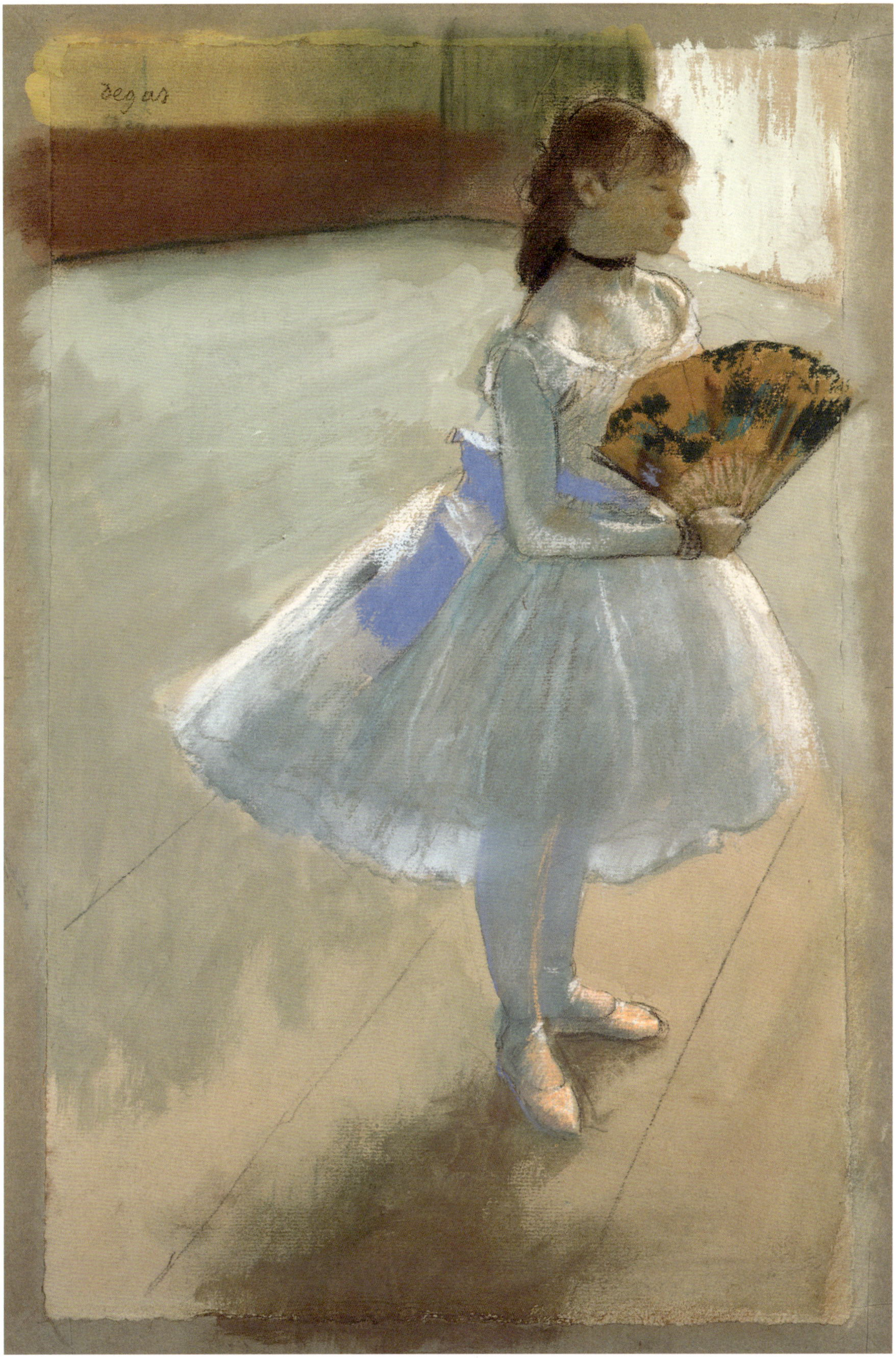
Degas

Little Dancer

Dance, winged scamp, dance on the wooden
lawns,
Love only that—let dancing be your life.
Your skinny arm assumes the attitude
And balances your flight against your weight.

Taglioni, come, Princess of Arcady!
Nymphs, Graces, come you souls of yore,
Ennoble and endow, smiling at my choice,
With form the boldfaced little neophyte.

Montmartre may give the breeding and the
mind,
Roxelane the nose, and China the eyes—
But vigilant Ariel offers this recruit

The dancing feet of daylight and of dark.
Then for my pleasure let her know her worth
And keep, in the golden hall, the gutter's
breed.[1]

TRANSLATED BY RICHARD HOWARD

The "boldfaced little neophyte" in the shadow of the "Graces . . . of Yore," the "skinny arm" that balances the dancer's "flight against [her] weight," her "gutter's breed" that she must grasp and maintain in "the golden hall" of the opera—the words of Degas's sonnet set up a series of imaginative contrasts between elegant ideal beauty on the one hand and scampish awkwardness on the other that evoke both the mood and the making of *Dancer with a Fan*.

The pastel probably began, in fact, as a simple drawing of a young girl holding a fan, executed in fine black chalk on a buff-colored paper. At the beginning, the figure was almost certainly isolated against a blank background and was typical of the many studies of dancers in positions of repose that Degas executed in the course of his research. He kept them as a kind of stock of images that could be combined and recombined to populate the paintings and multifigured pastels of dancers that he was producing in increasing numbers in the later 1870s and into the 1880s. Among those paintings is the well-known *Dancers in a Classroom* of about 1880 at the Sterling and Francine Clark Art Institute (fig. 9, p. 128). For each of the dancers depicted in this elaborate composition—the dancer pulling on her stocking, the exhausted dancer seated beside her, or the dancer preening with a fan at center—there exist study drawings in pencil or black chalk, sometimes charcoal, or even pastel. These simple working drawings could serve Degas for years, kept back by him as part of his catalogue of possibilities. On the other hand, they could, with a bit more attention, be transformed into appealing pictures for the market, and this is what Degas did in *Dancer with a Fan*.

The initial sketch of the dancer, likely very slight, was given a background that Degas used on many occasions to denote a classroom for the Paris Opera ballet. A line or two were enough to indicate the line between the rising floor and the rear wall, pierced by a curtained window that brought light into the space. Having established the space around the figure, Degas began to enhance the drawing with color. At some point in the process—before the application of color, or while he was still working—he decided that the sheet he had first drawn on was slightly too small for his composition and mounted it to a larger sheet of paper; when finished, the dancer's fan would touch the right edge of the composition but not be cropped by its frame. To complete the picture, the artist used both dry pastels, which he applied in chalky strokes that he could blend as needed, and liquid gouache, painted on with a soft, broad brush. The paints and pastels that described the floor and wall extended beyond the original sheet onto its secondary support.

Degas's mastery of both wet and dry techniques is particularly apparent in the dancer's body and in her costume. Using the warm color of the paper as his base, he applied smudges of yellowish brown and soft greenish blue to indicate shadow, casting the girl's face into contre-jour and shading the right angle of her arm. Reflected light on her shoulders, collarbone, and chest was captured with strokes of white pastel, caught against the texture of the paper to create subtle halftones. The layers of tulle that made up the dancer's tutu were described with a variety of means: quick strokes of black chalk indicated the contours of the outer skirt and its underlayer, as well as the folds of the gathered cloth; blue and white pastel were worked in thin and thick passages over the buff paper, blended with a wet brush or with a dry finger or rag, to suggest translucent and opaque layers; and white and blue pastel indicated highlights on the skirt's upper layer. The dancer's stockings, in shadow, were indicated with washes of blue gouache, while the insteps of her feet and her shoes, in the sunlight, were made more luminous by the addition of strokes of pink and peach pastel. As if a final touch, the dancer's fan was touched with the brown, ocher, and dark green pigments that Degas had used for the wall beyond, bringing the distant background into harmony with the figure. Having first signed the pastel near the intersection of yellow and brown on the wall, Degas smudged that signature and signed his work a second time, in the yellow, indicating that the work was finished and ready to be given or sold to his friend Henri Rouart.

GTMS

Note
1. Gordon and Forge 1988, 204.

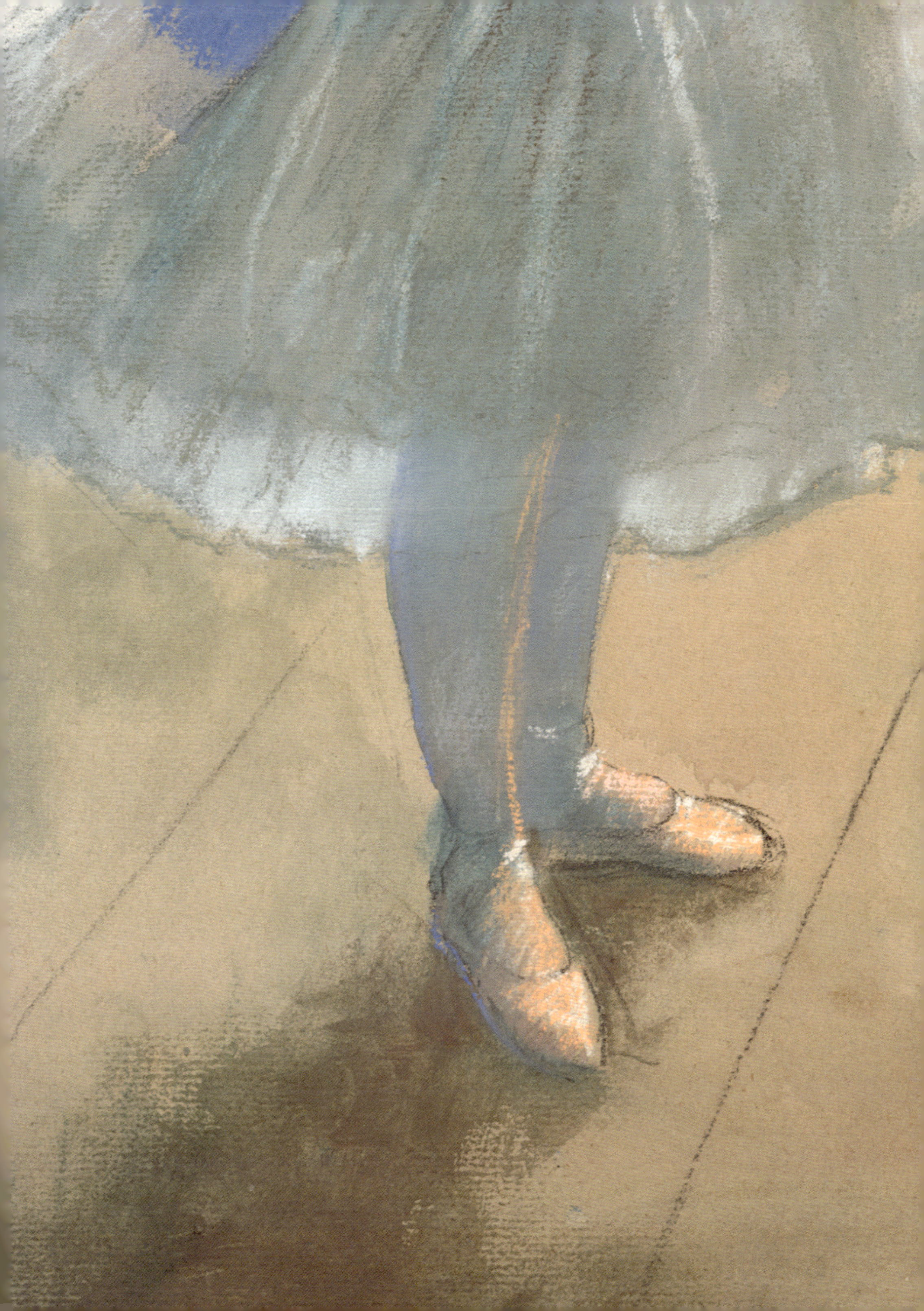

59

Edgar Degas French, 1834–1917

BALLET DANCERS ON THE STAGE, *1883*

Pastel on paper, 24¼ × 18⅝ in. (616 × 473 mm)
Signed lower left: *Degas*
Dallas Museum of Art, gift of Mr. and Mrs. Franklin B. Bartholow, 1986.277

PROVENANCE (Possibly Durand-Ruel, lot 596, purchased from the artist December 13, 1884; sold April 25, 1885 to Peter Coats); Durand-Ruel, Paris, before 1888; Dr. Georges Viau, Paris, before 1918; Wilhelm Hansen, Copenhagen; with Winkel and Magnussen, Copenhagen; with Galerie Barbazanges, Paris, until March 1921; Durand-Ruel, Paris, March 12, 1921, no. 2378; transferred to Durand-Ruel, New York, no. 4650; where purchased December 15, 1925, by Mr. and Mrs. Frank F. Ginn, Cleveland, and with them until at least 1936; Mr. and Mrs. William Powell Jones, Gates Mills, Ohio, before 1947; Mr. and Mrs. Algur Meadows, Dallas, before 1974 and until 1982; by descent to Mr. and Mrs. Franklin B. Bartholow, Dallas, 1982–1986; Dallas Museum of Art, gift of Mr. and Mrs. Franklin B. Bartholow, 1986.

EXHIBITED Durand-Ruel, Paris, January 1888; Pennsylvania Museum of Art, Philadelphia, *Degas,* 1936, no. 42; Cleveland Museum of Art, *Works by Edgar Degas,* February 5–March 9, 1947, no. 39; Wildenstein and Co., New York, *A Loan Exhibition of Degas,* April 7–May 14, 1949, no. 64; Dallas Museum of Fine Arts, *The Meadows Collection,* June 5–July 7, 1974; Seibu Museum of Art, Tokyo, September 23–November 3, 1976, Kyoto Municipal Museum of Art, Japan, November 7–December 10, 1976, and Fukuoka Cultural Center, Japan, December 18, 1976–January 16, 1977, *Exposition Degas;* Dallas Museum of Fine Arts, *Dallas Collects: Impressionist and Early Modern Masters,* January 24–February 26, 1978, no. 12; National Gallery of Art, Washington, *Degas: The Dancers,* November 22, 1984–March 10, 1985, 38–38, no. 8; Galeries nationales du Grand Palais, Paris, February 9–May 16, 1988, Musée des Beaux-Arts du Canada, Ottawa, June 16–August 28, 1988, and Metropolitan Museum of Art, New York, September 27, 1988–January 8, 1989, *Degas,* no. 259 *(Danseuses en Scène);* Dallas Museum of Art, *Impressionist and Modern Masters in Dallas,* September 3–October 22, 1989, 79, no. 26; Art Institute of Chicago, *Degas: Beyond Impressionism,* September 28, 1996–January 5, 1997, 181, no. 7; Detroit Institute of Arts, October 20, 2002–January 12, 2003, and Philadelphia Museum of Art, February 12–May 11, 2003, *Degas and the Dance,* pl. 107; Dallas Museum of Art, *All the World's a Stage: Celebrating Performance in the Visual Arts,* August 30, 2009–February 28, 2010.

BIBLIOGRAPHY Fénéon 1888, vol. 16, 309; Lafond 1918, 2; Hoppe 1922, 51–52; Jamot 1924, 152; Lemoisne 1946, 112, 408; Browse 1949, 374; Rich 1951, 26; Bouret 1965, 121; Browse 1967, 114; Russoli and Minervino 1970, 122–23; Terrasse 1976, 8–13; Bromberg 1986, 11–13; Gordon and Forge 1988, 212; San Francisco Museum of Modern Art 2000, 291–92; Moore and Sickert 2011, 65; Dallas Museum of Art 2012, 210; MacDonald 2013, 79–82.

The viewer of *Aria after the Ballet* (cat. 57) was placed in the stalls of the Paris Opera, the seats on the ground floor of the theater, and was seated right up front, just beside the musicians. That seat could only have been occupied by a man in Degas's day, and the seats at the front of the stalls were regularly occupied by opera subscribers: men who held season tickets so that they could go again and again to the performances, in part to hear the singing and playing, but mostly—at least in the popular imagination—to see the dance. The subscribers—in French, the *abonnés*—were well-heeled men who were, more often than not, the patrons and protectors of the female dancers. Beyond the theater itself, literally behind the scenes, in the grand *foyer de la danse* where the *abonnés* mingled with the dancers or in the dancers' dressing rooms, the black-coated gentlemen could be seen among the brightly clad young women who made up the *corps de ballet.*

Degas delighted in this juxtaposition of male and female elements, and he often showed the men as distant silhouettes in the corners of his stage views or ogling the dancers while they completed their toilettes. In both *Aria after the Ballet* and *Ballet Dancers on the Stage,* however, he determined not to depict the man—and yet the man's point of view makes him palpably present. Here, the dancers are crushed together so closely, and so close to the viewer, that only one of them—the dancer in blue at upper left—can be seen more or less in her entirety. The close point of view crops almost all the rest, eliminating heads or arms of some, and allowing one, at lower right, to appear only as a disembodied hand and forearm. All of this closeness presupposes that the viewer is either standing just behind the proscenium arch or sitting in one of the boxes immediately beside the stage floor, reserved for the administration of the opera and its friends.

The point of view Degas chose, which would have resonated with viewers in his time, also gave him the pretext for one of his most adventurous compositions. A line from upper left to lower right divides the writhing jumble of dancers' bodies from the plain buff triangle of the stage. The figures' proximity to the gaslights at the front of the stage throws their faces into ghostly pallor and casts deep shadows on the backs of their arms and hands. The brilliant orchestration of

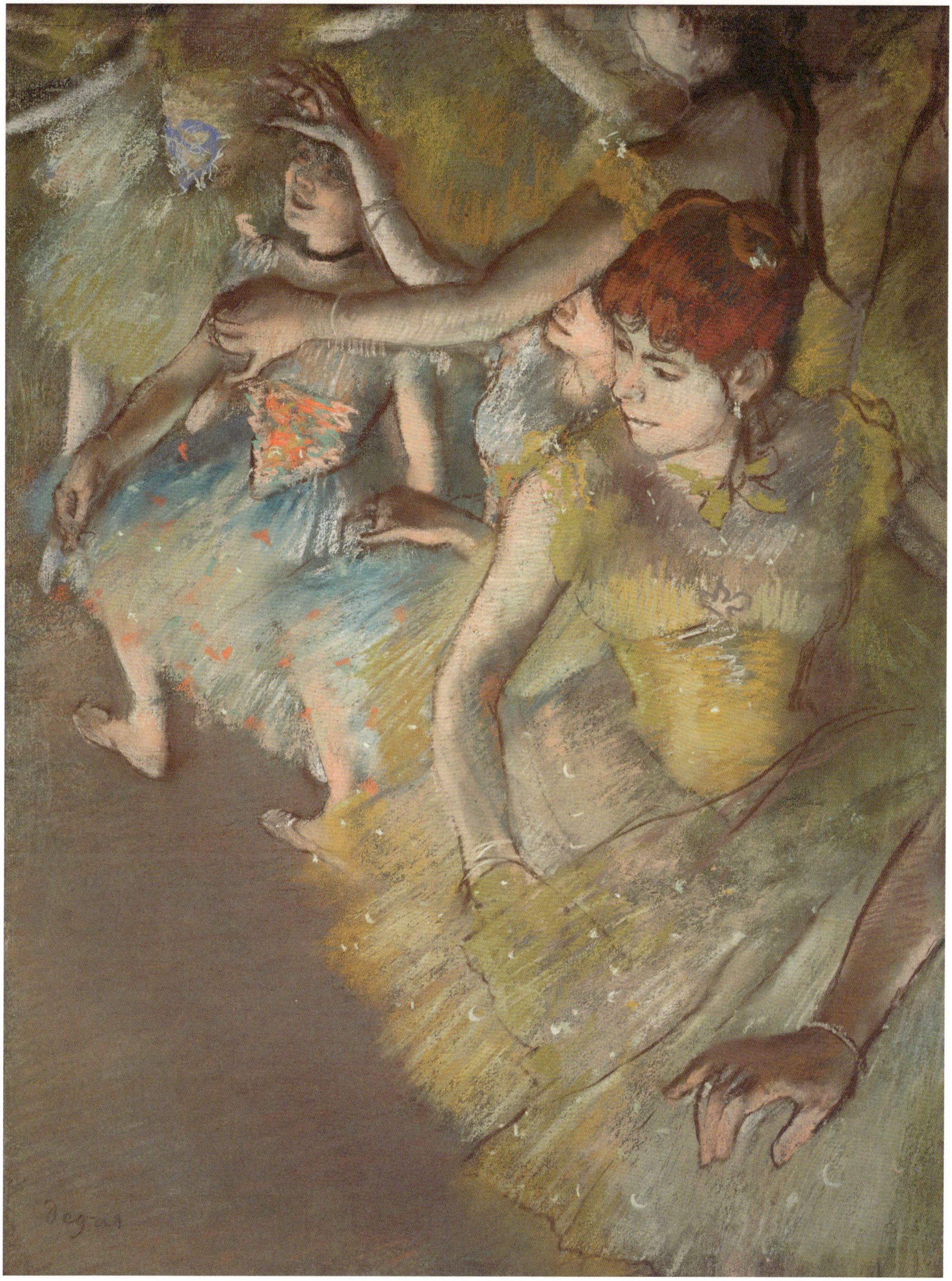

earthy flesh colors—bone white, ivory, pink, gray, and brown—is juxtaposed with the artificial hues of bright blue and bitter yellow for the costumes and garish red for the dyed hair of the principal dancer at right. Every manner of application of pastel is present, from the smooth-seeming, finely hatched triangle at the foreground, to the scumbled and dot-flecked costumes, to the boldly redrawn contours of the dancers' arms. Startling in conception, brilliant in execution, this is one of the artist's greatest achievements in depicting the world of the dance and the Paris Opera ballet.

GTMS

Edgar Degas French, 1834–1917

ALEXIS ROUART, *1895*

Pastel and charcoal on tracing paper mounted on buff paper, 22¼ × 15¾ in.
(565 × 400 mm)
Signed lower right: *Degas*; inscribed and dated upper right: *Alexis Rouart mars 1895*
Private collection, Dallas

PROVENANCE Louis Heim, Paris; Mme Bloch, Paris; Wildenstein & Co., Inc., New York (by 1972); private collection, New York (by 1976); sale, Christie's, New York, May 5, 2011, lot 00116; where purchased by current owner.

EXHIBITED Berner Kunstmuseum, Bern, *Degas*, November 1951–January 1952, no. 110; Wildenstein & Co., New York, *Faces from the World of Impressionism and Post-Impressionism, A Loan Exhibition for the Benefit of The New York Chapter of the Arthritis Foundation*, November–December 1972, no. 25; *Centennial Fair in Celebration of the Philadelphia Museum of Art's 100th Birthday*, Philadelphia City Calvary, Armory of the First Troop, October 1975; Seibu Museum of Art, Tokyo, September 23–November 3, 1976, Kyoto Municipal Museum of Art, November 7–December 10, 1976, and Fukuoka Cultural Center, December 18, 1976–January 16, 1977, *Exposition Degas*, no. 50; Kunsthalle Tübingen, Germany, and Nationalgalerie, *Edgar Degas, Pastelle, Olskizzen, Zeichnungen*, Berlin, January–May 1984, 81, no. 193; Kunsthalle Tübingen, Germany, *Degas Portraits*, March–June 1995, no. 178.

BIBLIOGRAPHY Terrasse 1972, 65, no. 6; *Pictures on Exhibit* 1972, 13, ill.; Brame and Reff 1984, 152, no. 139; Boggs et al. 1988, 544, fig. 304; Maheux 1992, 183.

"If I didn't have the Rouarts," Degas once said, "my God, I would be lonely! I'm lucky to have friends like them."[1] The brothers Rouart—Henri (1833–1912) and the younger Alexis (1833–1911)—first knew Degas in their youth at the École Louis-le-Grand. Reconnecting at the time of the Franco-Prussian war, they formed an essential part of Degas's society from his youth to his old age. They were closer to him than any of his blood relations; he saw them weekly at their homes, filled with works of art of the highest quality and diversity, including some of the finest of his own paintings and drawings—among them *Dancer with a Fan* (cat. 58).

The Rouarts, industrialists by background, entered the milieu of vanguard Parisian art through their friendship with Degas, in part, and through their activities as collectors. In the next generation, the connections to the visual arts multiplied, as three of Henri's sons married the daughters of artists. Eugène and Louis married the sisters Yvonne and Christine Lerolle, daughters of the painter Henri Lerolle, themselves portrayed on several occasions by Pierre-Auguste Renoir. Ernest was to marry Julie Manet, the daughter and frequent model of Berthe Morisot (Mme. Eugène Manet) and niece of Édouard Manet.

Degas first painted his friend Henri Rouart in 1871–1872, seated with his daughter and first child Hélène on his lap. Nearly a quarter century later, in 1895, the 60-year-old Degas embarked on another portrait of Henri, this time accompanied by his eldest son, another Alexis. We know precisely when work on the portrait began because of this forceful sheet, signed by the artist and inscribed, in a firm hand, "Alexis Rouart mars 1895." The drawing is part portrait and part costume study: in the painting that it precedes, Alexis is shown in street clothes, hatted and pulling on a glove as if about to take leave of his seated father, wearing a skull cap. (A second preparatory work on paper, extensively worked with pastel, in the collection of Scott M. Black, also helped prepare for the final painting, now in the Neue Pinakothek, Munich.)

In the drawing, Degas concentrated first on the young man's clothing, starting with bold strokes of charcoal, sketching the outline of his bulky overcoat and bowler hat before rubbing in shadows with his thumb. Then he went over the whole coat and the hat with strong parallel lines of black chalk, finally re-scribing the most important contours of shoulder, sleeve, collar, and hat brim with even darker lines. Between the deep shadow of the hat on his head and the black tie around his neck, Alexis Rouart's face seems to hover, almost puzzled, as if he is not quite sure what the painter might be up to. Perfectly still, he stares Degas in the eye, but the artist suggests something of his nervousness in the slight disparity between the size of one eye and the other, by the arch of an eyebrow at right. A few strokes of colored pastel suffice to suggest the young man's complexion: pale pink is joined with deep red and touches of white to describe his cheeks, nose, jawline, and ear, and a hint of ocher indicates his fair facial hair.

Degas, known for his scathing wit, was sentimental when it came to his friends. Among Degas's last major works is a magnificent charcoal and pastel group portrait of the wife of the young Alexis Rouart, Valentine, with their daughters, the toddler Hélène and young Madeleine. Surely it was the birth of Madeleine, in 1896, that prompted Degas to write a poignant note of

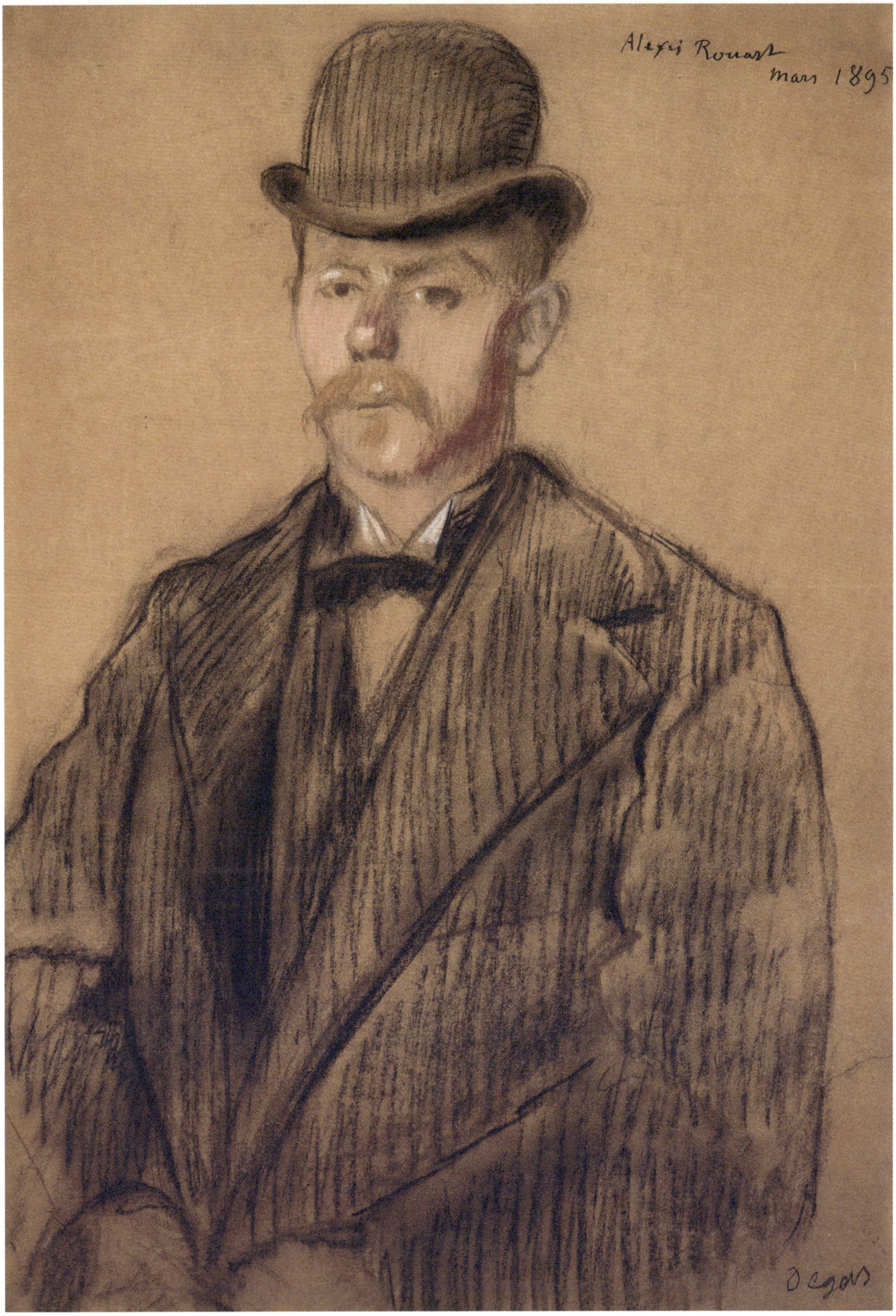

Notes
1. Loyrette 1991, 651.
2. Degas to Henri Rouart, May 25, 1896, quoted in Kendall 1987, 246.
3. Ibid.

congratulation to the baby's grandfather, his old friend Henri: "So here is your posterity on the march," Degas wrote. "You will be blessed, oh righteous man, in your children and your children's children."[2] But the Degas the Rouarts loved and admired, increasingly aware of his mortality, countered his friendly blessings with a touch of lonely melancholy. "During my cold," he said to his friend, "I am meditating on the state of celibacy, and a good three-quarters of what I tell myself is sad."[3]

GTMS

Edgar Degas French, 1834–1917

THE BATHERS, C. *1895–1900*

Pastel and charcoal on tracing paper, 42⅞ × 43¾ in. (1089 × 1111 mm)
Stamped lower left: *Degas* (Lugt 658)
Dallas Museum of Art, The Wendy and Emery Reves Collection, 1985.R.24

PROVENANCE Studio of the artist Edgar Degas, sale I, 1918, no. 212, purchased by Ambroise Vollard, Paris; Ambroise Vollard until the winter of 1946–47; Emery Reves, France; given to the Dallas Museum of Art, The Wendy and Emery Reves Collection, 1985.

EXHIBITED *Galerie Georges Petit, Atelier Edgar Degas: 1re Vente,* Paris, May 6–8, 1918, no. 212; Galerie Vollard, Paris, *Degas,* 1936; Smith College Museum of Art, Northampton, Mass., April 1951–December 1952; Metropolitan Museum of Art, New York, 1953–1955; Musée Massena, Nice, *Chefs-d'oeuvre de la peinture français,* November 27, 1956–January 6, 1957; Galerie Charpentier, Paris, *Cent Chefs-d'œuvre de l'art français, 1750–1950,* 1957; Metropolitan Museum of Art, New York, *Degas,* September 27, 1988–January 8, 1989, 556; Dallas Museum of Art, *Impressionist and Modern Masters in Dallas,* September 3–October 22, 1989, 79, no. 26; San Francisco Museum of Modern Art, October 2, 1999–January 4, 2000, and Dallas Museum of Art, February 1–May 7, 2000, *Degas to Picasso: Painters, Sculptors, and the Camera,* 86, no. 27.

BIBLIOGRAPHY Lemoisne 1946, no. 1071 (*Baigneuses*); Dallas Museum of Art 1985b, 116–17; Brettell 1995, 118–19; Hofmann 2007, 248–49; Shackelford and Rey 2011, 209–10.

On an unusually large sheet of paper, Degas drew a group of women together in a landscape. Loosely gathered around a tree, they are shown in three positions: one bends over in the background, as if drying her lower leg; another, seated with her legs stretched straight before her, combs her long red hair over her face, and it streams over her breasts into her lap; a third reclines in the lower right corner of the sheet, her head outside the picture's borders. The main lines of the composition are drawn in charcoal first, in broad, sweeping gestures, sometimes repeated, that describe the nude bodies very generally, avoiding detail almost completely. The contour lines function as a network of near-abstract strokes that, with the addition of hatched and stumped shading, coalesce into body parts: a row of legs, a tangle of backs and arms. Color, applied last on top of the charcoal lines, gives further clarity to the scene: a deep blue indicates a rumpled skirt and, mixed with white and paler blue, serves as the color of grass. Dark pinks, reds, and browns define the earth, a woman's tresses, a back, and a distant cow.

The Bathers is one of a group of studies of nude women that have puzzled students of Degas's art for decades. The artist's earliest images of the nude showed figures in the landscape in ancient Sparta or medieval France. In the 1870s, he showed women, alone or in groups, in brothel interiors, gradually turning to scenes of ordinary domestic life. Through the 1880s and into the 1890s, Degas made drawings, prints, pastels, and paintings of bathers in Parisian bedrooms and bathrooms, on rare occasions accompanied by a clothed housemaid, but generally washing or drying themselves, or combing their hair, all alone. In this work, however, in a pastel of almost identical size at the Art Institute of Chicago, and in an even bigger drawing in the collection of the Musée des arts décoratifs, Paris, the artist seemed to revert to his beginnings, showing his bathers not alone but in the company of others, and not in a bedroom but in the out of doors.

The simple explanation for the works—including the Reves Collection drawing—is that Degas shows a group of women who have gone to the countryside, have had a swim in a stream or a river, and are relaxing afterward, drying themselves in the sunlight. Perhaps because of their unusually large size, however, the pastels seem to aim for some more symbolic or even decorative purpose, curiously combining the stately preoccupations of the classicizing murals of Puvis de Chavannes with the organized chaos of Paul Cézanne's bathers in landscape settings. Paul Gauguin's large nudes—Degas owned one from 1895 on—may also offer a point of comparison. But these works are also ruminations on Degas's past, modern and monumental refigurations of the brutalized women in his 1865 *Scene of War in the Middle Ages,* or the disorderly gangs of working girls in his brothel monotypes of 1876. The strange and troubling clusters of nudes in those works prefigured the women in this extraordinary drawing, just as they seem to forecast the harrowing nudes of Pablo Picasso's *Demoiselles d'Avignon* of 1907 or the uneasy models of Lucien Freud.

GTMS

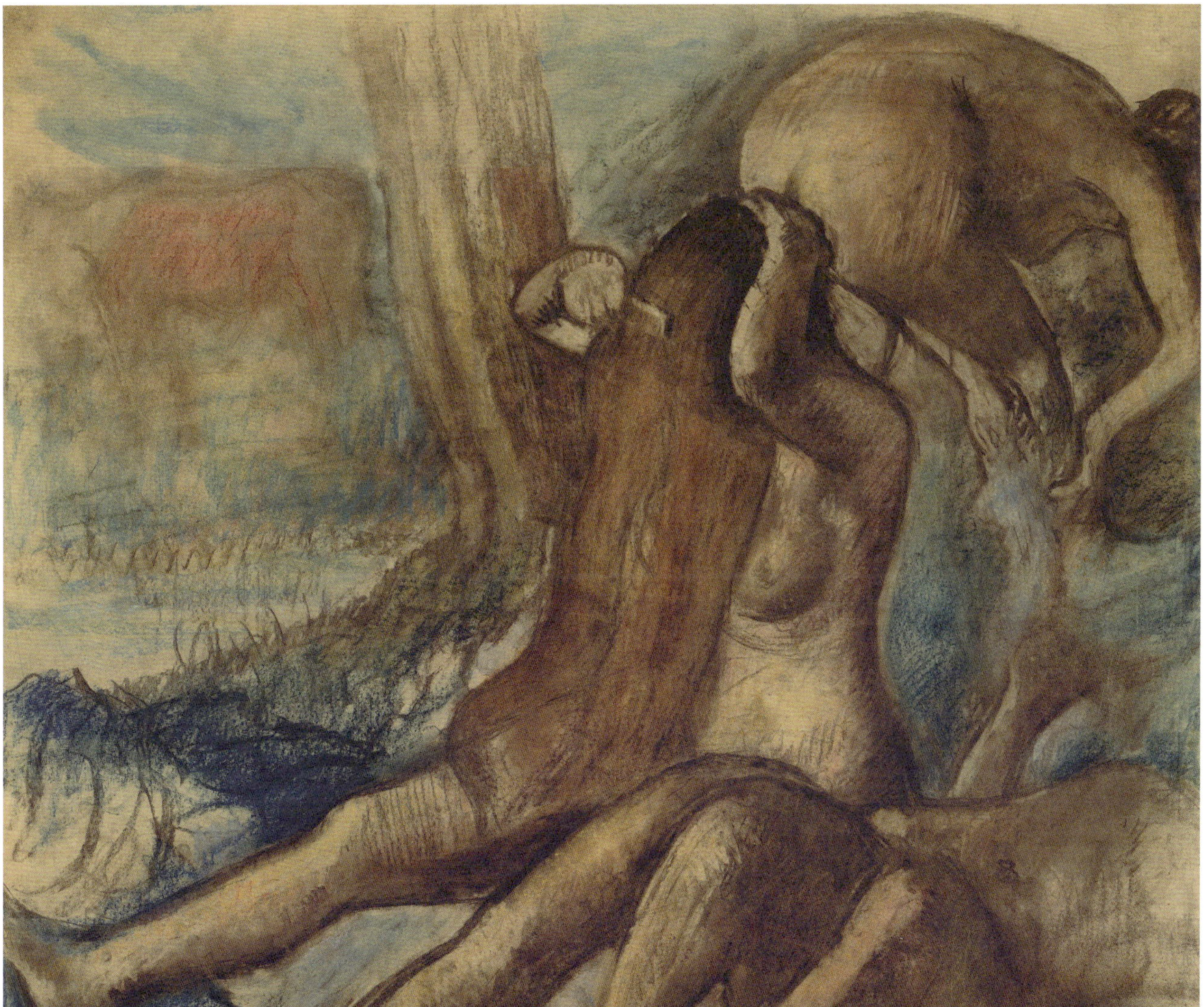

Edgar Degas French, 1834–1917

AFTER THE BATH, WOMAN DRYING HERSELF (APRÈS LE BAIN, FEMME S'ESSUYANT), C. *1900*

Charcoal and brown pastel on two sheets of tracing paper mounted on wove paper, 31 × 14½ in. (788 × 368 mm)
Stamped lower left: *Degas* (Lugt 658)
Private collection, Dallas

PROVENANCE Studio of the artist Edgar Degas, sale II, no. 320; sale, Christie's, London, November 29, 1988, lot. 323; Galerie Schmit, Paris; where purchased September 27, 1999, by the current owner.

BIBLIOGRAPHY *Master Drawings and Sculpture* 2014, 146, under no. 51, fig. 1.

After Degas's death in 1917, his heirs found thousands of works of art—his own—in his studio, a lifetime of paintings, pastels, prints, wax sculpture, and above all, drawings. Five of the nine drawings by Degas in this exhibition were still with him when he died. They are the academic drawing of a seated man (cat. 45), studies of a running youth (cat. 46) and of a horse (cat. 47), and two late charcoal drawings of nudes: one showing women in a landscape (cat. 61), and this powerful sheet showing a nude drying herself. Of the five, the charcoals and the study of the running youth were not kept by Degas's heirs, but were sold in the great auctions held of his studio contents, the previews for which became the equivalent of a four-part retrospective exhibition. The works Degas produced after about 1895—from the last dozen years of his life—astonished even his intimate friends. One of them, Daniel Halévy, the son of Degas's schoolmate Ludovic Halévy, recorded his reactions, as if speaking to his departed older friend:

> We looked at these walls covered with works that were powerful but horrible, which frightened us all the more because the energy of their lines and the beauty of their tones kept us from looking at or thinking of anything else. One hundred, two hundred examples of cynical nudity, that is what we were shown. The drawings of your youth hung beside them, contrasted with them. We saw your mother, your sisters, your friends, intimate scenes of a solid bourgeoisie, refined and musical, the products of an art wholly inspired by the old masters of Tuscany and France, by Mantegna and Clouet, by Pisanello and Ingres. But these beautiful studies were surpassed by the works of your somber virility.[1]

More daring in their drawing style than anything he had exhibited in his lifetime, the charcoal studies and pastels that were first shown in 1918—works like *After the Bath, Woman Drying Herself*—were a revelation. They revealed a brutal, beautiful Degas that was vitally modern. The bold charcoal lines of *The Bathers* (cat. 61) or *After the Bath,* works made within a few years of the turn of the century, are as forceful as the contemporaneous works of Henri Matisse or Pablo Picasso, artists who would have encountered Degas's most modern works at the gallery of Ambroise Vollard.

Like the Reves Collection *Bathers, After the Bath* is drawn in charcoal on tracing paper, Degas's favored medium from the 1890s onward. He particularly appreciated the ways in which tracing paper—made for mostly technical use by architects or for the replication of imagery by lesser hands than his own—could serve his own purposes. He used tracings to multiply compositions: *After the Bath* may well have begun as a tracing from a fully rendered pastel. Degas's drawings also suggest that he liked the ways in which the slick tracing paper received the densely black but powdery charcoal. Here, the contours of the figure—particularly the back, hip, thigh, and calf at left—show evidence of repeated applications of dense charcoal that has been rubbed, erased, and redrawn. Using his fingers or a rag to make gray tones from the smudged charcoal, Degas pulls those tones away with an eraser to make highlights—on the woman's back and shoulders or on the lip of the bathtub to her right. Little color has been added—just a few touches of brown intermingle with the charcoal lines that define the woman's upswept hair, and scattered lines of white pastel reinforce the highlights on the woman's skin. The drawing's power comes from the artist's control of his medium, his own willingness to stop work at the right moment, when the drawing had achieved the perfect balance of audacity and precision.

GTMS

Note
1. Daniel Halévy, "À Edgar Degas," *Le Divan* 61 (1919), reprinted in Loyrette 1991, iv.

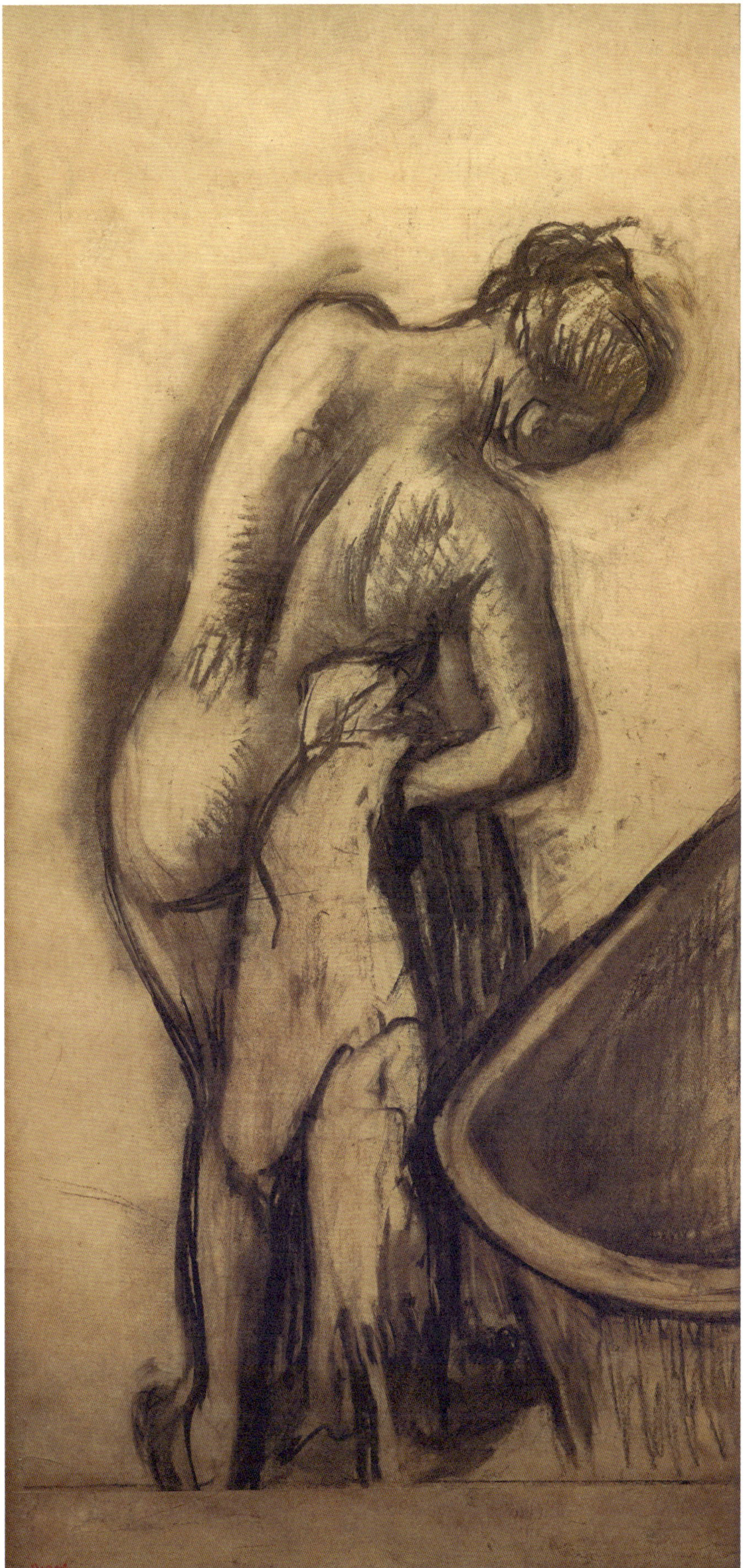

63

Pierre-Auguste Renoir French, 1841–1919

M. JULES LE COEUR AND MLLE LISE TRÉHOT, *1866–1867*

Watercolor on wove paper, 10 × 7 in. (254 × 178 mm)
Signed lower right: *A. Renoir*
Dallas Museum of Art, The Wendy and Emery Reves Collection, 1985.R.61

PROVENANCE Clémence Tréhot until about 1921; Dr. Matza, Paris, about 1921–at least 1933; Jacques Helft, Paris, by 1959; Emery Reves, France, by 1969; given to the Dallas Museum of Art, The Wendy and Emery Reves Collection, 1985.

EXHIBITED Musée de l'Orangerie, Paris, *Renoir,* 1933, no. 127 (M. Jules Le Coeur et Le Modèle Lisa); Dallas Museum of Art, *Impressionist and Modern Masters in Dallas,* September 3–October 22, 1989, 85, no. 100 (*The Stolen Kiss [Jules Le Coeur and Clémence Tréhot]*), ill.; Dallas Museum of Art, *Impressions from the Riviera,* November 5, 1995–February 4, 1996 (*M. Jules Le Coeur and Mlle Clémence Tréhot*).

BIBLIOGRAPHY Cooper 1959, 322–28, ill.; Fosca 1961, p11; Daulte 1969, 88–89, color ill.; Dallas Museum of Art 1985b, 100–01, color ill.; Brettell 1995, 36–37, color ill.; Dauberville and Dauberville, 2007, 623, no. 673; MacDonald 2013, 27, color ill.

Watercolor is a thoroughly British medium, and although many great French artists adapted it for their use, the history of watercolor in France is largely confined to the second half of the 19th century. The French Watercolor Society was not formed until 1878. Pierre-Auguste Renoir used the medium throughout his working life. Trained as a porcelain painter, he would have found it good preparation for work with transparent glazes.

Renoir was the preeminent impressionist painter of the middle class. Immensely prolific as a painter, he was probably equally prolific as a graphic artist. Unfortunately, neither his paintings nor his works on paper have been systematically catalogued, so it is difficult to make generalizations about his art. The drawings are understudied and have not been the subject of the specialized attention given to the drawings of any other major impressionist.

This watercolor has been dated convincingly to 1866–1867 and thus is from the first important decade in Renoir's working life. Because it is signed, the work was likely made with either exhibition or sale in mind, perhaps even as a souvenir of a tender moment in the garden.

Like many of the Renoirs in the Reves collection, this one led Emery Reves and his friend the scholar-connoisseur Douglas Cooper along a delightful path in their efforts to identify the subjects. Combining circumstantial information from the original owner with archival research, Cooper identified the man as the painter Jules Le Coeur, with whom Renoir maintained a close relationship between 1865 and 1870. Le Coeur and Renoir met while painting in the Forest of Fontainebleau (Renoir included his friend in *Jules Le Coeur in the Forest of Fontainebleau,* 1866, Museu de Arte, São Paulo), and it is likely that this watercolor was painted in a garden near Marlotte, where both painters were staying. Le Coeur was widowed and had a close friendship with Clémence Tréhot, whom Reves and Cooper identified as the woman represented here. Yet this identification may be incorrect. Renoir had an intimate relationship with Clémence's sister Lise, who was his favorite model at the time. He had depicted her in an identical costume in three other paintings of 1867,[1] and there is no evidence that Clémence was ever a model.

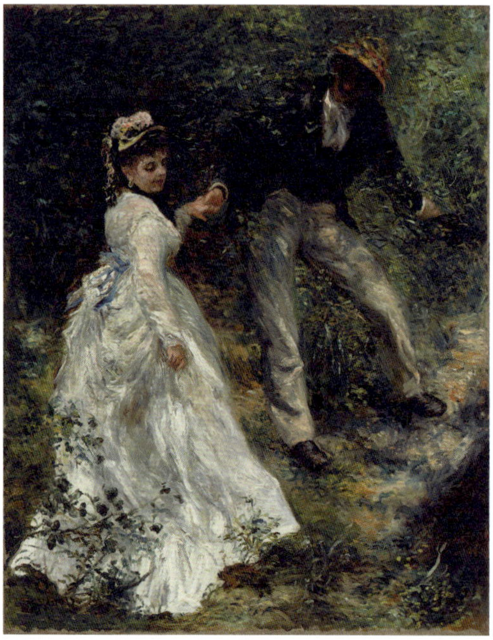

Fig. 10 Pierre-Auguste Renoir, *La Promenade,* 1870. Oil on canvas. The J. Paul Getty Museum, Los Angeles, 89.PA.41.

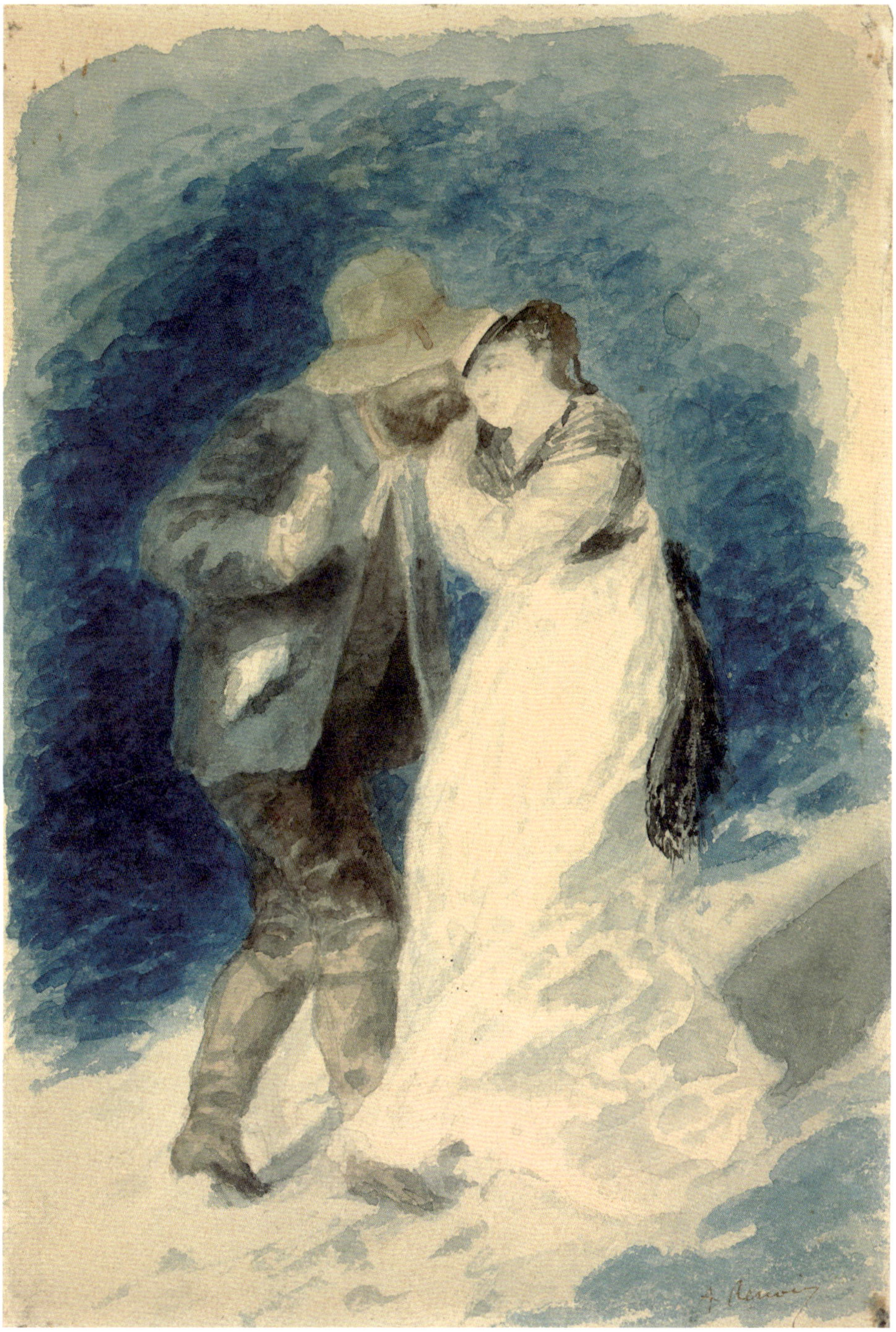

What seems at first to be an innocent encounter in a garden becomes, on closer inspection, an oddly ambiguous scene. Le Coeur is dressed in rough country garb and moves aggressively toward "Clémence." She seems to resist his advance, her hand raised to push his face away. The dark blue background does little to lessen the effect of an unwanted or overly insistent advance. The easy, sun-dappled effect gives way to a reading that is utterly unlike the familiar scenes of lighthearted *fêtes galantes.* What did Renoir mean by this watercolor? Did he intend to "illustrate" a passage from Émile Zola's 1867 novel *Thérèse Raquin*? Or was he simply recording a scene in a garden? If we were meant to know the identity of the models, as we do today, does the scene record Renoir's jealousy of Le Coeur? Or, more probably, were these friends of Renoir used simply as models in his delicate attempt to study in watercolor the tensions in male-female relationships? Renoir's composition raises more questions than it answers.

The watercolor acted as an informal prototype for Renoir's 1870 painting of a similar subject, *La Promenade* in the J. Paul Getty Museum, Los Angeles (fig. 10).

RRB

Note
1. Daulte 1969, 29, 31, 33.

Pierre-Auguste Renoir French, 1841–1919

THE BATHER, C. *1880–1881*

Red chalk on wove tissue paper mounted on board,
33¼ × 25¾ in. (845 × 655 mm)
Signed upper right: *Renoir*
Dallas Museum of Art, The Wendy and Emery Reves Collection, 1985.R.57

PROVENANCE Ambroise Vollard, Paris; Madame de Galéa, Paris; Sam Salz Gallery, New York; where purchased by Emery Reves, France; given to the Dallas Museum of Art, The Wendy and Emery Reves Collection, 1985.

EXHIBITED Dallas Museum of Art, *Impressionist and Modern Masters in Dallas*, September 3–October 22, 1989, 85, no. 105; Dallas Museum of Art, *Renoir and Algeria*, June 8–August 31, 2003.

BIBLIOGRAPHY Fosca 1961, 180–81; Drucker 1967, no. 71; Dallas Museum of Art 1986, 13; Brettell 1995, 76–77, color ill.; Dauberville and Dauberville 2007, 616, no. 660.

The Bather is among the most important surviving drawings by Renoir. It relates, without question, to the famous painting *Blonde Bather*, 1881, in the Clark Art Institute, Williamstown (fig. 11). Renoir is said to have painted this work in Naples while on his first trip to Italy, where he studied the art of the ancient world and the Renaissance, as his fellow Frenchmen had done since the late 16th century. He had moved beyond impressionism by 1880 and sought in Italy inspiration from great past art. In this way, his motivations were exactly the opposite of those of the founders of impressionism, who stressed an art rooted in daily life and the varied appearances of the modern world.

The Bather has many layers of tradition. First, its subject of a female bather alludes to a long tradition of similar images—Susanna at the bath, Diana, or Venus—that populate Renaissance and baroque painting, drawing, and printmaking. Within this tradition, the nude more often reclines than sits; in creating a seated nude, Renoir allowed the nude an identity as a person, free to move as she wishes. And by giving her a prominent wedding ring, as can be seen in *Blonde Bather*, Renoir made her not only contemporary but also above reproach in her nudity. He created a thoroughly modern "goddess" who carries allusions to both the Bible and classical mythology.

A second fascinatingly traditional aspect of the drawing is its medium-red chalk, or *sanguine*, which Renoir began using only in the late 1870s and early 1880s. This sheet can be considered his first masterpiece in the medium. The technique has a powerful history in French art, with its most important roots in the drawings of 18th-century masters such as François Boucher, Jean-Honoré Fragonard, and Hubert Robert (see cat. 1).

It is likely that this sheet was drawn from the model in Naples in preparation for the 1881 painting, which Renoir apparently began there and gave to his friend Henri Vever on returning to France. The figures in the drawing and the painting are of identical dimension, guaranteeing their one-to-one relationship.

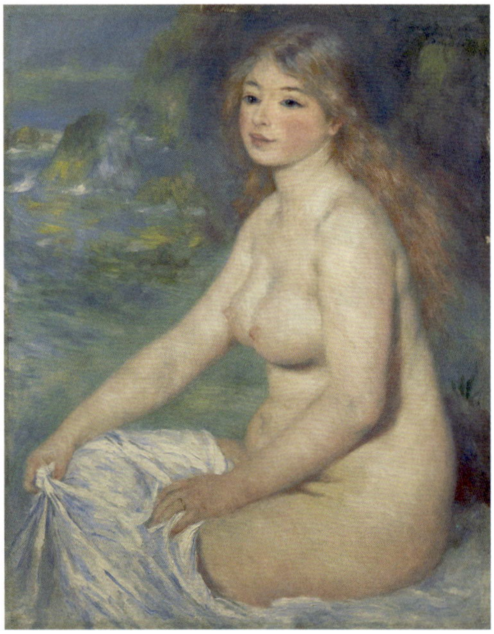

Fig. 11 Pierre-Auguste Renoir, *Blonde Bather*, 1881. Oil on canvas. The Sterling and Francine Clark Art Institute, Acquired by Sterling and Francine Clark, 1926, 1955.609.

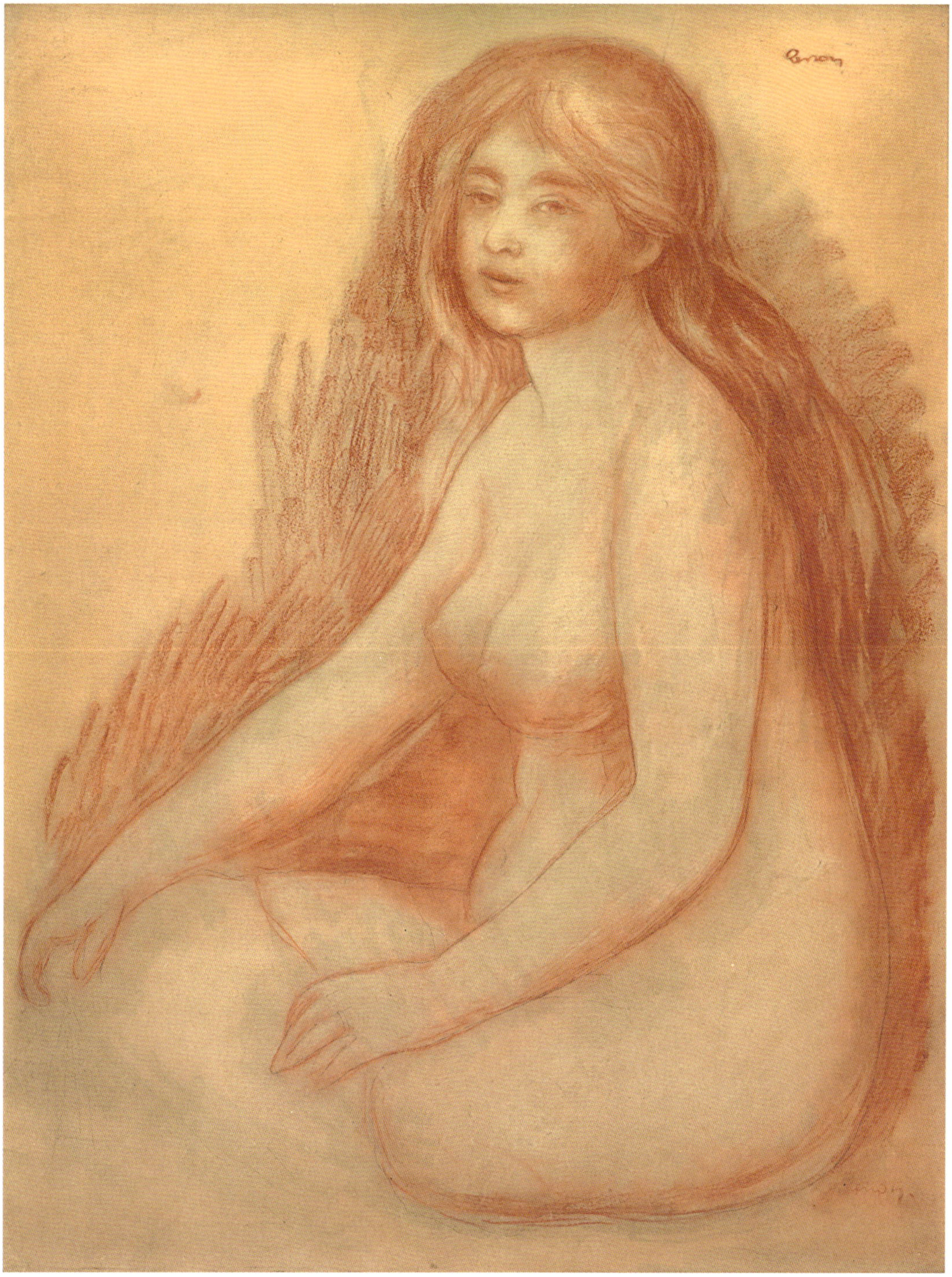

Although it would be tempting to conclude that Renoir made the drawing first and transferred it to the primed canvas, there is unfortunately no positive evidence for this. He used heavy wove paper rather than tracing paper and did not square the drawing to ease the transfer. It is more likely that he made the drawing from the model to secure his knowledge of the figure. He drew initially in pencil, using thin but firm lines to outline all major forms and then softened and expanded them with the red chalk. The drawing was probably finished along with or after the painting. Its two signatures suggest that when he sold it to his dealer, Ambroise Vollard, he signed it more prominently to add to its salability.

Renoir surely consulted the drawing again on making a second painting, in 1882, of the same figure, a version larger than either the drawing or the first painting. This superb painting (Agnelli Collection, Turin) was in the collection of Sir Kenneth Clark, whose 1956 book *The Nude* redefined the way 20th-century viewers think about the unclothed human form.

RRB

Camille Pissarro French, 1830–1903

URBAN UPRISING IN PARIS, *1870*

Charcoal, wash, and gouache on wove paper, 7⅝ × 10 in. (194 × 254 mm)
Initialed lower left: *C. P.*
Dallas Museum of Art, The Wendy and Emery Reves Collection, 1985.R.49

PROVENANCE Emery Reves, France; given to the Dallas Museum of Art, The Wendy and Emery Reves Collection, 1985.

EXHIBITED Dallas Museum of Art, *Impressionist and Modern Masters in Dallas*, September 3–October 22, 1989, 84, no. 89.

BIBLIOGRAPHY Brettell 1995, 42–43, color ill.

Camille Pissarro was the most politically involved artist among the impressionists. His political consciousness was activated by being an outsider—both Jewish and Danish—in France during his youth and by the examples of Gustave Courbet and his friend the radical philosopher Pierre-Joseph Proudhon. A lifelong anarchist, Pissarro warmed to Proudhon's distrust of authoritarian government and to his belief that artists had a responsibility to engage with an increasingly industrialized world.

This powerful drawing, clearly representing an urban uprising, is unique in Pissarro's career. It has traditionally been titled *Anarchist Meeting on the Boulevards,* but this is surely too precise, given the fact that we know almost nothing about it. A central figure of a man gestures with his raised arm as a crowd of men and women gather around him. Pissarro was careful to depict the crowd in motion, which lends an ominous and unstable quality to the subject. The drawing has none of the balanced and static character of Jacques-Louis David's famous *Oath of the Tennis Court* (1791, Musée du Louvre, on loan to the Musée national du Château de Versailles), nor does it have the careful observation of figural types that one sees in Louis-Léopold Boilly's street scenes. Rather, its art historical origins lie squarely in the art of Honoré Daumier, whose caricatures (see cats. 20–22) and politics Pissarro admired intensely.

To decode the subject of the drawing, it is necessary to place it in time. It has distinct stylistic parallels to drawings done by Pissarro as early as 1854–1855 in Caracas, Venezuela, but a generalized treatment of urban figures persisted in his graphic oeuvre through the 1890s. The highly organized, symmetrical composition leads one to date it to the 1850s or 1860s, but Pissarro drew no comparable scenes in those years, turning to the subject of urban politics in his graphic art only in 1890. Thus the conundrum: early style, late subject.

What precisely is the subject? Pissarro was careful to delineate the gender and social class of the figures while avoiding their individuality. Since there is a spectrum from urban workers to well-dressed figures of both genders, the gathering does not represent antibourgeois workers or politicized students. Yet, the drawing does retain the sense of collective action. Pissarro could easily have witnessed such a scene in Paris, but the virtual police state of the Second Empire (1852–1870) ensured that such gatherings were rapidly dispersed, and not even the highly politicized Daumier represented an urban uprising in the 1860s. Pissarro probably saw scenes like this one at the onset of the Franco-Prussian War in 1870, before his departure from France to England.

Given its mixture of the sexes and social classes, the drawing most likely represents a group of anti-Prussian Parisians before Prussia invaded France. It is known that Pissarro was roused by a patriotic fervor and that he even tried, unsuccessfully, to enlist in the French army in 1870. Surely it was this patriotism that he recorded on this powerful sheet.

RRB

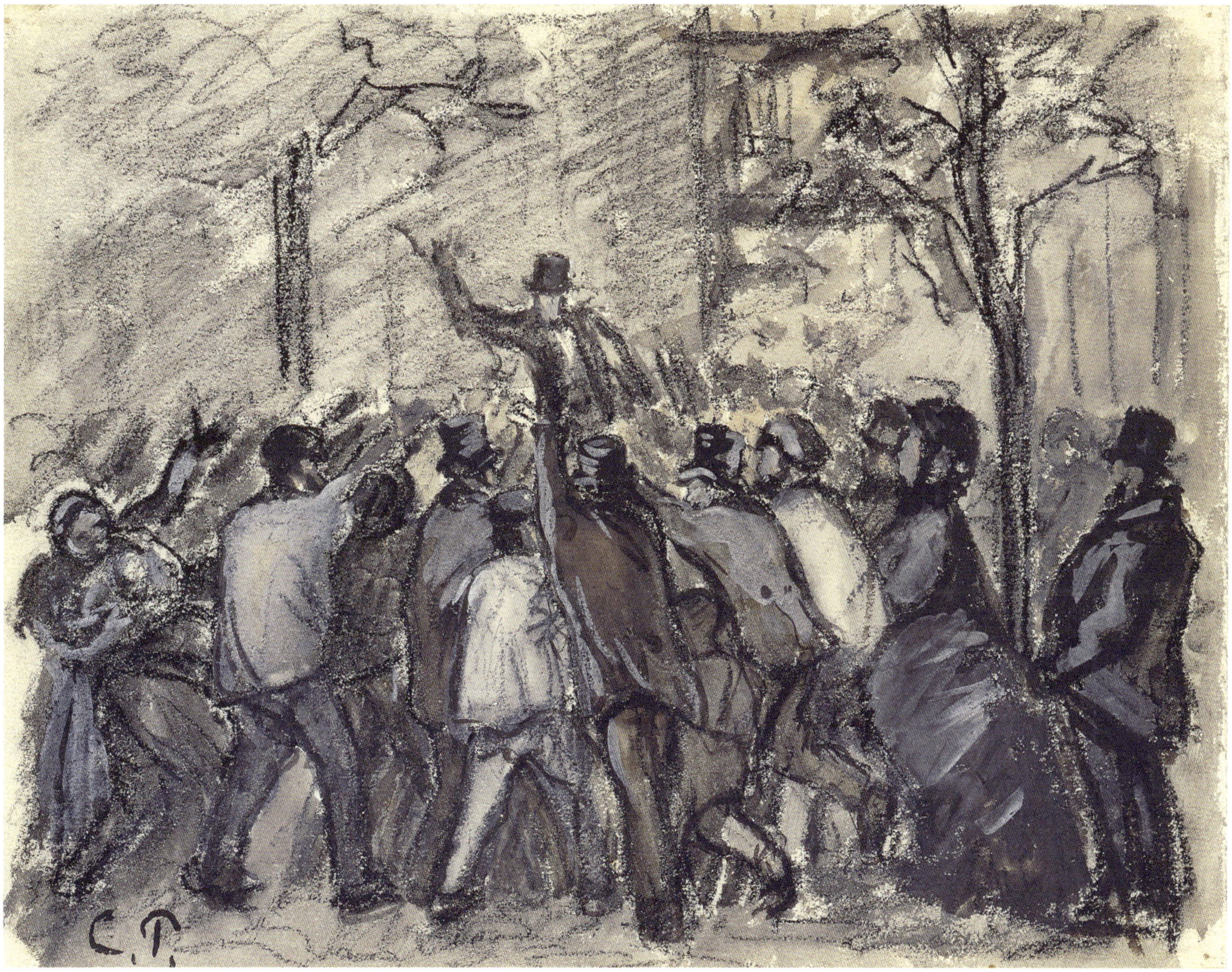
C.P.

66

Camille Pissarro French, 1830–1903

BATHER WITH GEESE, *1895*

Pen, ink, and lead white gouache on paper, 4¾ × 5½ in. (121 × 140 mm)
Dallas Museum of Art, The Wendy and Emery Reves Collection, 1985.R.43

PROVENANCE Emery Reves, France; given to the Dallas Museum of Art, The Wendy and Emery Reves Collection, 1985.

EXHIBITED Dallas Museum of Art, *Impressionist and Modern Masters in Dallas*, September 3–October 22, 1989, no. 87.

BIBLIOGRAPHY Brettell 1995, 114–15, color ill.

67

THE HARVEST (LA MOISSON), *1895*

Pen, ink, and lead white gouache on paper, 4¾ × 5¼ in (119 × 136 mm)
Initialed lower right: *CP*
Dallas Museum of Art, The Wendy and Emery Reves Collection, 1985.R.47

PROVENANCE Emery Reves, France; given to the Dallas Museum of Art, The Wendy and Emery Reves Collection, 1985.

EXHIBITED Dallas Museum of Art, *Impressionist and Modern Masters in Dallas*, September 3–October 22, 1989, no. 88, 84; Dallas Museum of Art, *Van Gogh's Sheaves of Wheat*, October 22, 2006–January 7, 2007, no. 48, 94.

BIBLIOGRAPHY Brettell 1995, 114–15, color ill.

These curious drawings belong to a set of at least eight sheets made by Camille Pissarro early in 1895 as part of a collaborative project with his son, Lucien Pissarro, who lived in England and was extensively involved in the woodcut and wood-engraving revival that began there in the 1850s. Initiated by William Morris, the movement steadily gathered converts, reaching an apex at the end of the century. The aim was to inject a new vitality into the art of the hand-printed book. Illustrations were created in harmony with newly designed typefaces to produce a completely integrated work of art.

Camille Pissarro had been a practiced and successful printmaker for more than a generation when Lucien embarked on his mission. The most important of their collaborative efforts was to have been called *Les Travaux des champs (The Work of the Fields)*, for which Lucien later commissioned an evocative text from Benjamin Guinaudeau. Camille Pissarro was to make the drawings, thereby lending his famous name to the work, while Lucien would be in charge of making the prints and producing the book. Ultimately, the project was a fascinating failure, producing many drawings, most of which remain in the Ashmolean Museum at Oxford University, but never a finished book. The first phase resulted in a portfolio of color and monochrome prints produced in 1891–1894 and released in 1894. The second phase, to which these drawings belong, began and ended in 1895 and seems not to have progressed very far. The third and final stage involved the commissioning of the text and numerous illustrations, but it, too, foundered.

These drawings add considerably to our knowledge about the second phase of *The Work of the Fields.* Although they relate technically to a number of sheets in the Ashmolean, both are more highly finished and exhibit numerous changes and alterations. Both appear to have been drawn by Camille Pissarro, who sent them to Lucien for "translation." They were either rejected or criticized and returned to Camille, who carefully cut out and glued on additional pieces of paper. He then "corrected" the drawings, possibly to balance the darks and lights to ensure that the sheets would harmonize with printed type. The elder Pissarro must have been pleased with these sheets because they apparently were separated from the other drawings and sold during his lifetime. There are no drawings directly related to *Bather with Geese,* which shares imagery, but not exact poses and compositions, with two prints: an etching of 1895 and a lithograph of 1895–1896.[1] *The Harvest* is another matter. It appears to have been based on a lithograph of 1894 that includes identical figures but has a more spacious landscape setting (Dallas Museum of Art, 2014.6). The drawing could also have been based on a sheet in the Ashmolean Museum[2] that appears to be a tracing from the 1894 lithograph.

RRB

Notes
1. Delteil 1923, nos. 115, 161.
2. Brettell 1980, 341.

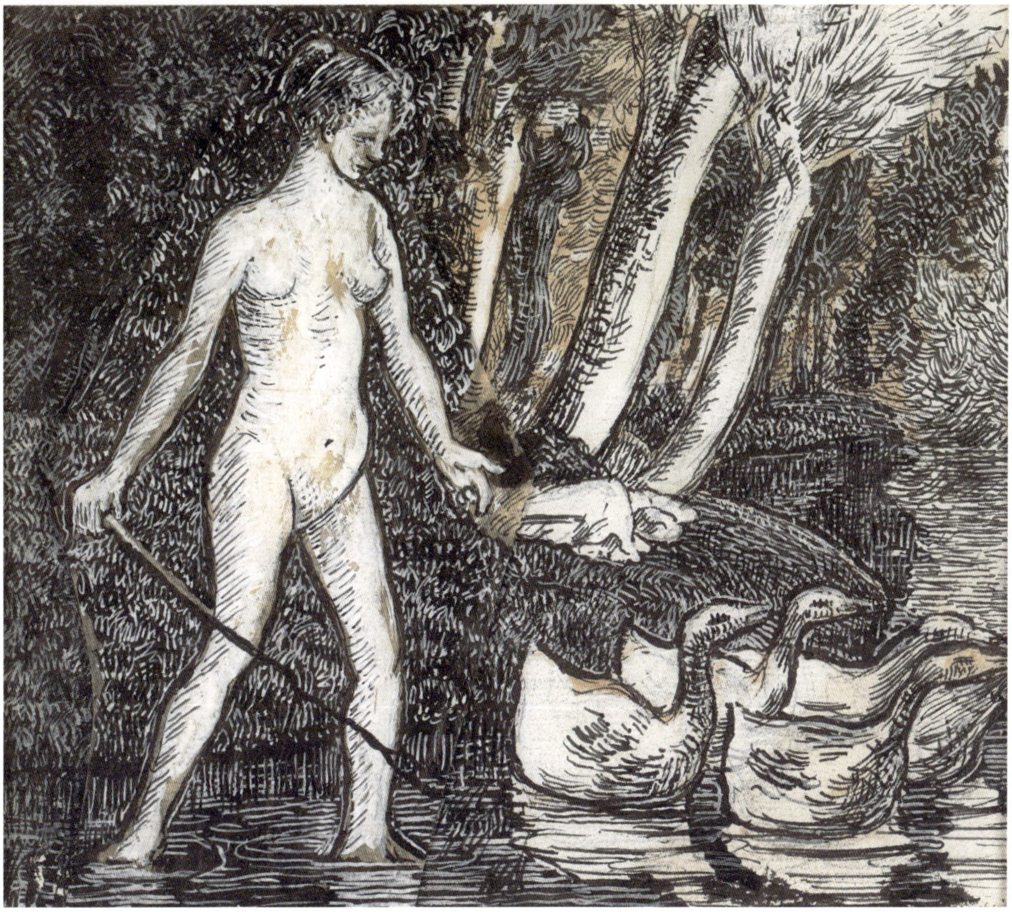

Cat. 66

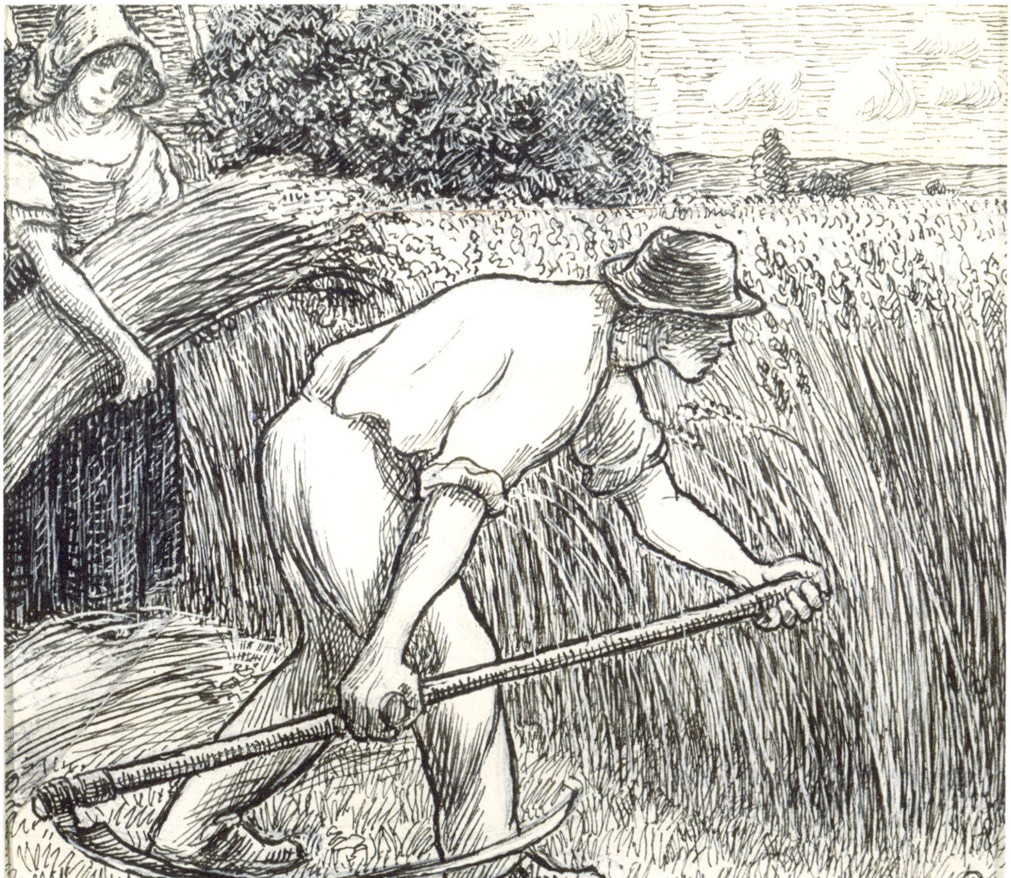

Cat. 67

68

Paul Cézanne French, 1839–1906

MAISON ET VERDURE, C. *1895–1900*

Pencil and watercolor on cream wove paper,
19⅞ × 12¾ in. (505 × 325 mm)
Private collection, Dallas

PROVENANCE Walther Halvorsen, Oslo; from whom purchased April 1, 1920 by Galerie Bernheim-Jeune, Paris; Mrs. Nathan J. Miller (d. 1938), New Rochelle, N.Y.; private collection, Paris; with Galerie Schmit, Paris, from whom purchased 1999 by the current owner.

EXHIBITED Possibly the drawing exhibited at Leicester Galleries, London, June–July 1925, no. 2 (as *L'angle de maison*).

BIBLIOGRAPHY Venturi 1936, vol. 1, 264, no. 996, ill.; Venturi 1936, vol. 2, pl. 298; Venturi 1978; Rewald 1983, 670, no. 419, ill.

Paul Cézanne was born into a comfortable bourgeois family in Aix-en-Provence (his father was a banker), affording him a financial independence that made it possible to pursue his ambition to become an artist. In 1861 he settled in Paris, where he befriended the other impressionists and exhibited with them twice in the 1870s. Continually drawn back to Provence, however, he returned there permanently after the death of his father and the inheritance of the family estate in the 1880s. Few painters have been as inner driven and single minded in their determination to reinvent the art of painting, and no artist of the 19th century came as close to doing it. His goal was to capture perception as a moment in time otherwise lost but for the discovery of its underlying structure.

Cézanne's watercolors, which radically ignore what was expected of that medium until then, have challenged the understanding of critics and artists alike ever since they were first shown to the Paris public in 1905. As Émile Bernard wrote after watching him make one the year before:

> His method was remarkable, totally different from the traditional procedures and extremely complicated. He began on the shadow with a single patch, which he then overlapped with a second, and a third, until these patches, which produced screens, modeled the object by means of color.[1]

While watercolor had been essentially colored drawing, with a high value placed on delicacy and spontaneity of touch, Cézanne was using it, as Matthew Simms has shown, to redefine and intensify the experience of seeing forms in space.[2] Often perceived as "unfinished," the watercolors instead make use of the blank paper as the brightest tonal value in a push-pull relationship with the hatchings in pencil and overlays of transparent colored wash to define shadow. From this, forms begin to emerge, as in *Maison et verdure,* where the artist has focused on the corner of a tile-roofed stone dwelling facing a rocky cliff covered with vegetation—a site probably near the Bibémus Quarry, where he painted often from 1895 to 1900. Works like this one leave the viewer continually trying to see in his mind's eye what the artist was perceiving, and that has been part of their fascination for more than a century. Pushing the boundaries of art to the limits and beyond is what made Cézanne the inspiration of a generation of European and American artists.

The first owner of this watercolor was the Norwegian Walther Halvorsen (see cat. 114), who, while a painting student of Matisse in 1909–1910 and afterward, became an intimate member of a group of artists living in Montmartre. Giving up painting to become an art dealer, Halvorsen went on to be enormously helpful to these artists by promoting and selling their works outside of France. He was particularly devoted to the works of Cézanne, and he owned many, which John Rewald says probably were bought directly from the artist's son or from Ambroise Vollard.[3] In 1920 Halvorsen sold 27 Cézanne watercolors in a single day, including this one, to the Galerie Bernheim-Jeune in Paris. It was acquired there later in the 1920s by the New York philanthropist Mrs. Nathan J. Miller, who since the 1913 Armory Show had been a major patron of avant-garde American painters, especially Max Weber. She owned two oil paintings and this watercolor by Cézanne. After her death, the watercolor was eventually returned to France, where it was acquired by its current owner.

WBJ

Notes
1. Émile Bernard, "Souvenirs sur Paul Cézanne" (1907), quoted in Simms et al. 2002, 14.
2. Simms 2008, 1–5.
3. Rewald 1983.

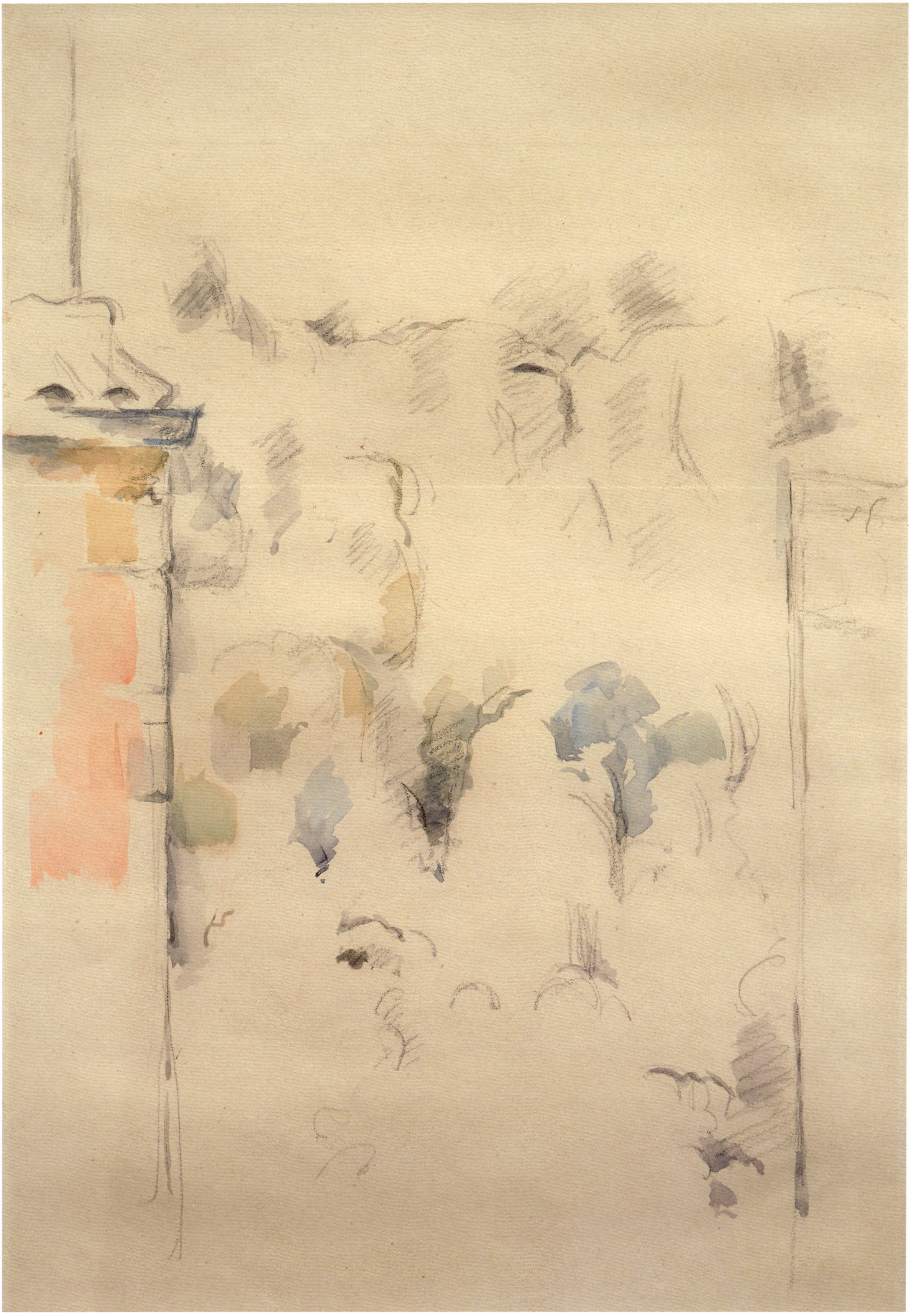

69

Paul Cézanne French, 1839–1906

ENVIRONS D'AIX, C. *1900–1906*

Watercolor and pencil on paper, 14 × 21⅜ in. (335 × 542 mm)
Collection of Mr. and Mrs. Barron U. Kidd, Dallas

PROVENANCE Paul Cézanne fils, Paris; Paul Cassirer, Berlin; [Frau] H. von S[iemens], Berlin; Frau von Siemens Estate; Dr. Walter Feilchenfeldt, Zürich; Fine Arts Associates (Otto Gerson), New York; Mrs. Henriette Hirschland, New York; Fritz & Peter Nathan, Zürich; private collection, Cologne; Fritz & Peter Nathan, Zürich; Norton Simon, Los Angeles; sale, Parke-Bernet, New York, May 5, 1971, lot 27 (bought in); Mr. and Mrs. Henry M. Reed, Caldwell, N.J.; sale, Parke-Bernet, New York, May 16, 1979, lot 233; Acquavella Galleries, New York; from whom purchased by the current owner.

EXHIBITED Arts Council of Great Britain, London, *Paul Cézanne: Exhibition of Watercolors,* March–July 1946, no. 55; Fine Arts Associates, New York (Otto Gerson), 1952, *Watercolors,* no. 12, ill.; Fine Arts Associates, New York (Otto Gerson), *Cézanne Watercolors,* January 20–February 18, 1956, no. 23, ill.; Kassel, *Documenta III,* 1964, no. 8; Museum of Modern Art, New York, October 7, 1977–January 3, 1978, and Museum of Fine Arts, Houston, January 26–March 19, 1978, *Cézanne: The Late Work,* no. 101, pl. 97; Acquavella Galleries, New York, *XIX & XX Century Master Paintings,* November 1–30, 1979, no. 7, ill.; Acquavella Galleries, New York, *Cézanne Watercolors,* October 18–November 24, 1999, pl. 14 (image inverted); National Gallery of Art, Washington, Musée Granet and Communauté du Pays d'Aix, Aix-en-Provence, and Réunion des musées nationaux, Paris, *Cézanne in Provence,* January 29–September 17, 2006, no. 132, ill.

BIBLIOGRAPHY Nathan and Nathan 1961, ill. opp. 46; Rewald 1983, 234, no. 579, ill.

Despite advancing age and the onset of diabetes, Paul Cézanne decided in 1901 to build a new studio, largely because the family house, Jas de Bouffan, had been sold in 1899 after the death of his mother and he did not wish to share the cramped quarters he was occupying with his wife, from whom he was increasingly estranged. On property he had bought on the hill of Les Lauves just north of Aix, overlooking the town and the mountains beyond, he built a spacious, two-story studio where he could find peace and work on the monumental *Bathers* and other great works of his last years.[1] From this site he painted this scintillating watercolor.

It is a familiar irony that aging artists, whether due to or despite failing eyesight—as was true with Cézanne, Edgar Degas, Claude Monet, and many others—or to an intense focus on essential goals, often realize in their final years some of the most cogent expressions of their intent. This was certainly the case with Cézanne, who described his vision problems to Émile Bernard in 1905:

> Now, being old, nearly seventy years, the sensations of color, which give the light, are for me the reason for the abstractions, which do not allow me to cover my canvas entirely, nor to pursue the delimitation of the objects, where their points of contact are fine or delicate, from which it results that my depiction in the painting is incomplete.[2]

But the precise depiction of form had never been Cézanne's objective. Increasingly at this time, he speaks of the need to paint the "envelope" or the air: "Nature is [experienced] more as depth than as surface, from which comes the necessity of introducing into our light vibrations, represented by reds and yellows, a sufficient amount of blue to render the air."[3] And then in the following year he writes: "Draw, but remember that it is the reflection of light that defines things. Light, through the laws of reflection, becomes the envelope."[4] While oil painting was always Cézanne's primary medium, in watercolors like this one he probably achieved the closest approximation of his goal. In this work, transparent patches of prismatic color overlap in a shimmering veil of opalescence that evokes the southern light of an elusive moment.

To Cézanne's younger contemporaries, works like this one were seminal. Had they been perfectly resolved exemplars of some tidier artistic ideology, they would have been imitated one day and discarded the next. Instead they remain, even today, incredibly moving emblems of authentic artistic struggle.

WBJ

Notes
1. Rewald 1983, 235.
2. Quoted by Philip Conisbee in Conisbee and Coutagne 2006, 240.
3. Cézanne to Émile Bernard, April 15, 1904, quoted by Simms 2008, 136.
4. Cézanne to Bernard, 1905, quoted by Simms 2008, 136.

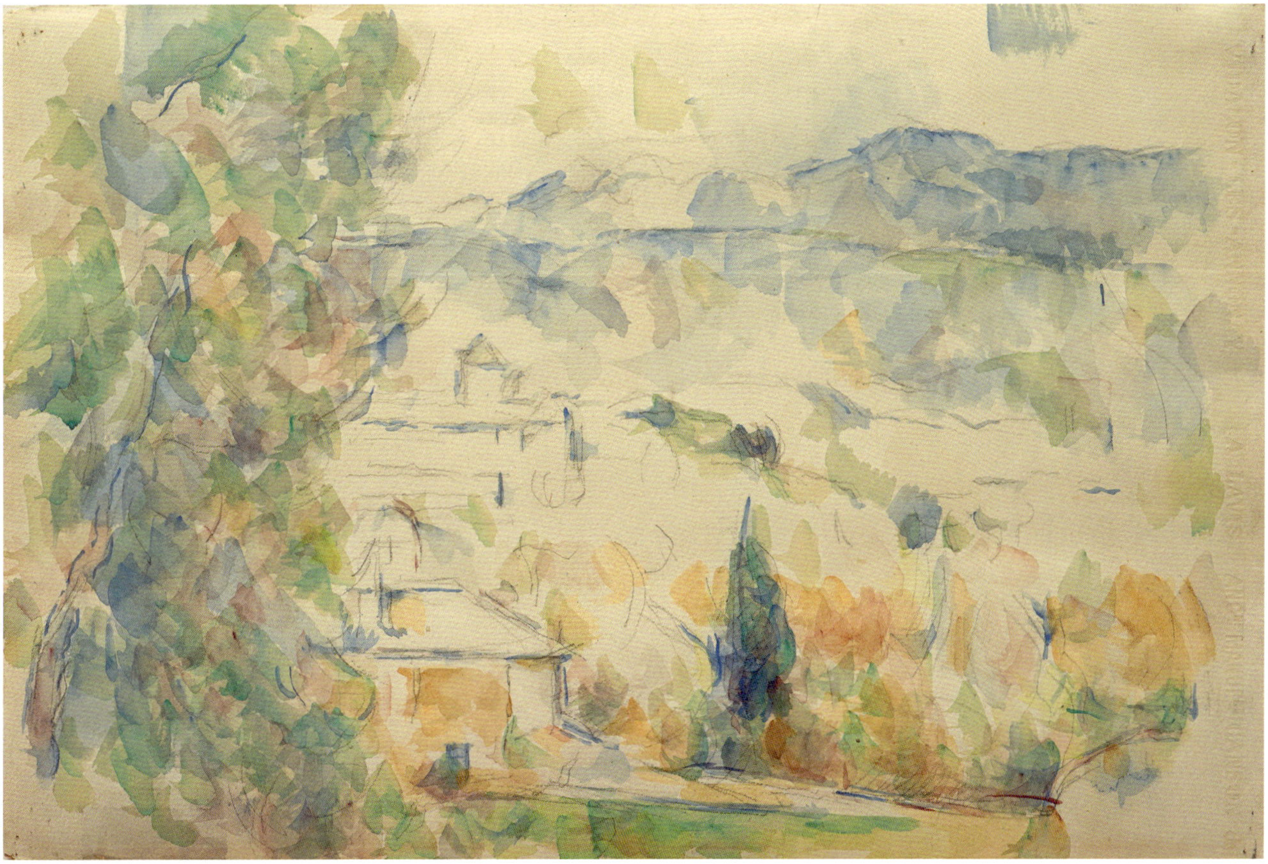

Paul Cézanne French, 1839–1906

STILL LIFE WITH APPLES ON A SIDEBOARD, C. *1900–1906*

Watercolor over pencil on white paper, 18⅞ × 24¾ in. (479 × 629 mm)
Dallas Museum of Art, The Wendy and Emery Reves Collection, 1985.R.12

PROVENANCE Paul Cézanne fils, Paris; Galerie Bernheim-Jeune, Paris; sale, Alexandre Durand-Ruel, Paris, Hôtel Drouot, June 15–16, 1917, no. 57, ill.; Durand-Ruel, Paris; Viscount Kurooki, Tokyo; Wolman, Paris; with Alfred Daber, Paris; Galerie Paul Rosenberg, Paris; Lord Ivor Spencer Churchill, London (by 1936); Zwemmer Gallery, London (by 1946–1952); Emery Reves, France; given to the Dallas Museum of Art, The Wendy and Emery Reves Collection, 1985.

EXHIBITED Galerie Bernheim-Jeune, Paris, and Paul Cassirer, Berlin, *Les Aquarelles de Cézanne,* 1907; Kunsthaus, Zürich, *Französische Kunst des XIX und XX Jahrhunderts,* 1917, no. 25; Arthur Tooth & Sons Ltd., London, *A Loan Exhibition of Pictures from Private Collections in Paris,* May 8–June 1, 1935, no. 2, ill.; Musée de l'Orangerie, Paris, *Cézanne,* 1936, no. 135, ill.; Kunsthalle Basel, Basel, *Paul Cézanne,* August 30–October 12, 1936, no. 92, ill.; Arts Council of Great Britain, London, *Paul Cézanne: Exhibition of Watercolors,* April 11–May 12, 1946, no. 27; Art Institute of Chicago, February 7–March 16, 1952, and Metropolitan Museum of Art, New York, April 4–May 18, 1952, *Cézanne: Paintings, Watercolors, and Drawings,* no. 123, ill.; Musée Masséna, Nice, *Chefs-d'oeuvre de la peinture français,* November 27, 1956–January 6, 1957, ill.; Grand Palais, Paris, *Cézanne, les dernières années,* April 20–July 23, 1978, no. 31, ill.; Dallas Museum of Art, *Impressionist and Modern Masters in Dallas,* September 3–October 22, 1989, 77, no. 12, ill.; Dallas Museum of Art, *Impressions from the Riviera,* November 5, 1995–February 4, 1996, ill.; Dallas Museum of Art, *Passion for Art: 100 Treasures 100 Years,* October 12, 2003–March 14, 2004; J. Paul Getty Museum, Los Angeles, *Cézanne in the Studio: Still Life in Watercolors,* October 12, 2004–January 2, 2005.

BIBLIOGRAPHY Bernheim-Jeune 1919, no. 42, ill.; Faure 1926, pl. 35, ill.; Venturi 1936, 284, ill.; Metropolitan Museum of Art 1952, no. 24, ill.; Schmidt 1952, 29, ill.; Huyghe 1962, 69, ill.; Elgar 1968, 240, ill.; Daulte 1969, 114, 115, ill.; Rubin 1977, 359, ill.; Rewald 1983, 226, ill.; Dallas Museum of Art 1985b, 132–133, ill.; Geist 1985, 21; Rewald 1986, 253, ill.; Nathan 1988, 116, ill.; Plazy 1991, 144, ill.; Brettell 1995, 130–131, ill.; Dallas Museum of Art 1997, 117, ill.; Kosinski 2003, no. 56; Armstrong 2004, pl. 17; MacDonald 2013, 105, fig. 91, ill.

Among the works that absorbed Paul Cézanne in the final years at his studio at Les Lauves was a series of large still-life watercolors, masterpieces that, it has been said, "strike a balance between stability of composition and fluidity of execution that is more assured and accomplished than in any other set of works he executed."[1] At this period in his life, when Cézanne was frequently leaving large areas of his works—whether canvases or works on paper—uncovered by paint (something he was not always entirely happy about), several of these large watercolors are completely resolved and confidently "complete," and none more than this radiant example in the Reves Collection. Most of the compositions in the series are traditional arrangements of tableware and comestibles on tabletops, and some of the objects can still be seen in Cézanne's studio at Les Lauves today. Throughout his long career, Cézanne had been drawn to the still life (as had artists ever since Caravaggio) as a comfortable format for exploring or confirming his ideas about visual representation. But although superficially traditional, these works are as experimental and daring as any of the time.

In this watercolor, areas of uncovered white paper can be seen, of course—such as the white label on the wine bottle, the white ceramic glaze on the decorated pitcher, or the white plate with four apples—but these lacunae play a representational role and are perfectly in balance with the smaller patches left blank to represent light glinting off the surface of the tabletop or the sheen of an apple's skin. Atmosphere is conveyed by freely applied patches of greens, blues, and reds in the shadows around the apples and the edges of the sideboard. Yet despite these nuances, the flatness of the picture plane is rather emphasized by the overall yellow hue applied both to the wall behind the table and to the table itself. Both the underlying pencil lines put first on the paper and the multiple, reinforcing strokes of watercolor that define the edges of things—the table, the contour of an apple, or the edge of a plate—illustrate Cézanne's knowledge that the eye does not perceive contours as precise lines unless they are being focused upon individually. So while the composition has no one arbitrary or fixed focal point, it is strongly bound together as a vibrant whole unified by the light.

WBJ

Note
1. Joseph J. Rishel, in Cachin et al. 1996, 461.

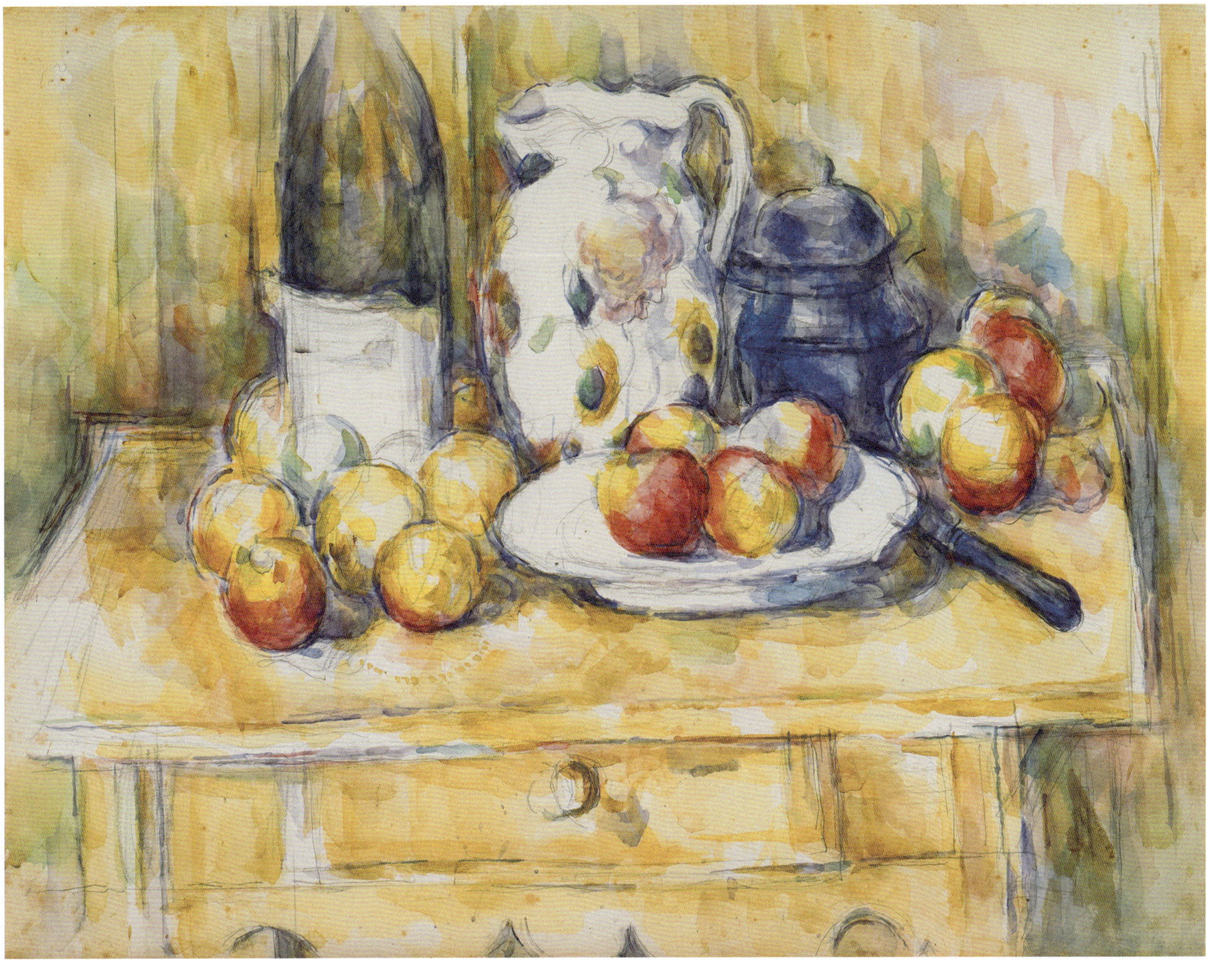

71

Georges Seurat French, 1859–1891

STANDING WOMAN (FEMME DEBOUT, LA TÊTE NUE), C. *1882*

Conté crayon on paper, 11⅞ × 8⅜ in. (302 × 213 mm)
Private collection

PROVENANCE Mme Olivier Sainsère, before 1961; Galerie Schmit, Paris; Pierre Berès, Paris; sale, Christie's, Paris, *Pierre Berès à livre ouvert*, December 12–13, 2012, lot 435; where purchased by the current owner.

EXHIBITED Kunsthalle, Bielefeld, October 30–December 25, 1983, and Staatliche Kunsthalle, Baden-Baden, January 15–March 11, 1984, *Georges Seurat: Zeichnungen*, 184, no. 31, ill.; Museum of Modern Art, New York, *Georges Seurat: The Drawings*, October 28, 2007–January 7, 2008, 252, no. 81, 150, ill.

BIBLIOGRAPHY De Hauke 1961, vol. 2, 102, no. 505, 103, ill.

"Comprehension is not everything, the unaccountable has a place in our lives. . . . Seurat, involuntarily perhaps, has presented us with the mysterious." This is Bridget Riley's assessment, as she focused recently on the drawings of Georges Seurat. Riley is an artist as knowledgeable about visual perception as any, yet she stands in awe of Seurat's accomplishment.[1] She realizes that his effects surpass our capacity to explain them, even now. Ironically, Seurat has always been credited with introducing advanced scientific principles to his representational practice; and science ought to offer paths to comprehension. His style of drawing, for example, exhibits the phenomenon of halation. In *Standing Woman* (cat. 71), we readily note the illuminating halo surrounding the darkness of the figure. This light dramatically fixes the figure in place but is itself the product of a tangle of hyperactive, destabilizing lines. Should we focus on the woman's stillness or follow the restless movement of the lines? As they accumulate, Seurat's lines gradually obscure the objects they render. This is his paradox.

Despite the mystery, Seurat professed no greater expertise than that of an hourly wage earner, skilled at depiction. Around 1881–1882, he concentrated on drawing and virtually reinvented the medium. His art inspired not only novel ways of representing nature but also, for subsequent generations, the possibility that line and tone could function independently as features of expressive abstraction. Riley summarizes Seurat's lesson: "He developed the conventional study of tone into a highly abstract mode of representation that commands the whole pictorial field, allowing the figurative motif to emerge out of an all-encompassing opposition of light and dark, black and white."[2] The figure is representational, but the "all-encompassing opposition"—metaphorically, a kind of atmosphere, even a mood—becomes abstracted. Seurat was unusual in covering the entire drawing sheet, including the irregular deckled edge of the laid paper he favored. He often applied his varied tones of conté crayon forcefully, as in the deep black areas of *In a Park* (cat. 72, p. 157). His emotionally evocative plays of light developed in two fundamental ways: as irregular linear networks in *Standing Woman,* or as areas of tone rubbed into paper in *In a Park.* Through both of these techniques, drawing creates effects associated with painting. As if in recognition of this fact, Seurat exhibited examples of his drawing along with his painting, as equals.

Even before abstraction existed as a viable pictorial mode, Seurat's method led astute observers to its "abstract" implications. In 1891, just after the artist's untimely death, critic Gustave Kahn wrote: "Instead

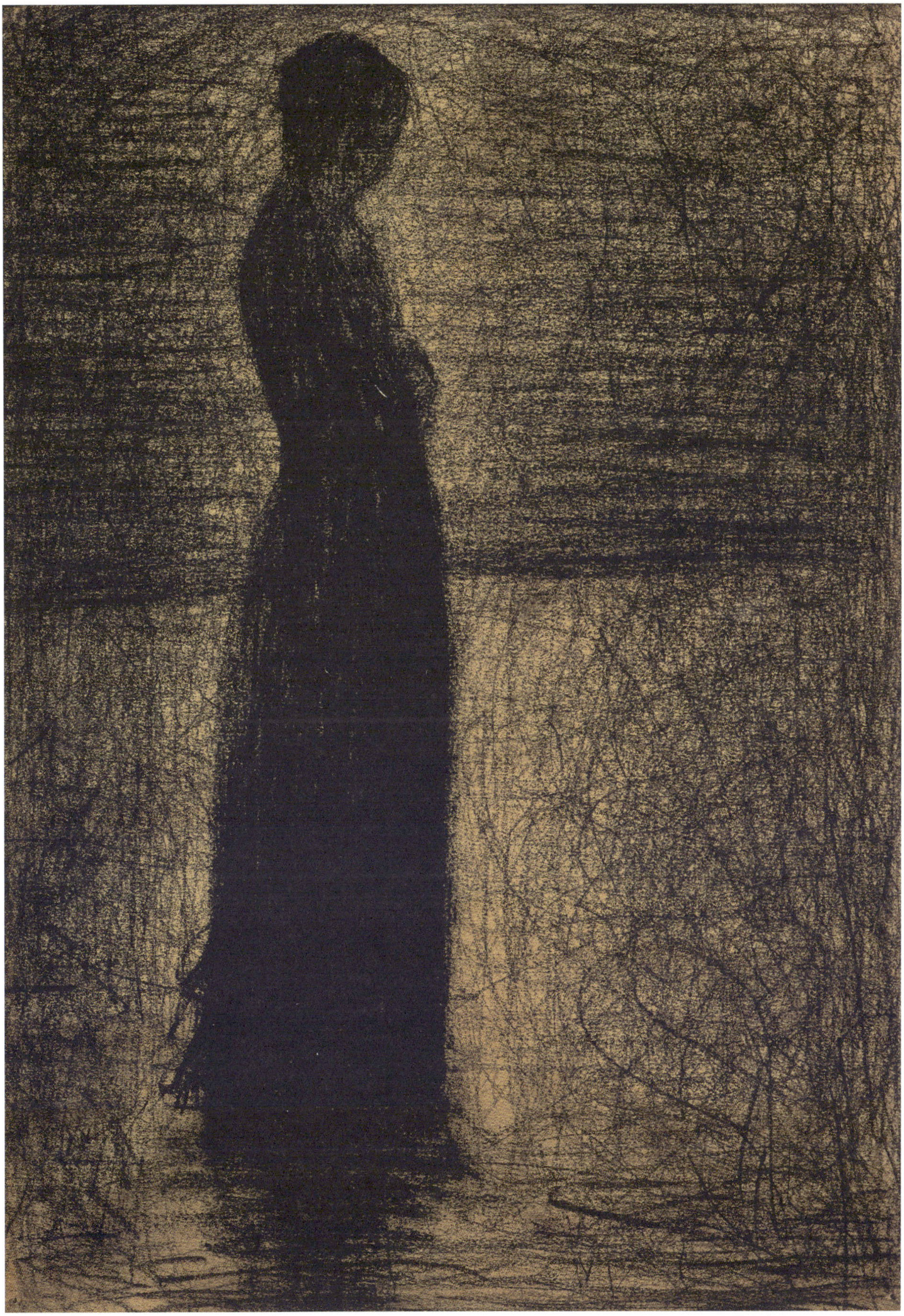

72

Georges Seurat French, 1859–1891

IN A PARK (DANS UN PARC), C. *1883*

Conté crayon and graphite on paper, 12¼ × 9¼ in. (311 × 235 mm)
Private collection

PROVENANCE Camille Platteel, Paris; Suzanne Verger, Brussels; Pierre Berès, Paris; sale, Christie's, Paris, *Pierre Berès à livre ouvert*, December 12–13, 2012, lot 436; where purchased by the current owner.

EXHIBITED Galerie Bernheim-Jeune, Paris, *Rétrospective Georges Seurat*, December 1908–January 1909, no. 148; Galerie Bernheim-Jeune, Paris, *Les dessins de Seurat*, November–December 1926, no. 70; Palais des Beaux-Arts, Brussels, *De Toulouse-Lautrec à Chagall: Dessins, aquarelles, gouaches*, March–April 1956, ill., Museum of Modern Art, New York, *Georges Seurat: The Drawings*, October 28, 2007–January 7, 2008, 252, no. 90, 160, ill.

BIBLIOGRAPHY Kahn 1928, pl. 55; De Hauke 1961, vol. 2, 130, no. 542, 131, ill.

of outlining a figure and leaving it surrounded by a certain amount of empty reserve, . . . he developed masses of black and white, creating a strong sense of modeling across the surface of the paper."[3] Seurat's nuances of light turn in space, as if the pictorial voids, articulated by this play of tonal value, were as substantial as the depicted objects. As a result, the atmospheric background of *Standing Woman* becomes more animated than the figure itself, which assumes a modern silhouette, a pose—Seurat was a master of expressive contour and caricature. As Kahn recognized, the interest of this drawing lies equally in the figure and the formless "modeling" that surrounds it. This is why his description alludes to the totality of the sheet and why Riley would later refer to an "all-encompassing opposition." Similarly, *In a Park* stresses the rhythmic variation of light as it articulates a simple architectural façade among trees. Light and the contrast of tones becomes the subject—not the building, not the landscaped grounds.

Seurat's two techniques of mark making (skimming lines *across* the surface, rubbing areas of tone *into* the surface) correspond to two basic modes of figuration, now associated with computerization: a vector system and a raster system. It is as if Seurat had intuited the electronic future, both its science and its mystery. Each of these two drawings manifests the two systems, but the scribbles of *Standing Woman* act initially as directional vectors, while *In a Park* capitalizes on its inherent raster—the parallel ridges already present in the laid paper, which generate a grid of low peaks and shallow valleys, enough tooth to capture deposits of dark crayon while leaving tiny points of light. Despite the seemingly random meandering of the lines in *Standing Woman*, their skillfully controlled accumulation creates "modeling." This effect is analogous to the fine grid of tonal values revealed through the graininess of *In a Park*.

RS

Notes
1. Bridget Riley, "Seurat as Mentor," in Hauptman 2007, 195.
2. Ibid., 190.
3. Kahn 1891 (author's translation).

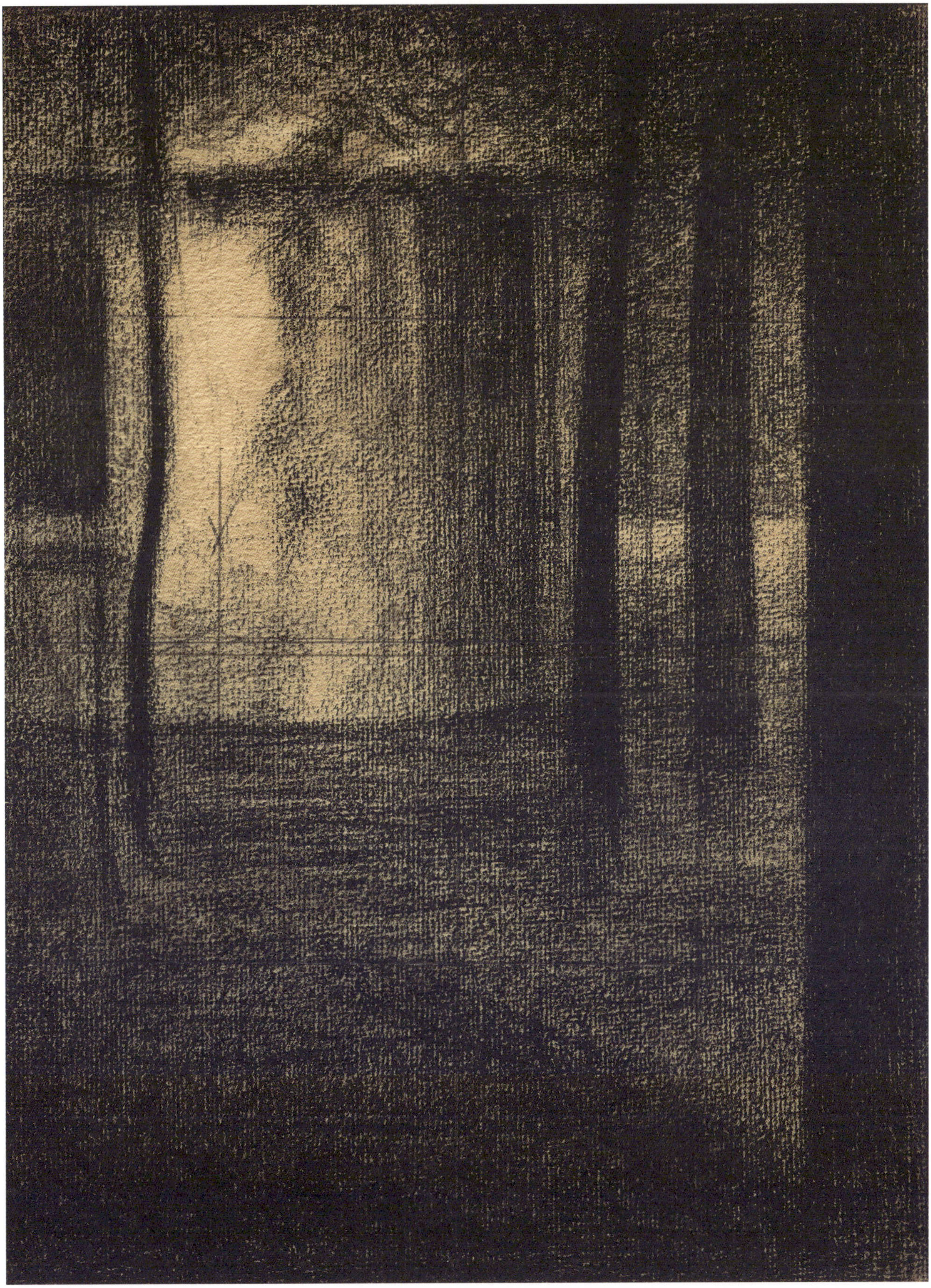

73

Vincent van Gogh Dutch, active in France, 1853–1890

CAFÉ TERRACE ON THE PLACE DU FORUM, *1888*

Reed pen and ink with graphite on laid paper, 24¾ × 18⅝ in.
(629 × 472 mm)
Dallas Museum of Art, The Wendy and Emery Reves Collection, 1985.R.79

PROVENANCE Sent by the artist to Theo van Gogh (d. 1891), Paris, in 1888–89; by inheritance to his son, Vincent Willem van Gogh, as part of his collection, administered by his widow, Johanna Van Gogh-Bonger, Amsterdam, 1891; sold by her to Paul Cassirer, Berlin, December 1906; to his widow, Angela von Tschudi, Munich; sold by the von Tschudi family to the Fritz Nathan Art Gallery, Zurich, until 1960; sold to Emery Reves, France, 1960; given to the Dallas Museum of Art, The Wendy and Emery Reves Collection, 1985.

EXHIBITED Galerie Vollard, Paris, 1896–1897, no. 33; Galerie Moline, Paris, opened February 1902, no. 16; Stedelijk Museum, Amsterdam, *Vincent van Gogh,* July–August 1905, no. 388; Paul Cassirer, Berlin, *Zwölften Kunstaustellung der Berliner Secession, Zeichnende Künste (Twelfth Art Exhibition of the Berlin Secession),* December 1906, no. 71; Dallas Museum of Art, *Impressionist and Modern Masters in Dallas,* September 3–October 22, 1989, 86, no. 121; Rijksmuseum, Amsterdam, *Vincent van Gogh: Drawings,* March 30–July 29, 1990, 237; Nationalgalerie, Staatliche Museen, Berlin, *Manet bis Van Gogh,* September 20, 1996–January 9, 1997, 150–51, no. 54; Metropolitan Museum of Art, New York, *Vincent Van Gogh: The Drawings,* October 21–December 31, 2005, 284–85, no. 96; Museum of Modern Art, New York, *Van Gogh and the Colors of the Night,* September 21, 2008–January 5, 2009, 136, no. 97.

BIBLIOGRAPHY Gosschalk 1905, 232; Meier-Graefe, 1908, 516; du Quesne-van Gogh 1911, 48, 64; Meier-Graefe 1922, vol. 2, pl. 66; Hartlaub 1922, 643; de la Faille 1928, vol. 3, no. 1519; Meier-Graefe 1928, pl. 31; van Gogh 1938, pl. LII; Fejto 1961; Nathan and Nathan 1961, 50–51; Ross 1966, 37; Chaet 1970, 126–27, no. 121; de la Faille 1970, no. 1519; Roskill 1971, 173; Hulsker 1980, fig. 1579; Mittler and Howze 1980, 20, fig. 1.20; Kröller-Müller Museum 1980, 65; Welsh-Ovcharov 1981, 134; Dallas Museum of Art 1984; Dallas Museum of Art 1985b, 124–25, 2, fig. 1; Rewald 1987, inside cover (frontispiece?); *Van Gogh Drawings* 1987, 29; Feilchenfeldt and Veenenbos 1988, 136; Paul 1993, 393; Brettell 1995, 94–95; Plazy 1998, 54–55; Mittler and Howze 2001, 20, fig. 1.20; Stolwijk and Veenenbos 2002, 51, 126, 197; van Heugten 2005, 147; Dallas Museum of Art 2012, 207.

This large and important drawing by Vincent van Gogh has for more than a century been treated in the literature on the artist. Most of that discussion has involved speculation about the nature of its relationship to the famous painting of the same subject in the Rijksmuseum Kröller-Müller, Otterlo, The Netherlands (fig. 12). The drawing is composed with such assurance that it could easily be seen as a drawing made after the painting. But as Susan Alyson Stein has convincingly argued, it was in fact a preparatory drawing for a painting he intended to make, a work inspired by a passage at the beginning of Guy de Maupassant's *Bel Ami* describing brightly lit Parisian cafés at night.[1] In a letter to his sister in September 1888, van Gogh excitedly describes painting the picture on the site and by gaslight, taking pride in having made a night scene with no black in it, only scintillating colors. The drawing resembles the painting because the location is the same, but there are significant differences, such as in the awning of the café, the carriage in the street, the absence of the tree at the right, and especially in the treatment of the buildings on the right side of the cobbled road, which suggests that the drawing was made on a previous occasion, in daylight, while the painting was made at night.

Van Gogh worked with one of his favorite drawing tools, the reed pen. An ancient implement used for both writing and drawing, it allowed van Gogh to draw with the thick, confident lines that structure the

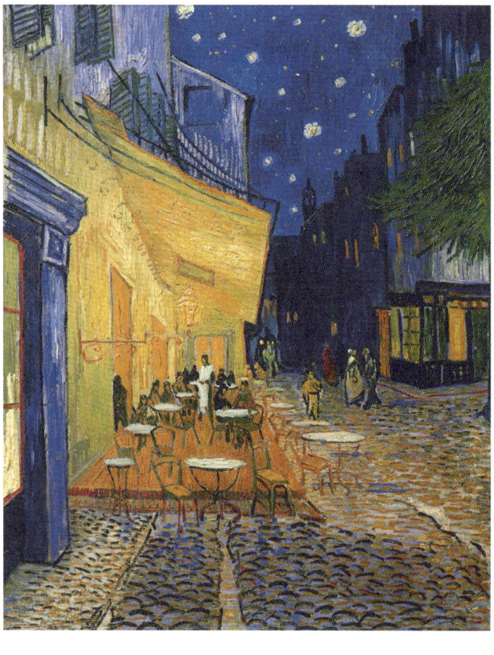

Fig. 12 Vincent van Gogh, *Café Terrace at Night (Place du Forum in Arles)*, 1888. Oil on canvas. Rijksmuseum Kröller-Müller, Otterlo, The Netherlands, cat. 232.

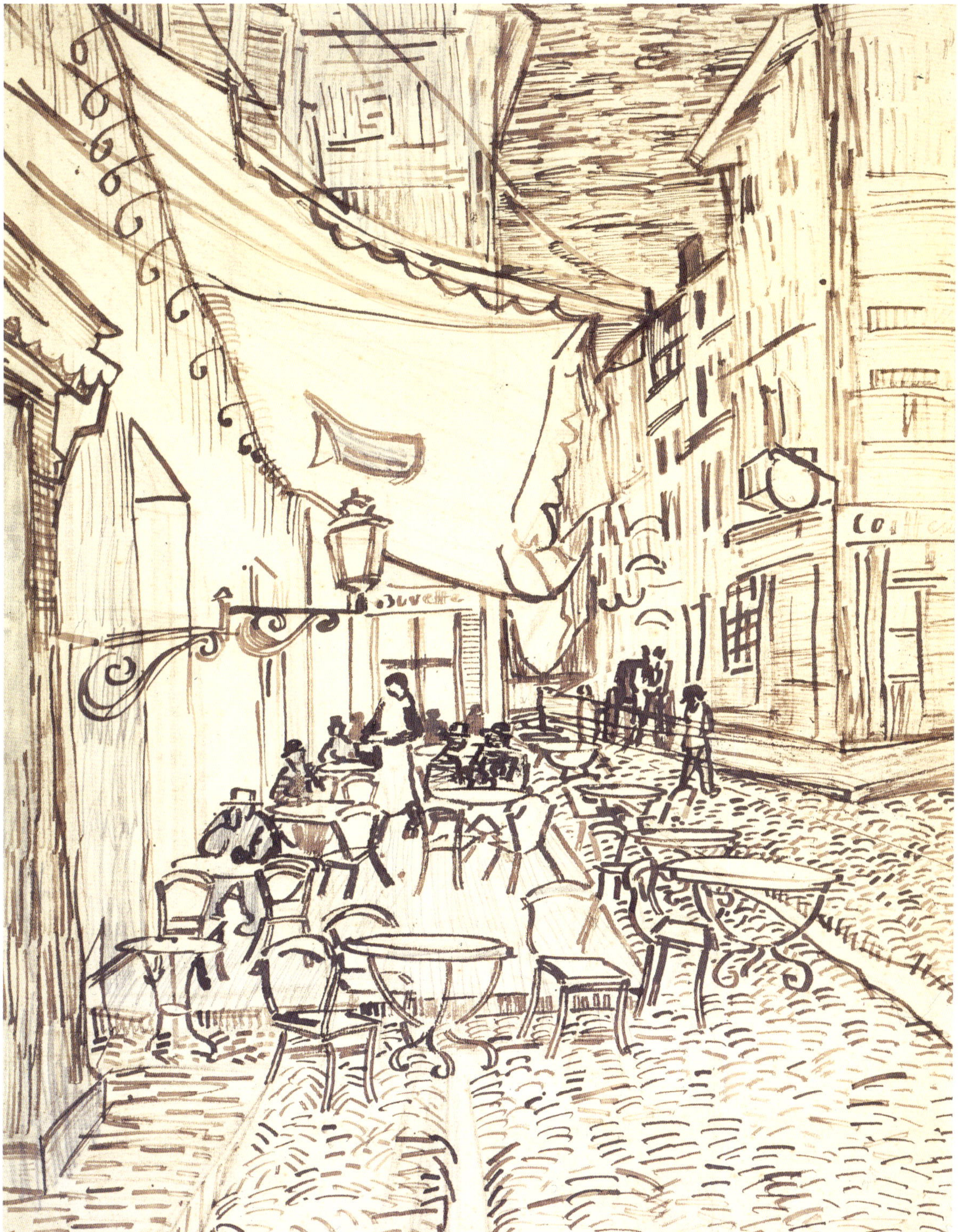

architecture and street as well as the more calligraphic loops that describe the café's awning and furniture. The light traces of graphite are not from a preliminary underdrawing to lay out the framework of the composition; on the contrary, van Gogh used pencil to add fine details and suggest texture, as with the lines that trace the wooden boards of the café's terrace. After completing the painted version of *Café Terrace at Night,* van Gogh retreated from the practice of making finished compositional studies of prospective subjects, perhaps under the influence of Paul Gauguin.[2]

HMacD

Notes
1. Stein, in Ives et al. 2005, 279.
2. Ibid.

Odilon Redon French, 1840–1916

TWO FIGURES IN A LANDSCAPE
(DEUX PERSONNAGES DANS UN PAYSAGE), *1865*

Black crayon on cream wove paper, 9 × 8⅛ in.
(229 × 205 mm)
Signed lower left: *ODILON REDON*; dated lower right: 65
Private collection, Dallas

PROVENANCE Galerie Céres, Paris, before 1954; André Ravsen, New Canaan, Conn.; Michael Altman, New Fairfield, Conn.; Marc de Montebello, New York; David Schaff Fine Arts, Mendenhall, Pa.; where purchased January 1, 1994, by the current owner.

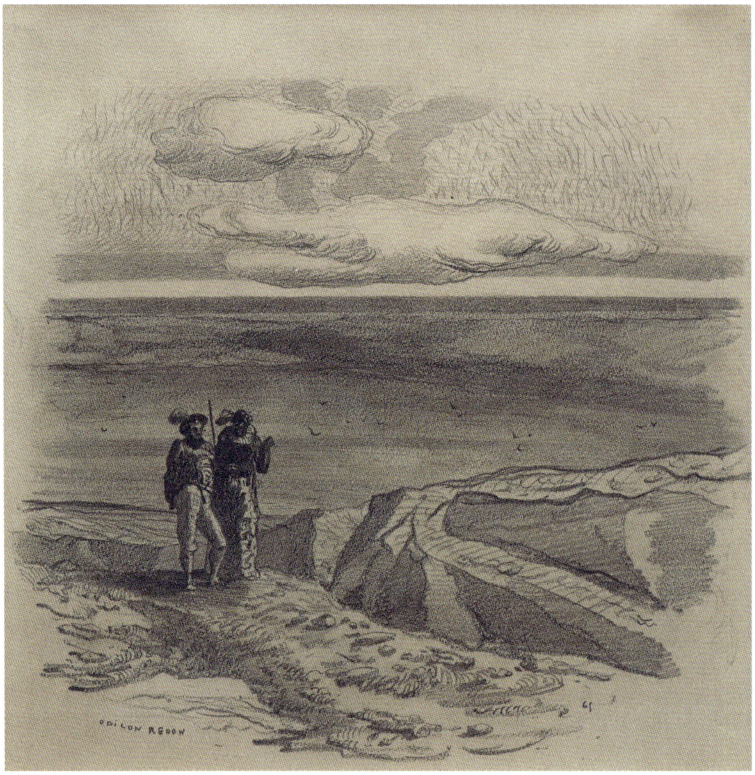

Odilon Redon was an artist better known—and more influential—for his works on paper and the ideas they embodied than for his oil paintings. Born in provincial Bordeaux the same year as Claude Monet, Redon was mainly identified with the symbolist movement and was certainly among the most original and influential draftsmen and printmakers of his age. He was represented more amply than any other artist in the 1913 Armory Show in New York (by some 50 pieces), but the full extent of his impact on the art world was probably not even felt until after his death, when an artist as radical as Marcel Duchamp would declare that Redon's embrace of the subconscious mind had been his generation's most powerful inspiration. Redon was trained in the studios of the painter Jean-Léon Gérôme and the draftsman and engraver Rodolphe Bresdin. His extraordinary mature works in charcoal and pastel, and their counterparts in lithography, remain some of the most compelling images in the history of art.

This previously unpublished drawing dates to the earliest period of Redon's career and was made the same year he left his first apprenticeship, in the studio of Gérôme, and began to work with Bresdin. The rocky, dreamlike landscape setting is typical of those in Redon's other drawings of the mid-1860s, perhaps based on his recent travels in the Basque country of southwestern France, but it is not meant to show a recognizable setting. Like many of Redon's drawings of this period, the composition featuring figures in a landscape seems to allude to a literary episode, but the subject remains frustratingly ambiguous. In this case, the couple shown in Renaissance-era garb makes one want to associate them with such fated literary lovers as Faust and Marguerite or Hamlet and Ophelia, yet the clues are too few to hazard more than a guess.

HMacD

75

Odilon Redon French, 1840–1916

DREAM, C. *1910*

Watercolor and gouache on paper, 10¼ × 8⅞ in.
(260 × 225 mm)
Initialed lower right: *Od. R.*
Dallas Museum of Art, gift of The Pollock Foundation in honor of Hortense D. and Lawrence S. Pollock, 2002.57

PROVENANCE La Boétie, Inc. (Helen Serger), New York; The Pollock Foundation, 1964; given to the Dallas Museum of Art, December 30, 2002.

BIBLIOGRAPHY Wildenstein 1992–98, vol. 4 (1998), 250, no. 2584.

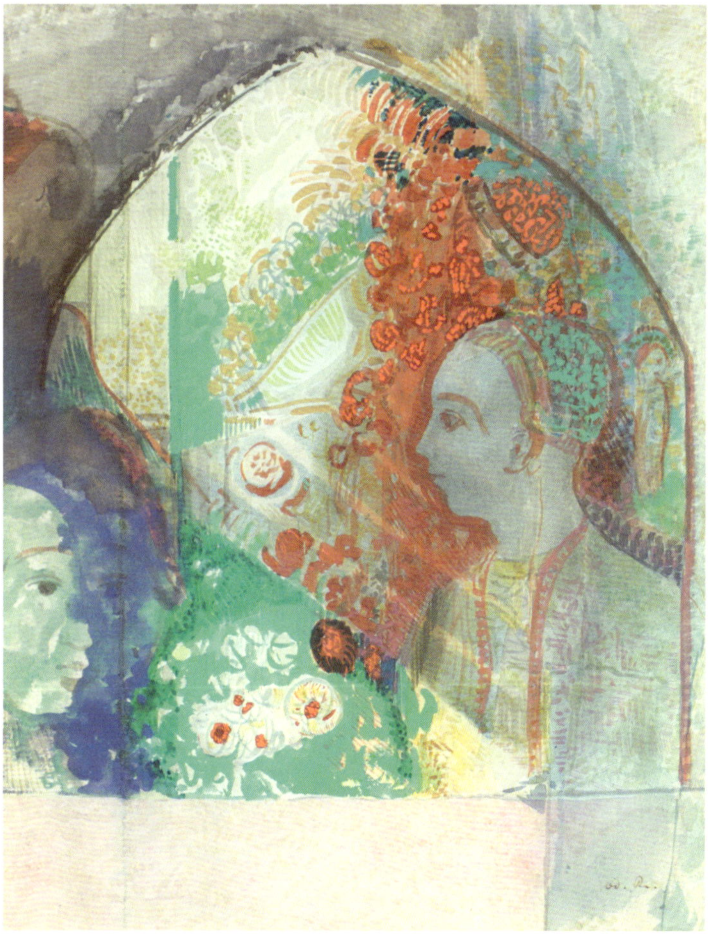

In this shimmering watercolor, Redon poses a female figure within the frame of an ogive window that suggests a setting inside a church or against the backdrop of a stained-glass window. This suggestion is reinforced by the small figure of Christ that hovers behind the woman's head at right, a fragmentary glimpse of a scene from such a window. Redon explored the motif of the female figure in profile, often framed by an arch, in a number of pastels and watercolors during the first decade of the 20th century. Michael Wilson has noted that Redon's sustained interest in the motif of a female figure in profile, her hair swept back under a close-fitting cap, may have been spurred by the 1893 entry of Pisanello's *Portrait of a Young Princess* into the Musée du Louvre (fig. 16, p. 188).[1]

HMacD

Note
1. Wilson 1978, 65.

76

Odilon Redon French, 1840–1916

FLOWERS IN A BLACK VASE, C. *1909–1910*

Pastel on paper, 47 × 39 in. (119 × 991 mm)
Signed lower right: *Odlon* [sic] *Redon*
Dallas Museum of Art, The Wendy and Emery Reves Collection, 1985.R.55

PROVENANCE Mme Robert André, Paris, until 1959; private collection, London, by 1959; Mattheisen Gallery, London, 1960; purchased by Emery Reves, France, 1960; given to the Dallas Museum of Art, The Wendy and Emery Reves Collection, 1985.

EXHIBITED Kunsthalle, Bern, *Odilon Redon,* August 9–October 12, 1958, no. 211 *(Fleurs),* ill.; Mattheisen Gallery, London, *Odilon Redon,* May–June 1959, no. 50 *(Vase de Fleurs),* ill.; Dallas Museum of Art, *Impressionists and Modern Masters,* September 3–October 22, 1989, 84, no. 98; Dallas Museum of Art, *Impressions from the Riviera,* November 5, 1995–February 6, 1996 *(Flowers in a Black Vase).*

BIBLIOGRAPHY Brion 1957, 45; Berger 1965, 216, no. 471; Gazdik 1971, no. 7; Sérullaz 1974, 152, color ill.; Dallas Museum of Art 1985b, 144–45, color ill., cover, ill.; Brettell 1995, 140–41, color ill.; Wildenstein 1992–98, vol. 3, 183, no. 1658; Dallas Museum of Art 1997, 116, color ill.; Dallas Museum of Art 2012, 214.

After years of concentrating on drawings and prints in black (what he called his *Noirs*), Odilon Redon returned to the use of color in the mid-1890s. By the first decade of the 20th century, when he often turned to flowers as a subject, he had developed a method of layering pastel in rich, velvety shades to reveal bouquets hovering against richly variegated fields that never quite cohere as recognizable spaces, either interiors or gardens. The somber palette of *Flowers in a Black Vase* is a reminder of Redon's early mastery of black, but his delicate description of the fragile blooms in high-keyed shades of yellow, blue, and white gives this still life its unexpected vibrancy.

HMacD

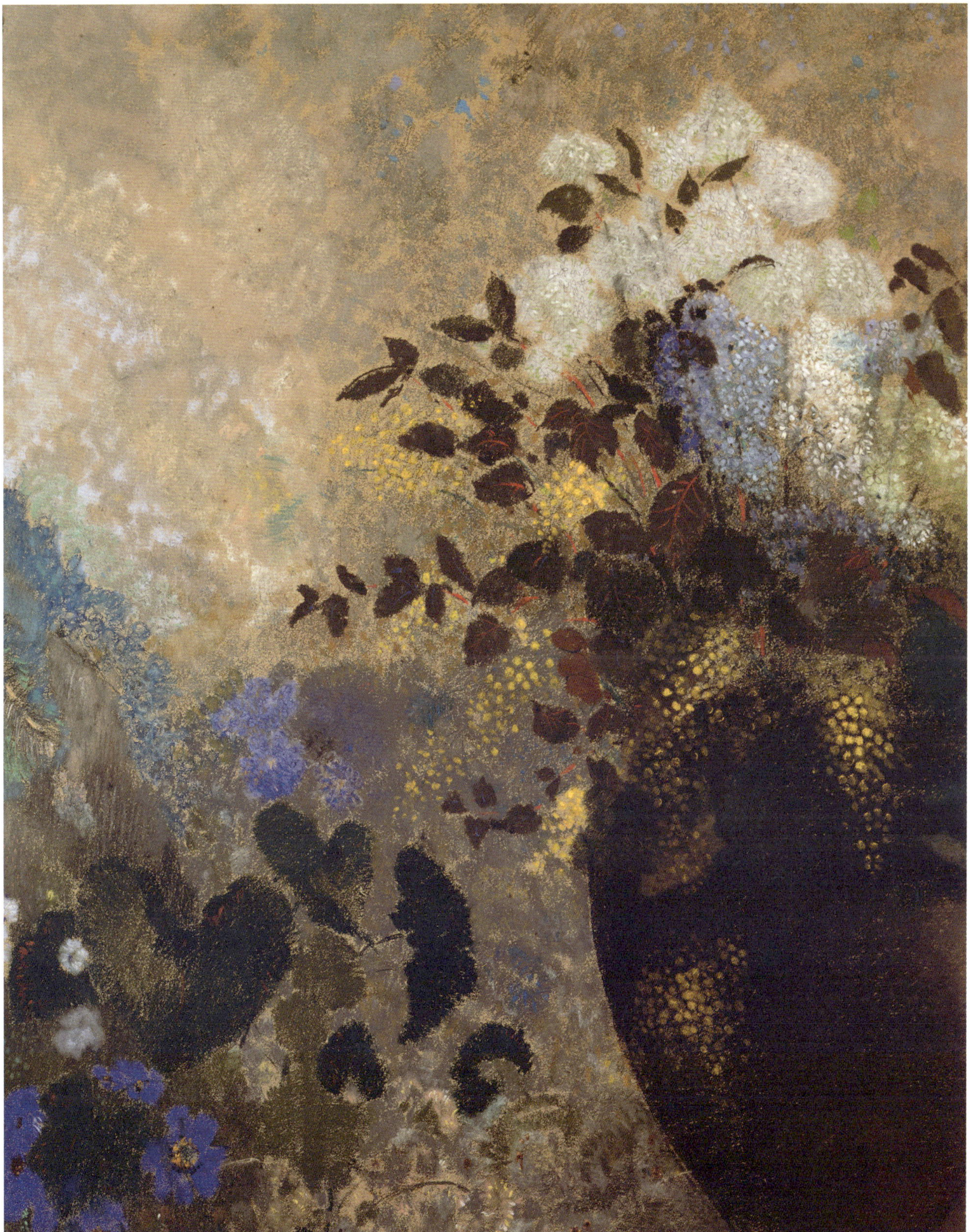

77

Henri de Toulouse-Lautrec French, 1864–1901

THE LAST RESPECTS, *1887*

Ink and gouache on wove paper, 25¾ × 19⅜ in. (655 × 492 mm)
Signed lower right: *H Treclau*
Dallas Museum of Art, The Wendy and Emery Reves Collection, 1985.R.76

PROVENANCE Aristide Bruant; sale, A. Bruant, 1905, no. 9, to M. Saucholle; Albert S. Henraux; Herbert Melbye, Copenhagen; sale, Sotheby's, London, *Impressionist and Modern Paintings, Drawings and Sculpture,* no. 33, 1962; Wendy and Emery Reves; given to the Dallas Museum of Art, The Wendy and Emery Reves Collection, 1985.

EXHIBITED Statens Museum for Kunst, Copenhagen, 1928; Paris, Musée des arts décoratifs, *Lautrec, trentenaire,* 1931, no. 201; Musée du Louvre, Paris, Pavillon de Marsan, *H. de Toulouse-Lautrec,* April 9–May 17, 1931; Statens Museum for Kunst, Copenhagen, 1951; Kunstorus Huis, Oslo, 1953; Dallas Museum of Art, *Impressionist and Modern Masters in Dallas,* September 3–October 22, 1989, 86, no. 119.

BIBLIOGRAPHY Joyant 1926, 13, 98; Mack 1942, 101; Sotheby's 1962, 71; Dortu 1971, vol. 7, 48, no. D.3.004; Mittler and Howze 1980, 175, 177, fig. 9.5; Dallas Museum of Art 1985b, 134–35; Brettell 1995, 92–93; Mittler and Howze, 2001, 89, 141, 177, figs. 5.9, 7.10, 9.9.

As a member of the old aristocracy of France, Henri de Toulouse-Lautrec, who suffered throughout his life from congenital health problems, had no need to work at all. But pursuing a strong calling to become an artist—and benefiting from new notions of exactly what that could mean—he settled as an adult in Montmartre, where he befriended Émile Bernard, Vincent van Gogh, and many other artists of the post-impressionist generation. There, observing and sometimes participating in a lifestyle that centered on alcohol, prostitution, and cabaret performers, he used his extraordinary talent to produce the most vivid record we will ever have of that unique culture. An artist of an essentially graphic sensibility, Toulouse-Lautrec seems never to have been without a sketchbook, and he produced thousands of drawings, many of which he developed with a draftsman's flair for line into paintings executed in gouache on cardboard and others in oil on canvas. Perhaps equally important was his contribution to the art of lithography and the development of the modern poster.

This drawing is a brilliant early example of the type of sheet Toulouse-Lautrec would give to a printer to be turned into an illustration or print, and that is precisely what became of this one. It was created as an illustration for *Le Mirliton,* a journal published by the celebrated singer and performer Aristide Bruant, who owned a cabaret of the same name where Toulouse-Lautrec was a frequent visitor. In this journal, Bruant often published the lyrics to his songs, which described the harsh life of working-class Parisians like the man Toulouse-Lautrec portrays in the foreground, clutching his cap before him in a gesture of respect as a horse-drawn hearse moves up the steep streets of Montmartre. The spare yet emotionally charged description of the principal figure reveals Toulouse-Lautrec's legendary economy of line, a quality that he also brought to his many depictions of Bruant, mostly done as designs for posters. He signed the drawing *H Treclau,* an anagram of his surname.

HMacD and WBJ

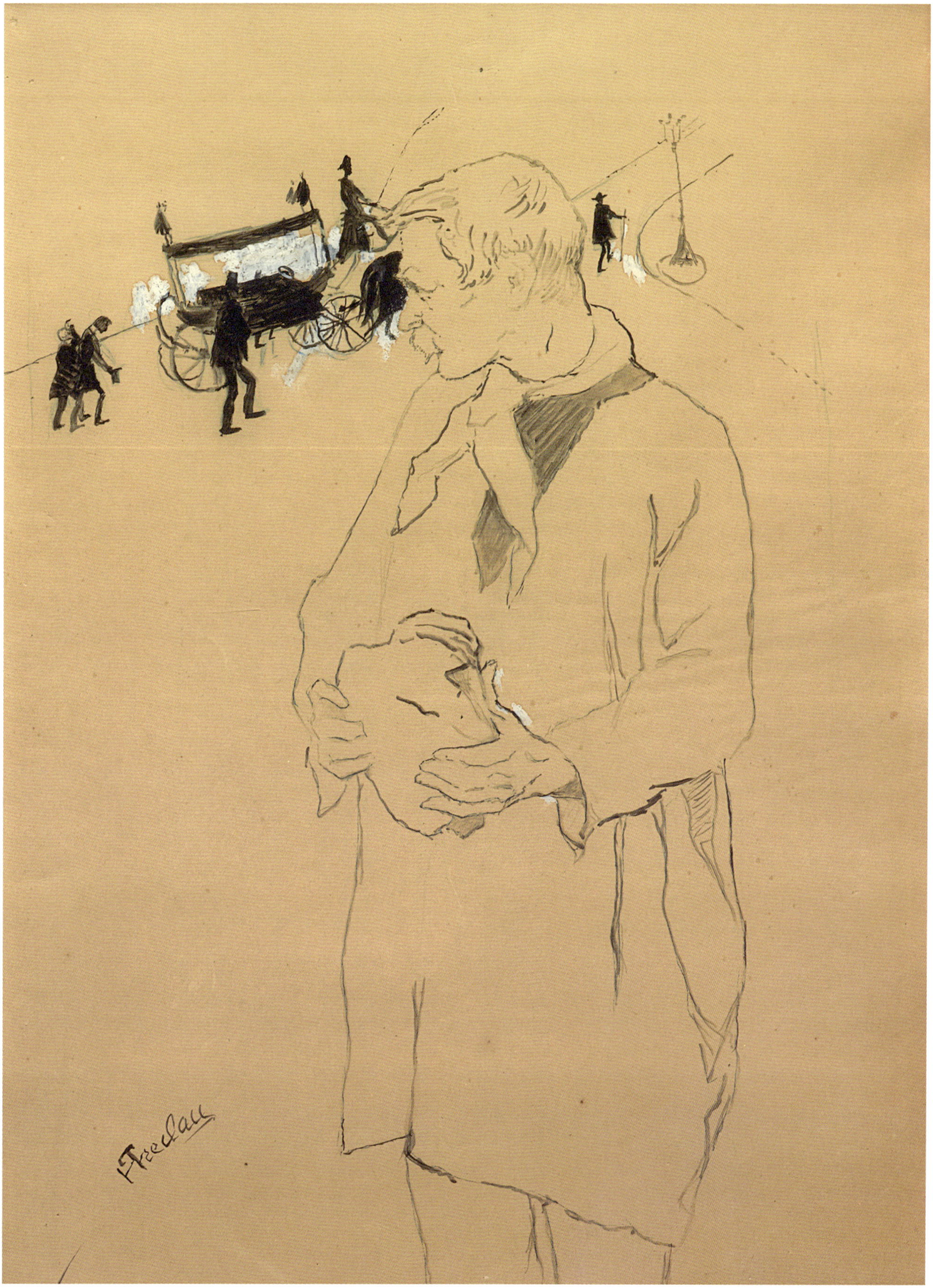
HTreclau

78

Henri de Toulouse-Lautrec French, 1864–1901

PROSTITUTES (FEMMES DE MAISON), C. *1893–1895*

Pastel on emery paper, 23½ × 19⅛ in. (597 × 487 mm)
Signed lower right: *H T Lautrec*
Dallas Museum of Art, The Wendy and Emery Reves Collection, 1985.R.75

PROVENANCE Given by the artist to Robin Langois; Sir Kenneth Clark, London, by 1942; Wildenstein & Co., New York; Emery Reves, France, by 1951; given to the Dallas Museum of Art, The Wendy and Emery Reves Collection, 1985.

EXHIBITED Galerie Manzi-Joyant, Paris, 1896; Galerie Durand Ruel, Paris, *H. de Toulouse-Lautrec,* May 14–31, 1902, no. 141; National Gallery, London, *Nineteenth-Century French Paintings,* December 11, 1927, no. 32; Musée de l'Orangerie, Paris, *Toulouse-Lautrec: Exposition en l'honneur du cinquantième anniversaire de sa mort,* 1951, no. 95; Musée Massena, Nice, *Chefs-d'oeuvre de la peinture française,* November 27, 1956–January 6, 1957; Palais de la Méditerranée, Nice, *Toulouse-Lautrec: Peintures, aquarelles, dessins,* January–March 1957, no. 16; Dallas Museum of Art, *Impressionist and Modern Masters in Dallas,* September 3–October 22, 1989, 86, no. 118; Dallas Museum of Art, *Passion for Art: 100 Treasures 100 Years,* October 12, 2003–March 14, 2004, cat. 31.

BIBLIOGRAPHY Joyant 1926, vol. 1, 283; Huyghe 1931, 145; Cogniat 1950, 122, color ill.; Rothenstein 1950, 23, color pl.; Jourdain and Adhémar 1952, no. 80, color pl.; de Laprade 1954, color pl. V; Julien 1959, 49 *(Femme nue de dos),* color ill.; Adhémar 1962, 137; Dortu 1971, no. 498; Caproni 1977, no. 359; Dallas Museum of Art 1985b, 136–37, color ill.; Brettell 1995 108–9, color ill.; Marton 2003, 3D; Dallas Museum of Art 2012, 211, color ill.; MacDonald 2013, 9, 120 (color det.), 121–22, color ill., 123–24, 127, 130–31.

A master of the art of watching, Toulouse-Lautrec gives us here a completely nonspecific glimpse into brothel life. Two women—one clothed and one nude—share a kind of intimacy without clues as to whether a client has just departed or is yet to arrive. To produce the strong contrast between the pale flesh of the central, nude figure and the dimly lit background, the artist took advantage of the rough texture of his support: emery paper, a kind of fine sandpaper often used by pastel artists. The rough tooth of the emery paper captured the thickly applied, friable pigment and allowed Toulouse-Lautrec to build up layers of blue, pink, and yellow pastel along with the dominant ivory tone of the figure's naked flesh. The movement of his pastel stick across the contours of the figure seems to model her anatomy, sculpting the planes of muscle along her thighs and the sharp angles of her shoulder blades. The secondary figure to the left is loosely described in less densely worked pastel, and the background setting—a room with a rumpled, unmade bed—is barely suggested, the tone of the emery paper (now somewhat darkened with age) left visible to indicate the sparsely decorated space.

HMacD

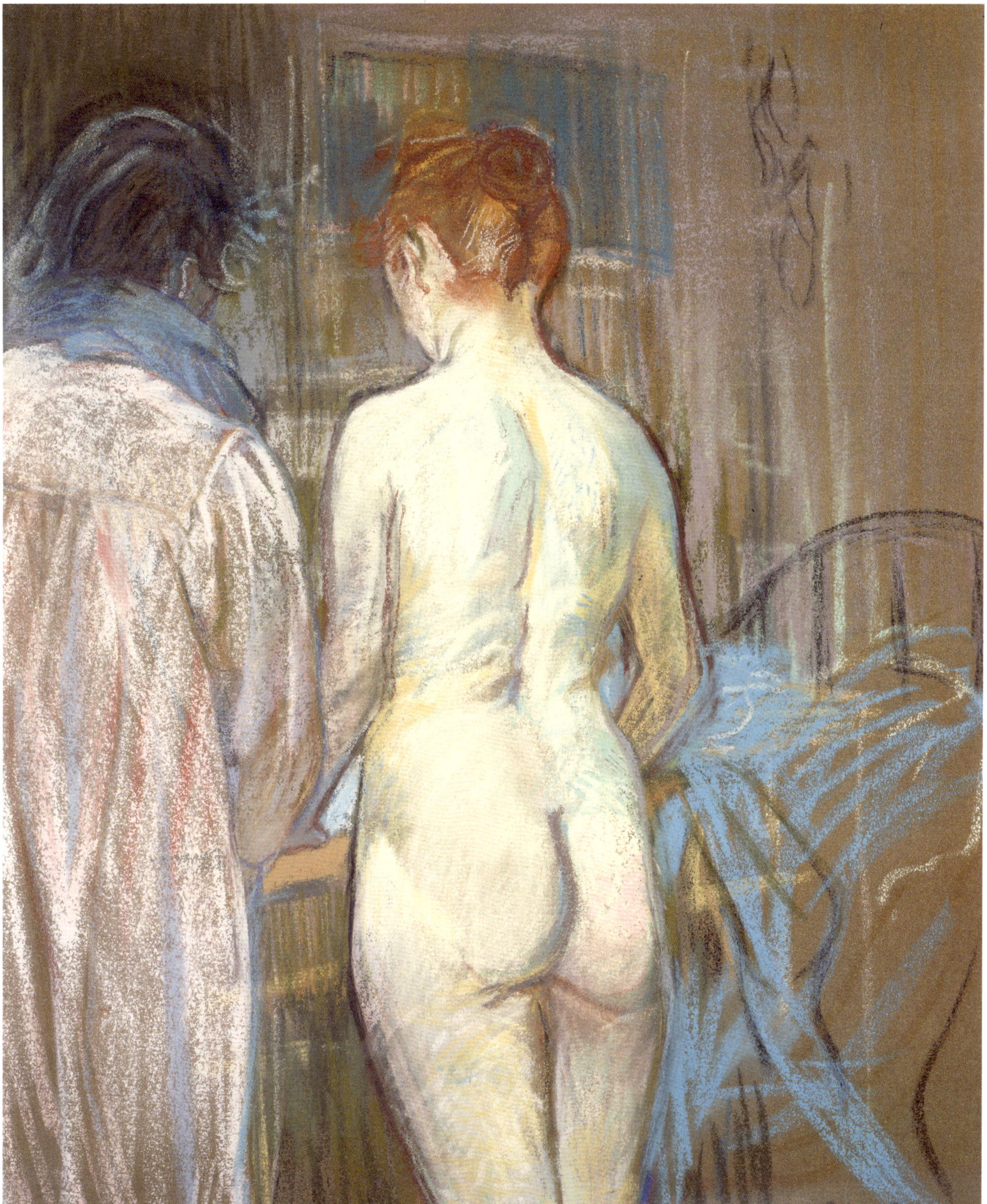

79

Henri de Toulouse-Lautrec French, 1864–1904

LE PAYSAN AU PARAPLUIE, *1881*

Pencil on paper, 6¾ × 10⅝ in. (172 × 270 mm)
Stamped lower left: Monogram of the artist
Collection of Mr. and Mrs. Barron U. Kidd, Dallas

PROVENANCE Dr. Georges Viau (1855–1939); private collection; current owner.

BIBLIOGRAPHY Joyant 1926, vol. 2, 183; Dortu 1971, vol. 5, 356, no. D.2.143.

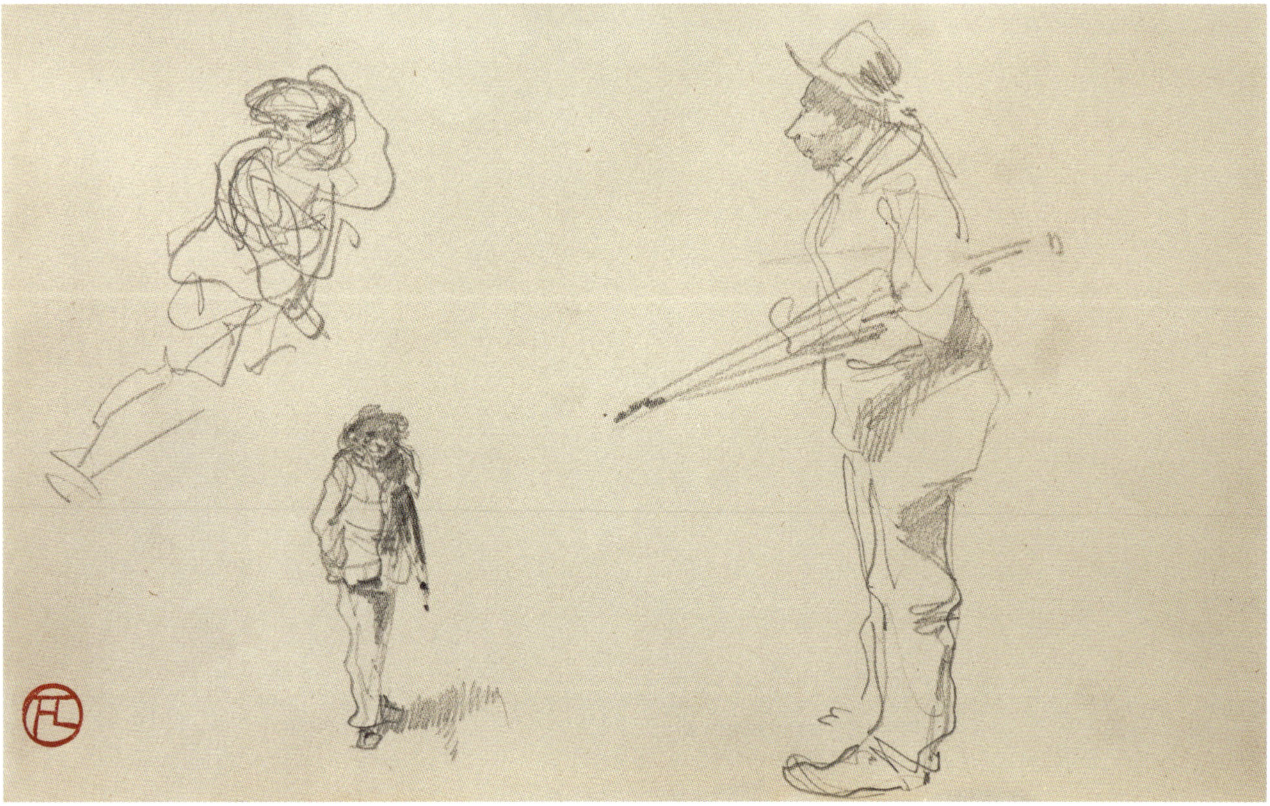

This sheet, once part of a sketchbook, reveals Toulouse-Lautrec's unparalleled talent for caricature in three separate drawings, each quite different in character. The three studies were quickly executed from spontaneous observation of a somewhat rustic male figure clutching a furled umbrella under his arm. The large sketch at right emphasizes the linear description of the man's distinctive profile, while the smaller study at lower left concentrates on capturing his form through areas of light and shadow. The man's broad-brimmed hat, baggy clothes, and heavy shoes alert us that he is a peasant rather than one of the urban characters the artist was famous for depicting. This suggests that the drawing was likely made when Toulouse-Lautrec was visiting his family's estate in southwestern France.

HMacD

80

Jules Chéret French, 1836–1932

PORTRAIT OF ANDRÉ DE JOLY
(PORTRAIT D'ANDRÉ DE JOLY), *1905*

Sanguine on paper, 14½ × 9⅞ in. (370 × 250 mm)
Signed, dated, and inscribed: *A M. A. de Joly / en toute sympathie / Chéret / Nice 15 / 5 / 1905*
Dallas Museum of Art, gift of Wendy Reves, 1990.R.181

PROVENANCE Sale, Phillips, London, *Modern Paintings and Drawings,* June 27, 1990, lot 30, purchased by Wendy Reves, France; given to the Dallas Museum of Art, The Wendy and Emery Reves Collection, 1990.

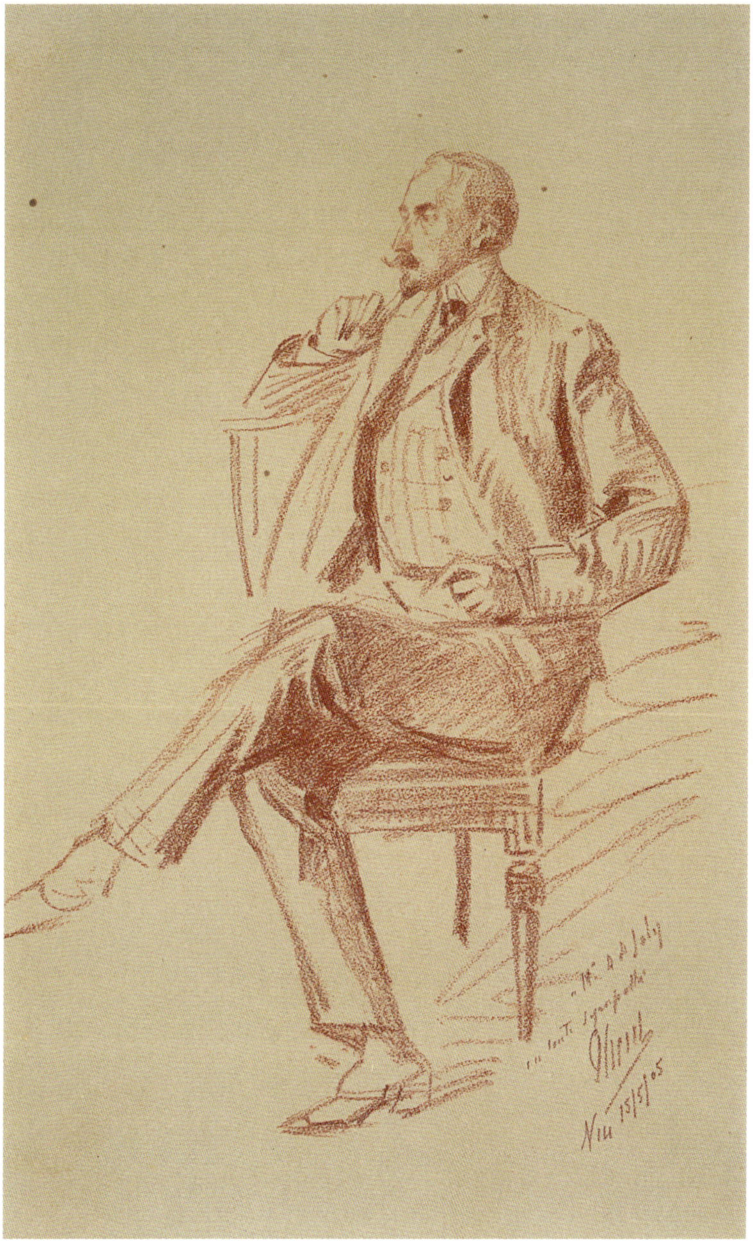

Jules Chéret was the most successful French poster designer of the second half of the 19th century. His light, swirling style, use of bright colors, and the predominance of racy women in his images gained him an unprecedented audience, further enhanced by his productivity: he designed more than 1,000 posters. He also received many commissions for the interior decoration of public buildings (such as the Hôtel de Ville in Paris) and private homes (such as the celebrated Villa La Sapinière for Baron Vitta, and Maurice Fenaille's townhouse in Neuilly). His work as a designer shows an unflagging admiration for the art of Antoine Watteau and the French artists of the 18th century.

This sanguine drawing is a perfect example of that tendency, as it combines the vivacity of the Age of Enlightenment with the spirit of the handsome society portraits of Giovanni Boldini or Paul César Helleu. The model for this portrait played an important part in Chéret's career. André de Joly (1857–1934) was Prefect of the Alpes-Maritimes from 1904 to 1917 and commissioned the artist to decorate the Gallery of the Prefecture in Nice, the former residence of the dukes of Savoy and the kings of Sardinia. Chéret retired to Nice and died there. The city's fine arts museum bears his name and has a collection of his works donated by the Baron and Baroness Vitta.

OM

81

Félix Buhot French 1847–1898

AU BOULEVARD DE CLICHY, *1887*

Ink, pencil, and watercolor on paper, 9 × 14⅜ in. (228 × 365 mm)
Signed lower left: *Au boulevard de Clichy / Première pensée de l'enterrement au Boulevard / Felix Buhot*; inscribed lower right: 5; stamped upper right in red: Buhot's monogram (Lugt 977)
Dallas Museum of Art, Foundation for the Arts, The Alfred and Juanita Bromberg Collection, Bequest of Juanita Bromberg, 2000.208.FA

PROVENANCE Purchased by Juanita K. Bromberg from the dealer Marcel Le Comte, Paris; Dallas Museum of Art, bequest of Juanita K. Bromberg to the Dallas Museum of Art, 2000.

The lineup of cabs following a hearse on a cold rainy morning combines many recurring features found in Félix Buhot's prints. Parisian streets, black silhouettes reflecting on a watery sidewalk, and long perspectives of new buildings are often central to his poetic descriptions of urban life. Draftsman, printmaker, and painter, Buhot was interested in landscape, particularly urban landscape, and often combined vignettes or remarks in the margins around a central image, describing them as "symphonic etchings." This new and refined way of adding visual notes, as on an old manuscript or palimpsest, was extremely well received by critics and print collectors. The detailed, obsessive etching of the plate always supports a poetic description of the subject. Combining a romantic inspiration with a fascination for modern urban life, Buhot illustrated many novels, including *L'Ensorcelée*, by Jules Barbey d'Aurevilly, and *Les Lettres de mon Moulin*, by Alphonse Daudet. He died in his early 50s, deep in depression despite his success.

This drawing, which represents an early stage in Buhot's process for elaborating a print, was probably the first idea for the print known as *Funeral Procession on the Boulevard de Clichy* (1887; fig. 13). He employs a very different way of drawing in comparison with his etching manner: quick, synthetic, and switching from watercolor to pencil and ink, showing an astonishing talent for capturing movements and impressions either using outlines or through volume. Few drawings by Buhot are known to be in public collections, and even fewer illustrate the array of his talents. Another drawing of the same composition, in the same orientation as the print, was in the Baldwin Wallace Collection (sold by Rachel Davis Fine Arts, March, 20, 2010, Cleveland, Ohio, lot 210). This last drawing is less elliptic and more crowded with figures and smoke. A famous print by Buhot from 1876—*Cabs, a Winter Morning at the Quai de l'Hôtel Dieu*—describes a similar line of cabs in a dark urban environment.

OM

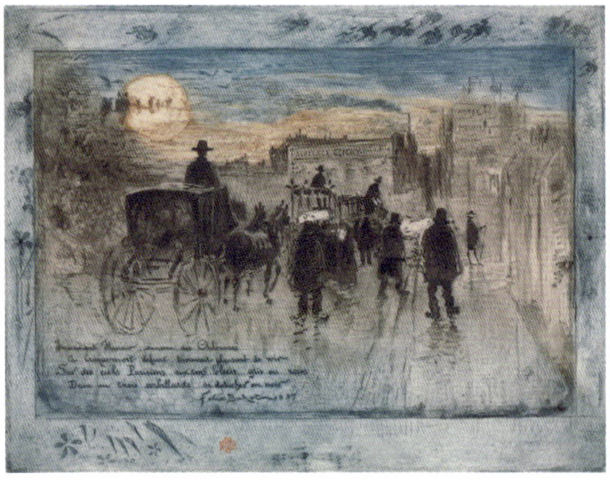

Fig. 13 Félix-Hilaire Buhot, *Funeral Procession on the Boulevard de Clichy*, 1887. Etching and aquatint inked *à la poupée*. The Baltimore Museum of Art: The George A. Lucas Collection, purchased with funds from the State of Maryland, Laurence and Stella Bendann Fund, and contributions from individuals, foundations, and corporations throughout the Baltimore community, BMA 1996.48.12993.

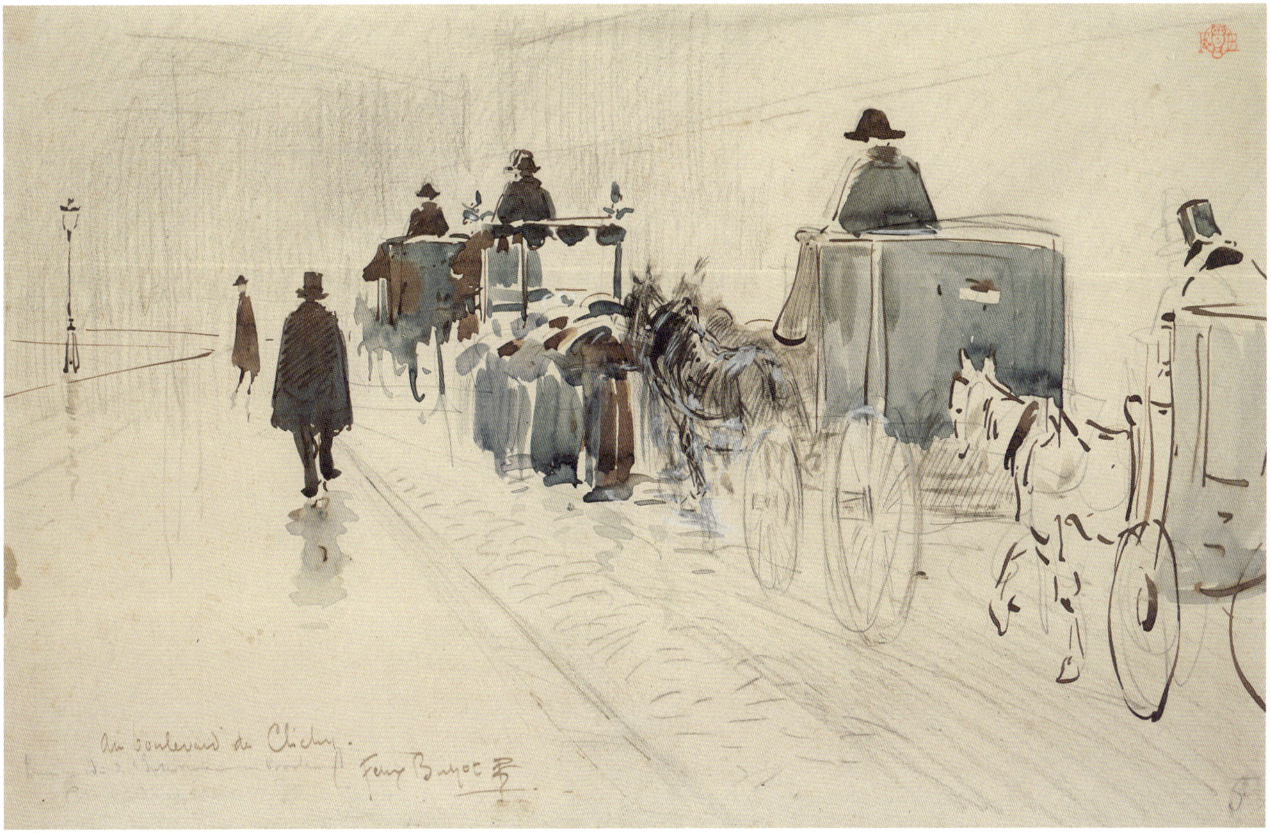
Au boulevard de Clichy.

Émile Gallé French, 1846–1904

FRAGMENT OF A STUDY OF A COUPE OFFERED TO PASTEUR FROM L'ÉCOLE NORMALE, *1893*

Pen and ink, gouache, and watercolor (?), 9½ × 9½ in. (240 × 241 mm)
Private collection, Dallas

PROVENANCE Galerie Antoine Laurentin, Paris, by 2000; where purchased 2000 by the current owner.

This virtually unknown study of the decoration of a vase made in honor of the famed scientist Louis Pasteur is a richly surreal expression of the intersection of the worlds of science and art in the last decade of the 19th century. Delineated by Émile Gallé, one of the leading French designers of glass and furnishings in the art nouveau taste, the motifs of this work reveal an homage to Pasteur's accomplishments in their depiction of what the designer described as "viruses swimming among globules of blood, germs carried in the atmosphere" and the elements that the scientist Pasteur "uncovered, conquered, catalogued and cultivated in experiments."[1] Along with specific representations of cells and bacteria, the symbolic forms of a python and Hydra issue forth from the darkness bringing suffering upon nature, here represented by the rabid dog and choleric chicken, both subjects of study for Pasteur. The tools of science—a microscope, test tube, and twin petri dishes—feature prominently as the technological means for discovery and, aided by rays of knowledge illuminating the microscopic world of disease, provided Pasteur with the power to reveal and effect a curative transformation declared by Gallé's quotation of "Et se transfigurer . . ." (And be transfigured . . .) from Victor Hugo's *Les Contemplations* (1856).[2]

The vase was commissioned for Pasteur's 70th birthday in December 1892 by Paul Dupuy, the bursar of the École normale supérieure, who, like Pasteur, was an admirer of Gallé's work. Considering the interests of the artist, the modern decoration of the completed vase (fig. 14) was especially fitting in its combination of motifs of the natural world—the botanical subjects with which Gallé was so familiar shared with Pasteur's realm of the study of biological sciences. In a single work, Gallé found an ideal opportunity to meld his own expertise in rendering sinuous vegetal forms in glass with symbolist imagery suggesting the "penetration of the mysterious depths of an elemental nature." An earlier monochrome study of the decoration (Musée d'Orsay, Paris) lacks this example's rich color palette and various details, including the rabid dog that Gallé later added. When the completed vase was at last presented to Pasteur on April 30, 1893, Gallé described his challenges to meet the commission as his "tentative gropings" that "crowded upon paper notes of interloping forms, of bizarre adaptations of certain beings" which he felt to bring to life required "not the pipe of a glassmaker, but the brush of a Hokusai, the demonical pencil of a Goya, the nightmare of an Odilon Redon."

KWT

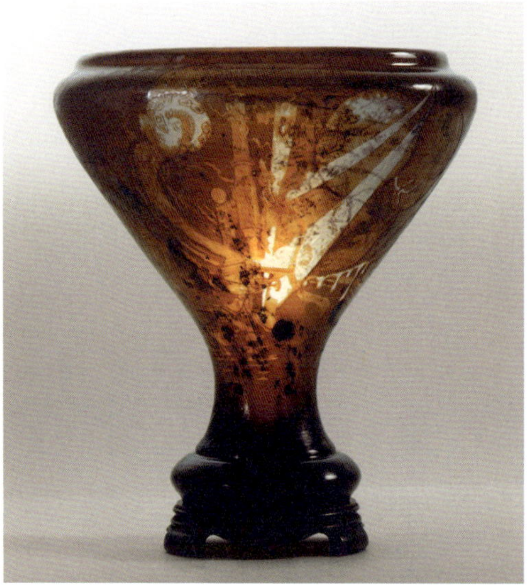

Fig. 14 Émile Gallé, *Le vase Pasteur: La face au microscope* on stand, 1893. Glass blown, acid-etched, and engraved. Institut Pasteur / Musée Pasteur, Paris, D173.

Notes
1. For a detailed discussion of the commission for the Pasteur vase, see Le Tacon 1994. This drawing was presumably unknown to Le Tacon and thus was not included in his review. All quotes by Gallé are drawn from Le Tacon's reprint of Gallé's April 30, 1893, manuscript on *le vase Pasteur* held by the Pasteur Museum, Paris, originally published in the *Journal des Débats* (May 3, 1893), the *Revue Encyclopédique* (May 15, 1893), and subsequently in Gallé's *Ecrits pour l'Art* (1908). There are numerous publications on the subject of Gallé's career; a full accounting of these references is beyond the scope of this essay.
2. Hugo 1856. Gallé references Hugo's text elsewhere on the completed vase and notes the inspiration for the vase as derived from the lines, *"On verra le troupeau des Hydres formidables / Sortir, monter du fond des brumes insondables / Et se transfigurer."* The context of this design as a visual realization of unconsciousness is discussed in Silverman 1989, 238–39.

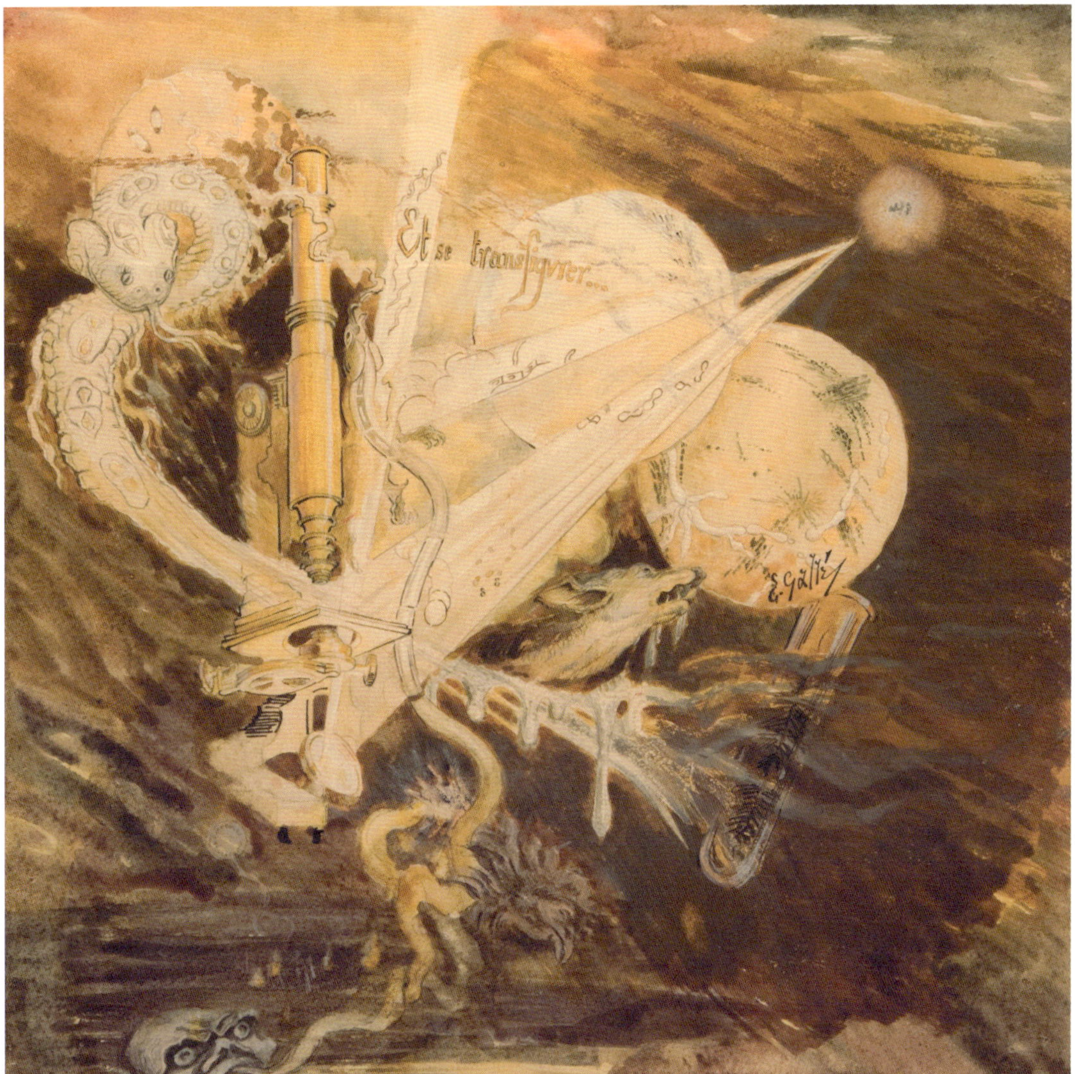
Et se transfigurer…
É. Gallé

83

Gwen John British, 1876–1939

WOMAN AND ORPHAN GIRL IN CHURCH, C. *1910–1920*

Charcoal and watercolor on paper,
6½ × 5¼ (165 × 133 mm)
Signed upper left: *Gwen John*
Dallas Museum of Art, Foundation for the Arts, The Alfred and Juanita Bromberg Collection, Bequest of Juanita Bromberg, 2000.281.FA

PROVENANCE Gwen John's estate (number E.J. 274); Edwin John (Gwen John's nephew); gift of the previous to J. Wood-Palmer, 1949; Leicester Galleries, London, 1953; sold to Alfred and Juanita K. Bromberg, August 28, 1953; bequest of Juanita K. Bromberg to the Dallas Museum of Art, 2000

EXHIBITED Tate Gallery, London, *Ethel Walker, Frances Hodgkins, Gwen John: A Memorial Exhibition,* May 7–June 15, 1952, no. 151.

BIBLIOGRAPHY Rothenstein 1952–74, vol. 1, 30, no. 151.

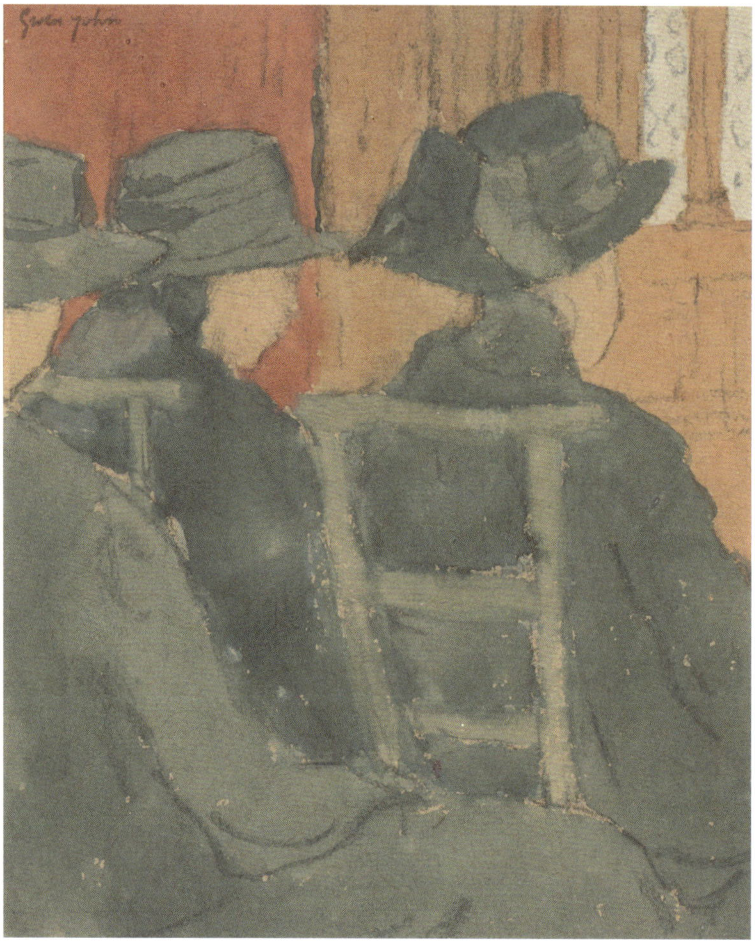

Painted in Meudon on the outskirts of Paris, this composition is part of a series of watercolors by Gwen John about women attending her church. Quiet, subdued, and intensely deep, John's art is among the most distinctive of the period. After studying at the Slade School of Fine Art in London, she made a brief trip to Paris in 1898 and in 1903 returned to France for the rest of her life. Sister to the painter Augustus John, Auguste Rodin's lover and muse during the early 1900s, and a close friend of Rodin's secretary, the poet Rainer Maria Rilke, John is a fascinating figure. Discreet and passionate, well acquainted with the avant-garde through her friends Henri Matisse, Pablo Picasso, and Constantin Brancusi, she pursued her own path with a persistent will.

Thanks to her patron John Quinn, an organizer of the 1913 Armory Show in New York, she settled in Meudon, where Rodin had his house and studio, and lived a quiet and simple life there. In 1913, the same year she exhibited a painting at the Armory Show, she converted to Catholicism. She started a series of paintings of Mère Marie Poussepin, the founder of the order of the Dominican Sisters of Charity. She was sometimes criticized for sketching in church. Once she responded, "I like to pray in Church like everyone else but my mind is not capable of praying for long periods at a time. . . . The orphans with those black hats with the white band and their black dresses with the white collars charm me, and other creatures charm me in Church. If I cut out all of this, there would not be enough happiness in my life."[1] In these gouaches and watercolors, John experimented with variations on a simple theme: women seated, seen generally from the back, their faces not visible even in a lost profile. Uncluttered in the extreme, using a small number of colors, each of them subtle and calm, her works convey a rare combination of meditation and intensity.

OM

Note

1. Jacques Maritain, *Notebooks,* trans. Joseph W. Evans (Albany: Magi Books, 1984), p. 304.

84

Jessie Marion King British, 1875–1949

FRONTISPIECE, THE BOOK OF BRIDGES, C. *1911*

Ink and watercolor on paper, 7⅞ × 6³⁄₁₆ in. (200 × 157 mm)
Inscribed above the image: *The Book of Bridges*; below the image: *by / Jessie M. King*
Dallas Museum of Art, Gift of Henry Hawley, 2005.87.9

PROVENANCE Miss Merle Taylor; her estate sale June 21, 1977, New York, Sotheby Parke-Bernet, lot 146; collection of Henry Hawley; given to the Dallas Museum of Art, 2005.

BIBLIOGRAPHY Printed books with this illustration on the cover: Arcambeau 1911; Arcambeau 1912; White 2007, 57.

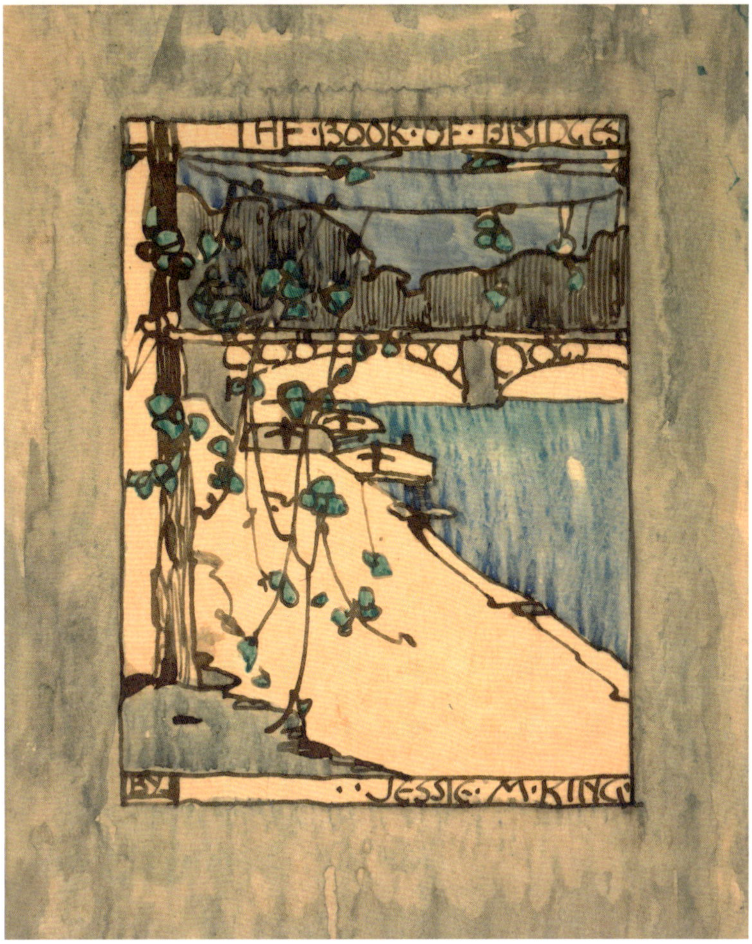

This illustration for the cover of a book on Paris bridges is a perfect example of Jessie Marion King's Glasgow School of Art style: elegant, simple, linear, accurate, and dreamy at the same time. The school's most famous figure was Charles Rennie Mackintosh, but Jessie Marion King, as an illustrator, was its most acclaimed practitioner. She received many awards, and her works were published in Glasgow, London, Berlin, and Paris. She also designed jewelry, silverware, and fabrics for Liberty & Company, in addition to wallpaper, textiles, costumes, and even interiors. Well connected with the Paris art scene, she was influential in the creation of the art deco movement.

The frontispiece of *The Book of Bridges,* or *Ponts de Paris,* is a view of the old Pont du Carrousel between the Musée du Louvre and rue des Saints-Pères. The bridge was destroyed in 1939. Known for its circular iron features, it was already 70 years old when King painted it. Trees on the bank and the bridge in the background lend a bucolic quality to this urban location. The definitive print on the cover differs in slight details, more saturated colors, and the placement of the author's name, Arcambeau, ahead of King's name. The book contains other representations of Paris bridges; the Dallas Museum of Art has in its collection preparatory drawings for two of them. The illustrations—in their composition, the serial aspect, and some of the perspectives—show the influence of Japanese prints, which were an inspiration for the entire Scottish school.

OM

85

Fernand Khnopff Belgian, 1858–1921

ANDRÉ GERMAIN, *1909*

Colored pencil on paper, 13 × 9½ (330 × 241 mm) (sight)
Signed and dated upper right: *Fernand Khnopff 1909*
Private collection, Dallas

PROVENANCE André Germain (1881–1964), by descent to the current owner.

EXHIBITED Galerie Georges Giroux, Brussels, 1916, *Salon du Portrait,* no. 88; Palais Galliéra, Paris, 1921, *Art Belge,* no. 15.

BIBLIOGRAPHY Biermé 1911, 5; Delevoy 1987, no. 254; Delville 1925, 27.

Ferdinand Bac, memorialist, designer, and creator of gardens, described the extraordinary personage depicted in this portrait:

> Neither man nor woman, choirboy nor old priest, André [Germain] is neither young nor old. Formerly married to Edmée Alphonse Daudet, he is a sort of degenerate monster, honeyed in voice and manners and, so it is said, cruel, underhanded, fanatical, and vindictive but an essayist [who is] very intelligent and well read. He edits a magazine called *Les Écrits Nouveaux* to which Mme de Noailles contributes. . . . He detests France and the French: they do not understand him. He seems to keep a lookout for the brilliant merely in order to betray them.[1]

A member of Proust's inner circle, Germain supported many writers through his magazine and the considerable financial resources that he inherited from his father Henri Germain, founder of the Crédit Lyonnais. He admired both the great turn-of-the-century figures and younger writers such as Louis Aragon and André Malraux. A prolific and provocative writer, he died penurious and forgotten.

Who better to portray him than the painter and draftsman Fernand Khnopff? One of the best-known Belgian symbolists, the painter of *Memories* (1889) and *Caresses* (1896) (both in the Royal Museums of Fine Arts of Belgium, Brussels) was connected to the writers Émile Verhaeren, Georges Rodenbach, Joséphin (Sâr) Péladan, and Stéphane Mallarmé. His links with England, the French symbolists, and the artists of the Vienna Secession placed him at the center of European artistic movements. His studio-house in Brussels had a profound impact on the artists, architects, and writers of his time.

A refined and subtle draftsman, Khnopff created a diaphanous universe of strange colors whose images haunt the spectator. In this portrait of Germain, we find the decadence typical of many artists and writers in his entourage. Fragile touches of color, such as the blue of the pocket handkerchief or the red of the lapel flower, reinforce the ethereal quality. The exquisite use of crayons echoes the portraits of the Italian and French Renaissance by Leonardo da Vinci, Jean Clouet, and Nicolas Lagneau.

OM

Note
1. Bac 2013, 218–19.

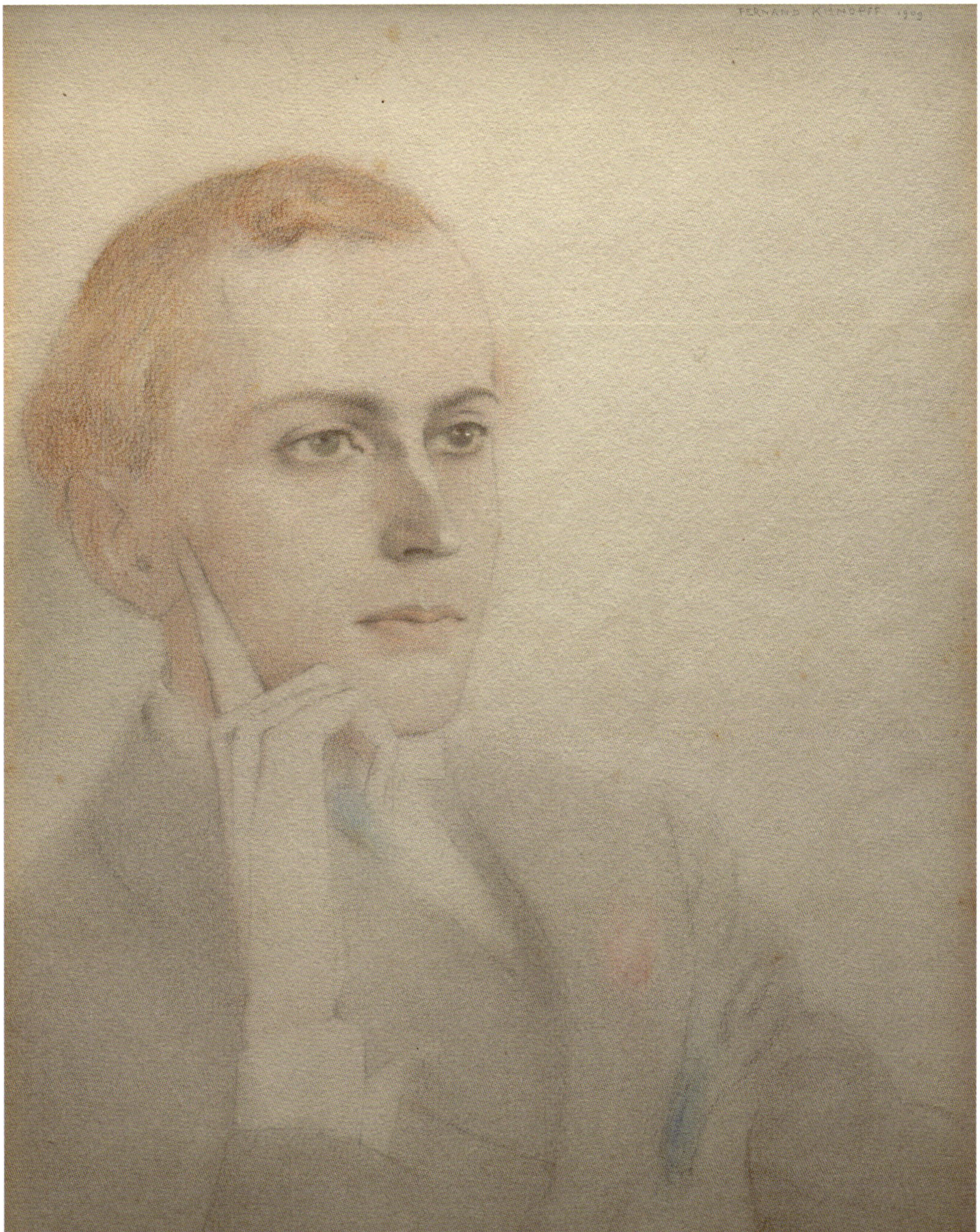
FERNAND KHNOPFF 1909

86

Pierre Bonnard French, 1867–1947

STUDY FOR LE PETIT SOLFÈGE ILLUSTRÉ, CHAPITRE I, C. *1891–1893*

India ink and graphite on wove paper, 8 × 11 in. (203 × 280 mm)
Private collection, Dallas

PROVENANCE Peter H. Deitsch Gallery, New York; where acquired 1962 by a private collector, Europe; sale, Christie's, London, *Impressionist and Modern Works on Paper*, June 19, 2007, lot 116; where purchased by the current owner.

EXHIBITED Peter H. Deitsch Gallery, New York, *Bonnard: 50 Watercolors and Drawings for "Petit Solfège Illustré"* (1893), November 6–December 1, 1962.

87

TRIAL PROOF OF LE PETIT SOLFÈGE ILLUSTRÉ, CHAPITRE I, *1893*

Lithograph touched with watercolor on paper, 8 × 10½ in. (205 × 267 mm)
Private collection, Dallas

PROVENANCE Peter H. Deitsch Gallery, New York; where purchased October 25, 1963, by the current owner.

EXHIBITED Peter H. Deitsch Gallery, New York, *Bonnard: 50 Watercolors and Drawings for "Petit Solfège Illustré"* (1893), November 6–December 1, 1962; Dallas Museum of Art, *The Time of Bonnard: Prints and Illustrated Books in France*, September 16–November 4, 1984.

88

STUDY FOR "GAMME MAJEURE" (MAJOR SCALE) OF LE PETIT SOLFÈGE ILLUSTRÉ, C. *1891–1893*

Pencil, ink, and watercolor on paper, 7 × 10⅜ in. (177 × 265 mm)
Collection of Mary Ralph Lowe, Fort Worth

PROVENANCE Sale, Sotheby's, London, February 4, 1981, lot 484; JPL Fine Arts, London; current owner.

EXHIBITED Peter H. Deitsch Gallery, New York, *Bonnard: 50 Watercolors and Drawings for "Petit Solfège Illustré"* (1893), November 6–December 1, 1962, brochure, cover ill.; JPL Fine Arts, London, *Pierre Bonnard*, 1985, no. 2; Metropolitan Museum of Art, New York, December 2, 1989–February 4, 1990, Museum of Fine Arts, Houston, February 25–April 29, 1990, and Museum of Fine Arts, Boston, May 25–July 29, 1990, *Pierre Bonnard: The Graphic Works*, 55, fig. 70, no. 22.

A leading member of the group of avant-garde artists who called themselves the Nabis (in Hebrew, the prophets), Pierre Bonnard worked in a broad range of media and idioms. In addition to his primary work as a painter, he was among the most inventive draftsmen and lithographers of the late 19th and early 20th centuries. During the 1890s, his graphic work was characterized by an energetic linear style that reflected the contemporary art nouveau aesthetic and the profound influence of Japanese prints.

In 1893, Bonnard published his first illustrated book, a children's music primer written by his brother-in-law Claude Terrasse. Bonnard's witty and inventive drawings for the project, created over nearly two years (72 are known) do not merely illustrate the text, but animate the ideas expressed in Terrasse's simple explanations crafted for a child's understanding. For instance, in Bonnard's study for the first page of chapter 1 (cat. 86), the text asks, "What is music?" The answer—"It is the art of producing sounds and combining them in a manner pleasing to the ear"—is echoed not only in the illustration of an audience listening intently, chins propped in their hands, but also in the repeating design of free-floating ears that seem to emerge from the wild locks of hair and flowing coattails of the musicians. The lithographed trial proof for the same page (cat. 87) shows a later and longer version of the text, for which Bonnard has expanded the scenes of performing musicians to fill nearly all the marginal spaces, with a choir occupying the left border and an orchestra filling the spaces at right. A drawing for the new shape of the expanded text box, corresponding to that used in the trial proof, appears on the verso of the first drawing. The brown watercolor brushstrokes prominently visible on the lithograph would appear to be gratuitous, though they add by chance a visual appeal to the modern eye.

Helen Giambruni has pointed to the influence of contemporary British illustrators, including Walter Crane and Kate Greenaway, on Bonnard.[1] These

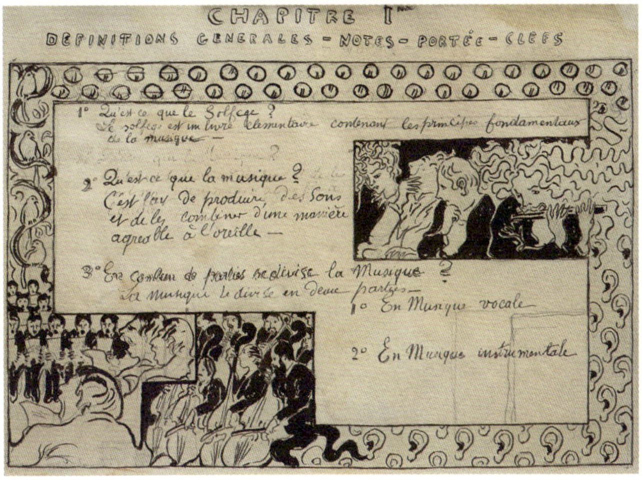

Cat. 86

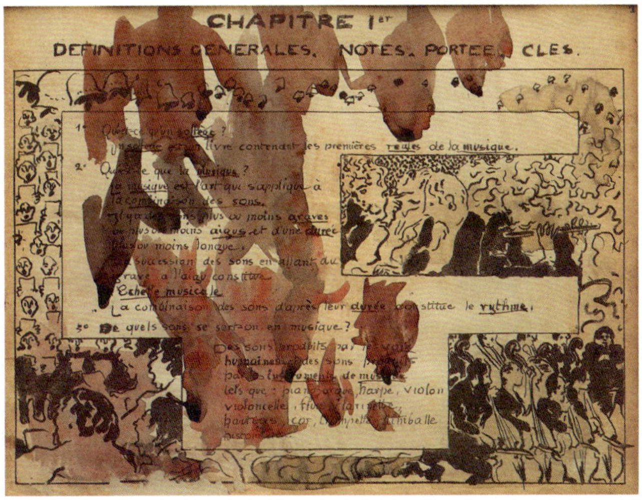

Cat. 87

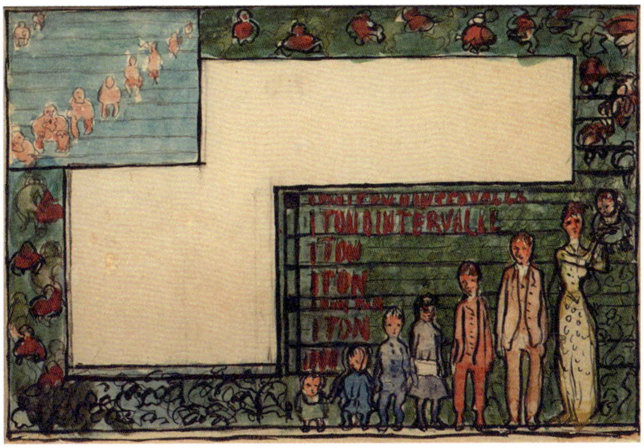

Cat. 88

artists, whose work was much appreciated in French artistic circles, offered him new and playful models for using style and scale to animate the pages of a book. Bonnard himself claimed as a reference point the whimsical marginalia of medieval manuscripts.[2] In his watercolor study for the page explaining the major scale (cat. 88), with its five tones and two half-tones, Bonnard sketches a family of children, their various heights striking the requisite tones; their mother holds up her lumpish infant to reach the final half-tone in the scale. The paper-doll flatness of the family in this charming illustration is typical of the naïveté that Bonnard deliberately courts in his illustrations for the *Petit solfège*.

HMacD

Notes
1. Helen Giambruni, in New York 1989, 53–54.
2. Ibid., 56.

89

Pierre Bonnard French, 1867–1947

SELF-PORTRAIT SMOKING AND OTHER STUDIES (RECTO), *1895*;
STUDIES OF MEN AND A RELIGIOUS SCENE (VERSO), *1895*

Pencil, india ink, and watercolor on paper,
12½ × 8¾ in. (318 × 222 mm)
Private collection, Dallas

PROVENANCE Jill Newhouse Gallery, New York; where purchased by the current owner in 2010.

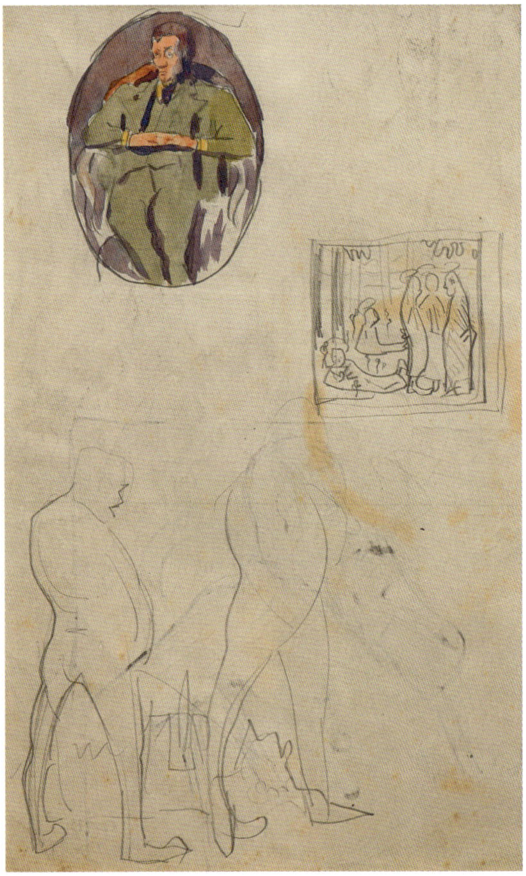
Cat. 89, verso.

This double-sided sheet is a fascinating demonstration of how Bonnard used the process of drawing to explore and develop visual ideas. On the recto (facing page), no fewer than seven different figures have been sketched, including two rough ink studies of the bearded face of Claude-Marie Terrasse, father of the artist's close friend and brother-in-law Claude Terrasse (see cats. 86–88). Bonnard has developed three of these figures to the extent that he added rough frames, isolating these nascent compositions from the larger sheet of studies. The most prominent and fully realized of these sketches, at the lower center of the sheet, represents what appears to be the artist himself, leaning back in a chair, wearing the pince-nez that he habitually used in those years, and smoking.

On the verso (above), Bonnard again allows his inventive pencil to explore several apparently unrelated ideas. In the upper left, he reworks in color and in an oval format the figure of a seated man in an armchair, hands folded across his waistcoat, which has bled through from the recto. At right is a compositional study of a religious subject with five haloed figures. At lower left, he has made two quick pencil sketches of a man urinating against a wall. These sketches are perhaps related to the framed figure at the upper left of the recto, a study of a vagrant later published as *Le Clochard, ou Scène de Rue*.

HMacD and WBJ

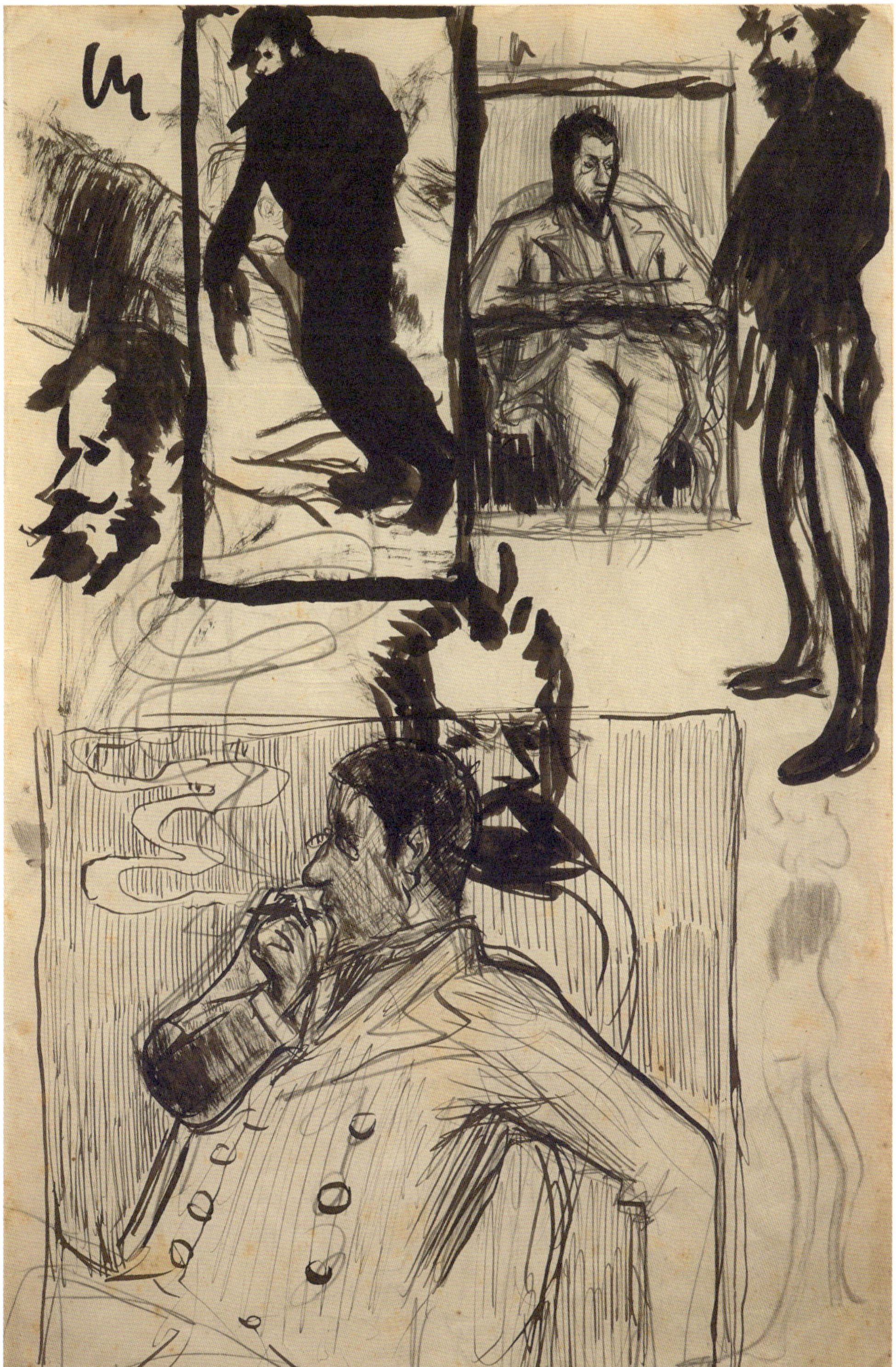

Cat. 89, recto.

Édouard Vuillard French, 1868–1940

LA PLACE VINTIMILLE (TRIPTYCH), *1908–1909*

Pastel on paper, laid on wood; left panel: 72⅞ × 26¾ in. (1852 × 680 mm); center panel: 74⅜ × 19⅜ in. (1888 × 492 mm); right panel: 72⅞ × 26¾ in. (1852 × 680 mm)
Estate stamp on each panel, lower right: *E. Vuillard* (Lugt 2497b)
Private collection, Dallas

PROVENANCE Studio of the artist E. Vuillard; Hallsborough Gallery, London; Graham Mattison, Paris; Spiess, Paris, 1981; current owner.

EXHIBITED Galerie L'Oeil, Paris, *Vuillard et son Kodak,* April 25–May 26, 1963, no. 21; Museum Boijmans Van Beuningen, Rotterdam, 1963, no. 112; Lefevre Gallery, London, *Vuillard et son Kodak,* March 5–26, 1964, no. 17 (panels 1, 3); Dallas Museum of Art, *Impressionist and Modern Masters in Dallas,* September 3–October 22, 1989, 115.

BIBLIOGRAPHY *Vuillard et son Kodak* 1963, 22, no. 100, color ill.; Brettell 1989, 43, no. 115; Groom 1993, 173, fig. 280; Salomon and Cogeval 2003, vol. 2, 797, no. VII–514.4 (panel 1), 797, no. VII–514.3 (panel 2), 798, no. VII–514.5 (panel 3).

Édouard Vuillard was the most prolific of the group of artists known as Les Nabis, which dominated discourse in French art in the 1890s, and he was also the most attracted to the graphic arts. Many friends of the artist recall that he was an obsessive draftsman who virtually always carried a small sketchpad and pencil, making thousands of sketches throughout his life. The vast catalogue raisonné of his work by Guy Cogeval is dominated by works on paper and board, but omits, except for comparative purposes, the thousands of *croquis,* or rapid pencil sketches, that Vuillard made multiple times per day. There is no doubt that if these were gathered, they would be the largest body of graphic representations of daily life in the history of art.

In mid-1908 Vuillard moved with his mother to a spacious apartment at 36, rue de Calais on the Place Vintimille with a view of the Square Berlioz. Clearly, he was entranced by this luminous, tree-filled urban space, because over the next several years he drew and painted it many times in different formats and mediums to create a complete urban portrait of the street where he lived. The present pastel triptych is related to three panels of the same square commissioned in 1909 by the French playwright Henri Bernstein for the space he was to share with his new wife. Having already purchased four vertical cityscapes made by Vuillard in the summer of 1908 in Passy, he asked the artist to paint four more works to form a series of Parisian views on long, vertical formats like Asian scroll paintings. The three pastel panels relate so closely to three of the four Bernstein panels that they are surely studies for them.[1] Vuillard kept the three pastel panels throughout his life.

Gloria Groom writes that on visiting Bernstein's sumptuous apartment on the Boulevard Haussmann, Vuillard was depressed by the appearance of the earlier four street scenes in the lacquered salon.[2] It is likely that this occasion pushed him to conceive of a unified triptych for three of the four pictures in the second commission and that the present work is his almost full-scale study for that arrangement (the completed panels are nearly four inches higher).

These views from Vuillard's apartment were not made in that space, but in a large studio on the Boulevard Malesherbes, which he rented in 1909. Groom has speculated that Vuillard may even have used photographs in creating the compositions.[3] He also could easily have used various pencil sketches made from his window, combining them with photographic information to create the oddly un-unified triptych. As much as two years later, Vuillard linked the Bernstein decorations with his visit with Pierre Bonnard to see Claude Monet. Vuillard had turned 40 in 1908 and had begun to conceive of his oeuvre in historical terms; his journal entries about the decorative scheme in these panels connect the atmospheric art of Monet with the close observation of urban realms practiced by Ukiyo-e printmakers and by artists of painted screens with urban subjects in Edo Japan.

Vuillard had completed the pastel study for the Bernstein panels by September 1909, when they were exhibited at Galerie Bernheim-Jeune.[4] However, the lack of foliage and the cold, misty atmosphere of

Notes
1. The larger left and right panels for the second Bernstein commission are now in the Thannhauser Collection, Solomon R. Guggenheim Museum, New York; the smaller central panel is in a private collection.
2. For a thorough discussion of the "Bernstein Decorations," see Groom 1993.
3. Ibid.
4. Ibid.

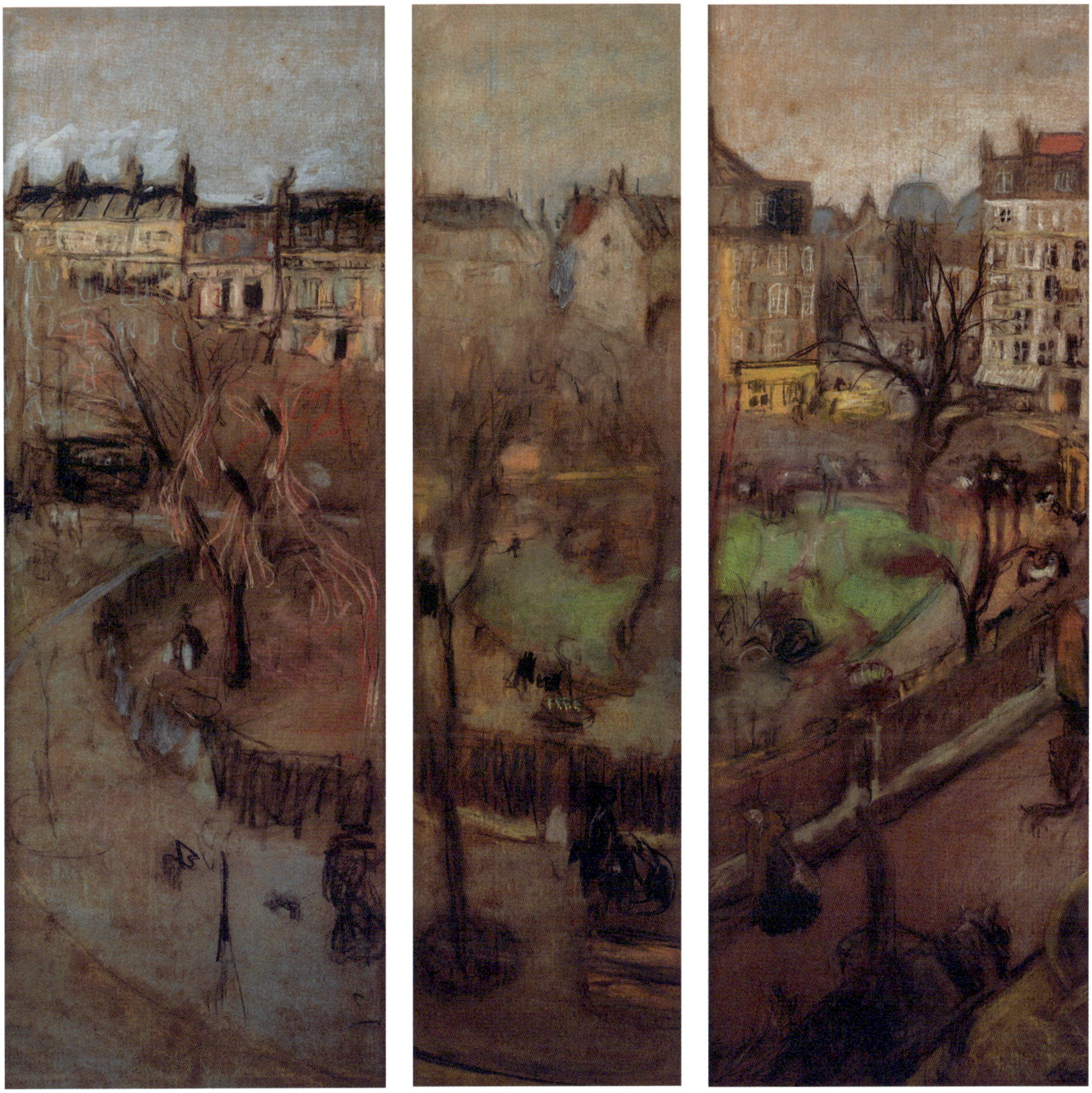

the pastels must have been observed in the winter of 1908–1909, before the Bernstein commission was received. Vuillard may have been thinking about a triptych of the lively view from his new apartment independently from the commission and then returned to the pastels when conceiving of the works for Bernstein, which he worked on largely in 1910, finally delivering them to his patron in December of that later year. Since Vuillard kept the pastels, they were undoubtedly an inspiration for his later—and considerably larger—painted screen of the same view commissioned by Marguerite Chapin in May 1911 (*Place Vintimille,* National Gallery of Art, Washington).

RRB

91

Édouard Vuillard French, 1868–1940

THE TENT, *1908*

Distemper on paper, on canvas, overall, 39¾ × 56½ in. (1010 × 1435 mm)
Signed lower right: *E Vuillard*
Dallas Museum of Art, The Wendy and Emery Reves Collection, 1985.R.83

PROVENANCE The artist, Édouard Vuillard; purchased by Bernheim-Jeune, Paris, September 28, 1908–at least 1919, no. 16762; Édouard Vuillard, 1919–1940; Lefranc Gallery, Paris, after 1940; Emery Reves, France, before 1948; given to the Dallas Museum of Art, The Wendy and Emery Reves Collection, 1985.

EXHIBITED Galerie Bernheim-Jeune, Paris, *Vuillard,* February 17–29, 1908, no. 10; Ministère des Sciences et des Arts, Brussels, *Exposition Universelle et Internationale,* April 23–November 1, 1910, 327; Lyon, France, *Exposition Internationale,* no. 442; Galerie Charpentier, Paris, *Cent Chefs-d'Oeuvre de l'Art Français,* May 3–October 5, 1957, 110; Dallas Museum of Art, *Impressionist and Modern Masters in Dallas,* September 3–October 22, 1989, no. 127, 87, ill.; Dallas Museum of Art, *Impressions from the Riviera,* November 5, 1995–February 4, 1996, color ill.

BIBLIOGRAPHY Dallas Museum of Art 1985b, 142–43, color ill.; Brettell 1995, 138–39, color ill.; Salomon and Cogeval 2003, vol. 2, 937 *(The Marquee),* color ill.; MacDonald 2013, 146, 152–54, color ill.

Édouard Vuillard traveled by train to the Brittany resort town of Penchâteau in July 1908 to visit his friends Joseph and Lucie Hessel, who had rented a house there called Ker Panurge. Joseph (called Jos) Hessel was a partner in the large art gallery Bernheim-Jeune, which handled Vuillard's work as well as that of his friend Pierre Bonnard. While in Brittany, Vuillard was inspired to make a large number of works, among the most important of which is *The Tent,* which he referred to in his journal entry of July 29 as "a sketch in tempera, the tent." He had traveled to Brittany with Alfred Natanson (cofounder of *La Revue blanche*), his wife, and their two daughters. Later in the month, the painter Pierre Bonnard, his common-law wife Marthe, and Vuillard's mother arrived to complete the house party. Many others came for luncheons, dinners, and long leisurely afternoons, and Vuillard represented these occasions almost as if he were a court painter for the Jewish intelligentsia. Photographs by both Vuillard and Natanson of an afternoon visit probably dating from July 28, 1908, are sited in and around a striped garden tent. Vuillard made many sketches of this afternoon; two are preserved in the Reves Collection (fig. 15).

Most of Vuillard's *croquis* from the early years of the 20th century are closely related to *The Tent* in technique and purpose. The artist drew with a burst of energy while staring fixedly at his motif. The aim was not to look at the drawing, but to create, using a few simple gestures, an instant diagram of a particular scene that might become the scaffolding for a subsequent work of art. *Croquis* can be preparatory, and they constitute an intensive form of visual research. Vuillard himself probably employed them in concert with his photographs as an aide-memoire when constructing his larger works (see cat. 90).

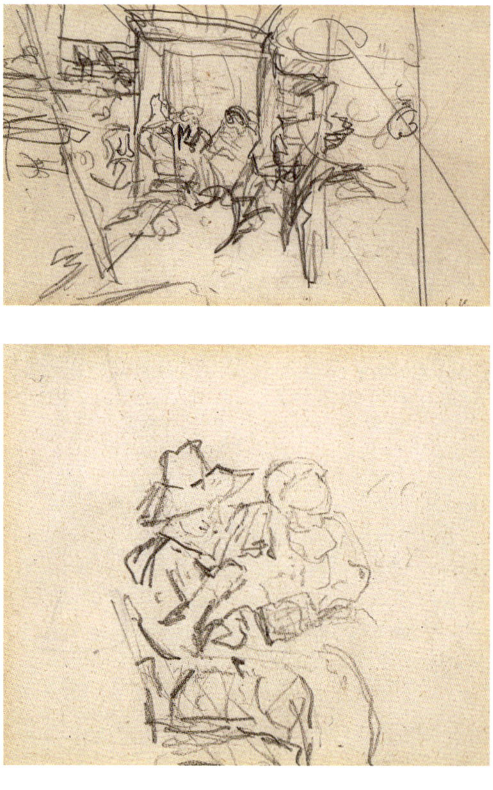

Fig. 15 Édouard Vuillard, *Two Studies for "The Tent,"* 1908. Pencil on paper. Dallas Museum of Art, The Wendy and Emery Reves Collection, 1985.R.84.

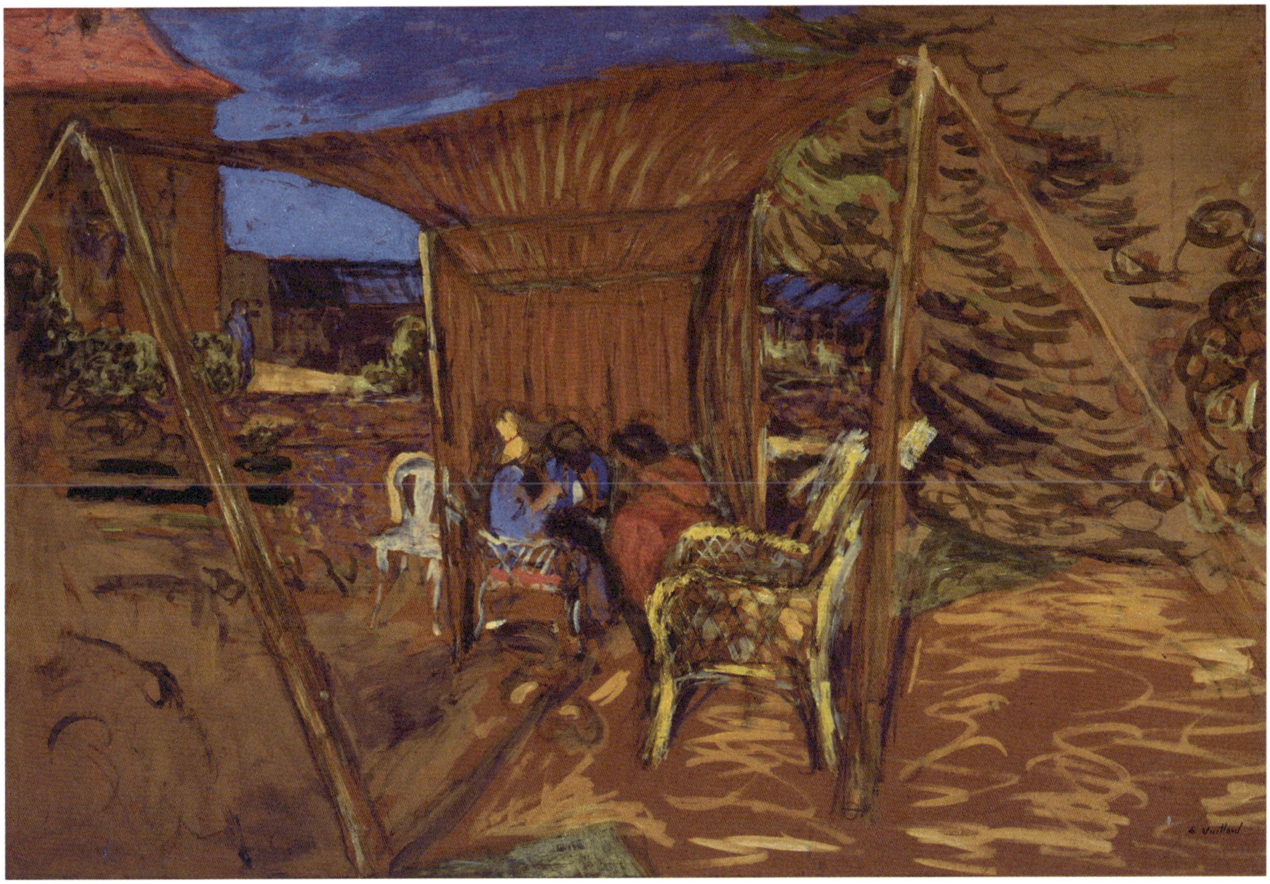

Vuillard's own description of *The Tent* as a "painted sketch" *(pochade)* links it to impressionist practice. Claude Monet used the same word in describing his sketches of the waterside cafe La Grenouillère in 1869. Vuillard, like Monet, wanted his work to convey the immediacy experienced at the site—in this case, a windy coastal garden in Brittany. *The Tent* is alive with gesture, as is a slightly smaller and differently constructed work called *La Tente rayée* (1908, private collection, Geneva). Our eyes pass rapidly across the surface, alighting at a figure or a part of the tent, but never for very long. Like the impressionists, Vuillard was interested in entrapping the entire visual field. As we look at his "sketch," we feel precisely the sensation of a blustery, windswept afternoon when we attempt a conversation, perhaps after having a little too much wine at lunch. The discreet pleasures of bourgeois life have seldom had a better visual archivist than Vuillard.

RRB

Auguste Rodin French, 1840–1917

MALE NUDE, C. *1900*

Pencil on white, medium-weight wove paper, 12 3/16 × 8 in.
(310 × 203 mm)
Private collection, Dallas

PROVENANCE The artist; given to his student Joseph Durand between 1900 and 1903; with Galerie Aittouares, Paris; Shepherd Gallery, New York, 1997; where purchased by the current owner.

EXHIBITED Galerie Aittouares, Paris, *Jean-Baptiste Carpeaux/ August Rodin,* n.d., 11, ill.; Shepherd Gallery, New York, *Nineteenth-Century European Paintings, Drawings, and Sculpture,* February 25–April 26, 1997; Neuberger Museum of Art, Purchase, N.Y., *End Papers: Drawings 1890–1900 and 1990–2000,* January 30–April 23, 2000, 9, fig. 7, 38, cat. 84.

The sculpture of Auguste Rodin stands as one of the hallmarks of the art of the last 150 years. Considered by many the father of modern sculpture, Rodin broke with the classicism preferred in academic circles, favoring expressive modeling and leaving evidence of his hand and methods of manufacture. Although he took on commissions of traditional subjects —historical monuments (*The Burghers of Calais,* 1884–1895), religious themes (*The Gates of Hell,* 1880–1917), and literary figures (*Monument to Balzac,* 1898)—Rodin approached them with an unwavering humanism, each figure animated by emotion from the common wellspring of human experience. These innovations, in concert with an extraordinary understanding of anatomy and the proportions of the human form, resulted in a body of work that remains in its humanism as powerfully resonant today as when it was made.

Drawing was essential to Rodin's practice and constitutes an extraordinary body of work on its own. Rodin was as prolific a draftsman as he was a sculptor, producing more than 9,000 works on paper during his career. This extraordinary corpus, comprising works both independent of and related to his sculptures, is dominated by figure studies, many of them simple pencil sketches, often articulated with watercolor, white pencil, or gouache. *Male Nude* is a vibrant, lyrical drawing typical of Rodin's late career when he redoubled his efforts as a draftsman, seeking new, expressive forms from the direct observation of live models often drawn without lifting his pencil from the paper or relinquishing his gaze. In 1902, Rainer Maria Rilke, the esteemed writer, poet, and frequent commentator on Rodin and his work, noted that "by not taking his eyes off the model and entirely abandoning the paper to his swift and experienced hand, [Rodin] drew an infinite number of gestures never seen, always overlooked, and the expressive power they exuded was immense."[1] *Male Nude* does not appear to be directly related to any of Rodin's sculptural compositions, but the pose—arched back, taut musculature, arms raised—recalls that of Rodin's first sculptural masterwork, *The Age of Bronze* (1875–1876). The assured, fluid line of the drawing reduces the body to its essential contours, anticipating the energetic, flowing forms of his final sculptures, the *Dance Movements.*

JM

Note
1. Quoted in Le Normand-Romain and Buley-Uribe 2007, 5.

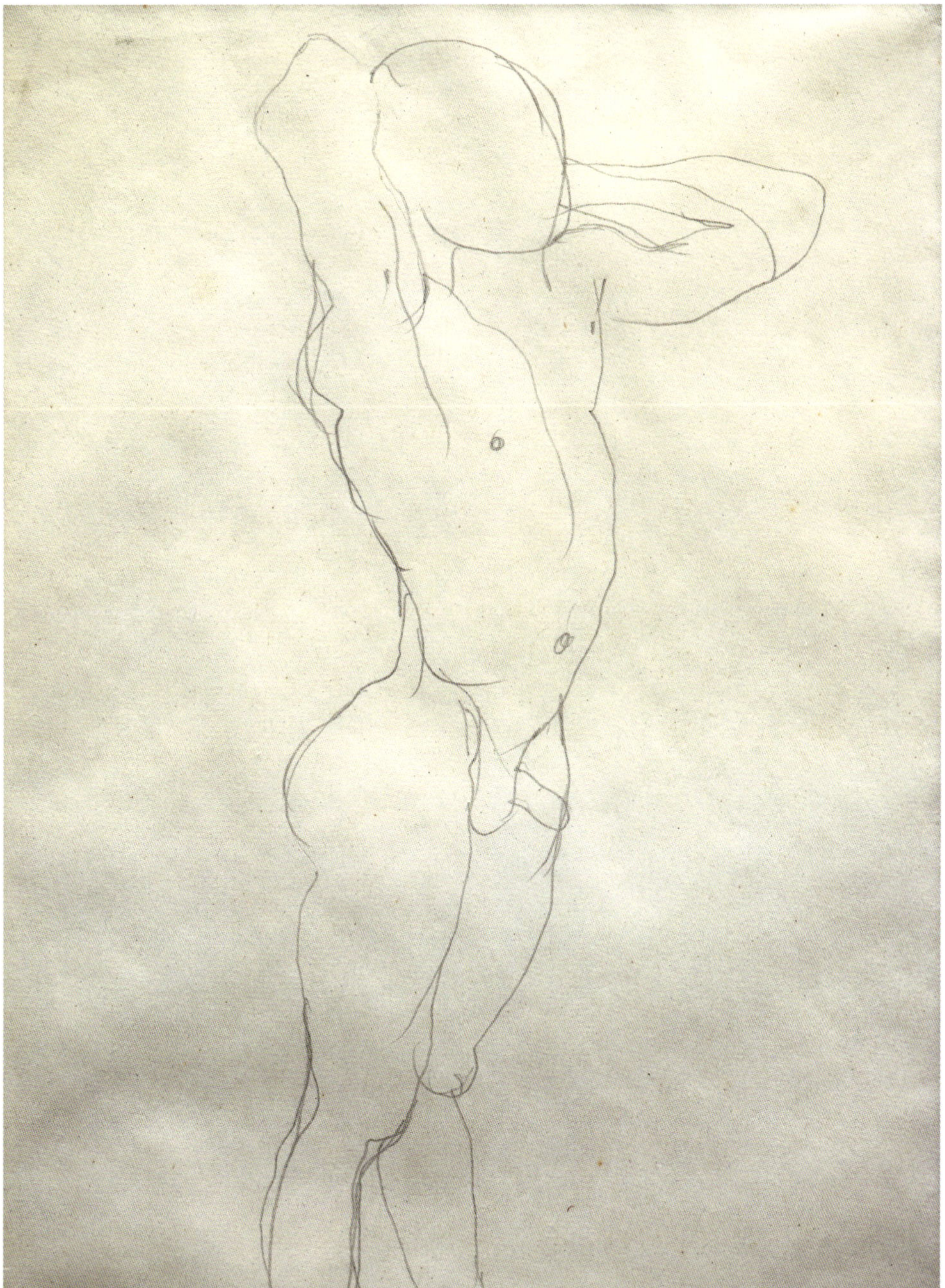

93

Ernest Biéler Swiss, 1863–1948

L'ÉPINE-VINETTE, *1910*

Watercolor over pencil and india ink on paper mounted on cardboard, 10⅞ × 9 in. (275 × 231 mm); original, artist-designed frame
Signed lower right: *Ernest Biéler*
Nona and Richard Barrett Collection, Dallas

PROVENANCE Private Swiss Collection; sale, Schuler Auktionen, Zurich, *Kunst & Antiquitaten Sale No. 102,* September 15, 2006, lot 3125; where purchased by the current owner.

Ernest Biéler was the most important late 19th- and early 20th-century painter from the Vaud and Valais regions of Switzerland. Trained at the Académie Julian in Paris, where many foreign artists learned their crafts, he returned to Switzerland in the 1890s and spent the rest of his life working in the region of his birth. His almost fanatically detailed representations of the landscapes and rural peoples of the villages around Savièse in the Valais collectively form the most important artistic embodiment of traditional Swiss rural life. He was to this small and intensely traditional region what Paul Gauguin or Émile Bernard were to Brittany, except that his understanding of the region was more profound than theirs.

Although Biéler was trained as an oil painter, his interest in Renaissance art led him on a quest to revive the medium of egg tempera painting, which he used with watercolor, gouache, pencil, and chalk to produce a large body of works on paper and *carton,* or artist cardboard. He stopped using oil paint in 1906. He also experimented with stained glass and mural painting.

Perhaps because he lived frugally within his independent income, his works were not extensively sold, and they have only become well known—even in Switzerland—during the past generation. Yet the first monograph on Biéler, published in a luxurious limited edition in Lausanne in 1936, was written by no less a figure than J. B. Manson, director of the Tate Gallery in London. Long thought to have been completed in 1911 and entitled *Girl from the Vallais,* this small, exquisitely detailed portrait of an anonymous girl from the town of Savièse was painted in 1910 as *L'épine-vinette,* included in an exhibition that traveled from Neuchâtel to Winterthur, Zurich, and Frankfurt in 1910–1911, and sold to a Swiss private collector in 1912.[1] Thus, it was not included in the landmark retrospective at the Arlaud Building in Lausanne in September and October of 1912, an exhibition that included 100 works by the artist.

This work is one in a long series of similarly scaled profile and frontal studies of rural citizens of the town of Savièse and its surrounding villages. In many ways, Savièse became the equivalent of Pont-Aven in Brittany to a school of artists who surrounded Biéler and who have become known as the School of Savièse. The town itself and its surrounding villages were beautifully sited in the Haute Valais and had a population of intensely traditional people who lived as they had for centuries. French speaking for more than 200 years, the villages were favored for inexpensive summer holidays by French and French Swiss artists, writers, and intellectuals. The combination of clear air, beautiful scenery, attractive, traditionally garbed inhabitants, ample opportunity for exercise, and affordable lodging was irresistible for urbanites in search of a simpler life. Biéler and his first wife, the art historian Hélène Lafond Biéler, lived in a spacious apartment at Denfert-Rochereau in Paris in the years before World War I and spent the summer months in Savièse, to which they escaped during the war.

It is scarcely surprising that the rural people of Switzerland had been the subject of many popular prints that represent rural Europeans in their indigenous

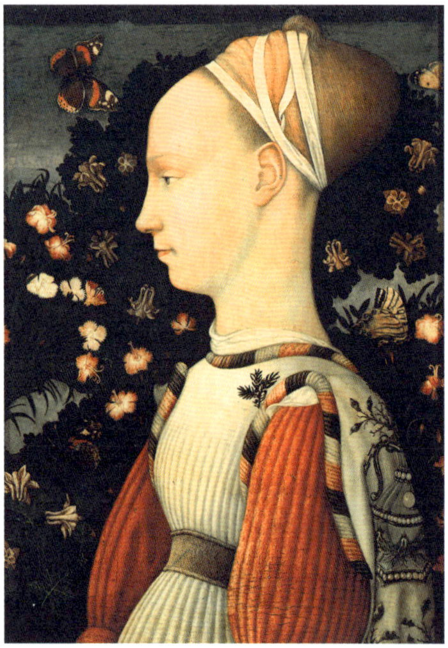

Fig. 16 Antonio Puccio, called Pisanello, *Ginevra d'Este, first wife of Sigismondo Malatesta,* c. 1435–1440. Oil on wood. Musée du Louvre, Paris, RF 766.

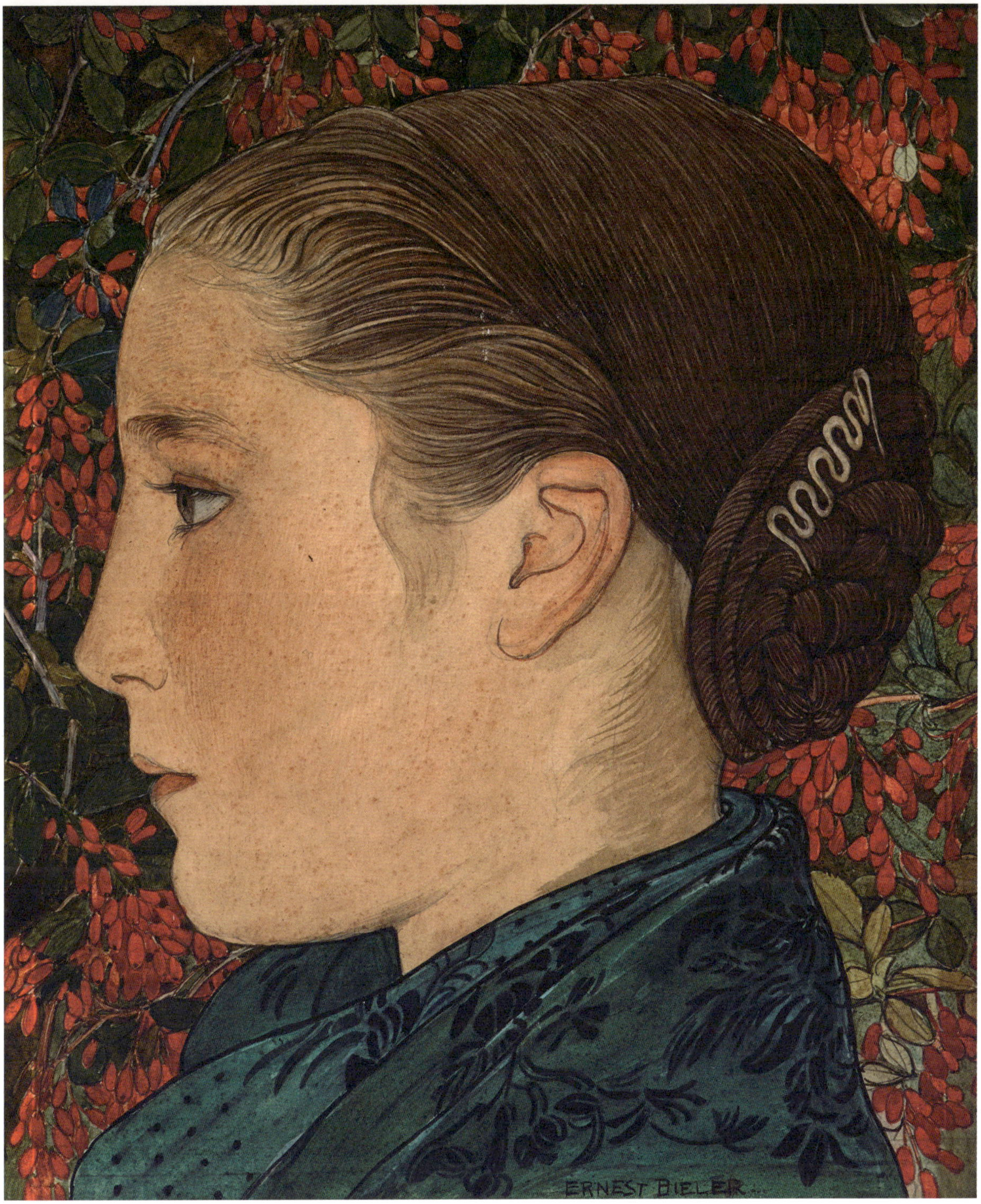

costumes, and Biéler surely understood that the European reach of these prints was proof of a larger market for more complex and aesthetically ambitious images of these beautiful people in their own world. The present work shows an attractive, broad-faced young woman whose name is unknown, whose head fills the pictorial format, and who is shown in a way that reminds one immediately of Renaissance profile portraits of the early 15th century (fig. 16). Biéler placed his model in front of a wallpaper-like background of blooming flowers with nervously animated red-orange petals that contrast with the model's placid, emotionless face and her simple blue scarf. The title of the work is the French word for Japanese barberry, the blooming shrub that animates the background. The combination of almost fanatical detail and compositional restraint is unique to Biéler, whose work cannot be mistaken for that of any other Swiss modernist artist.

RRB

Note
1. Ethel Mathier (author, forthcoming catalogue raisonné of Biéler's work), personal communication.

94

Ernest Biéler Swiss, 1863–1948

SELF-PORTRAIT, *1911*

Pencil, watercolor, and gouache on paper, 11½ × 10½ in. (290 × 270 mm); in original, artist-designed frame
Signed and dated right center: *E-Bieler-11*
Nona and Richard Barrett Collection, Dallas

PROVENANCE Galerie Vallotton, no. 73220; private collection; sale, Sotheby's, Zürich, *Swiss Art,* November 27, 2007, lot 1; where purchased by the current owner.

EXHIBITED Maison de Commune de Savièse, Savièse, Switzerland, *Ernest Biéler (1863–1948): Rétrospective du cinquantenaire,* November 14, 1978–January 17, 1999, no. 37.

This rare self-portrait is a full-scale version of Ernest Biéler's first major self-portrait, a more highly finished work in the same medium given by the artist to the Musée Cantonal des Beaux Arts in Lausanne in 1912, the year after its completion. Biéler was proud of the self-portrait, but he evidently duplicated it for the museum so that he could keep the present version, which can be considered the original. It is likely that one or the other version was included in the major retrospective of his work in 1912. A recent exhibition of Biéler's work at the Kunstmuseum in Berne reproduced the cover of the catalogue for that exhibition, which included 100 works by the artist and was the first monographic exhibition of his career.[1]

Biéler himself was nearing his 50th year and was clearly thinking retrospectively. His self-portrait is characteristically modest, and he represents himself not as an artist, but as a Swiss villager with penetrating eyes and a reddish-brown beard. Biéler simplified many details of the shirt and hat in the second version, but he added color and luster to the eyes and gray and white hairs to the beard and hair, choosing to emphasize his age and experience. The geometrically patterned fabric of his shirt is like that worn by many of his rural female models from Savièse, and his leather hat with tassels would not have been worn in the city. The geometric patterning of the background suggests two sources: the gridded decorative arts of the Wiener Werkstätte and the decorative banding in the background of Gauguin's paintings of 1894–1896. Both prove Biéler's fascination with the decorative arts, which he shared with a small group of printmakers, furniture designers, and other artists who worked with him in Savièse.

RRB

Note
1. See Kunstmuseum Berne 2011, 184, ill. 30.

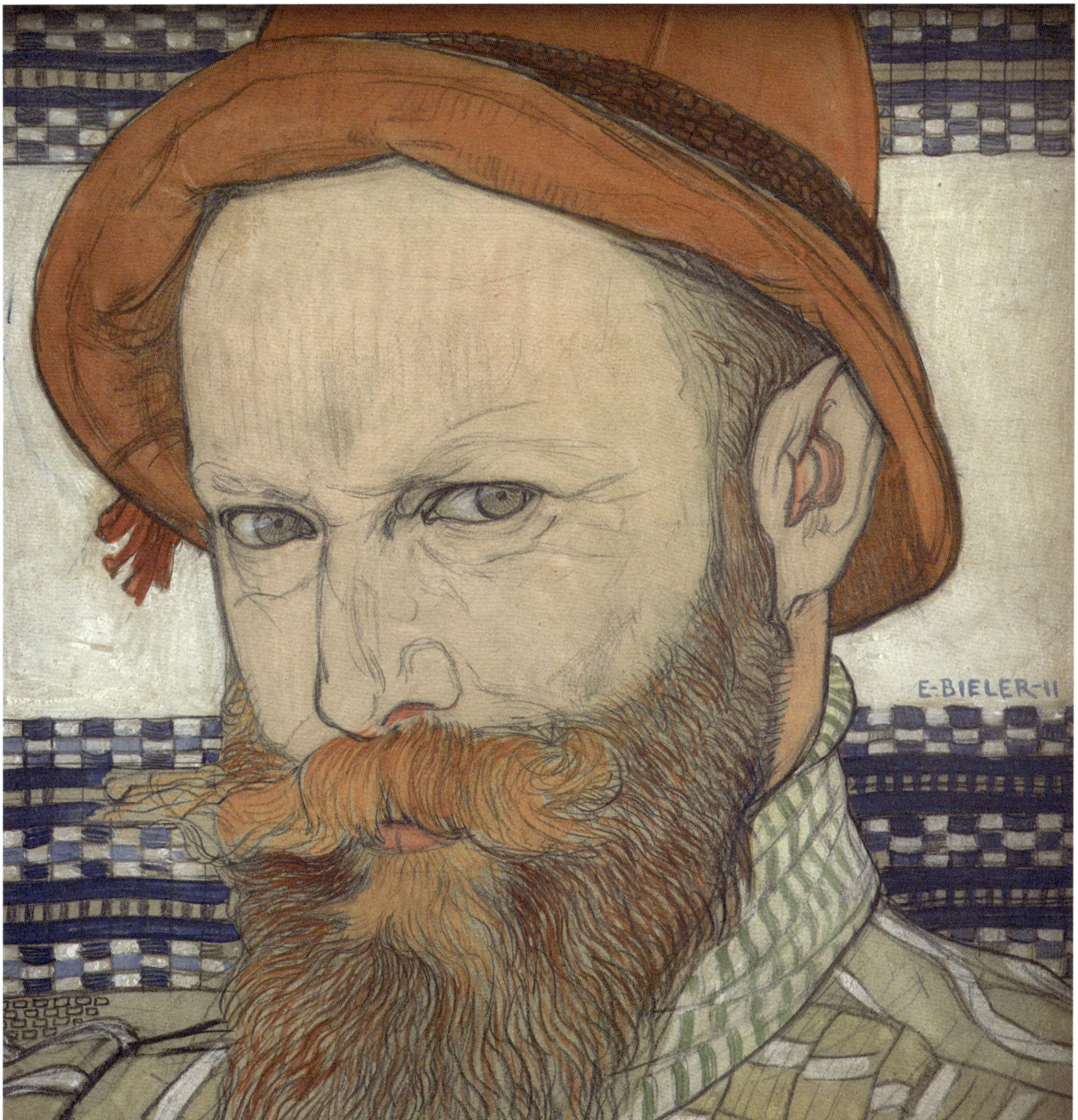
E-BIELER-11

95

Ferdinand Hodler Swiss, 1853–1918

BOY WITH BENT ARMS (HECTOR) (KNABE MIT ANGEWINKELTEN ARMEN [HECTOR]), C. *1898–1900*

Pencil, india ink, watercolor, and gouache on paper, 14 × 8½ in. (350 × 210 mm)
Signed lower right: *F. Hodler*
Nona and Richard Barrett Collection, Dallas

PROVENANCE Sale, Sotheby's, Zürich, *Schweizer Kunst*, June 17, 1998, no. 23; sale, Sotheby's Zürich, *Schweizer Kunst*, May 29, 2000, no. 58; where purchased by the current owner.

EXHIBITED Meadows Museum, Southern Methodist University, Dallas, *Texas Vision, The Barrett Collection: The Art of Texas and Switzerland*, November 21, 1994–January 20, 1995, 137.

BIBLIOGRAPHY Brettell 2004, 137.

Ferdinand Hodler's childhood was marked by the death of those close to him, a theme that haunts his oeuvre. He painted picturesque Swiss landscapes until receiving his first real artistic training in Geneva, where he discovered the art of Jean-Baptiste-Camille Corot and Gustave Courbet. His large figure paintings—including the masterpiece *Night (La Nuit)* (1889–1890, Kunstmuseum, Berne), which announced him as one of the major figures of European symbolism—proved controversial and even scandalous in Switzerland. Exhibiting in France in the early 1890s and from 1895 onward in Germany and Austria, Hodler made many artistic friendships, met collectors, and received commissions for murals. Hodler's powerful, vividly colored painting, based on rhythm, simplification, and a decorative structure—he summarized his aesthetic principles as "parallelism"—constitutes a major and radical contribution to modernity at the turn of the 20th century.

Hodler's model in this drawing is his only son, Hector, born October 1, 1887, of his union with Augustine Dupin, his lover and preferred model until his marriage to Bertha Stucki in 1889. Hector posed for his father almost from birth and became, as here, one of the principal protagonists of the artist's symbolist compositions, in which he celebrates the union of man and nature. Hector represents purity, innocence, and youth. Though not directly, this drawing could be related to the research for the first version of *Youth Admired by Women I* (Kunsthaus, Zürich), which was completed in 1903 and shows four women seen from the back as they turn their gaze on "a young man intuiting harmony," in Hodler's words.

In this final composition, Hector has grown in stature and strength, and although his upper arms are almost flat against his body, he holds a plant in each hand. These offerings express communion with beauty and nature, as does the nudity of the model. The young man's body is treated with a dry and uncompromising realism combined with a quest for symmetry and structure characteristic of Hodler's symbolism, which is anchored in both the real and the abstract. Drawing in ink was one of the artist's preferred techniques, and here it highlights the outline of the body, which stands out against the area of unified green. Hodler liked to place his figures in unspecified and limitless grassy surfaces, evoking infinite space.

Hodler produced many studies in various formats and techniques, putting some to use years later. Drawing was at the heart of his creative process, an integral element of his style, thought, and originality. In his manifesto *La Mission de l'Artiste* (1887), Hodler wrote that line should express "the logic of movement" and "bring out the beauty and character of the outline." A symbol, he said, was "an idea added to matter," and in this equilibrium between the ideal and the material, drawing occupied a central place.

SP

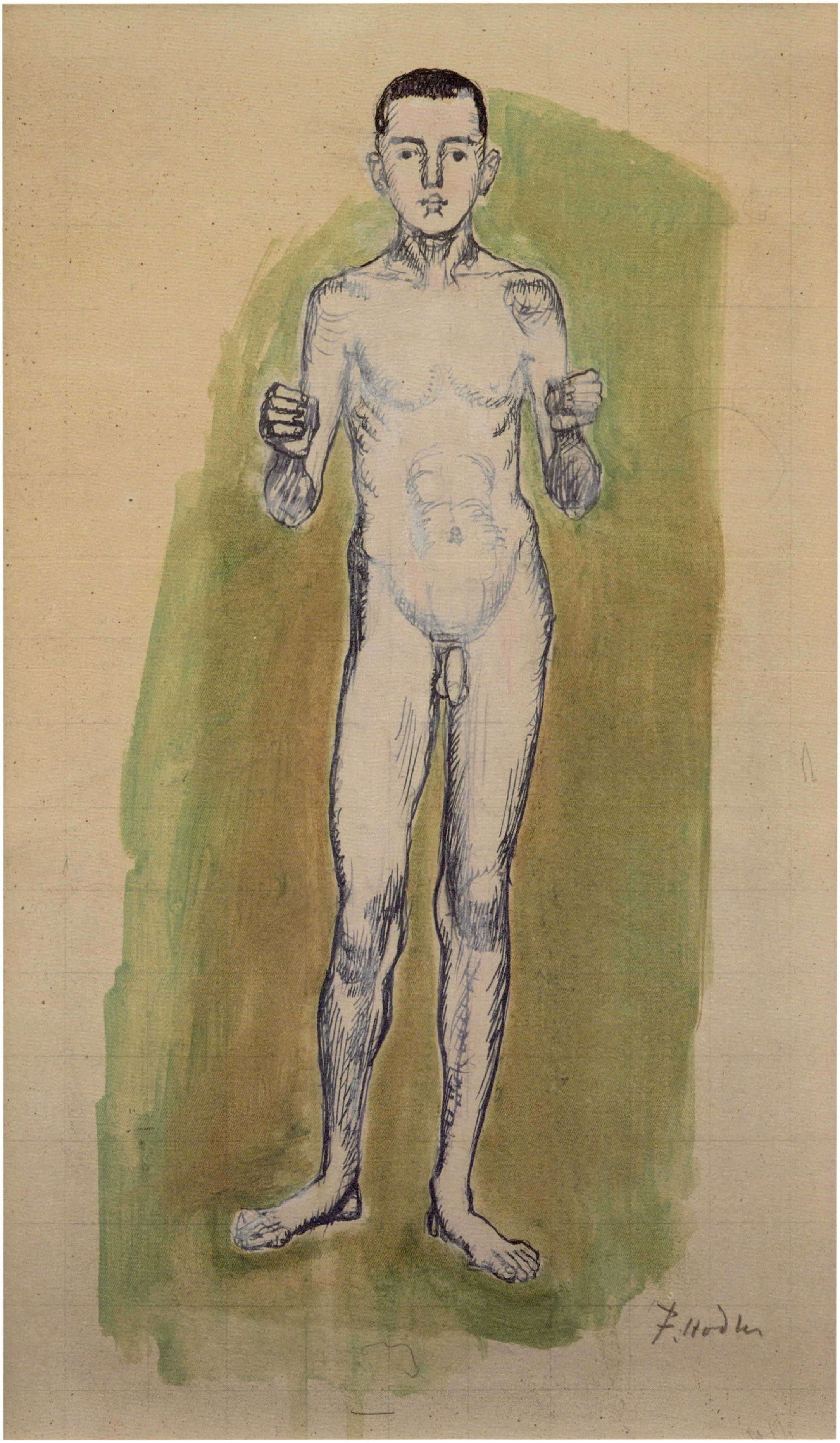
F. Hodler

96

Ferdinand Hodler Swiss, 1853–1918

HEAD OF A VIENNESE WOMAN, C. *1903–1904*

Pencil, charcoal, crayon, pastel, and oil on paper, mounted on cardboard, 14 × 9⅝ in. (357 × 243 mm)
Signed lower right: *F. Hodler*; verso, . . . *Frauenkopf / tête de Viennoise*. . .
Nona and Richard Barrett Collection, Dallas

PROVENANCE Josef Müller Collection, Solothurn, Switzerland; Professor Nef Collection; sale, Christie's, Zürich, *Schweizer Kunst*, March 14, 2005, no. 135; where purchased by the current owner.

EXHIBITED Galerie Römer, Zürich, *Ferdinand Hodler: Paintings and Drawings from the Josef Müller Collection and Other Swiss Collections*, June 12–July 31, 1986, no. 23.

BIBLIOGRAPHY Mühelstein 1914, no. 12, ill.; Loosli 1919, no. 249, ill.; Loosli 1921–24, vol. 4, no. 161; Bätschmann et al. 2012, 205, repr. (entry by Bernadette Walter).

This beautiful study of a head is a preparatory drawing for a portrait in the Kunsthaus Zürich (inv. 1964/24), exhibited as *Wienerin* during the artist's lifetime. The model has not been identified, but an autograph inscription on the back of the leaf indicates that she was Viennese. Hodler probably made this portrait during his stays in Vienna in 1903 or 1904 as a guest of honor of the Secession, when his work earned him a triumphal success that marked a turning point in his career. The model might be Sophie Loew, the wife of one of his collectors with whom he stayed in 1903, or Leonore Von Bach, the wife of a jurist and art lover whose daughter Hodler painted in 1904.

The drawing mixes several different media: graphite and black pencil for the outlines and to sketch in the features of the face, pastel and crayons for the colored notes in the woman's hair and cheeks. We find the same color accents in the oil portrait. The features of the model are softened in the painting, the format is larger (18 × 15 in. [460 × 380 mm]), and the broader framing reveals the curve of the shoulders. But the squaring up that allowed the drawing to be transferred to the painting can still be seen, as Hodler often left his workings visible. We know that he exhibited either the painted portrait or the drawing in 1917 at the major retrospective of his work held at the Kunsthaus Zürich.[1]

This drawing is emblematic of Hodler's audacious use of color and his taste for vigorous outlines. Made at a turning point in his career, for many years it belonged to the prestigious collection of Josef Müller, a friend of the artist and one of the most enthusiastic and faithful of his Swiss collectors.

SP

Note
1. For the portrait, see Bernadette Walter, in Bätschmann et al. 2012. For the drawing, see Brüschweiler 1986.

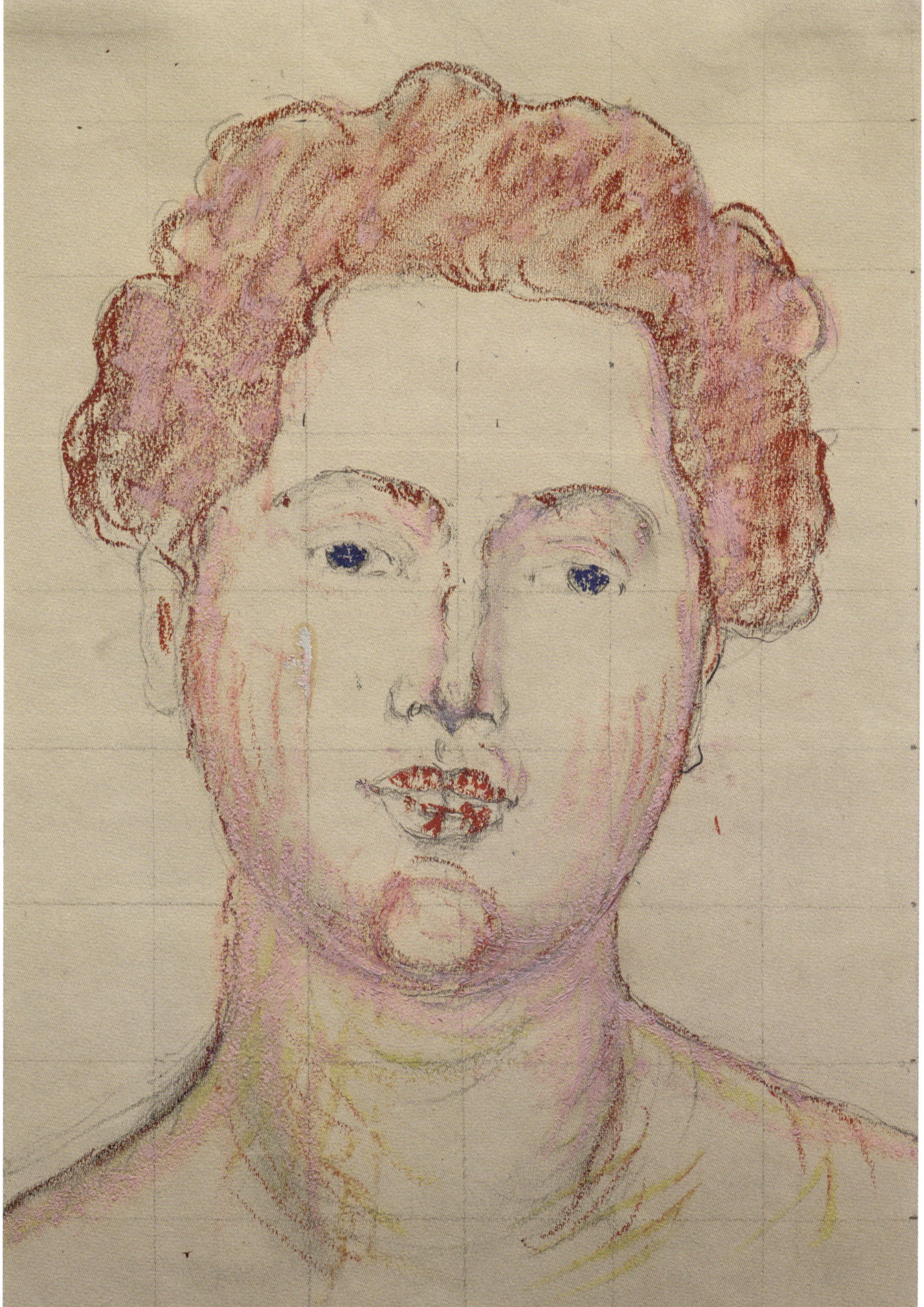
F. Hodler

Cuno Amiet Swiss, 1868–1961

PORTRAIT OF THE WRITER ADOLF FREY, 1903

Charcoal on paper, 11½ × 9½ in. (290 × 240 mm)
Initialed lower right: *CA*
Nona and Richard Barrett Collection, Dallas

PROVENANCE Collection of Adolf Frey (1855–1920), Zurich; private collection; sale, Sotheby's, Zürich, *Schweizer Kunst,* May 29, 2000, no. 33; where purchased by the current owner.

EXHIBITED Dallas, Meadows Museum, Southern Methodist University, *Texas Vision, The Barrett Collection: The Art of Texas and Switzerland,* November 21, 1994–January 20, 1995, 146.

BIBLIOGRAPHY Brettell 2004, 146.

Cuno Amiet is a major figure in Swiss art whose extraordinary sense of color stands at the heart of modernity. He studied in Munich (1886–1888) and Paris (1888–1892) and then worked in Pont-Aven, Brittany (1892–1893), where he discovered the powerful colors and simplified, heavily outlined forms of Paul Gauguin's paintings. He began to experiment under the influence of other artists, including Édouard Manet, Paul Cézanne, and Vincent van Gogh. Though he won a medal in the Paris Universal Exposition in 1900, Amiet first made his reputation in Germany, where he was a member of the German expressionist group Die Brücke from 1906 to 1913. His studio, house, and garden in Oschwand, Switzerland, were an intellectual and artistic center.

His subject Adolf Frey (1855–1920) was a poet, novelist, and historian of Swiss literature. As a professor of literature in Zurich, he was close to a number of artists and writers, including the writer Gottfried Keller. He published works about Rudolph Koller, Albert Welti, and the painter Arnold Böcklin, after the latter's death in 1901. Amiet illustrated Frey's poems in 1901 and painted his portrait two years later. This leaf (facing page) is one of the preparatory drawings made for the painting, also in the Barrett collection (fig. 17), which is slightly wider but very close to the drawing. The facial features are reproduced with energy and assurance on a neutral background. In the painting, Amiet added a dedication: *DAS IST ADOLF FREY / DER DICHTER / IM APRIL 1903 / GEMALT VON CA* (This Is Adolf Frey / the Poet / in April 1903 / painted by CA). Framed tightly around the model, it shows an economy of means characteristic of Amiet's style at the turn of the century. The decorative effect of its almost-square format was enhanced in the painting for which this drawing was made.

After his Pont-Aven experiments, Amiet returned to an austerity and purity of line that, combined with his realistic style, are somewhat reminiscent of the portraits of the German painter Hans Holbein the Younger. Holbein worked frequently in Basel in the early 16th century and was hailed as a foundational figure in Swiss art at a time when the young Swiss Confederation was building its national identity. The primitivism and *altdeutsch* austerity of this portrait contribute to its originality and enhance the power of the drawing, which shows an impressive humanity.

SP

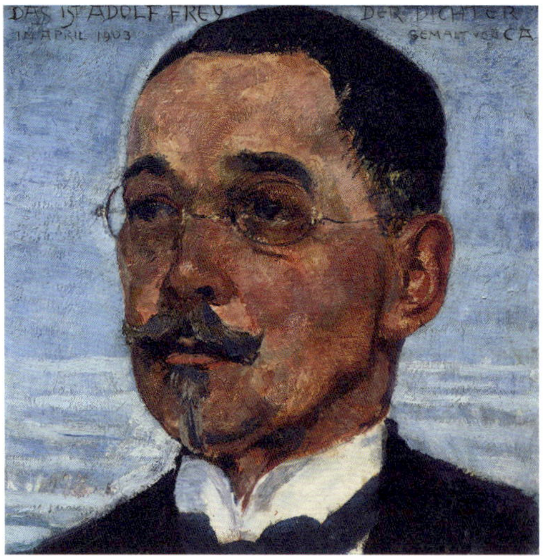

Fig. 17 Cuno Amiet, *Portrait of the Poet Adolf Frey (Bildnis des Dichters Adolf Frey),* 1903. Oil on cardboard. Nona and Richard Barrett Collection, Dallas.

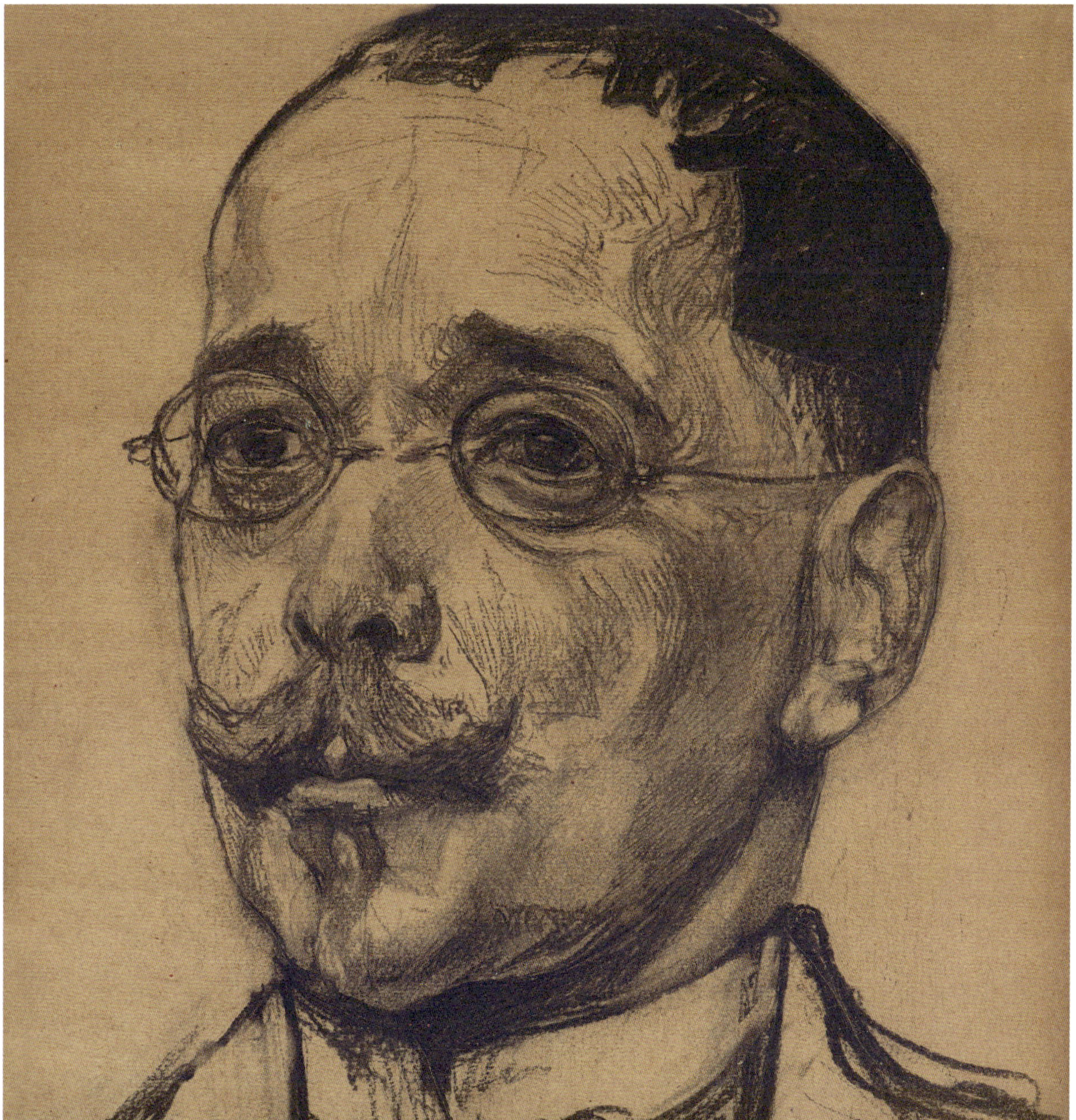
CA.

98

Cuno Amiet Swiss, 1868–1961

GRETI, C. *1907*

Charcoal highlighted with white chalk on paper, 25⅜ × 19⅛ in. (645 × 485 mm)
Nona and Richard Barrett Collection, Dallas

PROVENANCE Sale, Sotheby's, Zürich, *Schweizer Kunst,* May 31, 2005, no. 9; where purchased by the current owner.

EXHIBITED Kunstmuseum Solothurn, Switzerland, *Cuno Amiet: Frühe Arbeiten auf Papier,* August 20–November 6, 2005, 108, no. 51.

BIBLIOGRAPHY Vögele and Radlach 2005, 108.

Greti Adam (1900–1979), who was adopted by Cuno Amiet and his wife in 1904, frequently posed for the painter. This large drawing shows her as a young girl, standing against a background that Amiet has chosen not to describe. We see only the suggestion of a wall and a shadow. The drawing is similar to a painted portrait in which Greti, wearing a dazzling pink dress, is also shown in three-quarter profile but turning toward the left. The drawing belongs to the artist's Die Brücke years, when he joined this group of young painters who exalted the expressive power of color and form. Though he preferred subjects inspired by home and family, Amiet shared the German expressionists' taste for experimentation, seen here in the hatching that brings out the shadows and the modeling and resembles the technique Amiet developed in his wood engraving. It is also present in the dense, dynamic scatter of white dots that gives rhythm to the surface of the dress and, in places, to the background. These dots are reminiscent of the networks of lozenge-shaped dots and colored stripes that sometimes invade the textured surface of the artist's paintings of the same period. This playful use of the graphic medium, combined with the slightly elevated point of view and the young girl's mischievous gaze, radically renew the conventions of the child portrait. Bordering on abstraction, the drawing exemplifies Amiet's audacity.

SP

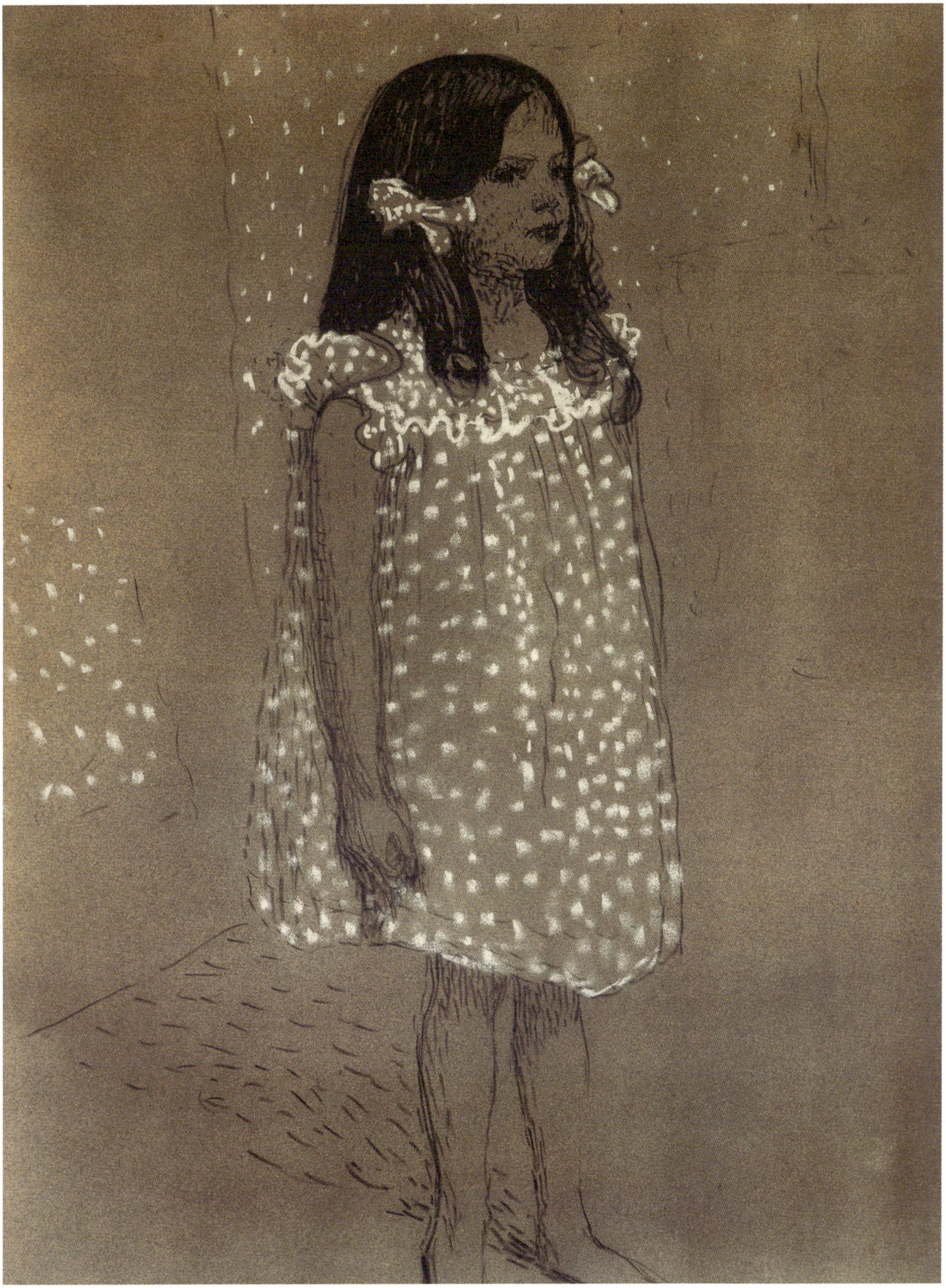

99

Adolf Hirémy-Hirschl Austro-Hungarian, 1860–1933

HEAD OF A YOUNG WOMAN, *1890S*

Charcoal and white chalk on brown wove paper, 14½ × 11¼ in. (368 × 286 mm)
Private collection, Dallas

PROVENANCE Shepherd Gallery, New York; where purchased 1968 by the current owner.

EXHIBITED Shepherd Gallery, New York, *100 Recent English Acquisitions,* January–February 1968, cat. 152L (as Edward Coley Burne-Jones); Pollock Galleries, Southern Methodist University, Dallas, *English Drawings of the Nineteenth Century,* October 14–November 1, 1973 (as Sir Edward Coley Burne-Jones); Leeds Gallery, Humanities Research Center, University of Texas, Austin, November 26–December 20, 1973 (as Sir Edward Coley Burne-Jones).

100

DRAPERY STUDY, C. *1900*

Charcoal and white chalk on buff wove paper, 13½ × 10⅜ in. (344 × 263 mm)
Collection of Dr. and Mrs. Richard R. Brettell, Dallas

PROVENANCE Family of the artist until the 1980s; Galleria Carlo Virgilio, Rome; with Roger Ramsay Gallery, Inc., Chicago; where purchased by the current owner.

EXHIBITED Roger Ramsay Gallery, Inc., Chicago, *Adolf Hirémy-Hirschl (1860–1933): The Beauty of Decline,* May 5–June 13, 1984, cat. 102.

As was the case with the much older Rudolf von Alt (cat. 42), the career of Adolf Hirémy-Hirschl coincided with the final cultural flourishing of the Austro-Hungarian monarchy. The precocious, 20-year-old Adolf Hirschl—as he was named at birth—won a first prize at the Akademie der bildenden Künste in 1880, an achievement that singled him out as among the most promising of his generation, who were intended to decorate the vast government buildings and palaces being constructed by the Emperor Franz Josef in Vienna's Ringstrasse. Neither geopolitics nor cultural politics favored such a destiny, however, as the monarchy would come to an end with World War I, and the cultural hegemony that sponsored the likes of Hirémy-Hirschl would be undermined by the Vienna Secession. Founded in 1897 by Gustav Klimt and others (but with the octogenarian von Alt as its honorary president), the Secession broke with the Vienna Künstlerlhaus over its conservative academic policies and launched Austrians on a path toward modernism similar to those followed in other European capitals. Hirschl, whose career had continued to flourish in Austria and abroad, felt no sympathy with the artistic rebels and chose to stay with his conservative colleagues. But, sensing that he had missed the tide, and recently embroiled in a scandalous affair with a married woman, he abandoned Vienna a year later for Rome. There he adopted the Hungarian name Hirémy and, with his new wife, spent the remaining years of his life as an honored member of the conservative artistic community. Largely forgotten until the 1980s, his work is still in need of systematic study.

Schooled in the making of large allegories, which could sometimes skirt dangerously close to what we would today call kitsch, Hirémy-Hirschl produced in connection with these a large number of exceptionally beautiful drawings—figure studies, heads, drapery studies—most executed in charcoal and white chalk or pastel on colored papers (buff, brown, gray, green, blue, orange). The two drawings catalogued here cannot yet be associated with known paintings in his scattered and little-studied oeuvre, but both are typical examples of his virtuosity. *Head of a Young Woman* (cat. 99) was long mistaken for an English drawing until examples of the artist's work began to appear. The earlier of the two, it was probably an independent work, but in its languid, blatant sensuality it is similar to the female types in *Wedding Procession in Ancient Rome,* the painting that in 1891 won for Hirémy-Hirschl the Kaiserpreis of the Vienna Künstlerhaus. *Drapery Study* (cat. 100) is perhaps related to another of the artist's five or more paintings of ancient processions. Barely sketching the head and arms of the figure, Hirémy-Hirschl has focused only on the folds of drapery clinging to the standing form. Whether intentional or not, the patch of dense black at the left margin of the sheet (where the artist sharpened the friable charcoal to a fine point) serves to accentuate the materiality of the medium, which, mixed with white chalk against the warm tone of the buff-colored paper, creates an extraordinarily rich tactile illusion.

WBJ

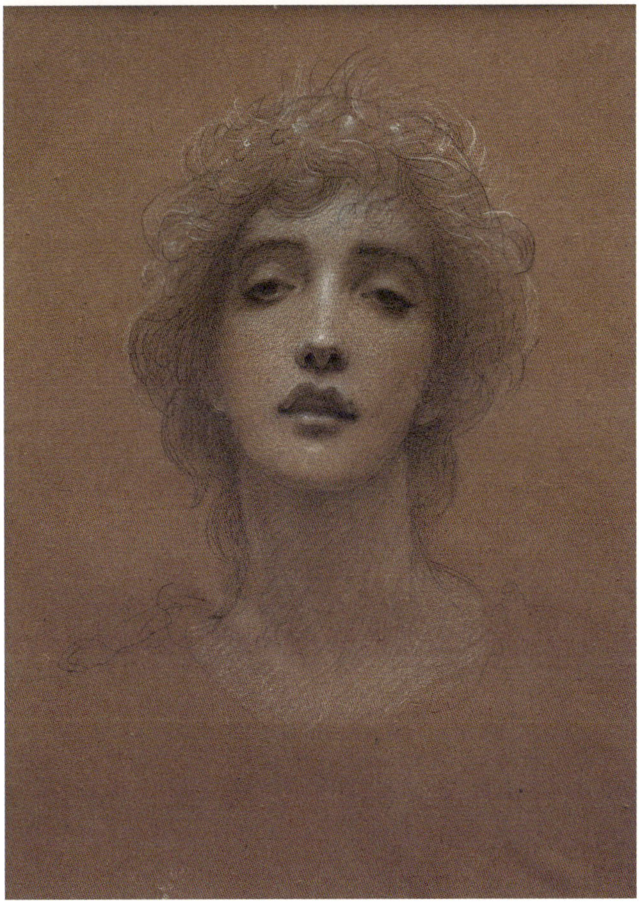

Cat. 99

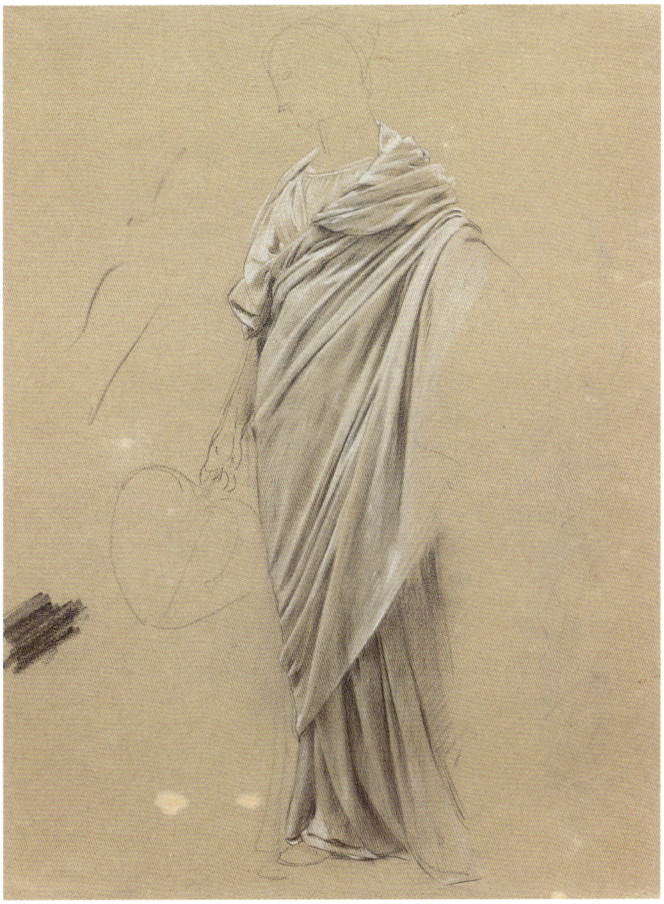

Cat. 100

Egon Schiele Austrian, 1890–1918

OLD GABLED HOUSE IN KRUMAU (ČESKÝ KRUMLOV), *1910*

Charcoal and watercolor on paper, 17¾ × 14½ in. (450 × 368 mm)
Signed and dated mid-upper left: *Egon / Schiele / 1910*; initialed lower left: *S*
Dallas Museum of Art, gift of the Estate of Mrs. Barron Kidd, 1994.221

PROVENANCE Wolfgang Gurlitt? (mentioned with a question mark in Kallir 1990); Mrs. Barron Kidd; given to the Dallas Museum of Art, December 27, 1994.

EXHIBITED Albertina, Vienna, *Egon Schiele: Gedächtnisausstellung*,1948, no. 47; Neue Galerie der Stadt Linz, Wolfgang-Gurlitt-Museum, Linz, *Egon Schiele*, March 1949, no. 70; Künstlerhaus, Salzburg, *Egon Schiele*, 1950, no. 23; Galerie Wolfgang Gurlitt, Munich, *Egon Schiele*, 1957, no. 23; Staatliche Kunsthalle, Baden-Baden, *Gustav Klimt und Egon Schiele*, January–February 1958, no. 74; Dallas Museum of Art, *Expressionism: German and Austrian Works on Paper*, June 24–October 28, 2007.

BIBLIOGRAPHY Kallir 1990, no. 741.

Egon Schiele's accomplishments during his short life are phenomenal both in content and in form. Early on, his extraordinary talent distinguished him as the Mozart of Art in Vienna, where he attended the Akademie and became the protégé of art nouveau artist Gustav Klimt. By 1910 Schiele had turned away from the older artist's mellifluous line and adopted an angular, highly concentrated approach. He placed his subjects within existential voids, increasing the compositional and psychological tension. Only after his brief imprisonment on charges of pornography in 1912 and his marriage to Edith Harms in 1914 did the artist allow his subjects an environment that commented on their characters.

For Schiele, a detail could stand poignantly for the whole, and empty space could be as expressive a motif as an object. In this case the cut-off corner of a multistoried, pale red, gabled house shares the pictorial space with an inversely jagged void that responds to the building's punctuation of its surrounding space. The corner view begins above the ground floor and ascends to the attic stories. Schiele has lovingly recorded the various ledges, windowpanes, shutters, and chimney funnel that climb up the bulging old building. The attention lavished upon the delineation of these details conveys the artist's rapport with his motif.

The gothic town of Krumau on the Moldau, with its commanding castle and church, was part of Emperor Franz Josef's Austro-Hungarian Empire; it is Český Krumlov in the present-day Czech Republic. As the hometown of the artist's mother it had a special place in Schiele's heart and represented a safe haven far away from the big-city intrigues of Vienna where he lived. His family visited the picturesque town on a winding river several times when Schiele was a boy. Krumau was also the site of a suicide attempt by his dying father, who was in the final stages of syphilis. Schiele nourished a haunting nostalgia for Krumau and once even experienced a "visit" from his father's ghost there. The artist had hoped to live in the old town permanently, but because of his lifestyle—taking the evening promenade on the main square dressed in a white caftan and with his model-lover Wally Neuzil on his arm—the inhabitants of the city took action against the unmarried pair and forced them to leave.

Schiele was only 20 when he created this poignant portrait of a gabled house. Krumau called forth some of his most heartfelt and somber townscapes, and this detailed drawing, although only a partial architectural view, unmistakably conveys the artist's affection for the town and its old buildings.

AC

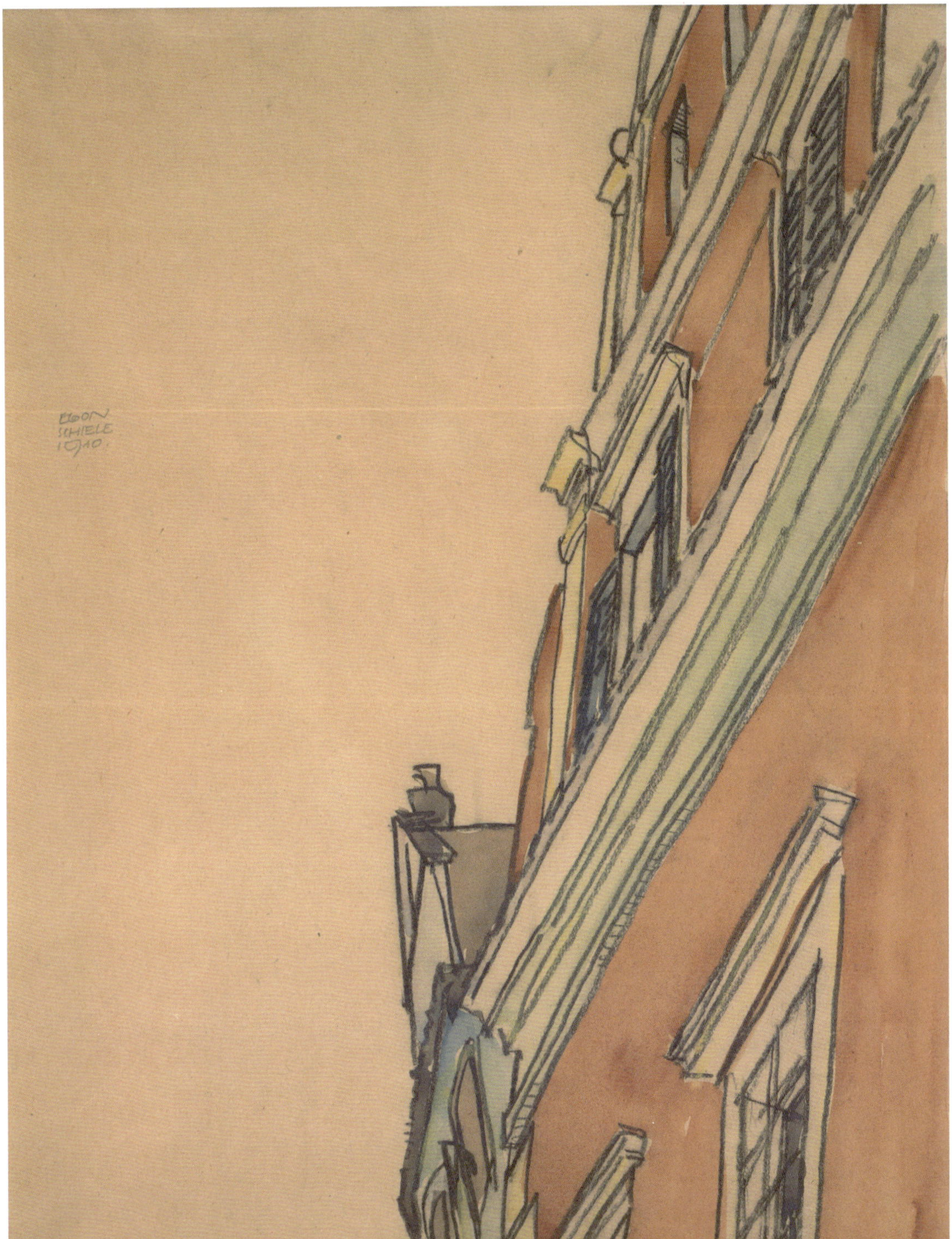

Egon Schiele Austrian, 1890–1918

REMEMBRANCE (ERINNERUNG), *1913*

Watercolor and pencil on paper, 18¼ × 12¼ in. (464 × 311 mm)
Recto: Signed and dated lower right, *Egon / Schiele / 1913*; inscribed lower left, *Erinnerung*
Verso: Black chalk drawing of a rowboat seen from above
Dallas Museum of Art, gift of Dr. Alessandra Comini in memory of her parents, Megan Laird and Raiberto Comini, 2001.357.a–b

PROVENANCE Marie Schiele? (mentioned with a question mark in Kallir); Viktor Fogarassy; Alessandra Comini; given to the Dallas Museum of Art, December 19, 2001.

EXHIBITED Hagendbund / Neue Galerie, Vienna, 1928? (mentioned in Kallir 1990 as not in catalogue and with a question mark); Württembergischer Kunstverein, Stuttgart, *Die Klassiker der österreichischen modernen Kunst von Klimt bis Wotruba*, November 1957, no. 97; Staatliche Kunsthalle, Baden-Baden, *Gustav Klimt und Egon Schiele*, January–February 1958, no. 149; Galerie St. Etienne, New York, *Egon Schiele (1890–1918)*, February–April 1965, no. 43, ill.; New York, La Boétie, *Egon Schiele and His Circle*, May–June 1971, no. 25, ill.; Dallas Museum of Art, *Expressionism: German and Austrian Works on Paper*, June 24–October 28, 2007.

BIBLIOGRAPHY Comini 1974, pl. 100a; Comini 1976, pl. 15; Kallir 1990, no. 1430.

Schiele's portraits and self-portraits are mirrors of the collective cultural quest of his time: for the inner self—psychological man, rather than the political, religious, or economic person of previous times. The artist was a contemporary of Arnold Schönberg and Sigmund Freud, and he shared in their preoccupation with the psyche as he shifted attention from the rational to the irrational, from the environmental to the existential, and from *Schein* (appearance) to *Sein* (being).

After his imprisonment for 24 days in 1912 on charges of immorality, among other things, Schiele withdrew from society and began to paint self-portraits showing himself as a monk, a hermit, or a saint (the martyred St. Sebastian). In 1913 he began work on a life-size self-portrait with another figure called *Self-Portrait with Saint*, for which this compelling watercolor is an important study. The oil painting is now lost, and we know it only through a photograph of the artist standing to the right of the work and "completing" the picture (fig. 18).

The delicate watercolor study, in which the artist looks back over his shoulder and away from the image on which he is working, is heightened with green and yellow bands across Schiele's short caftan and two vertical streaks of red running down the legs. His title for the work—*Erinnerung (Remembrance)*—is boxed in at the lower left. This study reveals two interesting features not carried over into the painting itself: Schiele stands with a piece of drawing chalk in his hand, and the second figure, who does not share his world, is only an image that the artist has begun to draw. The figure has the monk's beard equated with Gustav Klimt in Schiele's allegorical renditions of himself with the older artist, who was his mentor. Schiele was right-handed, but here he holds the chalk in his left hand. If this seems partially to contradict his role as artist, the painting confirms the ambiguity, for the chalk is no longer shown and the artist seems about to step into his own picture behind the striding figure of the saint who has replaced the Klimt-monk of this preparatory study.

Schiele's expression in this study—dreamy and fragile—underlies the precarious journey back to normalcy in a society that had so recently condemned him to imprisonment. Five years later he would be dead, a victim of the influenza epidemic that ravaged Europe at the end of World War I.

AC

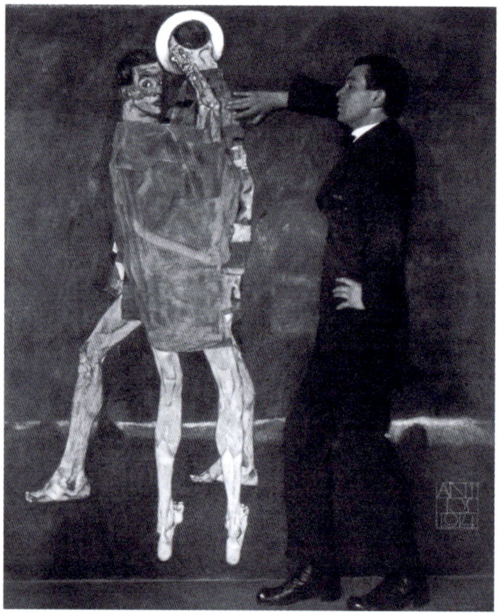

Fig. 18 Photograph by Anton Josef Trcka showing Egon Schiele standing in front of his uncompleted *Self-Portrait with Saint ("Encounter")* in 1914. Österreichische Nationalbibliothek, Vienna, Pf 7742 D2.

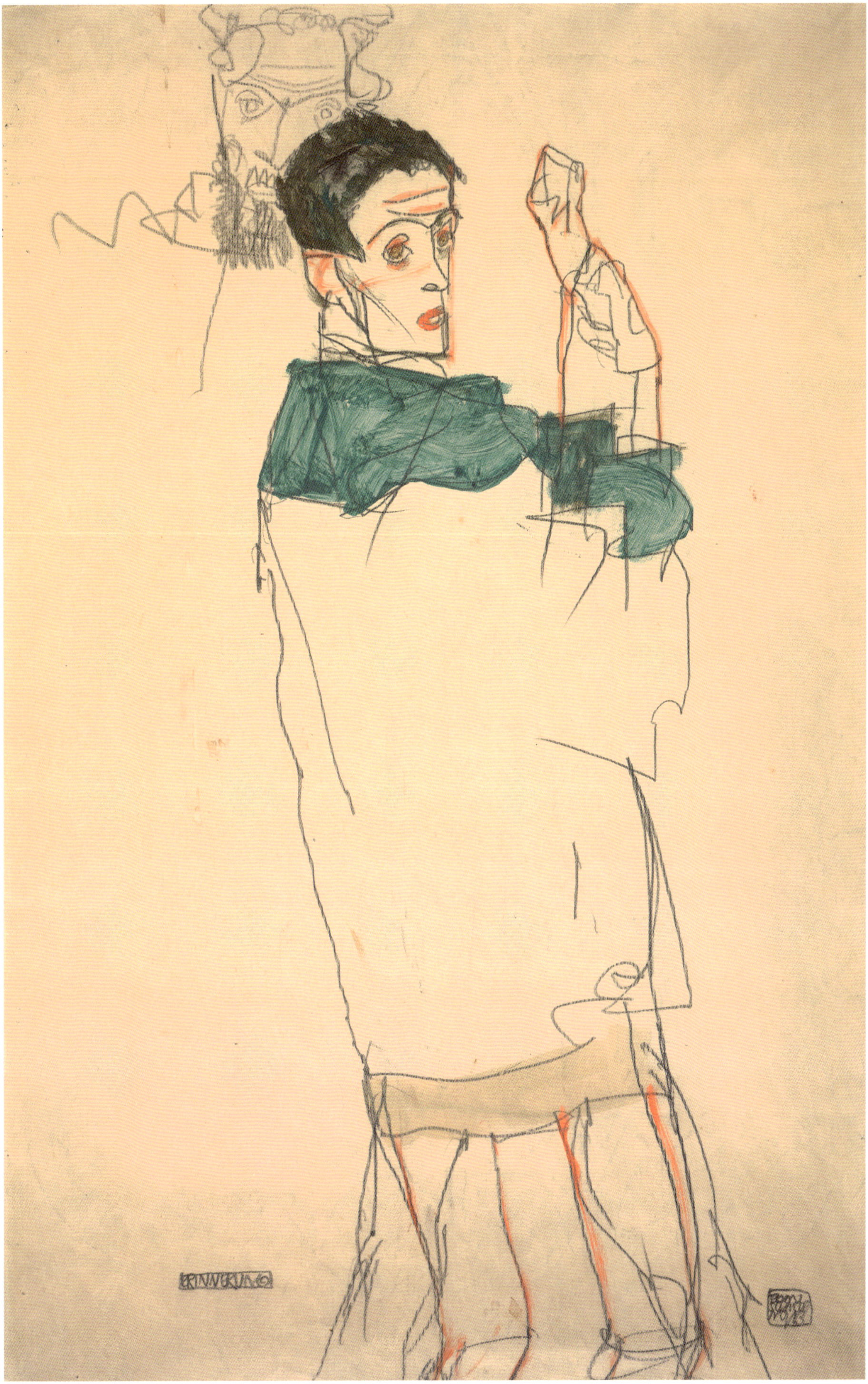
ERINNERUNG

103

Egon Schiele Austrian, 1890–1918

PORTRAIT OF GUIDO ARNOT, *1918*

Black crayon on paper, 18¼ × 11¼ in. (472 × 300 mm)
Signed and dated lower left: *Egon / Schiele / 1918*
Dallas Museum of Art, gift of the Estate of Mrs. Barron Kidd, 1994.222

PROVENANCE Wolfgang Gurlitt? (mentioned with a question mark in Kallir); Mrs. Barron Kidd; given to the Dallas Museum of Art, December 27, 1994.

EXHIBITED *Expressionism: German and Austrian Works on Paper from the Dallas Museum of Art*, June 24–October 28, 2007.

BIBLIOGRAPHY Kallir 1990, no. 2458.

In addition to drawing a study of his subject's hands, Schiele made several head studies of his friend, the Austrian gallery owner Guido Arnot, before creating the large and riveting oil portrait of 1918 (fig. 19). This one concentrates on Arnot's mustached face, which turns slightly away from the beholder, the eyes pulling to one side and fixed in thought. Schiele suggests the sitter's upper torso with a sparse but masterful line that conveys not only an arm resting on an invisible chair support but also Arnot's collar and cravat. The receding hairline and its part are suggested with just a few strokes of the black chalk (schwarze Kreide).

What does the expression on Arnot's face convey? Arnot, whose gallery was located in the center of Vienna, had given Schiele a one-man show in December 1914 and had bought works from him ever since. In arranging an exhibition of the artist to open in November 1916, he extracted the promise of a 25 percent commission on any work Schiele might sell directly to a client during the three months of the show. A glimmering of Arnot's wary ways may be seen in the alert and tensed position in which Schiele shows him (in the final oil, Arnot's hands are tightly folded together). The artist suggested this characterization of Arnot through posture in a quick notation in his sketchbook and immediately worked it out in a second sketchbook drawing. In the final oil, the pose seen in this study speaks of Arnot, but all the rest belongs to the artist: chair, books, and artifacts, including the carved wooden horse (upper right) with which Schiele posed for a photograph in March 1914. Inclusion of this special object from the outside world testifies to his relationship to his model and, in effect, seals a promise of patronage.

AC

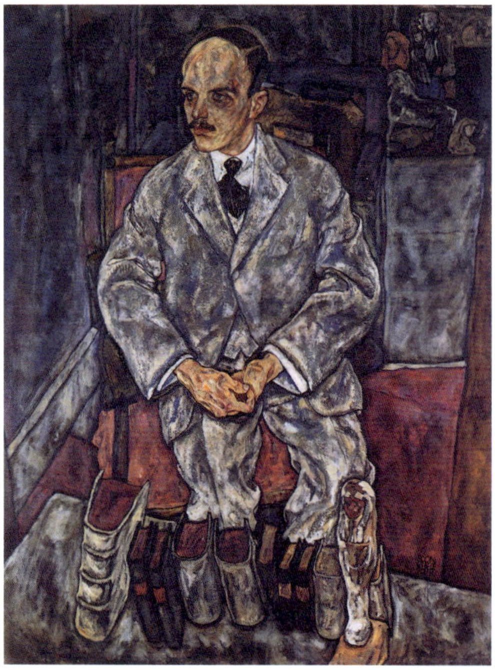

Fig. 19 Egon Schiele, *Portait of Guido Arnot*, 1918. Oil on canvas. Private collection.

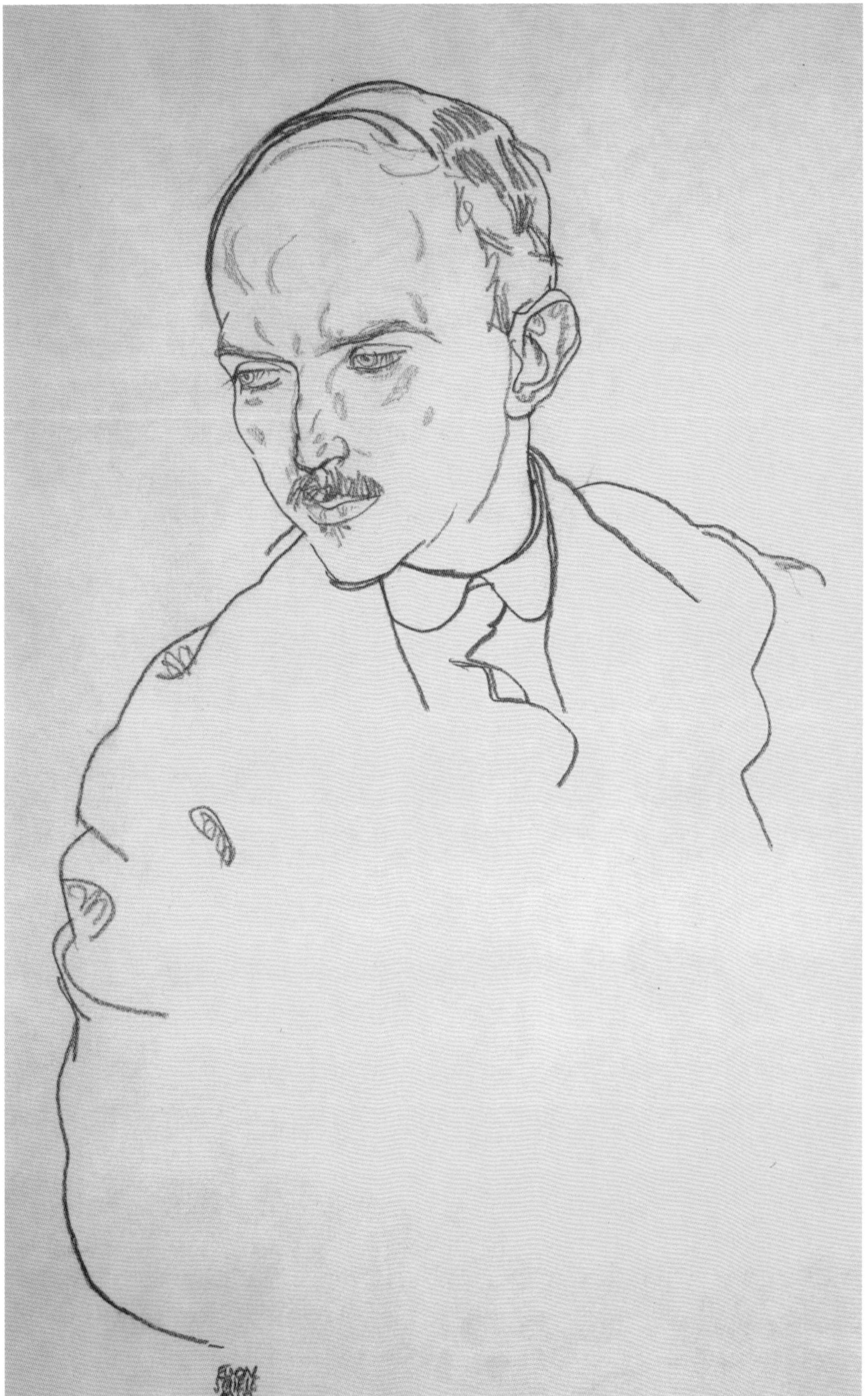

104

Piet Mondrian Dutch, 1872–1944

YOUNG TREE GROVE AMIDST WATER REFLECTIONS, C. *1902–1905*

Watercolor and gouache on paper, 11⅞ × 15⅝ in. (303 × 397 mm)
Signed lower right: *PIET MONDRIAAN*
Dallas Museum of Art, Foundation for the Arts Collection, gift of Mr. and Mrs. James H. Clark, 1975.66.FA

PROVENANCE Brock Street Gallery, London; Cologne, Lempertz Auction, December 3, 1960; Sidney Janis Gallery, New York, 1962; Mr. and Mrs. James H. Clark, Dallas, around 1962–1975; given to the Dallas Museum of Art, Foundation for the Arts Collection, in 1975.

EXHIBITED Dallas Museum for Contemporary Arts, *Dallas Collects,* August 21–September 16, 1962; Dallas Museum of Art, *Impressionist and Modern Masters in Dallas,* September 3–October 22, 1989, 82, no. 64.

BIBLIOGRAPHY Welsh 1977, 63, repr. 80; Welsh 1998, vol. 1, 270, no. A292; Bax 2001, 352.

Almost no painter of the 20th century was more committed to the path of abstraction in art, yet Piet Mondrian's journey was gradual, and he sustained a profound interest in understanding the structure of the world he observed. Mondrian painted *Young Tree Grove Amidst Water Reflections* when, as a young artist in Amsterdam, he made frequent cycling trips into the surrounding countryside in search of landscape subjects. He painted a number of river views along the Gein, but this watercolor seems to show another, unidentified location, since the double drawbridge lightly sketched in the background does not correspond to any known structure on the river. He signed the watercolor with the Dutch spelling of his family name, which he began to spell with a single *a* after his move to Paris in 1912.

The trunks of willow trees form a kind of scrim parallel to the picture plane through which the not-too-distant horizon can be glimpsed. Mondrian often sketched and painted this motif—a row of trees lining the banks of a river—during this period, perhaps under the influence of Claude Monet, whose work he would have encountered in a 1901 exhibition in Amsterdam. Mondrian demonstrates his command of the watercolor medium, overlaying areas of fluid paint with drier brushwork and sparkling highlights in opaque white.

HMacD

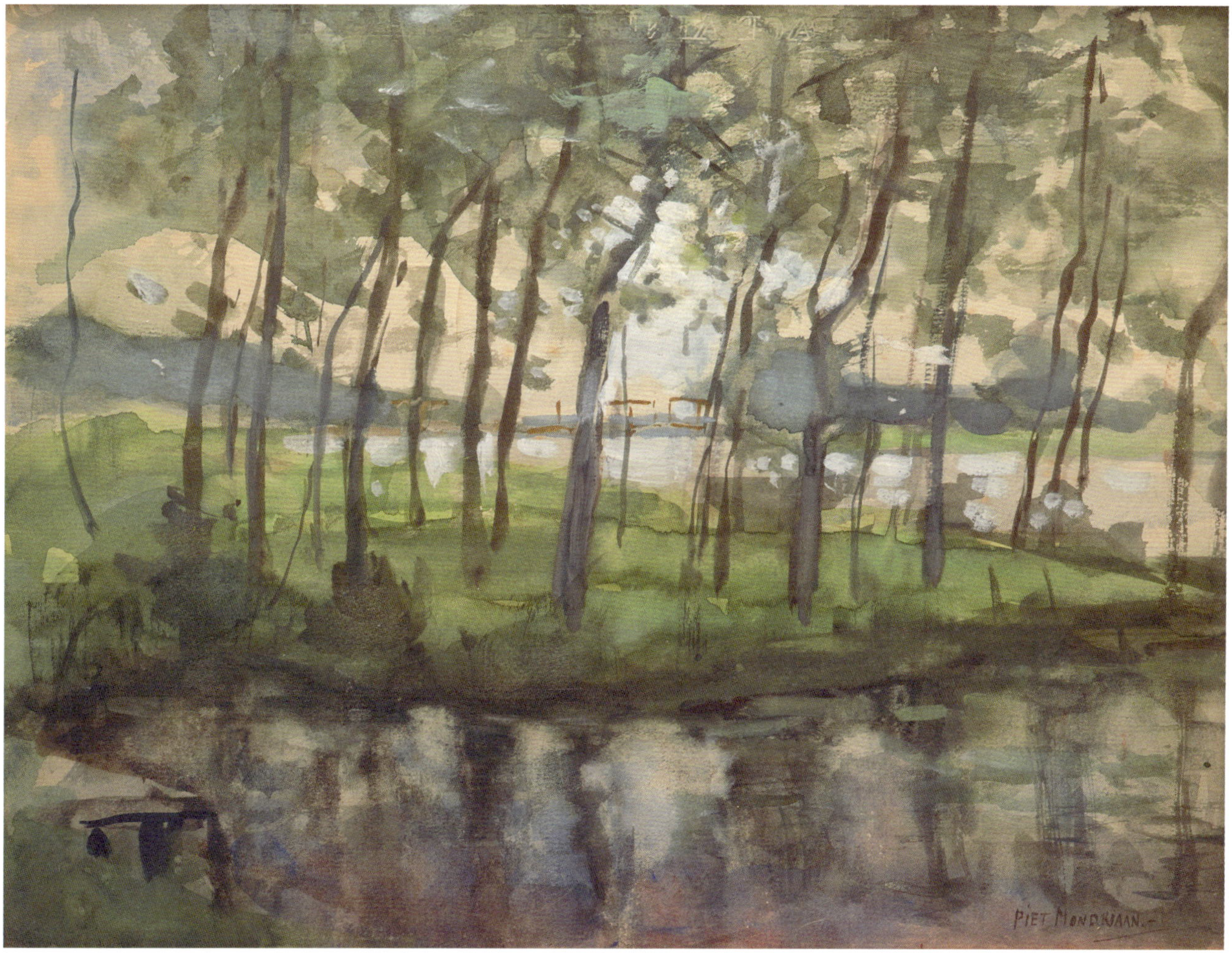
PIET MONDRIAAN.

105

Piet Mondrian Dutch, 1872–1944

FARM NEAR DUIVENDRECHT (RECTO), C. *1916?*;
THE SEA (OCEAN 2) (VERSO), *1914*

Charcoal on paper, 23⅛ × 30⅛ in. (587 × 765 mm)
Signed lower left (recto): *P. MONDRIAAN*
Private collection, Dallas

PROVENANCE Kunsthandel G. J. Niuwenhuizen Segaar, The Hague (1950); Sidney Janis, New York; where purchased by Mr. and Mrs. Henry Jacobus, Dallas, in 1958; by descent to the current owner.

EXHIBITED Dallas Museum for Contemporary Arts, *Texas Collects, 1960–1961;* Dallas Museum for Contemporary Arts, *Texas Collects 20th-Century Art,* May 14–28, 1963; Dallas Museum of Art, *Dallas Collects: Impressionist and Early Modern Masters,* January 24–February 26, 1978, no. 63 (recto), no. 64 (verso).

BIBLIOGRAPHY Seuphor 1952, 220 (verso); Seuphor 1956, pl. 13, no. C.C.117.(recto), and 402–3, pl. 21, no. C.C.226 (verso); Joosten 1973, 55 (verso); Bois 1982, 31–32 (verso); Buenger 1981–83, 55n47 (recto); Threlfall 1988, 224–25 (verso); Joosten 1998, vol. 2, 462, no. C2 (recto) and 244, no. B64 (verso); Bax 2001, 483 (verso) and 558 (recto).

Beginning as early as 1904, Mondrian made a series of drawings and paintings of a farm near Duivendrecht, not far from Amsterdam along the banks of the Gein River. His meditative views of the humble farm buildings huddled along a low horizon became so popular with collectors that he continued to produce new iterations of the subject well into the 1910s, even as he was moving quickly toward the geometric abstraction that would prove his stylistic hallmark. The drawing on the recto of this sheet (top of facing page) is one such late reprisal of the motif, similar in composition to a contemporary painting in the Dallas Museum of Art (fig. 20). Thus, as counterintuitive as it may seem, the abstract drawing of the sea on the reverse side of the sheet (bottom of facing page) actually predates the landscape.

Soon after his return to Holland from France at the beginning of World War I, Mondrian started to sketch the North Sea. Under the influence of analytical cubism, which he had studied closely during his two years in Paris, he had explored structuring his images as black grids of intersecting horizontals and verticals against a neutral ground. Now back in Holland, he continued this investigation with a series of images that studied the rolling movement of the waves represented as dominant horizontals interrupted by vertical lines and gentle curves that echo the ellipse of the composition.[1] This embryonic grid, central to Mondrian's works of later decades, was often contained within an oval frame during this period.

HMacD

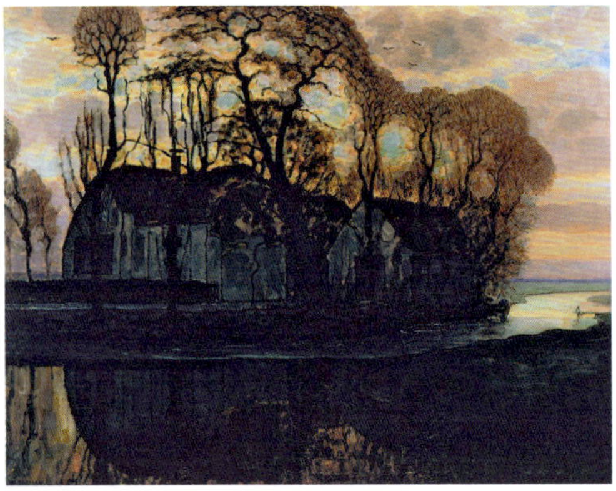

Fig. 20 Piet Mondrian, *Farm Near Duivendrecht, in the Evening,* c. 1916. Oil on canvas. Dallas Museum of Art, gift of The Edward and Betty Marcus Foundation, 1987.359.

Note
1. For more information on the Ocean series and related work, see Bois and Joosten 1994, 158–170.

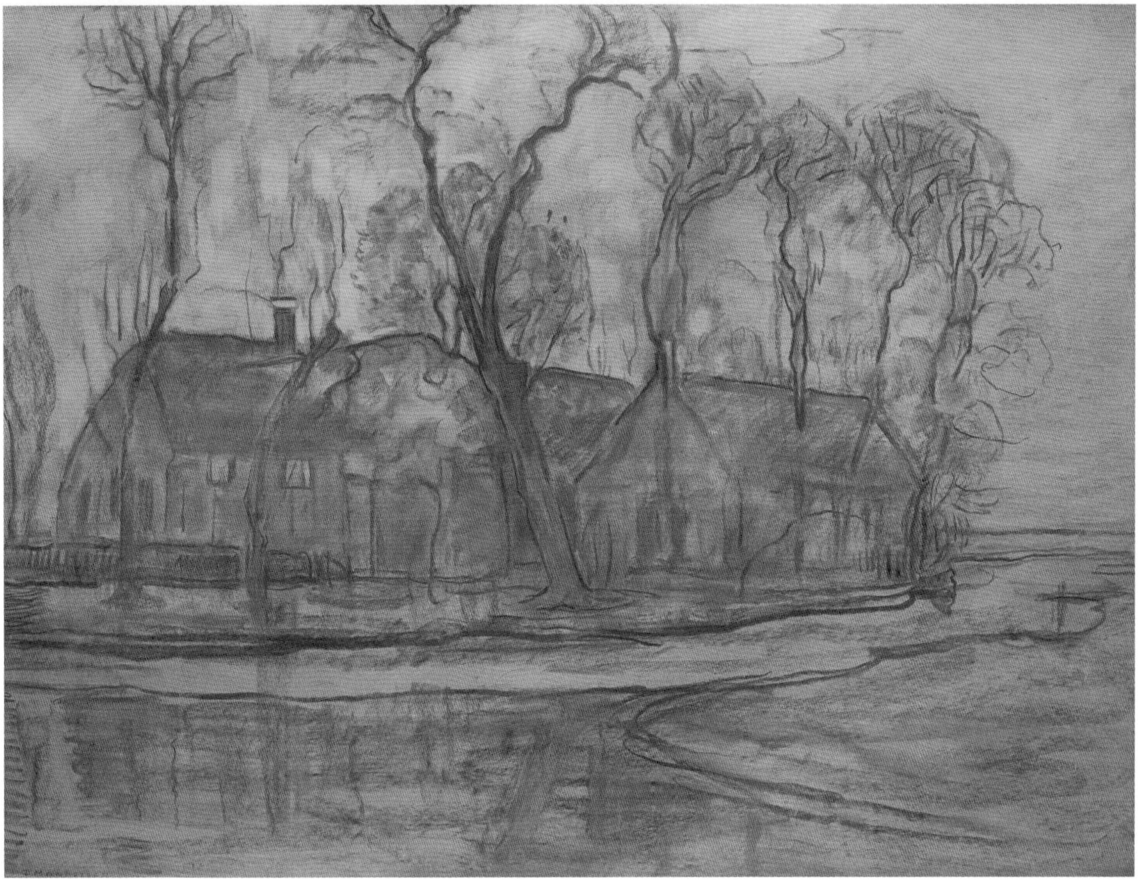

Cat. 105, recto.

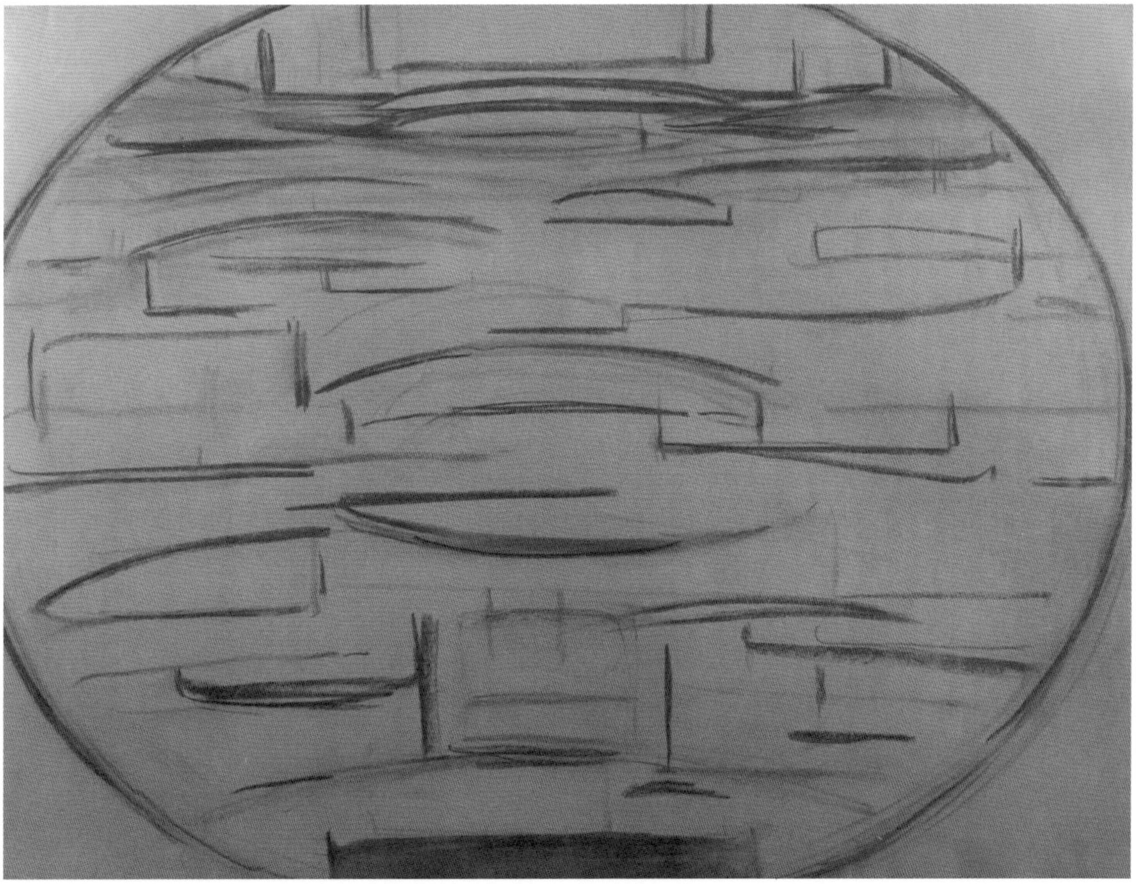

Cat. 105, verso.

Piet Mondrian Dutch, 1872–1944

AMARYLLIS, C. *1916*

Pencil and watercolor on paper, 19¼ × 12¼ in. (490 × 310 mm)
Signed lower left: *PIET MONDRIAN*
Private collection, Dallas

PROVENANCE Agathe W. Zethraeus, Amsterdam, ?–1970; sale, New York, Parke-Bernet Galleries, *Important Nineteenth and Twentieth Century Drawings and Watercolors,* May 6, 1970; Noah Goldowsky, New York, 1970–1972; Thomas Gibson Fine Art, London, 1972–1974; Sidney Janis Gallery, New York, 1974; where purchased by the current owner.

EXHIBITED Noah Goldowsky Gallery, New York, *The Early Works of Piet Mondrian,* November 1971 (*Lilies in a Bottle,* c. 1916); Thomas Gibson Fine Art, London, Spring 1972 (*Lilies in a Bottle,* c. 1916).

BIBLIOGRAPHY Joosten 1998, vol. 2, 475, no. C37; Bax 2001, 564.

Mondrian first began to draw and paint flowers as early as 1906–1907. As he later recalled, "I enjoyed painting flowers, not bouquets, but a single flower at a time, in order that I might better express its plastic structure."[1] As late as the 1920s, when he was deep into the most austere phase of his black-and-white abstractions, he continued to make flower studies, often, he admitted, to earn money. Sometimes a single drawing served as the model (probably traced) for more than one version, some in watercolor.

There are two versions of the present composition, this one obviously the first, and another, in a Dutch private collection, entirely painted in watercolor. A single stem of amaryllis stands upright in a simple bottle repurposed as a makeshift vase. This casual yet highly concentrated approach to staging the floral still life is typical of Mondrian's many flower studies. Although the lily has important associations in Christian iconography as the emblem of the Virgin Mary, conventionally included in scenes of the Annunciation, Mondrian eschews any specific symbolic reference. The poet and critic David Shapiro has recognized in Mondrian's studies of amaryllis blossoms a kind of "abstract cruciformality that bears a connotation of suffering and triumph," but he also notes that their firm verticals and horizontals tie this naturalistic motif to the artist's increasing interest in the architectural or geometric grid as the core subject of his art.[2]

HMacD and WBJ

Notes
1. Quoted in Holtzman and James 1986, 338.
2. Shapiro 1991.

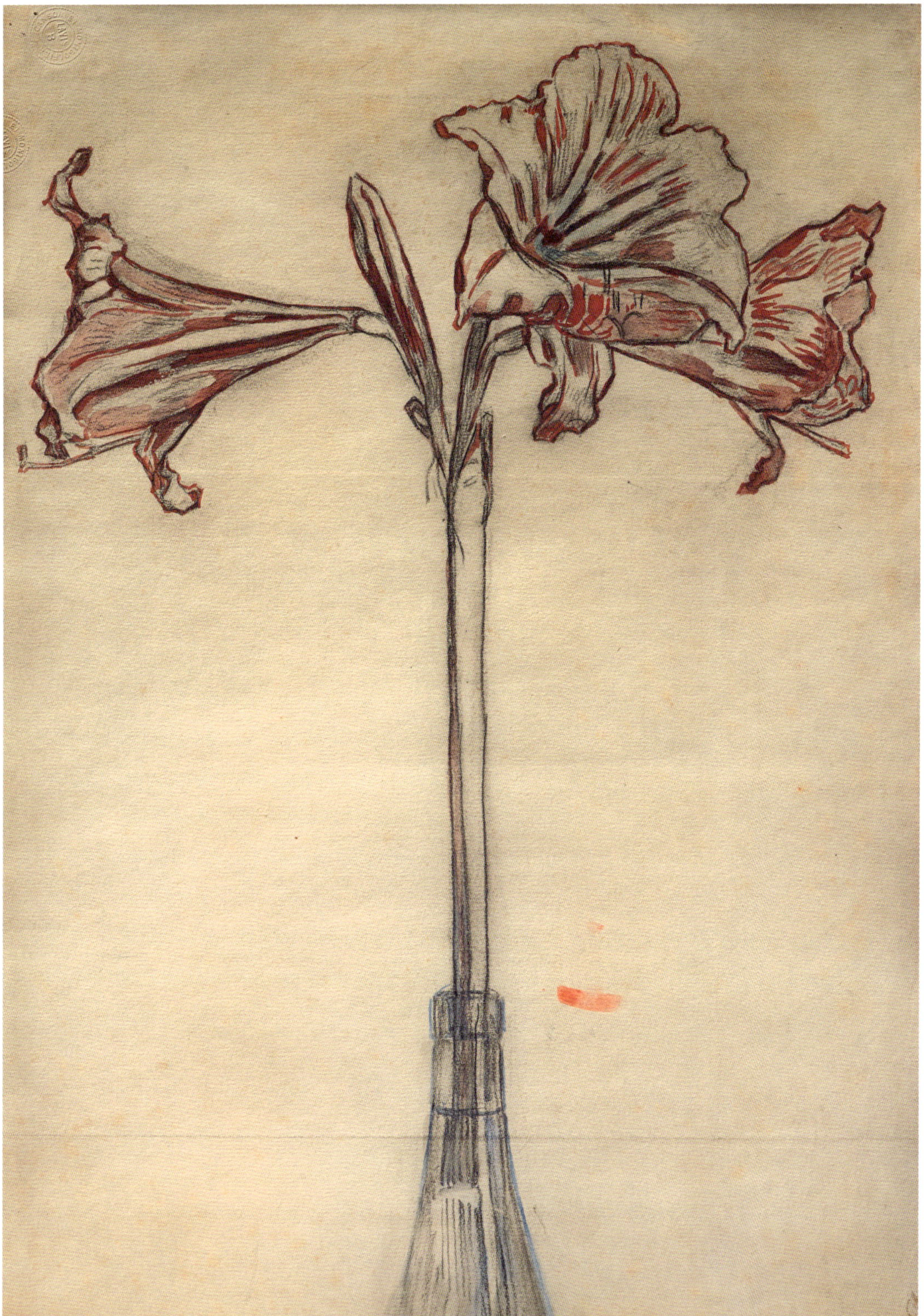
PIET MONDRIAN

107

Max Jacob French, 1876–1944

PAINTER IN HIS STUDIO, *N.D.*

Watercolor over pencil on paper, 13 × 9⅞ in. (330 × 250 mm)
Inscribed on verso: *Dupuis / 33 × 25*; signed lower right: *Max Jacob*
Private collection, Dallas

PROVENANCE Galerie Antoine Laurentin, Paris; where purchased 2001 by the current owner.

Max Jacob was not a groundbreaking or particularly creative painter. But he was one of the most magnetic personalities and most fertile minds in the cultural life of Paris of his time—an individual, it could be said, who was a primary catalyst in the chemistry of the avant-garde at the turn of the 20th century. The son of a Jewish tailor in Brittany, where he had been a brilliant student of philosophy and literature, he came to Paris in 1894, eking out a meager living with such odd jobs as piano teacher, shopkeeper, and art critic. Although he became a respected and influential writer in prose and verse, he briefly abandoned his literary aspirations early on, even enrolling as an art student at the Académie Julian, where he failed to impress his teachers.

People who read Jacob's name in almost any account of the artistic life of Paris before World War I may not realize that he was also a painter, but in fact he never entirely gave up the making of gouaches and watercolors, with which he helped support himself until the end of his life. In 1901 Jacob met and befriended Pablo Picasso, becoming his mentor during his toughest years of poverty and one of his truest lifelong friends. When they shared a room on the Boulevard Voltaire, Jacob taught Picasso to speak French and introduced him to Guillaume Apollinaire and others who would be key figures in the unfolding of one of the most dramatic chapters in the history of art. All the while, he inspired these artists and writers and egged them on with his ebullience and his truly original mind. Despite his conversion to Catholicism and his retreat to a monastery during the Nazi occupation of France, the Gestapo arrested him in 1944, and he died in a French internment camp en route to Germany, where he would surely have been murdered along with the rest of his family.

This undated watercolor shows a certain mastery of the elemental principles of the medium, whereby transparency and spontaneity of touch vivify the page and endow a scene with atmosphere. The crowded room, illuminated only by the natural light from a large window, aptly captures the working life of an impoverished artist living in Montmartre at the turn of the 20th century, when neither gas nor electricity had yet reached the inhabitants. Most of Jacob's oeuvre as an artist depicted himself, his friends, and their immediate environment—a cast of characters and a setting that became iconic as the romance of avant-garde Paris gathered more and more luster over the course of his life. The setting recalls that of other watercolors and ink drawings showing the artist and writer at his desk after 1900, but there is no resemblance between this person and Jacob. As the drawing is inscribed on the back "Dupuis," it may be meant to represent Maurice Dupuis, the Belgian painter who lived in Montmartre and whom Jacob surely would have known.

WBJ

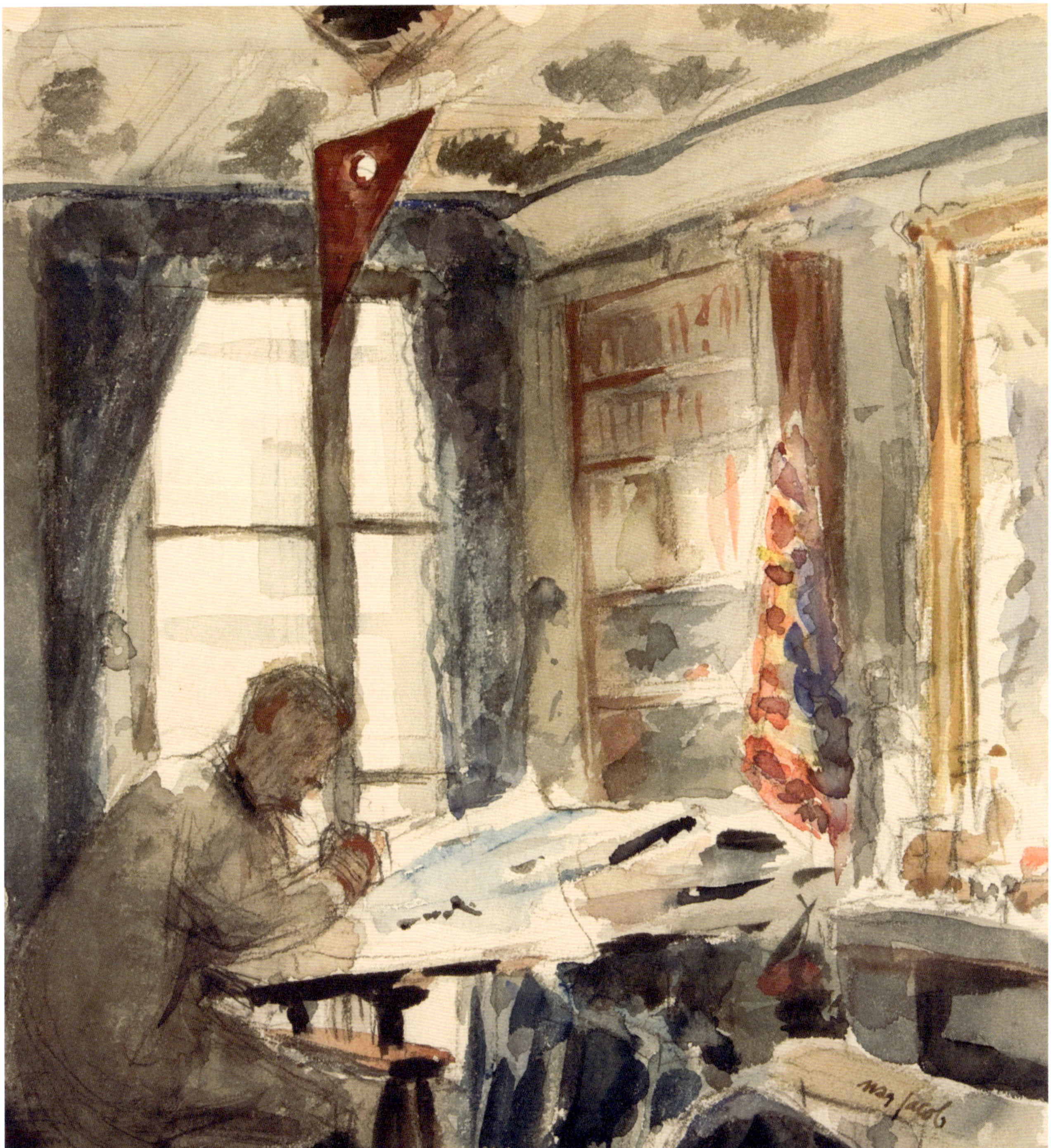
max Jacob

108

André Derain French, 1880–1954

EARTHLY PARADISE (PARADIS TERRESTRE), *1906*

Watercolor on paper, 19⅝ × 25⅝ in. (500 × 650 mm)
Signed in pencil lower right: *A Derain*
Collection of Mary Ralph Lowe, Fort Worth

PROVENANCE Sale, Fine Art Auctions, Miami, *Important Paintings and Sculptures,* December 4, 2011, lot 227; Jean-Luc Baroni, Ltd., London; where purchased 2013 by the current owner.

EXHIBITED Philadelphia Museum of Art, *Gauguin, Cézanne, Matisse: Visions of Arcadia,* June 20–September 3, 2012, cat. unnumbered, fig. 91; Musée Bonnard, Le Cannet, France, *Le Nu de Gauguin à Bonnard: Ève, Icône de la Modernité?,* July 6–November 6, 2013, 119, no. 41.

André Derain spent the summer of 1905 with his friend Henri Matisse in the French Mediterranean fishing village of Collioures, just north of the Spanish border. This Arcadian-Edenic watercolor is one of many works that can be traced to this experience. Derain's undulating trees, plants, and mountains, all redolent of a sun-filled day, form a natural stage on which figures revel in an atmosphere of richly evocative color and sensuously layered forms.

Suggestions of Adam, Eve, and the Serpent are evident on the watercolor's right. Other allegorical hints appear in the possible horse-and-rider subject above right, the trio of figures in the upper left corner hovering in a red tinted sky, and the embracing pair on the lower left.

The rising deep blue mountain form in the upper left center was clearly important to Derain in evoking the spirit of Collioures after his 1905 stay. Photographs confirm the presence of just such a mountain chain beyond the village in majestic backdrop, and a roughly similar blue mountain form is seen in Derain's paintings *The Trees,* c. 1906 (Albright-Knox Art Gallery, Buffalo), and *Landscape of the Midi,* 1906 (San Francisco Museum of Modern Art). A related watercolor, *Bacchic Dance,* 1906 (Museum of Modern Art, New York), displays more simply and abstractly, but with similar short brushstrokes of color, a scene of comparable lushness.

Derain began his serious pursuit of art only a decade or so before creating this watercolor, making his assured draftsmanship, imaginative command, and sophisticated color seen here are all the more remarkable. Alongside Matisse and Maurice de Vlaminck, both of whose early influence and support proved crucial, Derain and others pioneered the Fauve ("Wild Beast") aesthetic that took its name from a critic's harsh reaction to their paintings shown in a fall 1905 exhibition.

Matisse and Derain shared an interest in figures-in-paradise compositions (with Paul Gauguin's work an important precedent), as seen in this watercolor and in some of Matisse's greatest early paintings. Such Fauvist scenes were but one manifestation of a European penchant for depicting harmonic tableaux of innocence, pleasure, and fecundity amid an idyllic union of nature and humankind.

Derain's and his Fauvist colleagues' works are characterized by brilliant color applied directly to a surface in vividly assertive brushstrokes; little to no modeling, mixing of pigments, or apparent revisions; and a lack of concern for spatial depth and traditional perspective. Fauvism released color and form into new expressive realms and affected subsequent artists who would change the course of painting in the new century. Its traits are fully on view in this highly finished and representative example of Derain's lyrically sumptuous and visionary evocation of heaven on earth.

CW

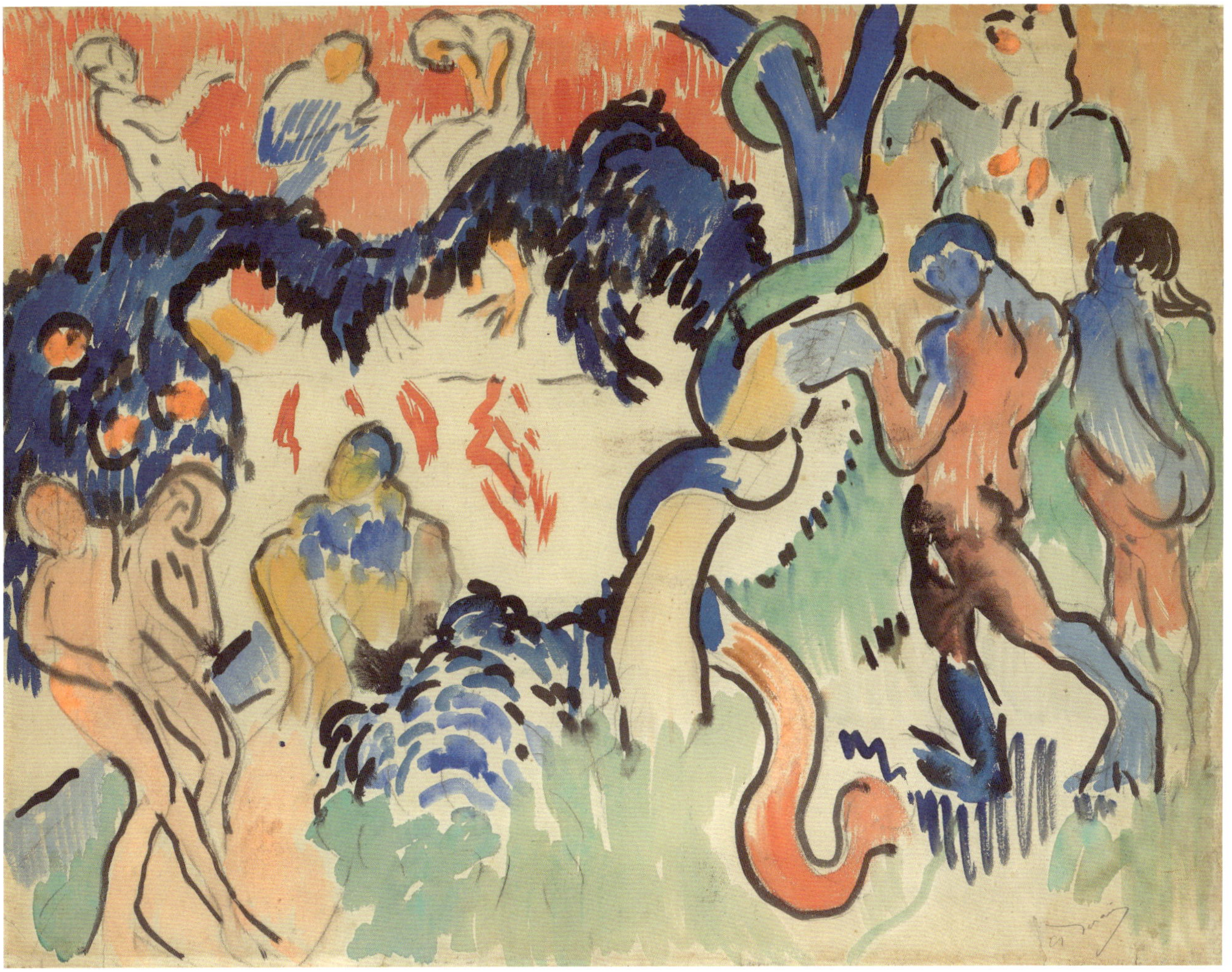

Pablo Picasso Spanish, 1881–1973

NUDE WITH FOLDED HANDS (NU AUX MAINS CROISÉES), *1906*

Gouache on paper, 19¼ × 11½ in. (305 × 220 mm)
Private collection

PROVENANCE Ambroise Vollard, Paris; private collection, London; acquired December 1964 from Marlborough-Gerson Gallery, New York, by the current owner.

EXHIBITED Grande Salle des Expositions de "La Réserve," Knokke-le-Zoute, Belgium, *Picasso*, July 15–August 27, 1950, no. 12; Fort Worth Art Center Museum, *Picasso*, February 8–March 26, 1967, no. 149; Dallas Museum of Fine Arts, *Dallas Collects Impressionist and Early Modern Masters*, January 24–February 26, 1978, no. 79; Dallas Museum of Art, *Impressionist and Modern Masters in Dallas*, September 3–October 22, 1989, 47, no. 75; Meadows Museum at Southern Methodist University, Dallas, *The Intimate Picasso*, May 13–August 29, 1999; Kunsthalle Bielefeld, Germany, *Picasso 1905 in Paris*, September 25, 2011–January 15, 2012, 158–159 color ill.

BIBLIOGRAPHY Zervos 1932–78, vol. 1, no. 258, pl. 113; Penrose 1958, pl. III, no. 8; Daix and Boudaille 1966, vol. 15, no. 19; Sutton and Lecaldano 1987, 108, no. 252; Picasso Project 2012, 229 ill.

Picasso and his companion Fernande Olivier spent part of the summer of 1906 in Gósol, a smugglers' town high "above the clouds" and donkey miles from nowhere in the Catalonian Pyrenees.[1] One of the signal works to emerge from that sojourn, *The Harem* (fig. 21), is a sunbaked reworking of Jean-Auguste-Dominique Ingres's *Turkish Bath* (1862, Musée du Louvre): paradoxically inspired by Gósol's parched archaism. In it Picasso set out to explore and disrupt the lazy alliance that Ingres's Orientalism had helped to create between exoticism and eroticism—by relocating the subject somewhat closer to home.[2] Among all of the changes Picasso made in *The Harem*, the most significant was a shift of fetishistic gears. In place of Ingres's bevy of mature, voluptuous beauties, Picasso substituted a clutch of waifs, their fragility and youth underscored by the languid puddle of masculine muscle slouching inebriated in the right foreground and the old crone of a procuress crouching in the back corner.

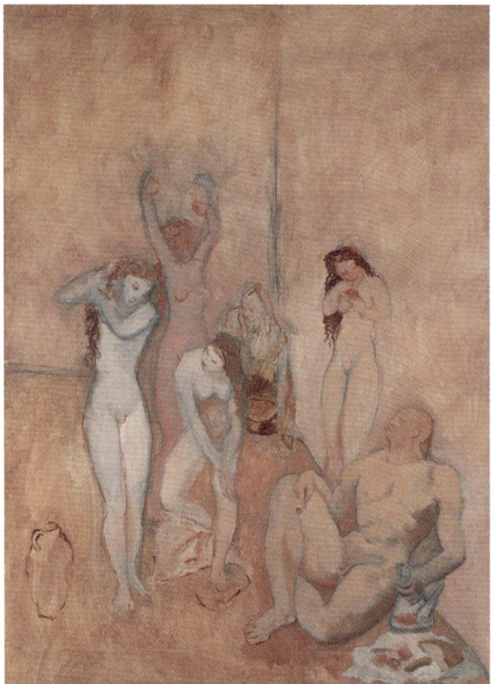

Fig. 21 Pablo Picasso, *The Harem*, 1906. Oil on canvas. The Cleveland Museum of Art, Bequest of Leonard C. Hanna Jr., 1958.45.

Like all of Picasso's big, pre-cubist figure paintings, *The Harem* represents the center of a constellation of studies, smaller pictures, prints, and finished drawings. In this case the related objects, of which *Nude with Folded Hands* is a beautiful example, constitute something like the stack of head shots from which the cast of the main event was ultimately drawn.[3] This girl in *Nude with Folded Hands*, and her numerous counterparts, are amalgams of Fernande, Picasso's principal model at the time, and one or more of the locals he would have found in Gósol.[4] Head and eyes uncomfortably averted, it is easy to imagine her fidgeting around the corner from *The Harem*, anxiously awaiting the chance to let her hair down and step into the picture. Referring to the placement of her hands, calculated to emphasize rather than conceal, Robert Rosenblum has labeled her (and the others like her) a *Venus Impudica* (immodest Venus)—to which we should add the qualification that if her comportment is unseemly, it is because the painter has made her so.

The delicacy with which Picasso has rendered her immature genitalia is genuinely disturbing.[5] But the wrongness we feel in ogling her—she is far too young to be exhibited, or to exhibit herself, this way—is no doubt magnified by Picasso's treatment of the rest of her anatomy. Displaying the air of anatomical assemblage that exemplifies so much of the archaic and classical sculpture that has survived, her sexual dimension is both heightened and problematized. Many of Picasso's nudes with clasped hands from

Notes
1. Olivier 2001, 183.
2. See Rosenblum 1997, 263–76, for a scintillating analysis of these works, and Richardson 1991, 436–54, for background.
3. Examples include *Nude with Joined Hands* (1906, oil on canvas, Museum of Modern Art) and *Nude with Clasped Hands* (1906, gouache on canvas, Art Gallery of Ontario), both pictured in color in Rosenblum 1997.
4. Richardson (1991) proposes the granddaughter of Josep Fontdevila, the innkeeper of the hotel where Picasso and Fernande lodged.
5. Rosenblum 1997, 273.

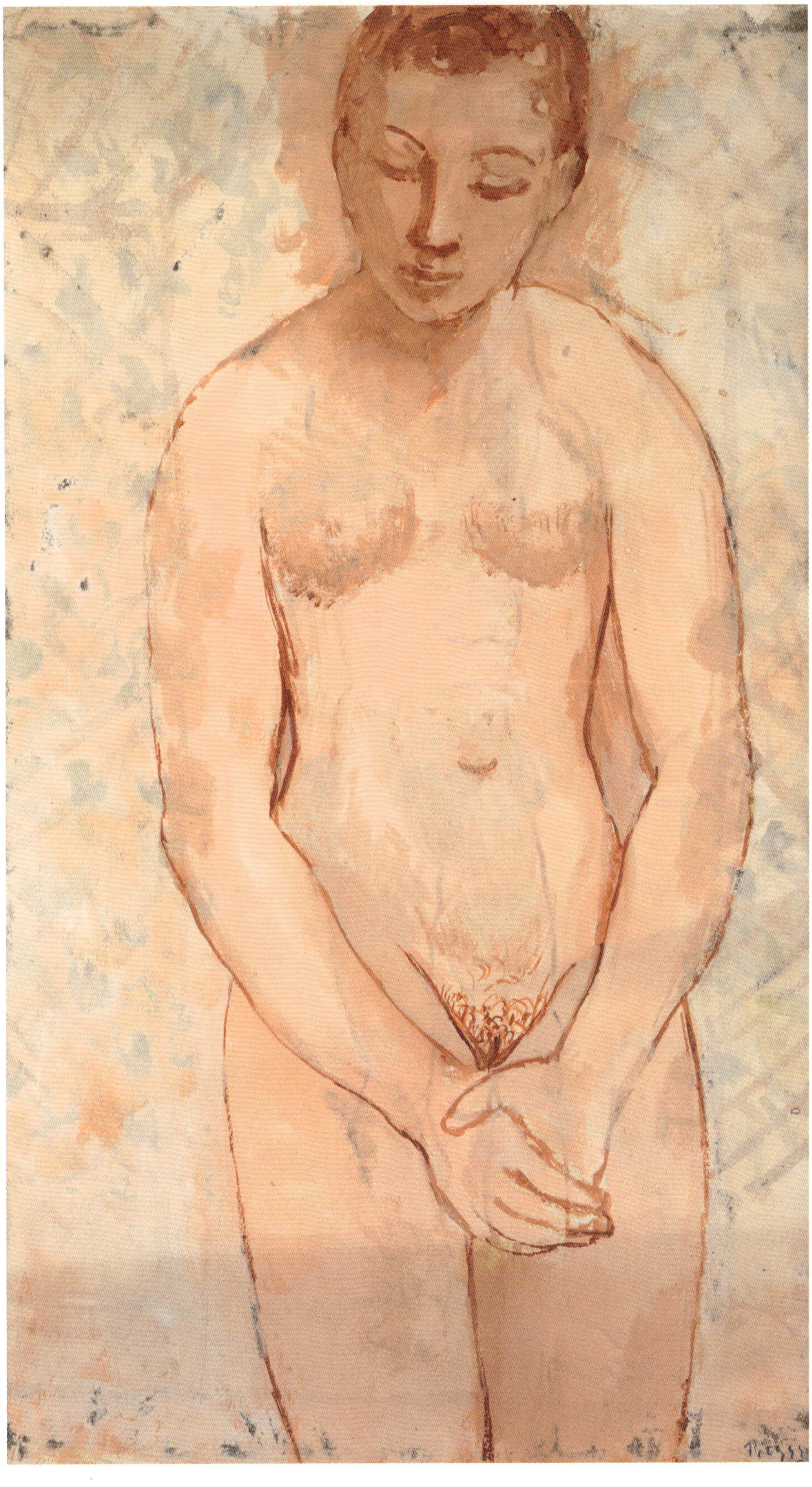

Gósol also share another anatomical discontinuity: heads that seem to have been transplanted from other drawings, other statues, other girls—an example of the synthetic nature of his art, even at this early date.

Looking at this shy waif from nowhere, awkwardly clasping her hands, trying bravely to hold herself together, it is hard to imagine her starring confidently in the most remorselessly modern picture of all time. But that is exactly where she would end up just a year later, in *Les Demoiselles d'Avignon* (1907, Museum of Modern Art, New York), for which *The Harem* was but a dry run. There, metamorphosed into the prostitutes of Picasso's urban bordello—now fully developed in their shattered forms and scary, mask-like faces—she trains her weaponized sexuality not on Ingres's titillation of bourgeois taste but on its destruction.

DH

110

Pablo Picasso Spanish, 1881–1973

STILL LIFE WITH A GLASS AND BOWL, C. *1909–1910*

Charcoal on paper, 19⅛ × 24⅞ in. (486 × 633 mm)
Collection of Mary Ralph Lowe, Fort Worth

PROVENANCE By descent from a private collection, France; sale, Sotheby's, Paris, *Art Impressionniste & Moderne*, May 30, 2012, lot 37; where purchased by the current owner.

Still Life with a Glass and Bowl is part of a continuum that runs from the frescoed walls of Roman villas, to Juan Sánchez Cotán's austere niches, across the overflowing sideboards of the Dutch Golden Age, over Paul Cézanne's rustic tables, through the cafés of Paris's Left Bank (about 1910), and, with El Lissitzky's *Prouns*, out into space and beyond. But Cézanne is the immediate source from whom Pablo Picasso and Georges Braque cribbed nearly everything they knew about how to make simple things disconcert by disordering single-point perspective.

Experiments require controls. For it is only against a clearly defined baseline that scientists can study and understand deviations from a standard—to wit, avant-gardists' perpetual interest in the tabletop still life, among the most reliable test subjects in the history of art. Picasso and Braque invented the strategies we know as cubism in a laboratory outfitted with equipment no more sophisticated than the objects to be found in any home. Their campaign to destabilize the centuries-old regime of veristic spatial representation was arguably won on an uncleared café table.

Still Life with a Glass and Bowl is a superb demonstration of what regulating the cubist experiment through subject and palette entailed and why many connoisseurs prefer the drawings from this period to the paintings. In cubist images the distortions reward attention. Everything in this drawing—the fruit bowl, the box, the wine glass (its half-foot and misaligned stem and bowl so precarious it could never stand anywhere outside the nominal space of cubism)—has been tampered with, even the tabletop and the shadows upon it. Within the vertiginous universe of the drawing, everything has been processed through a spatial ambiguity engine. The same tactic made it possible for Cézanne to disclaim any meaningful structural difference between the tablecloths he arranged in craggy peaks on a table in his studio and the crests of Mont Sainte-Victoire.

Cubist still life and landscape are capable of productive synthesis because landscape was the test ground on which the fundaments of perspective were established, a point epitomized in the most beautiful Picasso in Dallas, the exuberantly synthetic *Still Life in a Landscape* (fig. 22). To miniaturize the physical

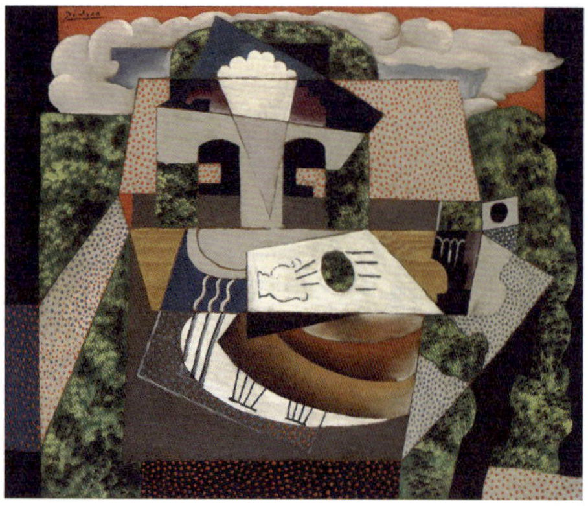

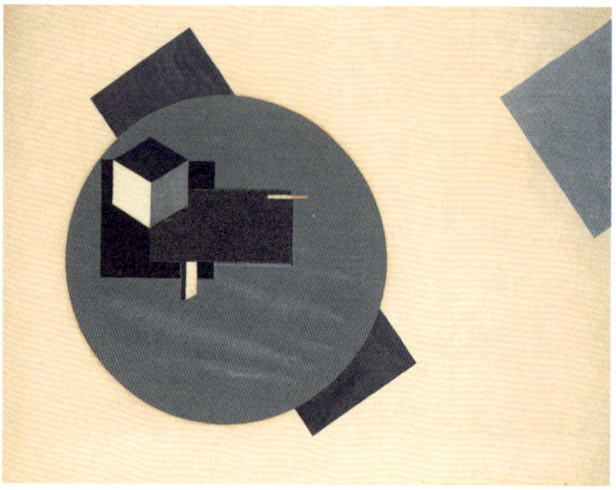

Fig. 22 Pablo Picasso, *Still Life in a Landscape (Naturaleza muerta en un paisaje)*, 1915. Oil on canvas. Meadows Museum, Southern Methodist University, Dallas. Algur H. Meadows Collection, MM.69.26.

Fig. 23 El Lissitzky, *Proun*, 1920. Collage of various cut-and-pasted papers, including abrasive paper (prepared with gouache and silver metallic paint), on cream wove paper, laid down on tan laminate board. The Art Institute of Chicago. Gift of Dorothy Braude Edinburg to the Harry B. and Bessie K. Braude Memorial Collection, 1998.733.

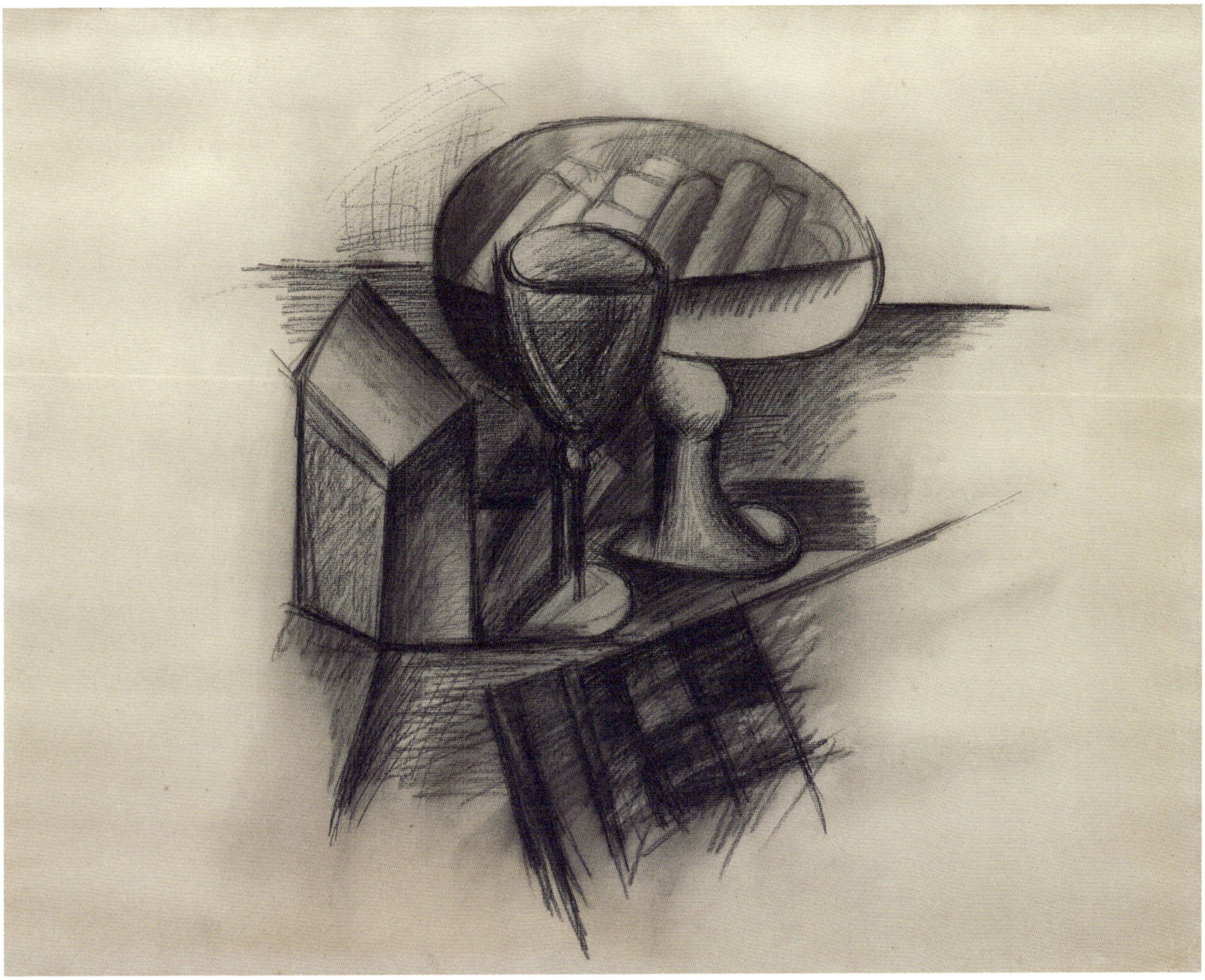

world in a still life is to transfer it to the workbench, all the more easily to tinker with it. In drawings such as *Still Life with a Glass and Bowl*, tinkering, for Picasso and Braque, meant taking apart. That is the significance of the odd patch in the foreground that appears to hang down from the table but is really neither here nor there. Its right side mimics the checkerboard pattern of a tablecloth, its left the molded profile of wainscoting: traces of place integrated awkwardly into object, just as an interior designer might do on an inspiration board. El Lissitzky would extend this principle of disassociation even further. In the galactically disorienting not-sites / not-objects of the *Prouns* (this drawing's clear descendants; see, for example, fig. 23), object-spaces as small as tables or as large as mountains—it is impossible to tell—have been cut adrift to tumble through the virtual space of design, without any point of reference, not even up or down.

DH

Naum Gabo American, born Russia, 1890–1977

STUDY OF A HEAD, C. *1917–1918*

Pencil and pastel on paper, 14⅛ × 8¾ in. (358 × 222 mm)
Inscribed top: Cyrillic and difficult to decipher; seemingly a story by Gabo entitled *Black* about a mine or factory.
Dallas Museum of Art, gift of Miriam Gabo and Nina and Graham Williams in honor of Dr. Steven A. Nash, 1985.141

PROVENANCE From the artist by descent to his wife Miriam and daughter Nina and her husband Graham Williams; given to the Dallas Museum of Art, 1985.

EXHIBITED Dallas Museum of Art, September 29–November 17, 1985, Art Gallery of Toronto, December 13, 1985–February 9, 1986, Solomon R. Guggenheim Museum, New York, March 6–April 27, 1986, Akademie der Künste, Berlin, September 7–October 19, 1986, Kunstsammlung Nordrhein-Westfalen, Düsseldorf, November 20, 1986–January 11, 1987, and Tate Gallery, London, February 11–April 20, 1987, *Naum Gabo: Sixty Years of Constructivism,* no. 87; Dallas Museum of Art, *Works on Paper: Recent Acquisitions,* December 12, 1978–March 20, 1988; Dallas Museum of Art, *Form on Paper: Drawings and Prints by Sculptors,* August 3, 2003–April 4, 2004.

BIBLIOGRAPHY Nash and Merkert 1985, 18, fig. 15, 19n41; 164, no. 87, ill.; Nash and Merkert 1986, 19, fig. 15, 20n41; 174, no. 91, ill.; Hammer and Lodder 2000, 76, fig. 52, 476n32.

Naum Gabo was one of the primary contributors to the creative upheaval of ideas about art and art's role in society that distinguish avant-garde developments in Russia in the early 20th century. Greatly influenced by cubism, futurism, and the utopian ideals of Russian poets and philosophers, Russian artists were among the first to break the barriers into total abstraction and apply their new "constructive" visual principles not just to painting and sculpture but to industrial design, architecture, and other realms of modern physical culture. Gabo came to these innovative developments through science, studying medicine, natural science, and engineering in Munich from 1910 to 1914. His first efforts to transfer technological thought into sculpture came with a series of assembled heads and torsos dating from 1915 to 1918. In this series he used a building system of honeycombed planes of metal, wood, or plastic, providing a diagrammatic three-dimensional form that eliminated most sculptural mass and opened up the form to a penetration of light and space—as in, for example, *Constructed Head No. 2* (1916, reconstructed c. 1923–1924, celluloid, Dallas Museum of Art, Edward S. Marcus Memorial Fund, no. 1981.35). *Study of a Head* relates to this series.

Its underdrawing—the layer of sketched lines under the dense application of pastel—clearly follows the pattern of other drawings related to the head and torso sculptures.[1] What is unique about this drawing, however, is the heavily worked-up shading that gives the head a solid, volumetric quality not found in any other drawing in this general group. It might be assumed that this dark coloration related to Gabo's story about a smoky factory or mine in the inscription at the top of the sheet. Another possibility is that it references the African masks that were in vogue among artists in Paris at that time, or even the modeled *Head of a Negro* (location unknown) that Gabo made in 1912–1913, although stylistically these two works are widely disparate.

In any regard, this drawing is historically significant as one of the most forceful and expressive of Gabo's early drawings and a document of groundbreaking developments in avant-garde Russia.

SN

Note
1. Nash and Merkert 1986, 153–60, 164–65.

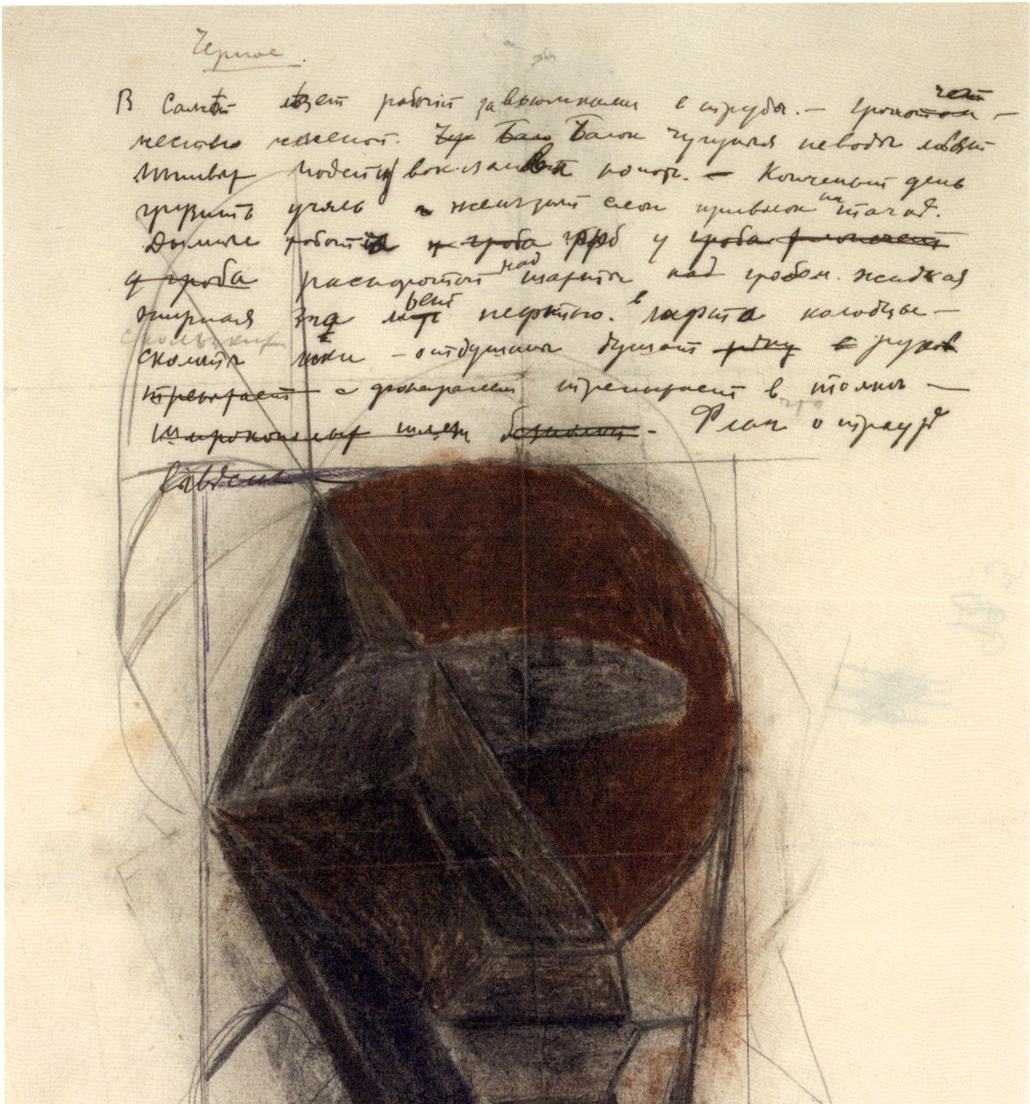

112

František Kupka Czech, 1871–1957

STUDY FOR "L'ACCORD DES COULEURS," *C. 1912–1918*

Watercolor on paper, 19½ × 12 in. (495 × 300 mm)
Signed lower right: *Kupka*
Private collection, Dallas

PROVENANCE Sotheby's, London, December 5, 1973, lot 190; Kande Gallery, New York; with B. C. Holland, Chicago; Murray Gribin, Los Angeles; with Rachel Adler Gallery, New York; Mario H. Gradowczyk, Buenos Aires; with Guillermo de Osma, Madrid, 1990; from whom purchased 1996 by the current owner.

EXHIBITED Galería Guillermo de Osma, Madrid, *De Nueva York a Madrid,* 1990, 20–21, ill.

In 1997, the Dallas Museum of Art organized the important exhibition *František Kupka: Painting the Universe,* the evocative title of which describes the artist's aim to employ the means of art to express cosmic and metaphysical states of mind and being. Steeped in religious and philosophical beliefs both traditional and modern, Kupka—who was born in Bohemia in what is now the Czech Republic—was one of the most important artists of the early 20th century to base work on the conviction that art could not only represent but even embody profound spiritual truths.

With this end in mind, Kupka created around 1910–1911 what are considered among the first—if not the very first—completely abstract works of art produced by any Western artist. His radiant abstract paintings of pulsating discs based on Newton's color theories were first shown in Paris at the Salon de la Section d'Or in 1912. They were a culmination of Kupka's belief in the oneness of science, nature, and vision—an intuitive fusion of the formal and theoretical revolutions that modern art had undergone, and that Kupka observed and took part in, since moving to Paris in 1895 to complete his studies.

In this large and commanding drawing, Kupka's lyrical abstract aesthetic is fully on view in a mysteriously evocative suggestion of energy made visible. Serrated forms vibrate across the sheet in graceful yet determined staccato rhythms, while a resolutely flat, black quadrilateral form on the mid-right edge implies an incalculable depth or an implacable opaque density. The dominant green form may bring to mind the life force of organic matter; yet Kupka's deeply held belief in the potential of color and form to engage and depict the ineffable and the infinite, the interior of the spirit and the outward trajectories of matter and energy, makes such references ultimately difficult to define.

In its form, color, and overall feeling, this watercolor relates to Kupka's art of the early 1910s, such as the painting *Position of Mobile Graphic Elements I,* 1912–1913 (Museo Thyssen-Bornemisza, Madrid), and from later in the decade, *Hindu Motif, Red Gradations,* 1919–1920 (National Gallery, Prague). In these works, we see the artist's intensely saturated color forms arranged in lines and arcs of increasing or decreasing depth that play across vast, seemingly unending vistas. Here such pulsating dynamism fairly radiates off the page in this striking example of Kupka's paradigm-shifting art.

CW

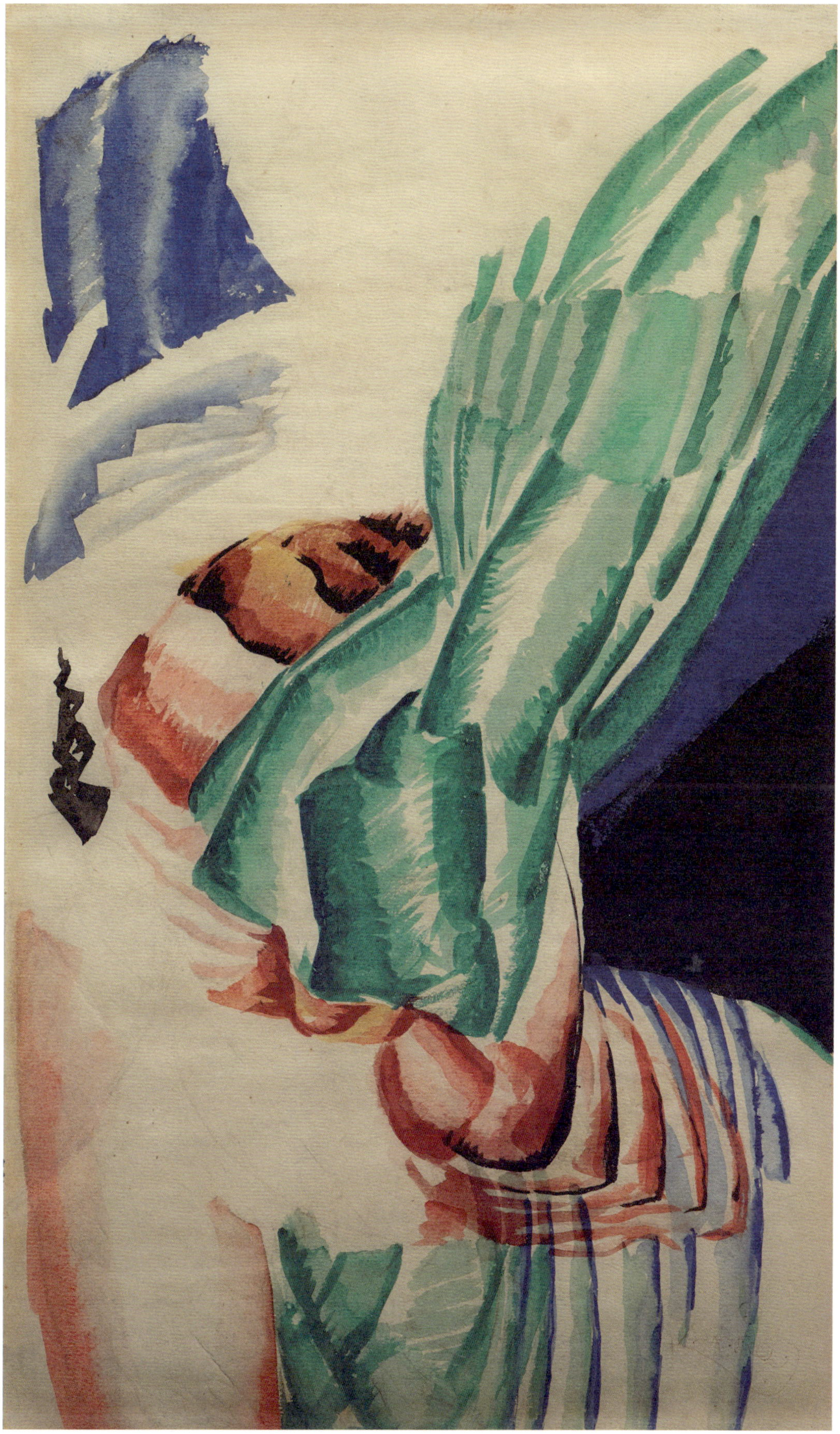

113

Henri Gaudier-Brzeska French, 1891–1915

UNTITLED (STUDY FOR RED STONE DANCER) (RECTO), *1912*;
UNTITLED (POSSIBLE STUDY FOR A SCULPTURE) (VERSO),
C. *1912*

Pencil on paper, 13½ × 8¼ in. (343 × 210 mm)
Dallas Museum of Art, Foundation for the Arts Collection,
Gift of Mr. and Mrs. Walter N. Pharr, 1963.107.FA

PROVENANCE Richard Feigen Gallery, Chicago; Walter N. Pharr, Dallas; given to the Dallas Museum for Contemporary Arts, May 27, 1960; Dallas Museum of Art.

By the time of his death at the French front during the first year of World War I, the 23-year-old Henri Gaudier-Brzeska had created a body of work that continues to place him at the forefront of British modernism. Moving to London from his native France in 1910, he was one of the most important artists associated with vorticism, a short-lived but ardent literary and visual art movement developed and articulated by the artist and writer Wyndham Lewis, the poet Ezra Pound, and others.

Along with tenets from other contemporary movements, British vorticism absorbed continental cubist and futurist ideas of form, space, and time, and transformed them into its own credo whose aim was to depict figures and forces in the 20th century's newly dynamic world free of traditions and restrictions of all kinds.

This remarkable sheet contains two drawings by Gaudier-Brzeska, both associated with sculptures in different styles that demonstrate his range. Distinct in subject and feel, they are nonetheless united by the artist's unique practice of drawing a number of delicate, almost imperceptibly fine lines that build up and shape in aggregate what may at first look like large strokes of the pencil.

The recto's figure (facing page) is related to the rounded forms and bending pose of the sculpture *Red Stone Dancer,* c. 1913 (Tate Britain, London), and exhibits Gaudier-Brzeska's extraordinarily nuanced and beautiful draftsmanship, emphasizing a dancer's almost transparent lightness moving through air. Hints of pre-modern forms of figurative and non-Western art are subsumed into Gaudier-Brzeska's vision of his subject, one that while common among artists across Europe at this time receives a particularly graceful yet taut rendition here.

On the verso (right) is a figure that in its stylized human features may relate to what is perhaps Gaudier-Brzeska's best-known work and an icon of vorticist sculpture: *Hieratic Head of Ezra Pound,* 1914 (National Gallery of Art, Washington). Gaudier-Brzeska's treatment of the human form in this drawing is quite different than the graceful arcs of the dancer. Here he builds blocks one on top of the other in an assertive, architectural manifestation of solid, immovable forms that echo ancient art's metaphysically based depictions of all-seeing, all-powerful beings.

This sense of command and conviction is felt throughout vorticist works, especially in the relatively few surviving works of Gaudier-Brzeska, such as these two highly resolved and beautifully rendered drawings that share the same sheet.

CW

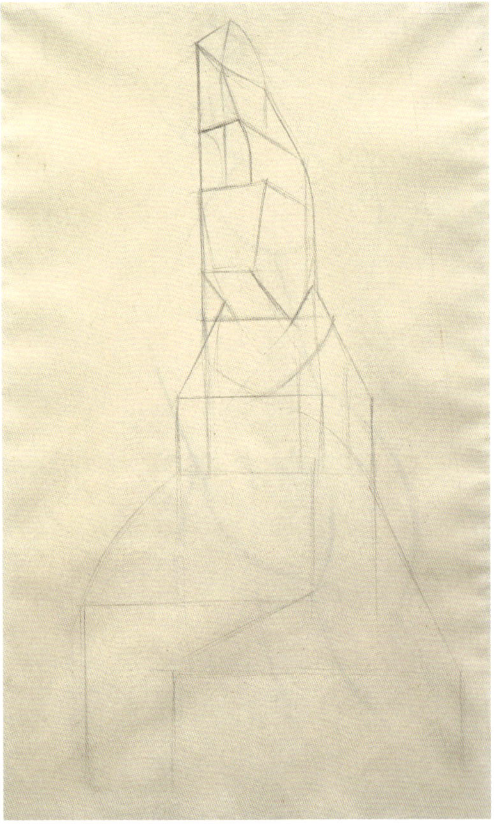

Cat. 113, verso.

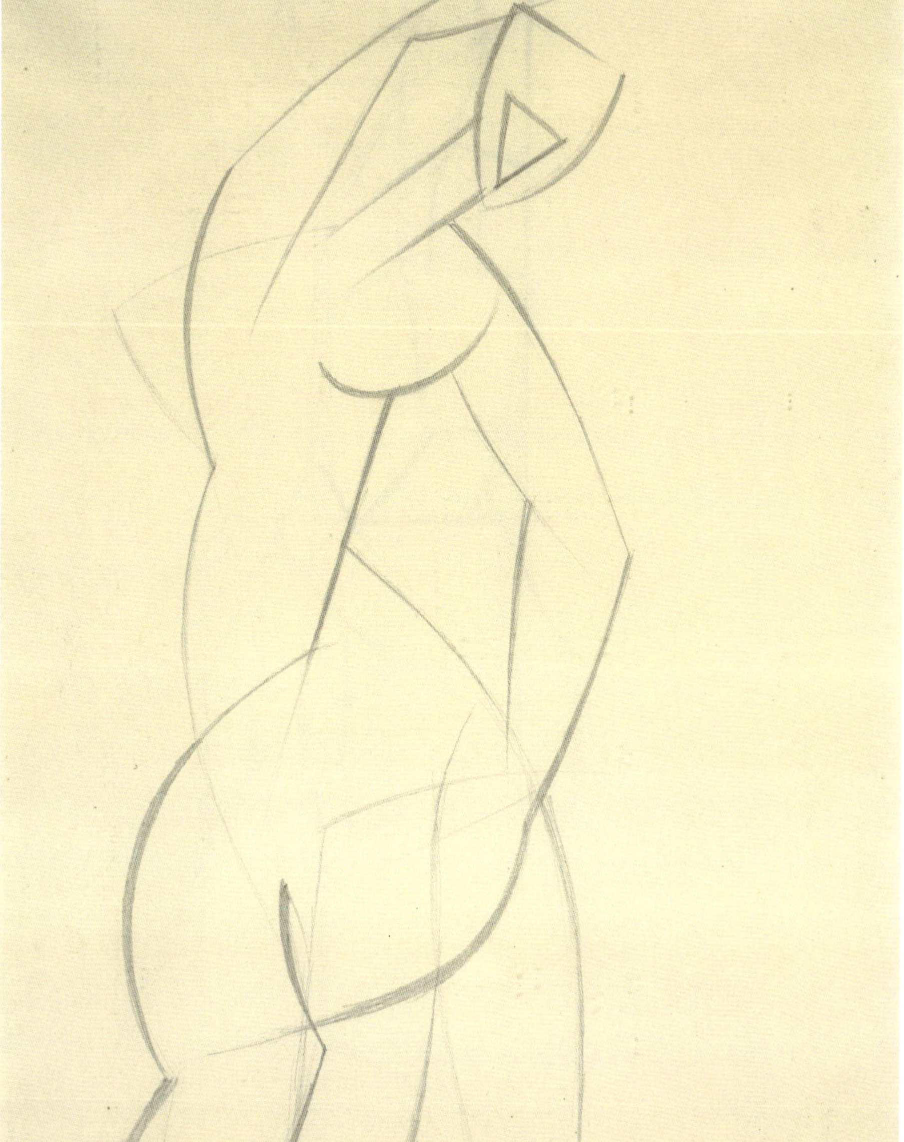

Cat. 113, recto.

Amedeo Modigliani Italian, 1884–1920

PORTRAIT OF WALTHER HALVORSEN (?), C. *1916–1917*

Pencil on white wove paper, 18⅞ × 12⅛ in. (480 × 307 mm)
Watermark: *ANC^ne MANUF^re CANSON & MONTGOLFIER VIDALON-LES-ANNONAY*
Signed in pencil lower right: *modigliani*
Private collection, Dallas

PROVENANCE Este Gallery, New York; from whom purchased April 1955 by David Daniels, New York; Fogg Art Museum, Harvard; Perls Gallery, New York; private collection; Sotheby's, New York, November 8, 2007, lot 378; where purchased by the current owner.

EXHIBITED Minneapolis Institute of Arts, *Drawings, Paintings, and Sculpture from Three Private Collections*, 1960, no. 40; Minneapolis Institute of Arts, February 22–April 21, 1968, Art Institute of Chicago, May 3–June 23, 1968, Nelson Gallery–Atkins Museum, Kansas City, July 11–September 29, 1968, and Fogg Art Museum, Harvard University, October 16–November 25, 1968, *Selections from the Drawing Collection of David Daniels*, no. 74.

By the outbreak of World War I, the tuberculosis that Amedeo Modigliani had contracted while a teenager in Italy had reached an advanced stage, so his attempt to enlist in the military was rejected. As a core member of the group of young artists living close together in Montmartre, he tried to mask the symptoms of the dreaded disease with his addiction to alcohol and hashish and by his driven and prodigious concentration on his work. His output of portraits and nudes—both paintings and drawings—has become emblematic of the bohemian culture in which modernism in music, literature, and art took root and flourished at the beginning of the 20th century.

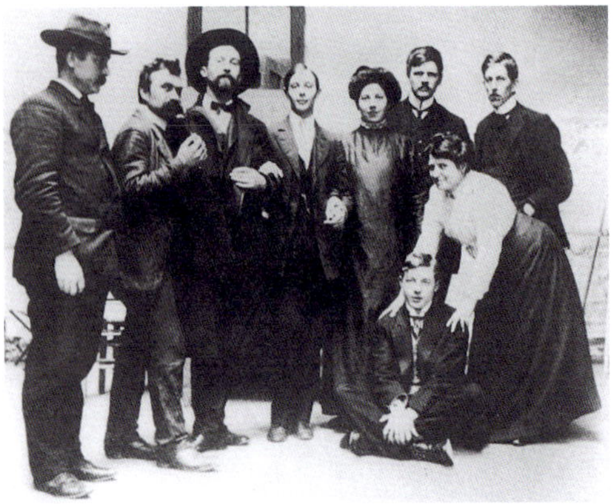

Fig. 24 Scandinavian students in Matisse's academy in 1910. Walther Halvorsen is seated on the floor.

The sitter for this superb example of Modigliani's portraiture, which belonged to one of the great drawings collectors of the last century, has eluded identification. When catalogued in 1968 by Agnes Mongan and Mary Lee Bennett, its traditional association with Jean Cocteau, a member of Modigliani's close circle, was rightly challenged. There is no resemblance between this drawing and the artist's other portraits of Cocteau, and since then the sitter has been described as unknown. There is a distinct resemblance, however, to another member of this group of friends, which included, among others, Modigliani, Henri Matisse, Pablo Picasso, Juan Gris, Fernand Léger, Georges Braque, Jean-Paul Laurens, Blaise Cendrar, and Max Jacob. That person was the Norwegian Walther Halvorsen (1887–1972), who had studied with Matisse in 1909 and 1910 but gave up painting around 1913 to become an art dealer. In 1916 he married, though only briefly, the aristocratic Lithuanian-Swedish actress Greta Prozor, known for her performances of Ibsen and other modernist playwrights and the sitter for one of Matisse's most important portraits made at that time (Centre Pompidou, Paris). Halvorsen proved enormously helpful to his friends by promoting and selling their works both in Paris and throughout Scandinavia, for which he was awarded the Légion d'Honneur. With encouragement from

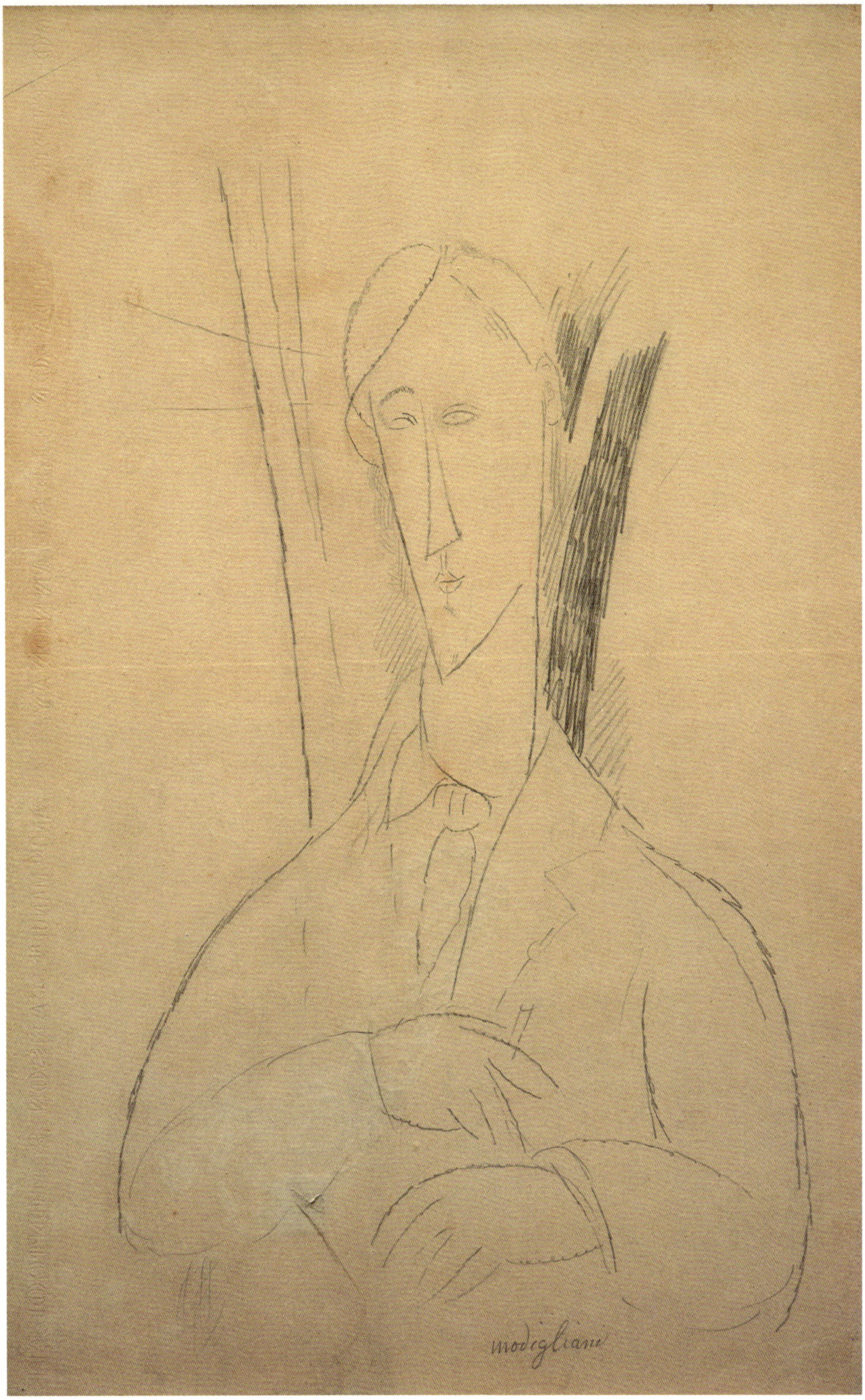

Picasso, Matisse, Albert Marquet, and others, he organized a huge exhibition of 94 paintings by members of the group—including Modigliani—that opened in Oslo on November 22, 1916. That date coincides with the approximate date assigned this drawing on stylistic grounds by Bennett and Mongan, who also note the sitter's "aristocratic elegance and . . . pungent individuality."[1] The round-shouldered and dapperly dressed young man, with his rosebud lips and fair hair parted on the proper left side, his fingers splayed, bears a suggestive resemblance to the photograph of Halvorsen sitting on the floor in the group photograph of Matisse's Scandinavian students taken six years earlier, in 1910 (fig. 24).

WBJ

Note
1. Bennett and Mongan 1968.

115

Fernand Léger French, 1881–1955

SEATED WOMAN AND STANDING WOMAN, *1913*

Ink, watercolor, and gouache on paper, 20⅞ 14⅛ in.
(530 × 358 mm)
Signed and dated lower right: *FL 13*
Private collection

PROVENANCE Private collection, Paris; Galerie Louise Leiris, Paris; acquired July 17, 1964, from Galerie Beyeler, Basel, by the current owner.

EXHIBITED Galerie Beyeler, Basel, *Fernand Léger,* May–June 1964, no. 7 *(Woman at Table and Woman Standing)*; Houston, Rice Museum, *Leger, Our Contemporary,* April 14–June 11, 1978, no. 3 *(Two Women, One at Table)*; Dallas Museum of Art, *Impressionist and Modern Masters in Dallas,* September 3–October 22, 1989, 73, no. 46.

This bold and imaginative drawing belongs to an important body of related works that Fernand Léger produced in the years just before World War I. The series begins with the landmark *Contrast of Forms* works in which Léger created some of the first entirely abstract Western works of art. These paintings and drawings featured massed interlocking geometric motifs such as the cube, cone, and cylinder set in an indeterminate open space and rendered in a restrained color scheme of primary and sometimes secondary colors with black and white.

In the next group of paintings and drawings Léger depicts the human figure with the *Contrast of Forms* vocabulary. This major drawing comes from this group. Here Léger ingeniously portrays two female figures in differing poses seen before a café table with still life. A popular subject among artists in the Paris of the preceding decades, the café scene receives a rigorous new treatment in this drawing, one that exemplifies Léger's wholly individual and groundbreaking synthesis of cubist and other modernist trends that experimented in representing multiple dimensions of solid forms in space and time. Future subjects from 1913–1914 that Léger treated with his *Contrast of Forms* conception would include landscapes and portraits.

While Léger's vision transforms the organic human form into essentially mechanical-looking beings (such as those seen in the Museum of Modern Art's painting *Exit the Ballets Russes* of 1914 and other even more similar works featuring figures at a table with still life), this drawing can be seen not as pessimistic and foreboding, but perhaps as a depiction of how human forms can exist and move logically and elegantly in and through space.

An artist whose work fundamentally represents modernism and the classic phase of cubism in particular, Léger received his early training as an architect. He arrived in Paris in 1900 from his native Normandy to study fine art, and in the following decades he critically contributed to Paris's protean milieu that changed the course of representation and abstraction in Western art.

Called to service in August 1914 at the outbreak of World War I, Léger stated that his experience with his fellow Frenchmen in the trenches prompted him after the war to create a direct figurative art that could be grasped by as many people as possible. Dating from his pre-war years, which are considered among his most important, this drawing is a brilliant early example of the abstracted yet recognizable human forms Léger would employ throughout his long and prolific career.

CW

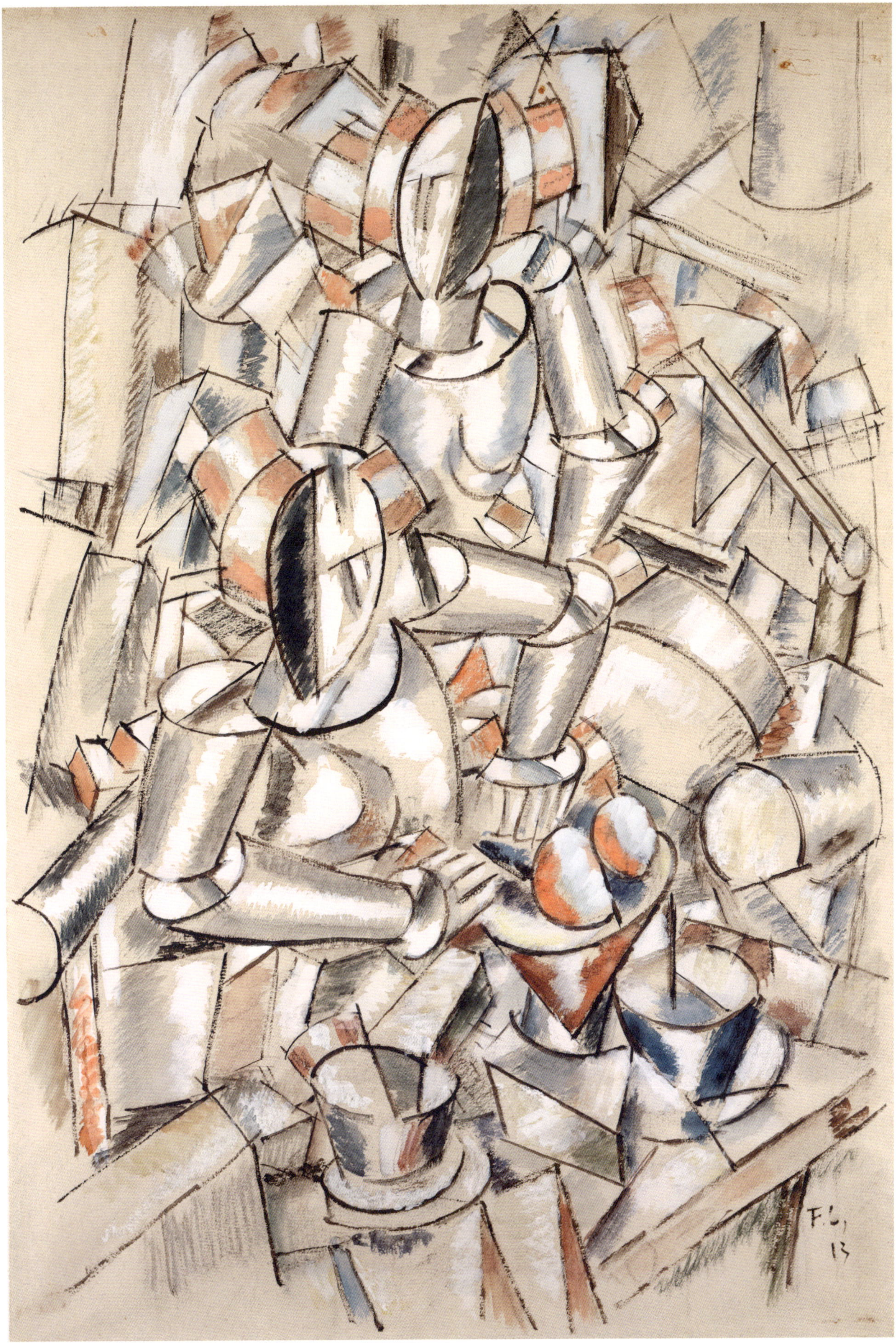

Bibliography

Ackerman, Gerald M. 1986. *The Life and Work of Jean-Léon Gérôme: With a Catalogue Raisonné*. New York and London: Sotheby's Publications.

Adhémar, Jean. 1962. *Henri de Toulouse-Lautrec*. Paris: Hachette.

Albert Anker House Foundation. 2003. *Anker*. Exh. cat. Martigny, Switzerland: Fondation Pierre Gianadda.

Alexandre, Arsène. 1888. *Honoré Daumier: L'Homme et L'oeuvre*. Paris: Laurens.

———. 1912. *La collection Henri Rouart*. Paris: Goupil & Cie.

Arcambeau, Edmé. 1911. *The Books of Bridges*. London and Glasgow: Gowan and Gray.

———. 1912. *Ponts de Paris*. Paris: Perche.

Armstrong, Carol. 2004. *Cézanne in the Studio: Still Life in Watercolors*. Exh. cat. Los Angeles: J. Paul Getty Museum.

Bac, Ferdinand. 2013. *Livre-Journal 1920*. Edited by Lawrence Joseph. Paris: Éditions Clair Paulhan.

Baltimore Museum of Art and Walters Art Museum. 2005. *The Essence of Line: French Drawings from Ingres to Degas*. Edited by Jay Fisher, William Johnston, Cheryl Snay, and Kim Schenk. Exh. cat. University Park, Pa.: Penn State University Press.

Baschet, R. 1942. *E.-J. Delécluze: Témoin de son temps*. Paris: Boivin.

Bätschmann, Oskar, Monika Brunner, and Bernadette Walter. 2012. *Ferdinand Hodler: Catalogue raisonné der Gemälde / Band 2 / Die Bildnisse*. Zürich: Scheidegger & Spiess.

Baudelaire, Charles. 1965. *Art in Paris 1845–1862: Salons and Other Exhibitions*. Translated and edited by Jonathan Mayne. London: Phaidon.

Bax, Marty. 2001. *Complete Mondrian*. Burlington, Vt.: Lund Humphries.

Bazin, Germain. 1997. *Théodore Géricault: Étude critique, documents, et catalogue raisonné*. Paris: Bibliothèque des arts.

Beetem, Robert N. 1961. "George Catlin in France: His Relationship to Delacroix and Baudelaire." *Art Quarterly* 24 (Summer): 129–45.

Bennett, Mary Lee, and Agnes Mongan. 1968. *Selections from the Drawing Collection of David Daniels*. Exh. cat. Minneapolis Institute of Art; Art Institute of Chicago; Nelson Gallery–Atkins Museum, Kansas City; and Fogg Art Museum. Cambridge, Mass.: Harvard College.

Berger, Klaus. 1965. *Odilon Redon: Fantasy and Colour*. New York: McGraw Hill.

Bernheim-Jeune. 1919. *L'Art Moderne et quelques aspects de l'art d'autrefois*. Paris: Bernheim-Jeune.

Bethune, Paul, and L. Paul Milès. 1913. *Catalogue des œuvres léguées par François Louis Français à sa ville natale*. Plombières-les-Bains, France.

Biermé, Maria. 1911. *Les artistes de la pensée et du sentiment*. Brussels: La Belgique artistique et littéraire.

Bois, Yve-Alain. 1982. *L'atelier de Mondrian: Recherches et dessins*. Paris: Macula.

———, and Joop Joosten. 1994. *Piet Mondrian: 1872–1944*. Milan: Leonardo Arte.

Bordes, Philippe. 1979 (1981). "Dessins perdus de David dont un pour 'La mort de Socrate,' lithographiés par Debret." *Bulletin de la Société de l'Histoire de l'Art français*, 179–84.

Bouret, Jean. 1965. *Degas*. Paris: A. Somogy.

Brame, Philippe, and Theodore Reff. 1984. *Degas et Son Oeuvre: A Supplement*. New York: Garland.

Brettell, Richard R. 1989. *Impressionist and Modern Masters in Dallas: From Monet to Mondrian*. Dallas: Dallas Museum of Art.

———. 1995. *Impressionist Paintings, Drawings, and Sculpture from the Wendy and Emery Reves Collection*. Dallas: Dallas Museum of Art.

———. 2000. *Impression: Painting Quickly in France, 1860–1890*. New Haven: Yale University Press. French ed.: Paris, Hazen, 2009.

———. 2004. "Provincial Cosmopolitanism: Modernism in Switzerland and Texas." In *Texas Vision: The Barrett Collection*, edited by Edmund P. Pillsbury, 131–50. Dallas: Southern Methodist University Press.

Brion, Marcel. 1957. *La peinture moderne de l'impressionnisme à l'art abstrait*. Stuttgart, Germany: Éditions d'Art Somogy

Bromberg, Anne. 1986. "Looking at Art: France in the 19th Century." *Dallas Museum of Art Bulletin*, 11–13.

Browse, Lillian. 1949. *Degas Dancers*. London: Faber and Faber.

———. 1967. "Degas's Grand Passion." *Apollo* 75, no. 60 (February): 104–14.

Brüschweiler, Jura. 1986. *Ferdinand Hodler*. Exh. cat. Zurich: Galerie Römer.

Buenger, Barbara C. 1981–83. "A Late Version of Mondrian's 'Farm at Duivendrecht.'" *Elvehjem Museum of Art Bulletin* (University of Wisconsin): 36–53.

Busine, Laurent. 1992. "From Edward Burne-Jones to Fernand Khnopff." In *Burne-Jones 1833–1898: Dessins du Fitzwilliam Museum de Cambridge*. Nantes: Musée des Beaux-Arts.

Cabanne, Pierre. 1958. *Edgar Degas*. Paris: Tisne.

———. 1960. *Degas danseuses*. Lausanne: International Art Book.

Cachin, Françoise, Isabelle Cahn, Walter Feilchenfeldt, Henri Loyrette, and Joseph J. Rishel. 1996. *Cézanne*. Exh. cat. Paris: Réunion des Musées Nationaux/Musée d'Orsay; London: Tate Gallery; and Philadelphia Museum of Art. New York: Harry N. Abrams.

Caproni, Giorgio. 1977. *L'opéra completa di Toulouse-Lautrec*. Milan: Rizzoli.

Chaet, Bernard. 1970. *The Art of Drawing*. New York: Rhinehart and Winston.

Clark, Kenneth. 1956. *The Nude: A Study in Ideal Form*. New York: Pantheon. Repr. 1972. Princeton: Princeton University Press.

Cogniat, Raymond. 1950. *La Peinture en France au temps des impressionnistes*. Paris.

Comini, Alessandra. 1974. *Egon Schiele's Portraits*. Berkeley: University of California Press.

———. 1976. *Egon Schiele*. New York: Braziller.

Conilleau, Roland. 1997. *Louis Français: Peintre de la nature, 1814–1897*. Sarreguemines, France: Éditions Pierron.

Conisbee, Philip, and Denis Coutagne. 2006. *Cézanne in Provence*. Exh. cat. Washington: National Gallery of Art, and Aix-en-Provence: Musée Granet.

Cooper, Douglas. 1959. "Renoir, Lise, and the Le Coeur Family: A Study of Renoir's Early Development, II. The Le Coeurs." *Burlington Magazine* 101 (September–October): 322–28.

Courthion, Pierre. 1962. *Édouard Manet*. New York: Harry N. Abrams.

Coutagne, Denis. 2008. *François-Marius Granet, 1775–1849: Une vie pour la peinture*. Paris: Somogy éditions d'art.

Daix, Pierre, and Georges Boudaille. 1966. *Picasso: Catalogue raisonné de l'oeuvre peint, 1900–1906*. Greenwich, Conn. Repr. Neuchâtel: Éditions Ides et Calendes, 1988.

Dallas Museum of Art. 1978. *Dallas Collects: Impressionist and Early Modern Masters*. Dallas: Dallas Museum of Art.

———. 1984. *Dallas Museum of Art Annual Review*. Dallas: Dallas Museum of Art.

———. 1985a. *Dallas Museum of Art Bulletin*, Fall. Dallas: Dallas Museum of Art.

———. 1985b. *The Wendy and Emery Reves Collection*. Dallas: Dallas Museum of Art.

———. 1986. *Dallas Museum of Art Bulletin*, Summer. Dallas: Dallas Museum of Art.

———. 1997. *Dallas Museum of Art: A Guide to the Collection*. Dallas: Dallas Museum of Art.

———. 2007. *Dallas Museum of Art: The Year in Review, 2005–2006*. Dallas: Dallas Museum of Art.

———. 2012. *Dallas Museum of Art: A Guide to the Collection*. New Haven: Yale University Press.

Dauberville, Guy-Patrice, and Michel Dauberville. 2007. *Renoir: Catalogue raisonné des tableaux, pastels, dessins, et aquarelles*. Paris: Bernheim-Jeune.

Daulte, Francois. 1953. *Le dessin français de David à Courbet*. Lausanne: Spes.

———. 1969. *L'aquarelle française au XIXe siècle*. Paris: Bibliotheque des arts.

De Font-Reaulx, Dominique, et al. 2007. *Gustave Courbet*. Exh. cat. Galeries Nationales du Grand Palais, Paris; Metropolitan Museum of Art, New York; Musée Fabre, Montpellier. Paris: Éditions de la Réunion des musées nationaux.

De Goncourt, Edmond, and Jules de Goncourt. 1925. *Gavarni: L'homme et l'oeuvre*. Paris: E. Fasquelle.

De Hauke, César M. 1961. *Seurat et son oeuvre*. 2 vols. Paris: Gründ.

Delacroix, Eugène. 1972. *The Journal of Eugène Delacroix*. Translated by Walter Pach. New York: Viking.

De La Faille, J. B. 1928. *L'Oeuvre de Vincent van Gogh*. Paris: G. Van Oest.

———. 1970. *The Works of Vincent Van Gogh: His Paintings and Drawings*. New York: Reynal & Hitchcock.

De Laprade, Jacques. 1954. *Lautrec*. London: William Heinemann.

Delécluze, Étienne-Jean. 1855. *Louis David. Son école et son temps. Souvenirs*. Paris: Didier. Reprinted Paris: J. P. Mouilleseaux, 1983.

De Leiris, Alain. 1969. *The Drawings of Edouard Manet*. Berkeley: University of California Press.

Delevoy, Robert L., Catherine de Croës, and Gisele Ollinger-Zinque. 1987. *Fernand Khnopff*. Brussels: Bibliothèque des Arts.

Delteil, Loys. 1906–30. *Le Peintre-Graveur Illustré (XIXe et XXe siècles)*. 31 vols. Paris.

Delville, Étienne. 1925. *Catalogue des œuvres de peinture, aquarelles, dessins, et sculpture exposés dans le Musée de Lisieux*. Lisieux, France: Musée de Lisieux.

Des Cars, Laurence. 1998. "Burne-Jones et la France." In *Un maître anglais de l'imaginaire*. Exh. cat. Paris: Réunion des musées nationaux.

———. 1999. "Edward Burne-Jones and France." In *Edward Burne-Jones: Victorian Artist-Dreamer*. Exh. cat. New York: Metropolitan Museum of Art.

DeVonyar, Jill, and Richard Kendall. 2002. *Degas and the Dance*. New York: Harry N. Abrams.

Dortu, M. G. 1971. *Toulouse-Lautrec et son oeuvre*. New York: Collectors Editions.

Drucker, Michael. 1967. *Renoir*. New York: New American Library.

Duguet, Roger. 1899. *Les contemporains, Louis David*. Paris.

Du Quesne-van Gogh, Elizabeth H. 1911. *Personliche Erinnerungen*. Munich: Piper & Co.

Duret, Théodore. 1910. *Manet and the French Impressionists*. London and Philadelphia: G. Richards and Lippincott.

École des Beaux-Arts. 1898. *Exposition des œuvres de Louis Français au profit du monument à élever à la mémoire de ce peintre du 22 janvier au 16 février 1898*. Paris: École nationale supérieure des Beaux-Arts.

Eitner, Lorenz E. A. 1983. *Géricault: His Life and Work*. London: Orbis Publishers.

Elgar, Frank. 1968. *Cézanne*. Paris: A. Somogy.

Elzea, Betty. 2001. *Frederick Sandys, 1829–1924: A catalogue raisonné*. Woodbridge, Suffolk: Antique Collectors' Club.

Faure, Élie. 1926. *P. Cézanne*. Paris: G. Crès.

Faure, J. B. 1902. *Notice sur la Collection J. B. Faure*. Paris.

Feilchenfeldt, Walter, and Han Veenenbos. 1988. *Vincent van Gogh and Paul Cassirer, Berlin: The Reception of Van Gogh in Germany from 1901 to 1914*. Zwolle: Waanders.

Fejto, François. 1961. "Intimisticher Realismus? Modernistiche Stromungen in der sowjetischen Kunst und Literatur." Basel: *National-Zeitung Basel*, July 23.

Fénéon, Felix. 1888. *Calendrier pour janvier: Pastels at dessins de Charles Serret, Rodin, Seurat, Courbet, Gauguin, Degas. La Revue indépendante*, vol. 16.

Fernier, Jean-Jacques. Forthcoming. *Catalogue raisonné de l'Oeuvre de Courbet et de ses Collaborateurs*, vol. 3.

Fernier, Robert. 1978. *La vie et l'oeuvre de Gustave Courbet: Catalogue raisonné. Vol. 1: Peintures 1866–1877, dessins, sculptures*. Paris and Lausanne: Bibliothèque des arts.

Flavia Ormond Fine Arts. 2005. *Master Drawings*. New York: Flavia Ormond Find Arts, Ltd.

Fosca, François. 1961. *Renoir: His Life and Work*. Paris: Thames & Hudson.

Fumaroli, Marc, Katherine B. Baetjer, et al. 1992. *Masterworks from the Musée des Beaux-Arts, Lille*. Exh. cat. New York: Metropolitan Museum of Art.

Gazdik, Igor. 1971. *Odilon Redon*. Bratislava: Pallas.

Geist, Sidney. 1985. "Cézanne's Watercolors." *New Criterion*, January.

Giambruni, Helen. 1989. "Domestic Scenes." In *Pierre Bonnard: The Graphic Art*, 53–54. Exh. cat. New York: Metropolitan Museum of Art.

Gianadda Foundation. 2003. *Anker*. Exh. cat. Montigny, Switzerland: Pierre Gianadda Foundation.

Glaser, Curt. 1922. *Édouard Manet*. Munich: Verlag der Marées-gesellschaft, R. Piper & Co.

González López, Carlos, and Montserrat Martí Ayxelà. 1989. *Mariano Fortuny Marsal*. 2 vols. Barcelona: Diccionari Ràfols.

Gordon, Margot, and Marcello Aldega. 1995. *Jean-Baptiste-Joseph Wicar. Drawings*. Rome: Edizione De Luca.

Gordon, Robert R., and Andrew Forge. 1988. *Degas*. New York: Harry N. Abrams.

Gosschalk, Johan Cohen. 1905. "Vincent Van Gogh, Door Joh. Cohen Gosschalk." *Elzevier's Geïllustreerd Maandschrift* 30: 219–34.

Gréard, Vallery C. O. 1897. *Meissonier. His Life and his Art*. London: Heinemann.

Groom, Gloria Lynn. 1993. *Édouard Vuillard, Painter-Decorator: Patrons and Projects, 1892–1912*. New Haven: Yale University Press.

Guerin, Marcel. 1969. *L'Oeuvre Gravée de Manet*. New York: Da Capo Press.

Hammer, Martin, and Christina Lodder. 2000. *Constructing Modernity: The Art and Career of Naum Gabo*. New Haven: Yale University Press.

Hanson, Anne Coffin. 1996. *Édouard Manet, 1832–1883*. Exh. cat. Philadelphia Museum of Art and Art Institute of Chicago.

Harper, Paula Hays. 1976. *Daumier's Clowns—Les Saltimbanques et les Parades: New Biographical and Political Functions for a Nineteenth-Century Myth*. Ph.D. diss., Stanford University.

Harris, Jean C. 1970. *Édouard Manet, Graphic Works: A Definitive Catalogue Raisonné*. New York: Collectors Editions.

Hartlaub, Gustav Friedrich. 1922. "Vincent van Gogh." *Der Cicerone* 14 no. 15: 623–54.

Hauptman, Jodi, ed. 2007. *Georges Seurat: The Drawings*. Exh. cat. New York: Museum of Modern Art.

Hautecoeur, Louis. 1954. *Louis David*. Paris: La Table ronde.

Hiddleston, J. A. 1995. "Baudelaire and Constantin Guys." *Modern Language Review* 40, no. 3 (July): 603–21.

Hodler, Ferdinand. 1887 [1981]. *La Mission de l'Artiste*. Zürich: Benteli.

Hofmann, Werner. 2007. *Degas: A Dialogue of Difference*. London: Thames & Hudson.

Holtzman, Harry, and Martin James, editors. 1986. *The New Art, The New Life: The Collected Writings of Piet Mondrian*. Boston: G. K. Hall & Co.

Hoppe, Ragnar. 1922. *Degas och hans arbeten i Nordisk ägo*. Stockholm: Föreningen Fransk Konst.

Howard, Seymour. 1975. *Sacrifice of the Hero: The Roman Years, A Classical Frieze by Jacques-Louis David*. Sacramento: E. B. Crocker Art Gallery.

Hugo, Victor. 1856. *Les Contemplations*. Paris: Nelson.

Hulsker, Jan. 1980. *The Complete Van Gogh: Paintings, Drawings, and Sketches*. New York: Harry N. Abrams.

Huyghe, René. 1962. *Cézanne*. New York: Harry N. Abrams.

———. 1931. "Aspects de Toulouse-Lautrec," *L'amour de l'art*, April.

Isaacson, Joel. 1969. *Manet and Spain*. Exh. cat. Ann Arbor: University of Michigan Museum of Art.

Ives, Colta, Susan Alyson Stein, Sjraar van Heugten, and Marije Vellekoop, with Marjorie Shelley. 2005. *Vincent van Gogh: The Drawings*. Exh. cat. New York: Metropolitan Museum of Art, and Amsterdam: Van Gogh Museum

Jamot, Paul. 1924. *Degas*. Paris: Éd. de la Gazette des Beaux-arts.

Jamot, Paul, and Georges Wildenstein. 1932. *Manet*. Paris: Les Beaux-Arts.

Johnson, Lee. 1986. *The Paintings of Eugène Delacroix: A Critical Catalogue*. Oxford, Eng.: Oxford University Press, 1986.

Johnston, William R., and Simon Kelly. 2006. *Untamed: The Art of Antoine-Louis Barye*. Exh. cat. Baltimore: Walters Art Museum.

Joosten, Joop M. 1973. "Piet Mondrian: Abstraction and Compositional Innovation." *Artforum* 2, no. 8 (April): 55–59.

_______. 1998. *Piet Mondrian: Catalogue Raisonné of the Work of 1911–1944*. New York: Abrams.

Jourdain, Francis, and Jean Adhémar. 1952. *T-Lautrec*. Paris: P. Tisné.

Joyant, Maurice. 1926. *Henri de Toulouse-Lautrec*. Paris: Floury Publications.

Julien, Edouard. 1959. *Lautrec*. New York: Crown Publishers.

Kahn, Gustave. 1891. "Seurat." *L'art moderne* 11 (April 5, 1891): 107–8.

———. 1928. *Les dessins de Georges Seurat (1859–1891)*. 2 vols. Paris: Bernheim-Jeune.

Kallir, Jane. 1990. *Egon Schiele, The Complete Works: Including a Biography and a Catalogue Raisonné*. New York: Harry N. Abrams.

Keisch, Claude, and Marie Ursula Riemann-Reyher, eds. 2009. *Adolph Menzel: Briefe*. 4 vols. Berlin and Munich: Deutscher Kunstverlag.

Keisch, Claude, Marie Ursula Riemann-Reyher, et al., eds. 1997. *Adolph Menzel: Das Labyrinth der Wirklichkeit*. Exh. cat. Berlin: Nationalgalerie und Kupferstichkabinett, Staatliche Museen zu Berlin. Cologne: DuMont.

Kendall, Richard. 1987. *Degas by Himself: Drawings, Prints, Paintings, Writings*. Boston: Little, Brown.

———. 1993. *Degas Landscapes*. New Haven: Yale University Press.

Klossowski, Erich. 1923. *Honoré Daumier*. Munich: R. Piper.

Kosinski, Dorothy. 2003. *Dallas Museum of Art 100 Years*. Dallas: Dallas Museum of Art.

Kröller-Müller Museum. 1980. *Vincent Van Gogh: A Detailed Catalogue of the Paintings and Drawings of Vincent Van Gogh in the Collection of the Kröller-Müller Museum*. Otterlo, Netherlands: Rijksmuseum Kröller-Müller.

Kunstmuseum Berne. 2011. *Ernest Biéler (1863–1948): Geträumte Wirklichkeit*. Exh. cat. Berne: Kunstmuseum Berne.

Kuthy, Sandor, and Therese Bhattacharya-Settler. 1995. *Albert Anker (1831–1910): Werkkatalog der Gemälde une Ölstudien / Catalogue raisonné des peintures et des études à l'huile*. Berne: Kunstmuseum Basel.

Lafond, Paul. 1918. *Degas*. Paris: H. Floury.

Laughton, Bruce. 1996. *Honoré Daumier*. New Haven and London: Yale University Press.

Laveissière, Sylvain. 2003. "Le chat mort: Un Géricault inédit." *Revue du Louvre, La revue des musées de France*, no. 5.

Lemoisne, Paul-Andre. 1928. *Gavarni, peintre et lithographe*. Paris: H. Floury.

———. 1946. *Degas et son Oeuvre*. Paris: Paul Brame et C. M. de Hauke.

Le Normand-Romain, Antoinette, and Christina Buley-Uribe. 2007. *Auguste Rodin: Drawings & Watercolors*. New York: Thames & Hudson.

Le Pelley Fonteny, Monique. 1991. *Léon Augustin Lhermitte (1844–1925): Catalogue Raisonné*. Paris: Cercle d'art.

Le Tacon, François. 1994. "Emile Gallé et Louis Pasteur." *Le Pays Lorrain* 1, no. 75, 23–36.

Loosli, Carl Albert. 1919. *F. Hodler: Mappenwerk*. Zurich: Rascher & Cie.

———. 1921–24. *Ferdinand Hodler: Leben, Werk, und Nachlass*. 4 vols. Bern: Von R. Suter & Cie.

Loyrette, H. 1988. *Degas*. Fribourg: L'Office du livre de Fribourg.

———. 1991. *Degas*. Paris: Fayard.

Lüthy, Hans A. 1989. *Albert Anker: Aquarelle und Zeichnungen von Albert Anker* (with contributions by Paul Müller). Zurich: Verlag Neue Züricher Zeitung.

Maaz, Bernard, ed. 2008. *Adolph Menzel: Radikal real*. Exh. cat. Munich: Kunsthalle der Hypo-Kulturstiftung. Munich: Hirmer Verlag.

MacDonald, Heather, ed. 2013. *Impressionism and Post-Impressionism at the Dallas Museum of Art*. New Haven: Yale University Press.

Mack, Gerstle. 1942. *Toulouse-Lautrec*. New York: Alfred A. Knopf.

Maheux, Anne F., and Jean Sutherland Boggs. 1992. *Chronology of Degas and Pastels*. New York: Braziller.

Maison, K. E. 1961. *Daumier Drawings*. London: Arts Council.

———. 1968. *Honoré Daumier: Catalogue Raisonné of the Paintings, Watercolors, and Drawings*. Greenwich, Conn.: New York Graphic Society.

Mangin, Arthur. 1867. *Les Jardins: Histoire et descriptions*. Tours: A. Mame.

Martin, John Rupert. 1968. *The Ceiling Paintings of the Jesuit Church in Antwerp. Corpus Rubenianum Ludwig Burchard*, Vol. 1. Brussels: Arcade Press.

Marton, A. 2003. "The Art of Showing Off: Ingenious Exhibition Installation Enhances a Century's Worth of Collecting." *Fort Worth Star Telegram*, October 12.

Master Drawings and Sculpture. 2014. London: Jean-Luc Baroni, Ltd.

Mathier, Ethel. 2011. "Ernest Biéler, Leben und Werk." In *Ernest Biéler (1863–1948): Geträumte Wirklichkeit*. Bern: Kunstmuseum.

Meier-Graefe, Julius. 1908. *Modern Art: Being a Contribution to a New System of Aesthetics by Julius Meier-Graefe*. New York: G. P. Putnam.

———. 1922. *Vincent*. Munich: Piper & Co.

———. 1928. *Vincent van Gogh der Zeichner*. Berlin: O. Wacker.

———. 1930. "Französische Zeichnungen," *Der Cicerone XXII*.

Menzel, Adolph. 2009. *Briefe*. Edited by Claude Keisch and Marie Ursula Riemann-Reyher. 4 vols. Berlin / München.

Meslay, Olivier. 1989. *Dessins et esquisses de maîtres anciens et modernes: 17 mai au 21 juillet 1989, Galerie Charles et André Bailly*. Paris.

Metropolitan Museum of Art. 1952. *Paintings by Paul Cézanne*. New York.

———. 1983. *Manet: 1832–1883*. Exh. cat. New York: Metropolitan Museum of Art, and Paris: Galeries nationales du Grand Palais.

———. 2008. *Gustave Courbet, 1819–1877*. Exh. cat. New York: Metropolitan Museum of Art.

Mittler, Gene A., and James D. Howze. 1980. *Creating and Understanding Drawings*. New York: Glencoe McGraw-Hill.

———. 2001. *Creating and Understanding Drawings*. Rev. ed. New York: Glencoe McGraw-Hill.

Montagu, Jennifer. 1994. *The Expression of the Passions. The Origin and Influence of Charles Le Brun's "Conférence sur l'expression générale et particulière."* New Haven and London: Yale University Press.

Moore, George, and Walter Sickert. 2011. *The Painter of Modern Life: Memories of Degas*. London: Pallas Athene.

Moreau-Nélaton, Étienne. 1927. *François Bonvin raconté par lui-même*. Paris: Henri Laurens.

Mühelstein, Hans. 1914. *Ferdinand Hodler: Ein Deutungsversuch*. Wiemar: Kiepenheuer.

Munhall, Edgar. 1988. *François-Marius Granet: Watercolors from the Musée Granet at Aix-en-Provence*. Exh. cat. New York: Frick Collection.

Murphy, Alexandra R. 1999. *Jean-François Millet: Drawn into the Light*. Exh. cat. Williamstown, Mass.: Sterling and Francine Clark Art Institute. New Haven and London: Yale University Press.

Nash, Steven A. 1973. *The Drawings of Jacques-Louis David, Selected Problems*, thesis, Stanford.

———, and Jörn Merkert. 1985. *Naum Gabo: Sixty Years of Constructivism*. Dallas: Dallas Museum of Art.

———, and Jörn Merkert. 1986. *Naum Gabo: Sechzig Jahre Konstruktivismus*. Munich: Prestel-Verlag.

Nathan, Fritz, and Peter Nathan. 1961. *25 Jahre, 1936–1961*. Winterthur, Switzerland: Buchdruckerei Winterthur.

Nathan, Paul. 1988. *Texas Collections: Fine Arts, Furniture, Windmills, and Whimseys*. Dallas: Taylor Publishing Co.

Nathan, Peter. 1972. *Dr. Fritz Nathan und Dr. Peter Nathan, 1922–1972*. Zürich: Peter Nathan.

Néret, Gilles. 1989. *David: La terreur et la vertu*. Paris: Mengès.

Olivier, Fernande. 2001. *Loving Picasso: The Private Journal of Fernande Olivier*. Translated by Christine Baker and Michael Raeburn. New York: Harry N. Abrams, 2001.

Olson, Roberta J. M. 1989. "Granet and the Spell of Italy." In *François Marius Granet: Exhibition—A Selection of Drawings*. New York: Jill Newhouse.

Paris. 1946. *Les chefs-d'oeuvres des collections privées françaises retrouvés en Allemagne*. Paris: Ministère de l'éducation nationale.

Paris-Musées. 2002. *Constantin Guys, 1802–1892: Fleurs du mal, Dessins des musées Carnavalet et du Petit Palais*. Exh. cat. Musée de la vie romantique. Paris: Paris-Musées.

Paul, Barbara. 1993. *Hugo von Tschudi und die modern französische Kunst im Deutschen Kaiserreich*. Mainz, Germany: P. von Zabern.

Penrose, Roland. 1967. *The Sculpture of Picasso*. Chronology by Alicia Legg. New York: Museum of Modern Art.

Picasso Project. 2012. *Picasso's Paintings, Watercolors, Drawings, and Sculpture: A Comprehensive Illustrated Catalogue, 1885–1973; The Rose Period, 1905–1906, Paris*. Directed by Herschel Chipp and Alan Wofsy. San Francisco: Alan Wofsy Fine Arts.

Pictures on Exhibit. 1972. No. 36 (November 1972): 13, ill.

Plazy, Giles. 1988. *In the Footsteps of Van Gogh*. New York: Penguin.

———. 1991. *Cézanne*. Paris: Chêne.

Plessier, Ghislaine. 1990. *Adrien Dauzats ou la tentation de l'Orient: Catalogue raisonné de l'oeuvre peint*. Bordeaux: Musée des Beaux Arts de Bordeaux and W. Blake.

Prat, Louis-Antoine. 2011. *Le Dessin français au XIXe siècle*. Paris: Louvre Editions.

Price, Aimée Brown. 1994. *Pierre Puvis de Chavannes*. With contributions by Jon Whiteley and Geneviève Lacambre. Exh. cat. Amsterdam: Van Gogh Museum.

———. 2010. *Pierre Puvis de Chavannes: A Catalogue Raisonné of the Painted Work*. 2 vols. New Haven and London: Yale University Press.

Princeton University Art Museum. 2002. *Cézanne in Focus: Watercolors from the Henry and Rose Pearlman Collection*. Exh. cat. Princeton: Princeton University Art Museum.

Raffaëlli, Jean François. 1884. *Catalogue illustré des œuvres de Jean-François Raffaëlli*. Exh. cat., Paris.

Rewald, John. 1983. *Paul Cézanne, The Watercolors: A Catalogue Raisonné*. Boston: Little, Brown.

———. 1986. *Cézanne*. New York: Harry N. Abrams.

———. 1987. *Von van Gogh bis Gauguin: Die Geschichte des Nachimpressionismus*. Cologne: M. DuMont Schauberg.

Rich, Daniel Catton. 1951. *Edgar-Hilaire-Germain Degas*. New York: Harry N. Abrams.

Richardson, John. 1958. *Édouard Manet: Paintings and Drawings*. London: Phaidon Press.

———. 1991. *A Life of Picasso: The Early Years, 1881–1906*. New York: Random House.

Robaut, A. 1885. *L'Oeuvre complet d'Eugène Delacroix: Peintures, dessins, gravures, lithographies*. Paris: Charavay frères.

Rosenberg, Pierre. 2000. *Poussin, Watteau, Fragonard, David, and Ingres*. Princeton: Princeton University Press.

———, and Louis-Antoine Prat. 2002. *Jacques-Louis David 1748–1825. Catalogue raisonné des dessins*. Milan: Leonardo arte.

Rosenblum, Robert. 1997. "Picasso in Gósol: The Calm before the Storm." In *Picasso: The Early Years, 1892–1906*. Exh. cat. Washington: National Gallery of Art.

Roskill, Mark W. 1971. "Van Gogh's Blue Cart and His Creative Process." *Oud Holland* 86, no. 2–3: 142–79.

Ross, Anne. 1966. *Van Gogh*. New York: Gaston Diehl.

Rothenstein, Elizabeth. 1950. *Impressionist Paintings*. London: Faber and Faber.

Rothenstein, John. 1952–74. *Modern English Painters*. 3 vols. London: Eyre & Spottiswoode.

Rouart, Denis. 1945. *Degas à la recherche de sa technique*. Paris: Floury.

Rouart, Denis, and Daniel Wildenstein. 1975. *Édouard Manet: Catalogue Raisonné*. Paris: Bibliothèque des Arts Lausanne.

Rubin, William, ed. 1977. *Cézanne: The Late Work*. Exh. cat. New York: Museum of Modern Art.

Russoli, Franco, and Fiorella Minervino. 1970. *L'Opera completa di Degas*. Milan: Rizzoli.

Salomon, Antoine, and Guy Cogeval. 2003. *Vuillard: Critical Catalogue of Paintings and Pastels*. Paris: Wildenstein Institute.

Salomon, Jacques, and Annette Vaillant. 1963. *Vuillard et son Kodak*. Paris: L'Oeil, Galerie d'Art.

San Francisco Museum of Modern Art. 2000. *Celebrating Modern Art: The Anderson Collection*. Edited by Gary Garrels. Berkeley: University of California Press.

Saunier, Charles. 1925. "Les dessins de David." *L'Art vivant* no. 24, December 15.

———. 1929. "Le dessin de Louis David." *Le Dessin* no. 5.

Schmidt, Georg. 1952. *Aquarelle von Paul Cézanne*. Basel: Holbein-Verlag.

Schnapper, Antoine. 1980. *David témoin de son temps*. Paris: Bibliothèque des Arts, and Fribourg, Switzerland: Office du Livre.

Sérullaz, Arlette. 1989–90. *Jacques-Louis David 1748–1825*. Exh. cat. Paris: Réunion des musées nationaux.

Sérullaz, Maurice. 1963. *Mémorial de l'Exposition Eugène Delacroix organisée au Musée du Louvre à l'occasion du centenaire de la mort de l'artiste*. Paris: Éditions des Musées Nationaux.

———. 1974. *Encyclopédie de l'Impressionnisme*. Paris: Somogy.

———. 1984. *Musée du Louvre. Cabinet des Dessins. Inventaire Général des Dessins. École Française. Dessins d'Eugène Delacroix 1798–1863*. With Arlette Sérullaz, Louis-Antoine Prat, and Claudine Ganeval. Paris: Éditions des Musées Nationaux.

Seuphor, Michel. 1952. "Mondrian: 1914–1918." *Magazine of Art* 45, no. 5 (May): 216–26.

———. 1956. *Piet Mondrian: Life and Work*. New York: Harry N. Abrams.

Shackelford, George T. M., and Xavier Rey. 2011. *Degas and the Nude*. Boston: Museum of Fine Arts.

Shapiro, David. 1991. *Mondrian: Flowers*. New York: Harry N. Abrams.

Silverman, Debora L. 1989. *Art Nouveau in Fin-de-Siècle France: Politics, Psychology, and Style*. Berkeley: University of California Press.

Simms, Matthew Thomas. 2008. *Cézanne's Watercolors: Between Drawing and Painting*. New Haven and London: Yale University Press.

Sotheby's. 1962. *Sotheby's Annual Review, 218th Season*. 1962. London and New York: Sotheby's.

Stolwijk, Chris, and Han Veenenbos. 2002. *Account Book of Theo van Gogh and Jo van Gogh-Bonger*. Amsterdam and Leiden.

Sutton, Denys, and Paolo Lecaldano. 1987. *The Complete Paintings of Picasso: Blue and Rose Periods*. New York: Penguin.

Tabarant, Adolphe. 1947. *Manet et Ses Oeuvres*. Paris: Gallimard.

Terrasse, Antoine. 1972. *Edgar Degas*. Milan: Fratelli Fabbri.

———. 1976. "Degas et la Danse," *L'Oeil* (December).

Threlfall, Tim. 1988. *Piet Mondrian: His Life's Work and Evolution, 1872–1944*. New York: Garland.

Tinterow, Gary. 1987. *Degas*. New York: Metropolitan Museum of Art.

Van Gogh Drawings. 1987. New York: Dover Publications.

Van Gogh, Vincent. 1938. *Letters to Émile Bernard*. New York: Museum of Modern Art.

Van Heugten, Sjaar. 2005. *Van Gogh: Master Draughtsman*. Exh. cat. Amsterdam: Van Gogh Museum. New York: Harry N. Abrams.

Venturi, Lionello. 1978. *Cézanne, son art, son oeuvre*. New York: Rizzoli.

Vögele, Christoph, and Viola Radlach. 2005. *Cuno Amiet: frühe Arbeiten auf Papier*. Solothurn, Switzerland: Kunstmuseum Solothurn and Heidelberg: Kehrer.

Waldmann, Emil. 1923. *Édouard Manet*. Berlin: Paul Cassirer.

Weisberg, Gabriel P. 1973. *Social Concern and the Worker: French Prints from 1830–1910*. Exh. cat. Utah Museum of Fine Arts, Cleveland Museum of Art, Indianapolis Museum of Art. Salt Lake City: Utah Museum of Fine Arts.

———. 1979. *Bonvin*. Paris: Geoffroy-Dechaume.

———. 2002. *Against the Modern: Dagnan-Bouveret and the Transformation of the Academic Tradition*. New York: Dahesh Museum of Art.

Welsh, Robert P. 1977. *Piet Mondrian's Early Career: The "Naturalistic" Periods*. New York: Garland.

Welsh-Ovcharov, Bogomila. 1981. *Vincent van Gogh and the Birth of Cloisonism*. Toronto: Art Gallery of Toronto.

White, Colin. 2007. *A Guide to the Printed Books of Jessie M. King*, London: British Library.

Wildenstein, Alec. 1992–98. *Odilon Redon: Catalogue raisonné de l'oeuvre peint et dessiné*. 4 vols. Paris: Wildenstein Institute.

Wildenstein, Daniel, and Georges Wildenstein. 1973. *Documents complémentaires au catalogue de l'oeuvre de Louis David*. Paris: Foundation Wildenstein.

Wilson, Michael. 1978. *Nature and Imagination: The Work of Odilon Redon*. New York: Dutton.

Wilson-Bareau, Juliet. 1986. *The Hidden Face of Manet: An Investigation of the Artist's Working Processes*. Exh. cat. London: Courtauld Institute.

Wilton, Andrew, and Robert Upstone, eds. 1997. *The Age of Rossetti, Burne-Jones, and Watts: Symbolism in Britain, 1860–1910*. Exh. cat. London: Tate Gallery.

Zafran, Eric M. 1992. *Cavaliers and Cardinals: Nineteenth-Century French Anecdotal Paintings*. Exh. cat.

Zervos, Christian. 1932–1978. *Pablo Picasso*. 33 vols. Paris: Cahiers d'art.

Photography and Copyright Credits

Cat. 20: photograph by Robert LaPrelle, courtesy Kimbell Art Museum; cats. 23, 30, 36, 82, and 107: images courtesy of Valley House Gallery; cat. 108: image courtesy of Jean-Luc Baroni, Ltd; fig. 1: Pushkin Museum of Art, Moscow; fig. 2: © RMN–Grand Palais / Art Resource, NY; fig. 3: Erich Lessing / Art Resource, NY; fig. 4: courtesy The Walters Art Museum, Baltimore; fig. 5: Curtis Galleries, Minneapolis; fig. 6: © RMN–Grand Palais / Art Resource, NY, photograph by Matieu Rabeau; fig. 9: The Bridgeman Art Library; fig. 11: The Bridgeman Art Library; fig. 12: Erich Lessing / Art Resource, NY; fig. 13: photograph by Mitro Hood, courtesy the Baltimore Museum of Art; fig. 14: Institut Pasteur / Musée Pasteur, Paris; fig. 16: Erich Lessing / Art Resource, NY; fig. 21: © 2014 Estate of Pablo Picasso / Artists Rights Society (ARS), New York, image courtesy The Cleveland Museum of Art; fig. 22: © 2014 Estate of Pablo Picasso / Artists Rights Society (ARS), New York, photograph by Michael Bodycomb; fig. 23: © 2014 Artists Rights Society (ARS), New York / VG Bild-Kunst, Bonn; fig. 24: Archive Aftenposten / NRB Scanpix / Sipa USA.

We greatly respect the protected status of all copyrighted material. We have endeavored, with due diligence, to identify and contact each copyright owner. In some cases we have been unable to trace current copyright holders. We welcome notification and will correct errors in subsequent editions.

Front cover: Pascal Dagnan-Bouveret, *Portrait of Gustave Courtois*, detail of cat. 43, p. 99

Back cover: Paul Cézanne, *Environs d'Aix*, detail of cat. 69, p. 151

Page 4: Fernand Léger, *Seated Woman and Standing Woman*, detail of cat. 115, p. 231

Page 7: Frederick Sandys, *Proud Maisie, VI*, detail of cat. 52, p. 117

Page 8: Ernest Meissonier, *The Smoker (A Man of the First Empire)*, detail of cat. 39, p. 93

Page 12: Egon Schiele, *Remembrance (Erinnerung)*, detail of cat. 102, p. 205

Pages 18–19: Albert Anker, *Girl and Boy with Pick-a-Stick Game*, detail of cat. 49, p. 111

Page 131: Edgar Degas, *Dancer with a Fan*, detail of cat. 58, p. 129

Page 232: Georges Seurat, *Standing Woman*, detail of cat. 71, p. 155

The publication has been generously underwritten by Charlene and Tom Marsh.

Library of Congress Cataloging-in-Publication Data
Mind's eye (Dallas Museum of Art)
Mind's eye: masterworks on paper from David to Cézanne / edited by Olivier Meslay and William B. Jordan; with conributions by Esther Bell [and seventeen others].
pages cm
Includes bibliographical references.
ISBN 978-0-300-20721-7 (alk. paper)
1. Art, Modern—19th century—Exhibitions.
2. Art, Modern—20th century—Exhibitions. I. Meslay, Olivier, editor of compilation. II. Jordan, William B., 1940– , editor of compilation. III. Dallas Museum of Art. IV. Title.
N6447.M53 2014
740.74'7642812—dc23 2014005474

DALLAS MUSEUM OF ART
Maxwell L. Anderson, The Eugene McDermott Director
Olivier Meslay, Associate Director of Curatorial Affairs
Tamara Wootton-Bonner, Associate Director of Collections and Exhibitions
Eric Zeidler, Publications Manager
Martha MacLeod, Curatorial Administrative Assistant
Giselle Castro-Brightenburg, Imaging Manager
Brad Flowers, Head Photographer
Michael Hartman, McDermott Curatorial Intern

Edited by Ellen Hirzy
Translations by Chris Miller: cats. 3, 11–14, 18, 25–26, 30–31, 49, 80, 85, and 95–98
Translation by Russell Stockman: cats. 40–41
Proofread by Brynn Warriner
Designed by Jeff Wincapaw
Layout by Tina Kim
Typeset in Arno Pro by Maggie Lee
Image management by iocolor, Seattle
Printed and bound in China by Artron Color Printing, Ltd.

Produced by Marquand Books, Inc., Seattle
marquand.com

Published by the Dallas Museum of Art
DMA.org

Distributed by
Yale University Press, New Haven and London
yalebooks.com/art